CW00927260

THE TAILOR OF ULM

THE TAILOR OF ULM

COMMUNISM IN THE TWENTIETH CENTURY

LUCIO MAGRI

Translated by
Patrick Camiller

VERSO
London • New York

First published by Verso 2011

First published as *Il Sarto di Ulm*

1 3 5 7 9 10 8 6 4 2

Verso
UK: 6 Meard Street, London W1F 0EG
US: 20 Jay Street, Suite 1010, Brooklyn, NY 11201
www.versobooks.com

Verso is the imprint of New Left Books

ISBN-13: 978-1-84467-698-9

British Library Cataloguing in Publication Data
A catalogue record for this book is available from the British Library

Library of Congress Cataloging-in-Publication Data
A catalog record for this book is available from the Library of Congress

Typeset in Sabon by MJ Gavan, Cornwall
Printed in the US by Maple Vail

Contents

Introduction

Where should I, a Trotta, go now?
Joseph Roth

In 1989, at one of the packed meetings to decide whether the PCI should change its name, a comrade put the following question to Pietro Ingrao: 'After all that has been happening, do you really think the word communist can still be used to define the great mass democratic party that we have been and still are, and that we want to renew and strengthen so that it can form the government of this country?'

Ingrao, who had already fully explained his reasons for proposing a different course from that of the Party secretary, Achille Occhetto, replied in a jocular (though not too jocular) vein – by invoking Brecht's apologia for the 'Tailor of Ulm', a German artisan who became obsessed with the idea of building a machine that would enable men to fly. One day, convinced that he had succeeded, the tailor took his device to the ruling bishop and said: 'Look, I can fly!' The ruler challenged him to prove it, but when he finally took to the air he crashed to the pavement below. And yet centuries later – Brecht concludes – human beings did learn to fly.[1]

I was present at the meeting, and I found Ingrao's reply not only shrewd but well-founded. How much time, how many bloody

1. The famous incident that is the background to Brecht's poem ('Ulm 1592') actually occurred in 1811, but Brecht situated it in an earlier century on the cusp of the modern age.

struggles, how many advances and defeats, were necessary before the capitalist system – in a Western Europe initially more backward than certain other parts of the world – finally achieved an unprecedented economic efficiency, new and more open political institutions, and a more rational culture! What irreducible contradictions – between solemn ideals (a common human nature, freedom of thought and speech, popular sovereignty) and practices that constantly belied them (slavery, colonial domination, land clearances, wars of religion) – beset liberalism during the centuries in question! These contradictions existed in the reality of society, but were legitimated at the level of ideas: for example, with the argument that liberty could and should only be granted to those who, by virtue of property or culture, or even race and colour, were capable of making wise use of it; or, conversely, that the ownership of wealth was an absolute, inviolable right that therefore precluded universal suffrage.

Nor did the contradictions affect only the first phase of the historical cycle: they subsequently recurred in various forms, and only gradually diminished through the action of new social subjects and new forces that contested the prevailing system and ideas. If, then, the real history of capitalist modernity was neither linear nor straightforwardly progressive, but rather dramatic and costly, why should we expect the process of moving beyond it to be any different? This is the lesson that the story of the Tailor of Ulm was meant to convey.

Immediately, and only half in jest myself, I put two further questions to Ingrao that seemed to me to be raised by Brecht's parable. Can we be sure that, if the fall had only crippled the tailor instead of killing him, he would have immediately picked himself up and tried again, or that his friends would not have tried to restrain him? And what contribution did his bold attempt actually make to the history of aeronautics? These questions were especially pointed, and especially difficult, in relation to Communism. For when it first took shape as a theory, it had claimed to be not an inspiring ideal but part of a historical process already under way, of a real movement that was changing the existing state of things; it had therefore implied constant factual verification, scientific analysis of the present and realistic prognosis of the future, in order to avoid dissolving into myth. But we also need to register an important difference between the defeats suffered by the early bourgeois revolutions, in France and England, and the recent collapse of 'actually existing socialism' – a difference measured not by the number of deaths or the degree of despotism, but by their respective outcomes. In the first case, the legacy is immediately apparent (albeit much more modest than the initial hopes); in the second case, it is not easy to discern the character or scale of the inheritance, or to identify legitimate heirs. The last twenty years have not only failed to provide answers; the questions themselves have not been seriously discussed. Or rather, what pass as answers have come in the highly superficial form of denial or selective amnesia. A historical experience and theoretical heritage that marked a century of human history have thus been consigned, in Marx's expression, to 'the gnawing criticism of mice', which, as we know, are voracious creatures and multiply rapidly in the right conditions.

The word 'communist' still appears, of course, as an obsessive theme in the crudest right-wing propaganda. It survives in the election symbols of small European parties, either to retain the support of a minority still attached to its memory, or to indicate a generic opposition to capitalism. In other parts of the world, Communist parties still govern a number of small countries (mainly to defend their independence from imperialism) and one very large country, where Communist rule serves to promote extraordinary economic development that is moving in an entirely different direction. The October Revolution is generally considered a grand illusion: useful at one time, and in the eyes of a few, but a disaster overall, identified with the most grotesque form of Stalinism, and condemned in any event by its final outcome. Marx has regained a certain credit as a thinker, for his far-sighted predictions regarding the future of capitalism, but these have been totally severed from any ambition to put an end to it. Worse still, the damnation of historical memory now tends to cover the whole experience of socialism, even branching out to radical elements in the bourgeois revolutions and liberation struggles of colonized peoples (which, even in the land of Gandhi, could not always remain non-violent). In short, the 'haunting spectre' seems to have been finally buried, with honours by some, with undying hatred by others, but with indifference by most, because it has nothing more to say to them. Perhaps the most scathing, but in its way also the most respectful, funeral oration was pronounced by Augusto del Noce, one of the finest minds in the opposing camp, when he said some years ago that the Communists had both lost and won. They had lost grievously in their Promethean quest to alter the course of history, in their promise to bring liberty and fraternity to human beings, without God and without an afterlife. But they had won in so far as they had been a powerful and necessary factor accelerating the globalization of capitalist modernity and its values of materialism, hedonism, individualism and ethical relativism. An intransigent Catholic conservative, del Noce believed he had foreseen this extraordinary heterogenesis of ends, but he would have had little reason to feel happy about it.

Anyone who did believe in the Communist project, and was in any way part of it, has a duty to draw up a balance sheet, if only a personal one, and to ask whether the burial has not been a little too hasty, and whether a different way of ascertaining *rigor mortis* might be required. In Italy there have been many ways of evading this central issue. For example: I became a Communist because it was the key means of fighting fascism, defending republican democracy and supporting the workers' just demands. Or: I became a Communist when the links with the Soviet Union and Marxist orthodoxy were already being questioned, so that today I can combine my own limited self-criticism of the past with a positive openness to the future. Is that not enough? In my opinion it is not, since it fails to account for all the good and the bad in a collective enterprise stretching over many decades. Above all it fails to draw useful lessons for today and tomorrow.

Too often I hear people say: it was all a mistake, but they were the best years of our lives. For a time, when the blow was still fresh, this mixture of self-criticism and nostalgia, doubt and pride, seemed to me justified; it could even be a resource, especially for ordinary people. With the passage of time, however, and especially in the case of intellectuals and political leaders, it has come to appear an easy compromise with oneself and the world. So I have begun to ask myself once again: are there rational, compelling reasons why we should resist the psychological mechanisms of denial and repressed memory? Are there, at least, good grounds and favourable conditions today for reopening the critical debate about Communism, instead of consigning it to the archives? It seems to me that there are.

* * *

A lot of troubled water has flowed under the bridge since that fateful year of 1989. The changes expressed and ratified in that historical turning-point have become clearer and more definitive, while other developments have followed unexpectedly thick and fast. A new configuration of the world order, of society and consciousness, has been emerging.

A victorious capitalism was left holding the field, in a position to reassert its founding values and mechanisms without coercive constraints. Technological revolution, together with a new surge of globalization, seemed to augur a long period of rapid economic expansion and stable international relations, under the leadership – shared or endured – of a single overweening superpower. Opinions still differed, of course, about the role that conflict and rivalry between the two systems of the twentieth century had played in advancing democracy and progress, and about the toll this had taken on individual lives. How to correct the worst social consequences of the previous period, how to introduce guarantees of transparency and propriety into market operations, and how to temper the unilateralism of the dominant world power: these were also open to debate. But the system was here to stay: it was not to be challenged, and indeed demanded support in good faith, on the basis of its own principles. Perhaps one day, in the distant future, it too would exhaust its historical function, but the system that would then replace it would have nothing in common with anything the Left had done or thought. Such was the new reality: any sensible politician had to face up to it, or keep baying at the moon.

The picture has changed profoundly, however, in the space of just a few years. This too is a fact that can hardly be denied. Inequalities of income, power and quality of life have asserted themselves in new and often sharper forms, both among and within different regions of the world. The new functioning of the economic system has proved incompatible with long-standing social gains: universal welfare, stable full employment and elements of participatory democracy in the most advanced societies; the right to national independence, and some protection from armed intervention, for underdeveloped regions and smaller countries. New and urgent problems are looming everywhere, from environmental degradation to a moral decay in which individualism and consumerism, rather than filling the human and axiological vacuum created by the irreversible (and in itself liberating) crisis of age-old institutions, deepen that crisis and transform it into a dichotomy between dissipation and neo-clericalism. The political system too has clearly entered a new period of crisis and impotence as the decline of nation-states has spawned institutions insulated from popular suffrage, itself hollowed out by the media manipulation of consensus and the transformation of parties into electoral machines geared to the reproduction of governing castes. Meanwhile, in the realm of production, growth rates have been declining, and the economic equilibria seem more than cyclically unstable; financialization begets the illegitimate twins of unearned income and frantic pursuit of immediate profits, stripping the market itself of the criteria to gauge its efficiency, or to judge what should be produced. Finally, and as a consequence of all this, we are witnessing a decline of hegemony, the multiplication of conflicts, and a crisis of the world order. The natural response has been the deployment of military force, including outright war, which far from solving problems merely aggravates them.

Let us concede, however, that this sketch is excessively gloomy and one-sided, that the alarming trends are still in their early stages. Let us also accept that other factors – technological innovation, for example, or the even more surprising rise and current success of major new countries on the world stage – may offset or check such tendencies. And lastly, let us accept that the breadth of the social layers that benefited from the earlier round of accumulation, or that elsewhere hope to attain a prosperity previously denied to them, might yet underpin a new consensus or generate fear of radical changes that offer no certainty of success. Communists have not infrequently committed the mistake of catastrophism, and paid the penalty for it.

Yet none of this alters the fact that a turn has taken place, earlier and more forceful than anyone feared or hoped. Not only for turbulent or suffering minorities, but also in mass opinion, among wide swathes of the intelligentsia and even for some sections of the dominant class, the future of the world and human civilization seems scarcely reassuring. We are no longer in the high winds of the twentieth century, but nor are we breathing the quiet air of the Belle Epoque (which, as we know, did not exactly end well). In just a few years, combative social movements and ideological challenges have burst onto the scene, surprising not only in their breadth and persistence, but also in the range of active subjects they have mobilized and the novelty of the themes they have raised. Dispersed and intermittent, lacking a unitary project and an organizational structure, these movements are certainly more social and cultural than political. They have sprung from the most diverse situations and subjectivities; they reject organization, ideology and politics as they have known them in the past, and above all as these present themselves today.

Nevertheless, these movements are in constant communication with one another; they recognize common enemies and spell out their names; they cultivate ideals and experiment with practices radically opposed to the existing order of things – and to the values, institutions and powers that embody that order: modes of production, consumption and thought, relations between classes, sexes, countries and religions. At certain moments, and on certain questions such as the 'preventive' war against Iraq, they have succeeded in mobilizing a large section of public opinion. In that sense they are fully political, and carry weight. Should we, then, feel reassured that the 'old mole', finally freed from the doctrines and disciplines that held it back, has begun to tunnel once more towards a new world? I would like to think so, but I have my doubts.

Here too the facts are clear enough. On the one hand, we need to confront the true evolution of the situation, without despondency but also without pretence. It cannot be said that things are gradually taking a turn for the better, or that the lessons of reality are producing a general shift in the balance of forces in favour of the Left. Let us mention a few examples, as we near the end of the first decade of the twenty-first century.

The marriage of convenience between the Asian and American economies has facilitated an astonishing take-off by the former, while guaranteeing the latter imperial profits and allowing it to consume beyond its means. But the current arrangement has also contributed to European stagnation, and finally issued in a major new crisis. The Iraq war, rather than stabilizing the Middle East, has 'lit a prairie fire'. Europe has not forged ahead under its own steam towards greater unity, but has deepened its subordination to the Anglo-American model – and to its foreign policy. Latin America, after many years, once again has popular, anti-imperialist governments running several countries, but in Central

Asia, as in Eastern Europe, clients of the United States are continuing to multiply. Zapatero has been re-elected in Spain, but in Italy, after the narrow and short-lived victory of a coalition of the Centre-Left, Berlusconi is back – and worse than before. In Germany the Christian Democrats have returned to the helm, in France the whole *gauche* is in disarray, and in Britain New Labour has stuck to the Blair line and, if it loses, will give way to the Conservatives. The trade unions, after some signs of recovery, remain on the defensive almost everywhere, and the real conditions of workers are under pressure not only from the political context but from the blackmail of economic crisis and budget deficits. In the United States there is likely to be a return from Bush-style policies to the more prudent orientation pursued by Clinton, neither of which is up to the task of dealing with the world's new and pressing problems. In economics as in politics, no New Deal is in the offing. Everyone speaks of reform, whether out of necessity or choice, but each variant is more tepid and evasive than the next.

How should we assess the forces ranged against the system? The outlook is not auspicious. It is certainly important that the new social movements remain on the scene, and have in some cases expanded to new regions or contributed to a replenishment of political energies. Moreover, they have drawn attention to critical problems that were previously dismissed: water shortages, climate change, defence of cultural identities, civil liberties for immigrants, gays and other groups. It would therefore be wrong to speak only of regression or crisis – but just as misleading to suggest that some 'second world power' already exists or is in the making. For in the major struggles in which these movements have acted in unison – peace and disarmament, abolition of the WTO and IMF, the Tobin Tax, alternative energy sources, employment security – the results have been trifling, and initiative has declined. Pluralism has proved to be a limitation as well as a resource. New thinking about organization is all very well, but one cannot reduce it for ever to the internet plus blogging. Refusal of politics, power from below, revolution without a seizure of power: these may contain indispensable partial truths, but they risk turning into a fossilized subculture, in which rhetorical incantation gets in the way of self-reflection or any exacting definition of priorities. Finally, alongside the new movements – and through no fault of theirs – a different type of radical opposition has emerged, inspired by religious or ethnic fundamentalism, whose most extreme form is terrorism, but which influences and involves significant numbers of people.

If we turn to the organized forces of the radical Left that staunchly resisted the post-'89 collapse, launching attempts at renewal and working alongside the new movements and trade union struggles, the balance sheet appears still leaner. After years of working in a society in ferment, these forces remain marginal and divided. Their share of the vote in Europe ranges from 3 to a maximum 10 per cent, trapping them in a dilemma between minority radicalism and electoral pacts, whose onerous constraints weaken them further. In sum, to paraphrase some Marxist classics, we are once more in a period in which 'the old world can still produce barbarism, but a new world capable of replacing it has not yet emerged'.

The reason for this impasse is easy to see, although far from easy to remove. Neoliberalism and unilateralism, against which present struggles are rightly directed, are an expression of deeper and more durable tendencies in the world capitalist system that have been carrying its original proclivity to the extreme. These include: dominance of the economy over every other aspect of individual and collective life; dominance within the economy of the globalized market, and within the market of great concentrations of finance over production; dominance of services over industry within production, and of induced needs for immaterial goods over real needs. We are also witnessing a decline of politics, as nation-states are overshadowed by agreements made above their heads, and political systems are hollowed out by fragmentation and manipulation of the popular will that should guide and sustain them. Finally, there is the unification of the world under the sign of a specific hierarchy, with a preponderant power at its apex. It is a system, then, which appears to be decentred, but in which the critical decisions are ultimately concentrated in the hands of the few who control decisive monopolies: in ascending order of importance, over technology, over communications, and over financial and military power.

Underpinning it all, more than ever before, is capital in tireless pursuit of self-valorization, now entirely autonomous with regard to location and any alternative goals that might otherwise have constrained it. With the vast means of the culture industry at its disposal, capitalist property is able to mould needs, consciousness and lifestyles, to select the political and intellectual caste, to shape foreign policy, military expenditure and research programmes, and last but not least to reconfigure labour relations by choosing where and when workers will be recruited, and how best to undermine their bargaining power. In comparison with earlier periods, the most significant novelty is that, when the system enters a crisis or suffers a failure, it nevertheless manages to reproduce its own bases of strength and interdependence, and to fragment or blackmail the forces opposing it. It summons, and at the same time buries, its own gravedigger.

To challenge and overcome such a system, what is required is a coherent systemic alternative; the power to impose it and the capacity to run it; a social bloc that can sustain it, and measures and alliances commensurate with that goal. Much as we can and should discard the myth of an apocalyptic breakdown, in which a Jacobin minority steps in to conquer state power, there is still less reason to pin our hopes on a succession of scattered revolts or small-scale reforms that might spontaneously coalesce into a great transformation.

Thus, the current situation itself demands that a Left now drifting in confusion should reflect on 'the Communist question'. I do not use these words casually. 'Reflection' – not rehabilitation or restoration – indicates that a historical period has come to an end, and that the new times require radically new thinking about the origins, evolution and results of this (or any other) theoretical or practical tradition. I say 'Communist' because I am chiefly referring, not to texts, variously interpreted in such a way as to revive lasting truths or noble intentions from which there had been a falling away, but rather to a whole historical experience that explicitly posited the theme of an anti-capitalist revolution led by the working class organized in a party. Parties operating in this tradition, in Italy and elsewhere, mobilized millions and millions of people over a period of decades; they fought and were victorious in a world war; they ruled major states, shaped societies and influenced the destiny of the world; and in the end – certainly not by chance – they degenerated and went down to a harsh defeat. For better or worse, they left their mark on almost an entire century.

A first task, then, is to draw up a balance sheet of twentieth-century Communism – in a spirit of truth, whatever the initial convictions or the final conclusions; without fabricating any facts, without offering excuses and without separating the experience from the context in which it was lived. The aim must be to sort the wheat from the chaff: to distinguish the contribution to major historical advances from the tremendous costs that this involved, and genuine theoretical truths from errors of thought. We shall have to clarify the various periods in the evolution of Communism, to identify, within each, not only the mistakes but also their subjective and objective causes, and to consider what real opportunities there were to pursue a different path towards the desired goal. In short, we need to recompose the thread of a titanic undertaking and a spectacular decline, neither aspiring to (an impossible) neutrality nor pleading for special allowances to be made, but seeking to draw closer and closer to the historical truth. In tackling this set of tasks today, we have the special privilege of knowing how things eventually turned out, together with the stimulus that comes from finding ourselves once again in a crisis of civilization. We must make use of the present to improve our understanding of the past, and understand the past so as to orientate ourselves better in the present and future.

If we avoid such reflections and regard the twentieth century as a heap of ashes; if we delete from the record the great revolutions, the bitter class struggles and the huge cultural conflicts in which Socialism and Communism were the major driving force; or if we simply reduce everything to a clash between 'totalitarianism' and 'democracy', ignoring the origins and goals of the different forms of 'totalitarianism' or the actual policies of each democratic regime, then we not only tamper with history but deprive politics of its passion and arguments – needed to confront, both the old problems that are now back on the agenda, and new problems that call for profound changes and a rational discourse.

The type of investigation I am proposing here is tremendously difficult – and the motivations that should guide it no less so. The 'short twentieth century' is a long and complicated period, shot through with dramatic and closely interlinked contradictions, demanding an overview of the context as a whole; yet it is still so fresh in the collective memory that it is hard to attain the requisite critical distance. Moreover, such an investigation runs counter to the mainstream view today, which not only considers the chapter closed, but denies that history can ever be deciphered as a whole and in the long term – and therefore sees no value in situating the present within that history, or in developing appropriate interpretative categories. To challenge this prevailing wisdom, it would more than ever be necessary to break the continuity in our critical reading of the past: that is, to outline from the start a cogent analysis of the present and a project for future action (this was Marxism's strong point, even in aspects that proved to have been ephemeral).

I know full well that I do not have enough time left to me, nor the skills and intellectual resources, to be of much assistance in this massive undertaking. But I feel a certain generational as well as individual responsibility to make some contribution, first of all by reconstructing and examining some key moments in the history of Italian Communism. The motivation for this is not autobiographical, nor is it provincially restrictive. On the contrary, although this choice is circumscribed so as to focus on one particular object, it implies a working hypothesis that goes against the fashionable grain by compelling, and perhaps ultimately permitting, certain general conclusions. Today there are two readings of Italian Communism, mutually opposed and driven by divergent purposes and thematic interests. The first maintains, with varying degrees of crudity, that at least after the war the PCI was essentially a social-democratic party, without wishing to admit it, and perhaps even without realizing it. Its history was one of a long march, excessively slow but always steady, towards recognition of what it really was; the delay kept it out of government, but the Party's substantive identity gave it strength and ensured its survival. The second reading argues that despite its roles in the Resistance, the republican Constitution and the extension of parliamentary democracy, and despite the evidence of its autonomy and hostility to insurrectionism, the PCI was in the last analysis structurally tied to Soviet policy and the goal of establishing the Soviet model in Italy. Only towards the end was it forced to abandon this goal and to change its identity.

Both these readings, however, are contradicted by innumerable historical facts, and obscure what was most original and interesting in the Communist historical experience. The thesis I would like to put forward is that intermittently, and without ever fully developing it, the PCI represented the most serious attempt at a 'third way' in its historical period. That is, it sought to combine partial reforms, broad social and political alliances and a commitment to parliamentary action with resolute social struggles and an explicit, shared critique of capitalist society; to build a highly cohesive, militant party, rich in ideologically trained cadres but with a mass base; and to uphold its affiliation to a world revolutionary camp, enduring the constraints that this implied but gaining for itself a relative autonomy. This was not a matter of mere duplicity: the unifying strategic idea was that the consolidation and development of 'actually existing socialism' did not provide a model that could one day be implemented in the West, but was the necessary background for the achievement of a different type of socialism in the West – one that respected liberties. It is this that accounts for the growing strength of the PCI, even after capitalist modernization, and for its international influence even after the first glaring signs of a crisis of 'actually existing socialism'. But by the same token, its subsequent decline and eventual dissolution into a force more liberal-democratic than social-democratic require us to explain how and when this strategic project foundered. In identifying the objective and subjective reasons for this trajectory, we will ask ourselves whether better paths were available that might have served to correct it.

If our thesis is correct, then the history of Italian Communism may tell us something important about the evolution both of republican Italy and of the Communist movement in general, helping us to assess its better side and to grasp its insurmountable limits. (A comparable field for investigation, however different the context, might be the equally singular Chinese experience: greatly admired today for its economic successes, but with an unexplained past and an indecipherable future.)

My second reason for focusing on Italian Communism is less important, but not altogether negligible. Many historians have written on the history of Communism, providing a wealth of information and scholarly analysis about the period between the Russian Revolution and the years after the Second World War, as well as more episodic accounts, full of gaps and prejudices, with regard to subsequent decades. But in both cases we still lack a comprehensive and balanced assessment. At fault for this are not the controversies that have justifiably arisen over various aspects so much as the discrepancy between accurate examination of the sources and partisan pamphleteering. This is scarcely surprising, of course, since both in the past and more recently historians have been exposed to powerful influences on their work – first the climate of bitter political conflict, then the sudden, unexpected collapse. The effect was to inspire some with the sobriety of the specialist, while prompting others to produce convenient simplifications. Over and above everything else, however, the limited nature of the sources and the difficulties of interpreting them are an obstacle to research and reflection for even the most acute and scrupulous historians. Communist parties – by virtue of their ideology, their organizational form and the conditions under which they operated – were far from transparent. Fundamental debates were conducted within narrow and often informal party gatherings, their participants bound by confidentiality and careful to speak, even among themselves, in terms compatible with the concern for unity. Policy decisions took genuine account of the preoccupations of party activists, and debates were often lively and well attended in lower levels of the organization, but in the end everyone accepted and defended the majority decision, albeit with shades of nuance. Leadership selection took proven ability into account, but top-down co-opting on the basis of loyalty also played its part. In certain countries and periods, there was no hesitation in censoring the facts and providing only cursory explanations of policies, even to the party membership, because consolidation and mobilization took precedence over all else – at the expense of truth, if need be. But even where spaces developed in which some dissent was tolerated – within the Central Committee, for example, as in Italy from the 1960s on – it was expressed in prudent, partly coded language. Record-keeping was accurate at all levels, but it was also kept simple and often involved a degree of self-censorship, whether deliberate or out of official duty.

At the time of the 'turn', the governing principle became that of 'renewal in continuity'. Since the party was a living community, those who distanced themselves or were distanced from it suffered a deep human isolation which, in the long term, served to fuel jaundiced views on both sides. Serious reading of the newspapers and documents of the time, supplemented with a few posthumously published interviews and newly available archive material, does not provide sufficient basis on which to reconstruct the real history, free of ambiguities or censorship. We also need the mediatory memory of those who took part as protagonists or direct, informed observers, who can say something about areas where the documents are silent, or read the meaning and significance of what lies beyond the words. To take an extreme example, imagine how much light would have been cast on the last fifteen years of the Soviet Union had Gorbachev given an authentic account of events and discussions, and offered his considered judgement of them, at a time when he was still in a position to do so.

But we all know how many snares the individual memory contains – not just because of age, but also because personal responsibilities, or perhaps a past injustice, can make it selective or tendentious. It is easy to reread history through the lens of one's own experience. There is nothing wrong in this. Proust and Tolstoy, Thomas Mann and Joseph Roth, afforded greater insights into their times than many of the historians who were their contemporaries.

I spoke above of the 'mediation of memory' in a different sense – by both choice and necessity. I don't find my own personal experience very interesting, and even if it were I would not know how to communicate it. My influence on policy was limited to a few precise moments in time, more at the level of ideas (often too early but recurring) than through successful activity within the Party. I therefore feel the need for documented facts and the memories of others to subject my own memory to an objective discipline, as if I were dealing with someone else's life; this alone makes it possible to approach a plausible account of what actually happened, or might have happened. Autobiography will only feature below when it is strictly necessary.

For reasons of age, I became a Communist ten years after the turbulence of fascism and the Resistance had ended – indeed, after the Twentieth Congress of the Communist Party of the Soviet Union and the events in Hungary, and after I had read not only Marx, Lenin and Gramsci, but also Trotsky and the unorthodox Western Marxists. I therefore cannot say that I joined the Party the better to fight fascism, or that I was ignorant of Stalinism and the 'purges'. I joined because I believed, as I have continued to do, in a project of radical social change for which the costs had to be borne. I will therefore have to clarify, first of all to myself, whether this was the right decision. I remained active in the Party through fifteen years of lively debate and important experiences, arguing from minority positions and never playing any role in the power structure. But I had direct contact with the leadership group and was fully aware of what was happening; I can even say I had a certain influence. They were decisive years, about which even today too little is known, or too much is repressed, and about which I am able to add something based on personal experience.

I was expelled from the Party in 1970, along with other comrades, because we had created a journal, *Il Manifesto*, that was seen as unacceptable. First, because its very existence was a breach of democratic centralism; second, because it called for sharper criticism of the Soviet model and Soviet policies; and third, because it urged a rethinking of party strategy and took on board proposals put forward by the new working-class and student movements. No one, I think, would accuse me of having remained silent, or of having parroted old orthodoxies. But I in turn am compelled to ask why – as a result of which errors or limitations – so many good arguments and often far-sighted analyses remained isolated and failed to make their mark.

Together with a number of other comrades who had deluded themselves about extremist politics, I became aware of its limits in the early 1980s and decided to rejoin the PCI in 1984. But I did not do so in a spirit of repentance, since Berlinguer's recent turn seemed to have settled many of the differences between us. As part of the PCI's leadership this time, I had direct knowledge of the processes that first hampered and then hollowed out this turn, revealing at once its belatedness and its limitations. It is a period about which there is still great reticence, and about which no criticism is seen as too harsh. In the early 1990s, now serving in the front line, I fought against the decision to dissolve the PCI – not because the new course seemed too innovative, but because it innovated in the wrong way and the wrong direction. In liquidating such a rich identity wholesale, it opened the way not simply to social democracy (itself already in crisis) but to a moderate liberal-democratic force. The leadership disbanded an army that had not yet dispersed, and compensated for its lack of a project with a fanciful cult of the 'new'. I remain today one of the few who believe this operation to have been completely groundless – which compels me all the more to wonder why it carried the day.

Finally, I took part in the foundation of Rifondazione Comunista – with some misgivings, because I feared it would lack the ideas, the will and the strength to take its name seriously; feared, in other words, a maximalist drift followed by opportunist accommodation. I distanced myself from it because, although I continued to believe in the project, I did not see sufficient determination or ability to carry it forward within that organization, or within the far Left diaspora. Scarcely anyone knows or understands much about the twists and turns of this latest venture, and it may prove useful just to speak honestly about it.

I am, then, a living private archive, in storage. For someone already old, isolation has a certain dignity. But for a Communist, isolation is the gravest of sins, which must be accounted for to others and to oneself. The 'last of the Mohicans' may be a mythical figure; the lone Communist, an 'angry old man', risks becoming a figure of fun if he does not draw aside.

But if sin opens the way to the Lord – forgive this ironical concession to the fashion and expediency that today spurs so many to a sudden search for God – then isolation might permit a distance that will be useful for the task I have set myself. I cannot claim that 'I wasn't there' or 'I didn't know'. In fact, I said one or two things when they were still unseasonable things to say, and so now I am at liberty to defend things that should not be disowned, and to ask myself what could have been done, or might yet be done, beyond the bric-a-brac of everyday politics.

It is not true that the past – of Communists or of anyone else – was completely predetermined, just as it is not true that the future is entirely in the hands of the young who are yet to come. The 'old mole' has been burrowing away, but being blind he is not sure where he comes from or where he is going; he may be digging in circles. And those who cannot or will not trust in Providence must do their best to understand him, and help him on his way.

1

The Legacy

This book does not claim to be, indeed cannot be, a complete history of the Italian Communist Party, even though that is its chosen field of investigation. It is much less than that, and something more.

Less, because it concentrates on the decades from the Salerno turn in 1944 to the 1990s, the period when the PCI defined a cultural and political identity of its own and won major influence in Italy and around the world by virtue of its strength and capacities. More, because it selects some key sub-periods in this time span and uses the author's personal memories of them, along with testimonies directly obtained from other witnesses, to make up for the grievous lack of information. It seeks to correct judgements and interpretations prevalent at the time, setting them in their historical context and using the benefit of hindsight. Finally it explores certain carefully chosen elements of 'counterfactual history', and offers a number of conclusions regarding the present and the future.

First of all, however, I will make some remarks on the general and specific experiences out of which the PCI was born, and on the cultural heritage that was available for its attempt at innovation. These are grouped into two distinct sets, each with a deliberately provocative title. 'The burden of Communist man', which makes no claim to originality, recovers certain facts which are well known to historians but have recently been obliterated, or adulterated, in the collective memory and even the official party culture. 'The Gramsci genome' considers the extraordinary reservoir of ideas that Gramsci bequeathed to the PCI, and which it used fruitfully, though in partial ways that suited its purposes.

THE BURDEN OF COMMUNIST MAN

1. In the last decade and a half of the nineteenth century and up to the eve of the First World War, a new social, political and cultural subject took clear shape in Europe and elsewhere. Its long and troubled gestation had involved extraordinary moments of revolutionary insurgency (1848, the Paris Commune) sealed by crushing defeats; bitter, never fully resolved, ideological conflicts among anarchists, neo-Jacobins, utopian socialists and others; a variety of practical experiences (trade unions, cooperatives, community organizations); and highly diverse national contexts shaping and integrating everything in particular ways. Marxist-oriented socialism did emerge in the end as a hegemonic protagonist, however, organized into national parties with strong international links, and associated with trade unions, cooperative movements, newspapers and journals. It was the age of the Second International. There can be no doubt about the two progenitors whose historic encounter resulted in its birth. On the one hand, a new class formed in the relationship between capital and labour, rapidly produced by economic growth and rapidly excluded from its fruits, which was becoming more and more concentrated in large-scale industry, capable of collective struggle and demands and, with the French revolution behind it, possessing a (still unclear) awareness of its social and political rights that made it more than a motley of plebs resigned to its fate; on the other hand, a powerful Marxist mode of thought, consciously rooted in and critical of modern culture, offering the new social subject not vague support but robust intellectual tools. Thanks to these tools the new class might be able to understand the structural reasons for its suffering, to interpret the course of history and locate itself within it, to develop a plausible project for transforming the system, and at last to equip itself with a political organization and to assume the role of a future ruling class. Difficulties and arguments persisted even after the founding of joint organizations, and even between people who declared themselves sincere Marxists. There were theoretical disputes (from *Kathedersozialismus*, influenced by mechanical positivism or Kantian moralism, to trade-unionist economism) and political

controversies (on universal suffrage, the importance of parliament, colonialism or issues directly concerning workers). But there is no need to dwell upon these, not only because a vast literature is already available, but above all because they did not prevent the newly developing social subject from acquiring a cultural identity and a united political direction, albeit with certain mediations and ambiguities.

It is worth recalling, though, how successful the venture was in its early days, since this was later obscured by a series of bitter divisions and has today been largely forgotten. The astonishing rise of the Second International over a period of little more than twenty years had a number of consequences, many of which would be permanent. The political gains included a major expansion of suffrage in many important countries and greater freedoms of speech, press and organization, although an initial price had to be paid in the form of harsh repression, imprisonment and exile. The social gains included a reduced working week, the right to 'combination' (that is, collective bargaining), the first steps towards health provision and social security, protection for women and children, and compulsory elementary education. Party organization grew by leaps and bounds (nearly a million members in Germany), with electoral results to match (a general trend, but surpassing 35 per cent of the vote by 1910 in Germany, where Social Democracy was the largest force in parliament). Finally, at the cultural level, Marxism began to penetrate the universities, no longer confined to factories, prisons and Siberia; while high-calibre leadership groups compelled intellectual opponents to take them seriously in argument. There were also a few revolutionary upsurges against state authorities, defeated but not purposeless (as in Russia in 1905) or crowned with victory (as in Mexico). One of the reasons for this astonishing rise was an underlying unity, which, over and above past disagreements or nascent quarrels, was sufficient to define an identity and to mobilize the hopes of broad sections of the population. No socialist, however reformist and gradualist, ceased to believe that the overcoming of the capitalist system was both necessary and possible and constituted the ultimate goal of his activity. No socialist, however revolutionary and impetuous, denied that partial battles were important for improving the workers' living conditions, or at least, if defeated but well fought, worthwhile for raising the level of cohesion and mobilization around the shared cause. In this sense, Socialists and Communists were not at odds, still less poles apart: the former emphasized the complementarity between the transitional phase, long or short, and the destination towards which it led, whereas the latter laid greater stress on the differences between the two.

The recollection of that founding period tells us something important about all the minor issues that provoke debate today. The first thing that stands out is the fundamental contribution of the Marxist workers' movement to the birth of a distinctive modern democracy, characterized by popular sovereignty and the nexus between political liberty and material conditions that allows it to be exercised. How decisive was the unity of organization, structured thought and mass participation in turning a plebeian 'multitude' of individuals into a collective protagonist of real history! And how absurd it is today to compensate for a vacuum of theory and analysis by dressing up and renaming ideas, such as anarchism, that were already worn-out and defeated a century ago; or to misuse old terms, like social democracy itself, to designate ideas or choices that have nothing to do with what they were originally meant to convey.

2. In the space of a few years, that movement which had seemed on its way to becoming a 'power' fell headlong into crisis and was shattered. The reason lies in an event which it found hugely difficult to read and master: the First World War.

It is both strange and telling that today's heated debate on the twentieth century, especially its tragic aspects, has obscured or sidelined that 'constitutive' conflict. The failure to put together a convincing account of its causes, significance and results is hardly surprising in itself. The generation that lived through it soon measured the scale of the tragedy: millions upon millions killed or crippled, economies in ruin, states and empires dissolved; nearly every layer of society was hit, together with certainties and cultures that had appeared impregnable. If the surprise was so great for everyone, it is because the causes and responsibilities remained unclear: no economic or social crisis had been impelling a military conflict on such a scale and at such a cost; the colonial division of the world had been more or less sealed by agreement; and the undeniable struggle for hegemony among the great powers had been proceeding on the terrain of finance and technology.

Although the dominant classes had for some time been engaged in high-profile rearmament, they neither expected nor wanted a world war, their alliances were casual and contradictory, and they were reluctant until the end to take irrevocable action. Yet the spark at Sarajevo and the almost fortuitous chain of provocations that followed it had triggered a general conflagration, transformed by new weapons technology into an unprecedented 'total war'. Huge masses had taken part, prepared to accept the role of cannon fodder in the ardent belief that they were 'defending the fatherland and civilization'. These contradictory alternatives ('war as accident' or 'war as self-defence against aggression') left a permanent mark on the collective memory, with the help of broad sections of the intelligentsia. Subsequently, the theory of an 'irrational parenthesis' – Benedetto Croce is a case in point – offered a critical but limited view of the conflict. However, the reading that eventually gained acceptance portrayed the First World War as a struggle between Western 'democracies' (which also happened to be the main colonial powers of the time) and autocratic empires (a pity that the Kaiser and Tsar fought on opposite sides, and that the Americans only intervened towards the end). This is still the official version: the First World War as precursor of the conflict that flared up again in the Second World War and the Cold War. (Not by chance did an Italian president recently repeat the characterization of the First World War as a 'fourth war of independence' – a conflict that a Pope rightly referred to as a 'pointless slaughter'.[1]) It would be interesting to look more closely at this conception, now that so many commentators absolve capitalism and liberalism of all responsibility for the dark side of the twentieth century, and to examine its links with the current theory of pre-emptive war. But it would take us too far from our main focus: the consequences of the First World War for the Marxist workers' movement, its divisions and metamorphoses, and the birth of Communism. It cannot be said that the Great War came as a bolt from the blue for Marxists. On the contrary, at the turn of the century the discussions

1. The First World War has traditionally been known in Italy as the 'fourth war of independence', which, following the conflicts of 1848, 1852 and 1860, completed the political unification of the country. Giorgio Napolitano, the ex-Communist president of Italy, repeated this characterization in a speech on 4 November 2008. On 18 February 2008, Pope Benedict XVI had stated that the war 'appears more and more as a pointless slaughter'.

within Social Democracy not only paid increasing attention to the theme of war but went right to the heart of the matter, in a general analysis of the period whose seriousness and application make one nostalgic for what has been lost.

It is commonly said that Marxism was always in thrall to a schema that made it incapable of grasping the constant changes of the system it opposed. But this trite refrain finds one refutation in the great debate on imperialism, in which the problem of war was integral to various analyses of the great transformations of capitalism over the previous decades. This evolution, involving contradictory phenomena, made it necessary to revise many of the predictions in the *Communist Manifesto* and the strategies linked to them. Among the most important new trends were: the systematic application of the new sciences to production technology (chemicals, electricity, long-distance communications, agricultural mechanization); the recomposition of society due to the concentration and differentiation of labour in huge industrial plants; the decline of artisans and small tradesmen, and the growth of a sizeable middle layer of white-collar workers, especially in the public sector; the greater scope for wage concessions, partly due to the proceeds of less primitive colonial exploitation; and the financialization of the economy, with the rise of stockholding companies and large trusts supported by the banks. At the same time, general education had been reducing illiteracy and undermining class barriers. Rapid expansion of international trade and capital exports, within and beyond the confines of particular empires, had fuelled the struggle for hegemony and the arms race, increasing the political weight of military castes. And finally, a wider suffrage made it necessary to seek (and often obtain) a consensus by means of new ideological instruments such as nationalism and racism.

Leaders of the workers' movement analysed many of these new trends with exemplary thoroughness, but their differing interpretations and conclusions gradually crystallized into sharp divergences (Lenin, Luxemburg, Hilferding, Kautsky and Bernstein were some such leaders, each with the support of particular intellectuals and workers, parties, parliamentary fractions and trade unions). On one side, the new capitalism was thought to confirm the possibility of a gradual, virtually painless, road to socialism, almost a natural process, meaning that priority should be given to parliamentary action; war and authoritarian attacks on the movement might arise along the way, but they were avoidable and would not check the general tendency. On the other side, imperialism was seen as the final stage of capitalism – a stage of decay in which real power grew more concentrated behind a mask of corrupt and discredited parliamentarism. It was marked by ever greater unevenness of global development, antagonism among the great powers, and a tendency to seek overseas outlets for the recurrent crises of underconsumption, while rallying the wavering middle classes around the sound and fury of patriotism, and isolating the working class and the peasantry. War was part of this wider picture of imperialism, and it would either offer an opportunity for revolution or sink into pointless slaughter. Neither side in the debate, however, argued that war was imminent; and, for opposite reasons, neither thought that it would fundamentally alter the course of events. Thus it happened that the whole socialist movement adopted a firm anti-war stance yet neglected to develop the kind of mass campaign which, given the hesitancy of the world's rulers, might have at least delayed its outbreak or encouraged a refusal to participate in it.

When the great conflict erupted it overwhelmed the world, and the Second International along with it. Most of the major parties, with the timid exception of the Italian, reneged on their undertaking to oppose and denounce it. Lenin remained alone. 'Betrayal' is not a word I am fond of, and its obsessive use later became a regrettable barrier to the dialogue or convergence on the Left that was both necessary and possible. But it really does apply to that historical moment, and not merely to the support of Social Democrat MPs for war credits and belligerent governments, the way in which their leaderships went along with, or actually fanned, the patriotic fury among their membership and electorate, and the perversion of national defence into a lust for victory. Then, even when carnage, mass hunger and 'cannon fodder' policies had opened people's eyes, on the losing side but also elsewhere; even in the context of widespread disillusion, anger, desertions and strikes, those same leaderships stood by their agreement to 'maintain order' and ensure the continuity of bureaucratic apparatuses and military castes. They rejected not only revolution – unlikely as this was – but also any serious attempt at political democratization and social reform. That is, they broke with their own roots. And they paid the price for it. As a political force and world view, what still went by the name of Social Democracy remained marginal, scattered and powerless for decades; it regained an important role only after the Second World War, when it effectively switched to a liberal-democratic identity and, taking the rough with the smooth, became a left wing within the Western camp.

Those who had been right about the war, and had expected to see a socialist revolution break out in the wake of popular insurgency, were now faced with being a minority and began to look for short cuts. Suffering defeats and repression in Western Europe, they regrouped around Leninist thought (a resounding call to arms as well as a profound revision of Marxism, and the only revolutionary legacy of the war), in a vast backward country destined to remain isolated for a long time to come. Russia was the birthplace of the strength and appeal, but also the difficulties and limitations, of a new political subject that decided to call itself Communist – one that aspired to play a global role, and indeed did so for many decades.

This brings us to the most controversial aspect of Communism: the interpretation and evaluation of the Bolshevik revolution, and of its consolidation into a major state and an international organization. No genuinely new reflection can avoid tackling the Revolution, but although it defined the limits of revision, criticism and abjuration it has remained secondary and merely implicit in the historical and political debates of recent years.

Was it a disastrous choice that already contained the chromosomes for degeneration, and eventually collapsed of its own accord after doing untold damage? If that were true, there would be no need to rack our brains reconstructing a historical process in all its contradictions: the conclusion would be that the 'impetus' of October did not exhaust itself, but never existed; it would suffice to identify the faulty chromosomes, to point to the final undoing, and to archive the rest for the consideration of scholars. Or was the Russian Revolution a great event which propelled democracy and civilization forward, only to be betrayed by personal abuse of power and a bureaucratization unrelated to the historical context in which it originated and was inserted? In that case a robust denunciation of Stalinism, together with frank criticism of those who, out of anti-fascist pride, failed to condemn it in time, would suffice for us to feel free to start again, from square one, in 'a new world'.

My study of Italian Communism in the second part of the twentieth century will, I hope, contribute to a more serious and detailed assessment of what the Russian Revolution aimed to achieve. But it would be making a false start if it did not first briefly review the events of the period between the two world wars. For it was then that zones of censorship and misunderstanding first formed in our memory – zones that we must struggle to overcome. And it was in the events of that time that Italian Communism found the resources, limited though they were, to build a great mass party and to seek its own 'road to socialism'.

3. The Russian Revolution would not have taken place, and would not have triumphed, without Lenin and the Bolshevik Party, which had its roots in a small but concentrated working class, and whose quality and firmness of leadership were not divided but expanded by the convergence with Trotsky's group and the return of numerous exiles trained in various corners of Europe. Still less would it have occurred without the First World War. It became an option because of the decomposition of the autocratic state, the hunger in the cities, the uprooting of millions of peasants to fight at the front, the insurgency within the ranks of an army in disarray, and the loss of legitimacy of the commanding officers. The soviets were not the invention of one party but an organizational form driven by necessity and anger; they already had the experience of the 1905 revolution behind them, and it was in the struggle for hegemony within the soviets that a clear authority and programme came to be recognized. Although Lenin had already formulated the theory of uneven development, according to which the system would break at its weakest links, he long resisted the idea that the revolution in Russia might have a socialist character, still less that a socialist revolution could consolidate itself in such an economically and culturally backward country. (For this reason, he rejected Trotsky's theory of permanent revolution.) At the beginning of the war, he was still convinced that Russia should and could be one link in a game that would be played out in the West, where socialism rested upon 'more solid' foundations. He eventually decided to seize power directly and at a stroke, in the face of much hesitation on the part of his comrades, only when the existing regime was in terminal crisis. A majority of the population resolutely favoured the republic, land redistribution and immediate peace,

which the liberal-democratic parties were neither willing nor able to concede. All power to the soviets and the capture of the Winter Palace became the 'minimum programme', to which the Bolsheviks added nationalization of the banks, an instrument of foreign capital. There was no alternative to the October Revolution, if autocratic power was not to be restored and the multinational state broken up in conditions of anarchy. In fact, the revolution was largely bloodless: fewer people were wounded in the storming of the Winter Palace than in the later reconstruction of the event for the cinema. And it had the consent of the broadest layers of the population, in so far as this was possible in a vast, illiterate country united by nothing but Tsarist mythology and religious superstition. It was in no sense a Jacobin venture, in which a minority takes advantage of an opportunity to seize power. The Bolsheviks held fast to their programme even when it conflicted with more radical tendencies, such as those that manifested themselves in relation to the Brest-Litovsk peace agreement.

But did not the shaping of the new regime – weakening of the soviets, single-party system, restrictions on liberty, execution of the royal family, secret police – reflect the authoritarian side of Leninism? Was it not a consistent, extreme application of concepts supposedly formulated by Marx ('violence as midwife of history', 'dictatorship of the proletariat')? That is not how it seems to me – or at least it is only a secondary part of the truth. One has only to reread two of Lenin's essays, written at a short interval from each other: *State and Revolution* centres on the idea of an advanced democracy which, though still a dictatorship (like any state), is based on direct, participatory institutions, represents the majority of the people, and guarantees the class content of the new state; but *The Proletarian Revolution and the Renegade Kautsky* presents the proletarian dictatorship as 'unrestricted', and the democratic dimension as absorbed into the party that represents and organizes it.

Two towering events were decisive for this shift. First, a long and terrible civil war, involving the popular masses, confirmed the legitimacy of the revolution but had a devastating effect on every part of the country, more even than the world war had done. It was not fought against liberal or bourgeois forces, but against ruthless Tsarist armies bent on restoration that recruited layers of the population previously subject to imperial repression and enjoyed the support of the British and French governments. The Bolsheviks eventually won through, but at the price of iron-fisted militarization; chaos overtook every productive sector, the countryside consumed whatever it had, the cities starved, the industrial proletariat was decimated and dispersed, and anyone with technical skills opted to emigrate (except for one sector won over to the revolution, which the Red Army did not hesitate to swallow up). Merely to survive translated into a harsh centralization of power.

Second, the mass upsurge in the West, especially Germany, which for a brief while had seemed to herald the possibility of revolution, soon ran out of steam and became confined to a minority in society. Lacking clear objectives, trained cadres or a secure political leadership, this spirit continued to manifest itself in occasional scattered revolts that were easily suppressed by the military apparatuses and bands of nationalist volunteers. Summary executions and selective assassinations (from Rosa Luxemburg to Walter Rathenau) were used to block the road not only to an improbable revolution, but also to political democratization and limited social reforms. The mindless impositions of the Versailles Treaty, arrogantly administered by the victor nations, also weighed heavily in the scales at this time.

In short, the whole picture changed. The Russian revolution, still isolated and threatened after its survival emergency, had to face all the problems of primitive economic accumulation, the task of rebuilding a state that had been almost totally destroyed, and the demands of an early literacy campaign targeting 80 per cent of the population. Lenin at least partly understood the real state of affairs. He brusquely put an end to the enthusiasms and passions of the war communism period, pushed through a New Economic Policy that soon bore fruit, and moved towards a prudent foreign policy that included the signing of the Rapallo Treaty with Germany. He also offered cooperation deals to foreign capitalist companies, guaranteeing the security of their investments in Russia (although this was soon revoked). Finally, almost on his deathbed, he warned against the concentration of power in the hands of one leader.

But the problem remained in all its seriousness: how to consolidate a new state and a socialist society in a backward country, which would probably have to rely on its own resources for a long time to come. Am I trying to excuse everything as the consequence of overwhelming objective factors, overlooking the mistaken analyses and theories and avoidable macropolitical errors which impaired the Russian Revolution from the very beginning? On the contrary. I am trying to explain the dynamic of events – perhaps only to get it straight in my own mind – by placing them in context and measuring the undoubted successes against the difficulties; just as historians, myself included, have done with regard to the ascent of bourgeois modernity. In the Russian case, the gains included rapid economic development, even during the world slump of the 1930s; moves to raise the cultural level of the masses; upward social mobility and income redistribution amid grinding poverty; elementary social safeguards for all; and a generally cautious, non-aggressive foreign policy. All this was achieved over a period of years, forming the basis for a high level of consent and mobilization inside the country and, despite everything, sympathy and prestige abroad. I have no wish to be silent about certain avoidable errors that could have been corrected when it was easy to do so, and that it is helpful, as well as just, to recognize today. The first error, to which Lenin himself paved the way, was an obsession with the 'correct line' in the centralized decision-making of the Third International, applied to tactical details in highly diverse situations; this led from the beginning to seriously flawed and inconsistent policies, such as the extremist course in Germany (for which Zinoviev and Radek were directly responsible) or the accommodation with the Kuomintang in China, until the moment when it began to massacre Communists. Over time the various national parties grew used to applying the directives of the leading party to the letter, without mediation, as in the case of the Hitler-Stalin pact. This undermined one of the top strategic acquisitions of the Russian revolution: a capacity for analysis in keeping with the specific situation of the day.

The second fundamental error, at the end of the NEP, concerns the decision to go for rapid industrialization (necessary in itself) and forced collectivization of the countryside. Instead of increasing agricultural output, which would in turn have provided acceptable resources for the growth of industry, this move in the late 1920s entailed a tragic human cost and transformed agriculture into a lasting handicap for the Soviet economy. Central planning and containment of the kulaks were perhaps necessary, but the frenzied planning and collectivization of every last parcel of land were another matter – not to speak of the mass deportations of the peasantry.

A third error, initiated by Lenin and corrected only after fatal delay, was the branding of 'centrism' as the main enemy within the workers' movement. Social Democracy certainly deserved much of the blame, with its succession of broken pledges, unfulfilled concessions and unprincipled alliances, but it was sheer sectarianism on the Comintern's part to write off a broad and still fluid milieu with which serious discussion would sometimes have been possible, to issue 'take it or leave it' ultimatums, and to propose no more than a united front from below that excluded other party leaderships. The result was a spirit of self-sufficiency that not even the victory of fascism could dispel, until it was too late. Stalin was no more responsible than his opponents for all these errors.

If we do not consider both sides of the Russian Revolution, and of the first decade after its consolidation, we will be unable to interpret the next, even more contradictory, decade, which witnessed the hardest test of all and the most important achievement: the anti-fascist resistance and the Second World War. The central argument of today's historical revisionism, which has seeped into and distorted the diffuse memory of the period, is that fascism was a wild, delirious response to the impending threat of Bolshevism. This contention is groundless. Fascism in Italy came into being around the theme of a 'victory betrayed' in the First World War, and its campaign of violence 'against the Reds' began when the factory occupations – a movement with no aspirations to revolution – were already over; when peasant revolts were rare and sporadic, the Socialist Party was in disarray and heading for repeated splits, and the trade unions were led by their most moderate wing. Fascism later secured funding from the employers and complicity from the Guardie Regie (founded in 1919 as a repressive state force), at a time when the Church had just signed a pact with the Liberals and, within the Catholic world, was keeping a watchful eye on Sturzo and his newly founded Partito Popolare Italiano. Fascism thus presented itself as a guarantee of order in the last instance. It eventually came to power in a non-emergency situation, by royal appointment and with the direct support of traditional conservative forces in parliament (even

Giolitti[2] and Croce at one moment), which thought they could make use of it for a while and then rein it in by restoring the previous oligarchic power structure.

In Germany, National Socialism was a marginal and defeated force throughout the period when left-wing unrest was being suppressed in turns by Social Democrat governments, a rebuilt army and a decidedly conservative parliamentary majority. Its eventual growth occurred on a tide of resurgent nationalism, amid an economic crisis intensified by the persistence of war reparations. Anti-Semitism and the selective violence of the SA brownshirts received explicit support from high places. The Nazis therefore surprised everyone by winning 44 per cent of the vote in 1932, but they were again on the wane in 1933. Hitler was appointed chancellor by President Hindenburg, with the complicity of Von Papen and Brüning and the decisive backing of the Prussian general staff. In Hungary, Horthy came to power when Béla Kun's 'Soviet republic' had already been crushed. And later, Franco launched a civil war in Spain against a duly elected moderate democratic government, while among the masses the anarchists carried rather more weight than the 'Bolsheviki'.

The Communists undoubtedly bore some responsibility in all these cases, because they failed to recognize the gravity of the situation and, with their theory of social fascism, impeded unity among the forces that could and should have fended off the danger. But the responsibility of the governing classes for the rise of fascism was much greater: they sowed the seeds, exacerbated the grievances that gave rise to it, and facilitated and legitimated fascist initiatives – not in order to confront a greater danger, but to preclude any future challenge to the social and imperial order. In any event, when the economic crisis was raging in the mid 1930s, fascism was already entrenched in much of Europe and showing clear signs of its authoritarian and aggressive proclivities. This was the darkest hour of the twentieth century, and both the extraordinary, positive rise of the Soviet Union and the possibility of its degeneration had their origins in it.

The Communists were embattled everywhere, especially in the West, where they were organizationally and electorally weak, if

2. Giovanni Giolitti (1842–1928): the leading Italian statesman of the late-nineteenth and early-twentieth century, who served five terms as prime minister.

not outlawed, exiled, imprisoned or liquidated. The Soviet Union, despite the success of the first five-year plans, felt vulnerable to military aggression and unable to stand up to it alone. In less than two years it therefore executed a major political and ideological turn, well summarized in the later slogan: 'Raise the banner of bourgeois freedoms from the mire.' Stalin not only accepted but promoted the turn, the Seventh Congress of the Communist International sanctioned it, and Togliatti, Dimitrov and Thorez translated it into the Popular Front experience. Much could be said about the short-lived Popular Front governments, which were poorly thought out from a strategic point of view. Here I will simply mention a few key points.

a) They failed in their immediate objective of preventing another world war and launching a policy of reforms. But they did send the first signal of a great democratic mobilization of working people and intellectuals against fascism and in support of new economic policies. Showing an affinity with the American New Deal, though not always consciously, they laid the first stones of an edifice that took shape during the war and led to victory: they were something more than a military alliance.

b) Although they went into crisis and eventually succumbed, it cannot be said that this was due to extremism on the part of the Communists. With defence of the Soviet Union as their top priority, they took part in the experience with great conviction (and heroism in Spain), perhaps even erring on the side of caution. In France, major (and permanent) social gains resulted from a great grass-roots movement; the PCF intervened so that it would not go 'too far'. The Blum government, which the Communists loyally supported from outside, soon fell as a result of its own uncertainties in economic and financial policy, the flight of capital, and an investment strike. Franco's victory in Spain was assisted by the direct intervention of Italian and German fascism, while the British line of benevolent neutrality was first imposed on Blum and then copied by Daladier. Though the Communists dealt harshly with anarchist attempts to radicalize events in Spain, the Soviet Union stood alone in supporting the legitimacy of the republic, for as long as it was able. The criticism that may be made of the Communists is that their new policy was mainly geared to an emergency situation, not inscribed within a long-term strategy.

c) The Italian party, though diminished by repression, formed the bulk of the International Brigades in Spain (along with the small Partito d'Azione); it suffered heavy losses there, but also trained a new batch of cadres that would prove essential to the Resistance in Italy. Especially in the person of Palmiro Togliatti, it also began to adumbrate a strategic conception of 'progressive democracy', which was consistent with Togliatti's earlier *Lectures on Fascism* and picked up the tenuous thread of the Lyons Congress (inspired by Gramsci). Beyond the Popular Fronts, however, and especially after their defeat, the real touchstone in the 1930s was how to avert another war. This is the issue on which there is still so much reticence today, and so much distortion of the events and the connections between them. Hitler's belligerent frenzy could have been halted in time. There is abundant historical evidence that, despite his assumption of absolute powers, the idea of openly planning for war in the short term met with opposition in Germany, even among powerful forces that could have blocked or overturned it. First of all, the heads of the armed forces were convinced that another war – at least at that time – would be lost; and they made their views known. The militarization of the Rhineland, the annexation of Austria, the invasion of the Sudetenland, the effective occupation of the rest of Czechoslovakia: at all these stages, a coalition like the one that eventually fought the war against Hitler's dream of world domination could have put a stop to it with a show of resolve.

The Soviet Union's proposals along these lines were repeatedly dodged or rejected by Western governments. Even Poland, the last victim in the run-up to war, turned down Moscow's offer of a mutual defence agreement. The successive acts of appeasement and capitulation fuelled the Nazi project; Munich is the best-known example, and it was no accident that Mussolini was considered a credible, if not neutral, mediator. Public opinion, unwilling to run the risk of war, breathed a sigh of relief. But within weeks Hitler had torn up the agreement and was demanding more. Were those who could have stopped him simply abject or ignorant? I don't believe they were, and almost no one else believes it either. The fact is that Chamberlain and Daladier – Roosevelt remained aloof, facing an isolationist public and an ever hostile Wall Street – had a plan they could not admit to, but which boasted a certain logic: namely, to use and weaken Germany by turning its imperial ambitions eastward, thus killing two birds with one stone. At this point the USSR signed the non-aggression pact with Germany, to avoid becoming its isolated victim, to gain time and turn the scales. The aftermath proved that it was right to do so: Russia was invaded not long afterwards, but by then it was part of a military alliance strong enough to resist Hitler. The error if there was one – and the PCI was able to avoid it more easily – was to drag the Communist parties for a year or more into the absurd theory of an inter-imperialist war, which dimmed their anti-fascist commitment and forfeited some of the esteem they had won in the struggle.

The above reconstruction is borne out by the fact that, even after war was declared and Poland invaded, the British and French did not make any serious moves until the German Blitzkrieg through Belgium had broken the Western front, France had collapsed and its parliament (including eighty Socialist deputies) had delivered the nation to the puppet government of Marshal Pétain. The Netherlands, Denmark and Norway were invaded, Switzerland remained neutral but did not refrain from lucrative business dealings, Romania and Hungary were already aligned with Germany, and Italy, shrewd as ever, joined the fray in order to share in the spoils. Europe was in fascist hands; only the British, protected by the Channel and bolstered by American aid, fought on intransigently – thanks, moreover, to the resolve of an intelligent Conservative of character, Winston Churchill. Fortunes began to change from the moment Hitler invaded the USSR. With the benefit of hindsight it is easy to say that this was the greatest of all his follies. Yet there is often a method in madness: Hitler was evidently convinced that it would only take one push to make the Soviet Union founder, from its internal more than external weakness, just as France had done a year before and Tsarist Russia thirty years before that. How could an inferior race stand fast, especially one that was poorly armed and ruled by an Asiatic despot? The collapse of the regime would have given Germany control over a vast country, an inexhaustible reserve of manpower and raw materials. At that point Britain could not have held out alone, and the United States would have had further reason to stay out of the war. Indeed, many of Hitler's enemies feared that his calculations were correct.

The first push was certainly effective, perhaps because Stalin had not been expecting it so soon; the Germans reached the outskirts of Moscow and drew close to the oil-producing regions of the country. But then, launching the masterful idea of a 'great patriotic war', the Soviet Union proved capable of a miraculous mass mobilization and an astounding industrial effort. The Western Allies understood its vital importance and sent weapons and resources; Leningrad, encircled and bled of half a million lives, held firm; the Germans were stopped on the Volokolamsk road, then surrounded and annihilated at Stalingrad; the long march to Berlin got under way. Meanwhile, Roosevelt used the Japanese attack on Pearl Harbor to bring the United States finally into the war, and an effective partisan struggle emerged in Greece and Yugoslavia. After Stalingrad the game was up for Hitler. When victory finally came, the Soviet Union had played a decisive role and paid with twenty-one million dead. Was Communism a myth? Even if we accept this, there were good reasons why it should have grown greater at that time. To depict the Second World War as a conflict between two 'totalitarianisms' is sheer nonsense: the Communists did not create a river of blood, they shed their own.

d) But for the Communists the 1930s had another side that cannot be passed over in silence, and which in the long run proved decisive. I am referring, of course, to the internal terror, and the cruel mass repression of potential or supposed opponents. This not only revealed the practice of an unfettered institutionalized power, but signalled a qualitative leap in the character and methods of Stalin's personal rule, and unleashed mechanisms that it would be difficult to reverse. The scale of the leap is apparent not only in the number of deaths and deportations, or in the arbitrary appointment of executioners who, in many cases, soon fell victim in their turn. It may be gauged, above all, from two new aspects that marked a profound shift away from Leninist practices, however extreme, as well as from the brutal struggles against oppositionists in the 1920s or the murderous 'class war' against the kulaks. The first aspect, most pronounced between 1936 and 1938, was that the repression struck not only at the old Bolshevik elite – who had lost all influence in society and in the ruling apparatuses, and were generally disposed to accept party discipline – but also at the Communist Party itself, not sparing people who had implemented Stalin's decisions and remained loyal to him throughout. Thus, of the delegates to the Seventeenth Congress of the CPSU in 1934, the so-called Victors' Congress, four-fifths were dead or in exile a few years later – including 120 of the 139 members of the new Central Committee elected there. The terror reached its peak when the various economic and political options had been more or less successfully implemented, and the danger looming on the horizon was wholly external. Thus it was a terror with no rational basis or plausible justification, a terror that did not strengthen but weakened the system at every level (one extreme example: the liquidation of a loyal and competent Red Army leadership on the eve of a war, three lieutenant-generals out of five, 130 major-generals out of 168, and so on). Stalin himself was both source and victim of this lunacy. His daughter's memoirs record that, in each purge, he was driven by doubts about the quality of cadres and a neurotic suspicion of their loyalty, along with the fear of a self-stabilizing bureaucratic caste and repressive apparatuses that increasingly acted on their own initiative. Then, having realized that the purges led to the promotion of even more dangerous people, he hastened to get rid of them too.

The second novel aspect of Stalin's rule, related to the first but insufficient to explain it, was the extraction of confessions and the character of other evidence used to justify the merciless verdicts in the major trials. The defendants had allegedly been provocateurs, terrorist plotters, fascist spies or Japanese agents from the start. It seems absurd, almost senseless, to ask of people – as so many still do, even of later generations – what did you know about all that? For how could anyone have believed, then or afterwards, that virtually the entire group that led the October Revolution had been working throughout to undo it, or that most of the cadres on whom Stalin had relied to do his bidding had been preparing to betray him? The result was not only an inexplicable hiatus between means and ends but a profound and lasting cultural deformation, in which reason was confined to the limits imposed by a faith. Voluntarism and subjectivism, both at the top and in the consciousness of the masses, sowed the seeds that long afterwards would produce their opposite: mass apathy and bureaucratic cynicism. And yet the power of an ideal, the sacrifices made in its name, the successes achieved for one and all, to be capped by other successes in the future, led even those in the know to justify the means, which they regarded as transient. After all, it was said, catastrophe had been averted, and new space was opening up for democratic and social gains and the liberation of new oppressed peoples; the world really had changed, and those contradictions would be resolved in the wake of further advances.

Such was the complex legacy that Italian Communism took over: the resources offered by history, and the limitations that it had to overcome in order to found a mass party and to define a strategy of its own – not a model to be reproduced, but a background that was necessary for it to 'go further'. Not for nothing did I adapt Kipling's famous, and deliberately ambiguous, formulation as the title for this section: 'the burden of Communist man'.

THE GRAMSCI GENOME

At the moment of its real take-off, however, the PCI also inherited a largely unfamiliar voice that had been locked away by the fascist enemy, and a self-standing resource in the shape of the *Prison Notebooks*. Antonio Gramsci, a brain that had continued to function despite everything, bequeathed to the Party a veritable mine of ideas.

I shall turn to Gramsci's thought several times in the course of this book, to elucidate points which always remained unclear in the policies and strategic thinking of the PCI, and which even today, or especially today, offer priceless material for discussion of the present – and an original reading of Italian history, in both its specificity and general significance. For now, I shall consider the 'fate' of Gramsci: that is, how and when he influenced the gradual definition of the PCI's distinctive identity and strategy, at first invisibly, then in public view, before waning to the point where he was little more than a guru of anti-fascism, a moral example and a multitalented intellectual. In other words, I shall be speaking not so much of Gramsci as of Gramscianism, as part of the genetic material that composes a great collective force and a national culture.

The *Prison Notebooks* required some mediation to become intelligible and to make a mark beyond a restricted circle of intellectuals. Prison conditions and censorship, frequent bouts of illness, limited information and reading material meant that Gramsci was forced to write allusively in the form of notes, breaking off a train of thought and returning to it later, unable to achieve the purpose he had set for his writings, which sustained the heroic effort of a brain that continued to think in solitude. Painstaking philological labour was therefore not enough to assemble the various fragments and to interpret them faithfully. From the outset, a risky attempt to clarify their essential elements and offer a guiding thread through the vast mass of material was required, so that even opponents would be obliged to come to terms with it. In short, it was necessary to restore Gramsci's role as the head and animating force of a great political enterprise, and the character he himself had given his work as a philosophy of praxis.

This mediation happened, with potent results. Gramsci soon became, and remained, a point of reference for political and cultural research in Italy and beyond, among Communists but not only for them. The mediation was achieved not by a few prominent intellectuals, or by a school, but through an operation planned by Togliatti with the participation of a mass party. It involved the dangerous work of conserving the manuscripts, organizing their publication in a provisional set of themes, and strongly encouraging their collective study. The recent fable that Togliatti entrusted the *Notebooks* to the Soviet archives to keep them out of circulation is a ludicrous inversion of the truth, and the notion that their first edition was heavily censored and manipulated has been artificially inflated. Of course, Togliatti did not simply wish to pay homage to a great friend, or to make a contribution to Italian culture; he also had the political objective – in the strong sense – of using a great body of thought and an authority beyond dispute to establish a new identity for Italian Communism. Something similar had happened once before, in the formative process of German Social Democracy and the Second International, when Marx was read and disseminated through Kautsky, to some extent with the approval of the ageing Engels. This came at the price of a certain reductionism. Indeed, shortly before his death, Togliatti himself recognized as much in a review article whose importance should not be exaggerated. We Italian Communists, he said in essence, owe a debt to Antonio Gramsci: we largely built our identity and strategy on the foundation of his work, but in order to do this we reduced him to our size, to the needs of our own politics, sacrificing 'much beyond that'.

When I speak of a reductionist reading, I am not referring to manipulation or censorship of the text, such as many doggedly sought to identify in later years. Valentino Gerratana's exemplary work has shown that it was more a question of skilful organization, which after all was initially necessary: skill in putting Gramsci's notes together, in sustaining a long production chain, in commenting on the writings in a way that stimulated their publication. It is not difficult to detect in all this the limits of the epoch, which Togliatti accepted. Above all he tried for a long time to play down the areas in which Gramsci had innovated in relation to Leninism, or conflicted with its Stalinist version. But he also sought to bring out the things in Gramsci that would point to a continuity between 'anti-fascist revolution' and his own conception of 'progressive democracy', and he more or less consciously deferred consideration of certain themes until the times were riper for them.

The main focus, then, was on two great themes. The first was Gramsci's conception of the Risorgimento as an 'unfinished revolution' (due to its omission of the agrarian question), and a 'passive revolution' (little involvement of the masses, and a marginalization of democratically more advanced political and cultural currents, resulting in a compromise between parasitic landowners and the bourgeoisie). The second was the relative autonomy and importance of the 'superstructure' – in opposition to the vulgar mechanicism that had also penetrated the Third International through Bukharin – and hence the role of intellectuals, political parties and the state apparatuses.

These themes unwittingly elicited a particular interpretative slant. On the one hand, they underlined the links between Gramsci and radical-liberal, anti-fascist writers such as Gaetano Salvemini, Guido Dorso or Piero Gobetti (with their analysis of the fatal backwardness of Italy's 'lumpen capitalism' and bigoted national culture), while downplaying the critique of Cavour's compromise, the swift corruption of parliamentarism into transformism, the ambiguities of Giolitti's periods in office, the polemic with Croce, the rising poison of nationalism, the 'Roman question' that continued to fuel sovereignty disputes between the Italian state and the Church – in short, all the one-sided, distorted processes of modernization that led to the crisis of the liberal state and the birth of fascism. On the other hand, the correct reaffirmation of the autonomy of the 'superstructure' tended to foster a separation of the political-institutional dynamic from its class base, turning Marxist historicism more and more into historicism *tout court*.

Other Gramscian themes remained for a long time marginal in the Party's theoretical reflection, and absent from its politics. I am thinking of what he wrote on 'Americanism and Fordism', which looked ahead to what would soon happen in Italy too and was already discernible, as a vague ambition, in fascist politics; or of his youthful passion for the factory councils experience, so different from the Russian soviets, which he himself had set aside after realizing its limits, but which, if revisited, would have helped the PCI to interpret the coming phase of the Resistance and, much later, the revolt of 1968. The reductive reading of Gramsci, both in the early days and in the longer term, did not have only cultural consequences. Two points should be mentioned in particular: the persistent failure to recognize and analyse the sweep of the economic modernization process in Italy; and the conception of a new kind of mass party, capable of engaging in political action, not just propaganda, and of educating the people, but still a long way from the collective intellectual, engaged with grass-roots movements or institutions and committed to cultural and moral reform, which Gramsci had considered especially important in a country untouched by the Reformation.

At least at the beginning, then, Gramsci's legacy offered itself – and was accepted – as the basis for a middle way between Leninist orthodoxy and classical Social Democracy, more than as a synthesis transcending their common limits of economism and statism. It was a 'genome' that could either develop or merely tick over, either fully assert itself or waste away. We shall see it at work. But it seems to me that Togliatti's initial interpretation of Gramsci was neither false nor groundless. For the driving force behind the *Notebooks* really is critical and self-critical reflection on the causes and consequences of the failure of revolution in the Western countries – in which he, like Lenin, had believed. Among the Marxists of his time, he was the only one who did not explain this failure only in terms of Social Democratic betrayal or the weakness and errors of the Communists; nor did he conclude at all that the Russian Revolution had been immature, and its consolidation in a state misguided. Instead, he looked for the deeper reasons why the model of the Russian Revolution could not be reproduced in the advanced societies, even though it was the necessary hinterland (and Leninism a priceless theoretical contribution) for a revolution in the West that would unfold differently, and be richer in results. His whole effort of thought rested on two foundations that may be summarized in a few sentences. First an analysis: 'In the East the State was everything, civil society was primordial and gelatinous;

in the West, there was a proper relationship between State and civil society, and when the State trembled a sturdy structure of civil society was at once revealed. The State was only an outer ditch, behind which there stood a powerful system of fortresses and earthworks.'[3] Second, a theoretical principle constantly invoked with a quotation from Marx's preface to *A Contribution to the Critique of Political Economy*: 'No social order is ever destroyed before all the productive forces for which it is sufficient have been developed, and new superior relations of production never replace older ones before the material conditions for their existence have matured within the framework of the old society.'[4]

For Gramsci, then, the revolution is a long worldwide process made up of stages, in which the conquest of state power, though necessary, occurs at a point that depends on the historical conditions; in the West it requires a protracted labour of capturing fortresses and earthworks and constructing a historic bloc of various classes, each with distinctive interests and cultural and political roots. At the same time this social process is not a gradual, one-way result of a tendency inherent in capitalist development and democracy, but rather the product of an organized will that consciously intervenes in history, a new political and cultural hegemony, a new human type at an advanced stage of formation.

Togliatti was therefore not wrong in wanting to use Gramsci's thought as an anticipation and theoretical foundation for the 'new party' and the 'Italian road to socialism', continuous with, but also distinct from, Leninism and original Social Democracy; part of a worldwide historical process initiated and supported by the Russian Revolution, but not a belated imitation of the model that this revolution created. Togliatti was not wrong, but nor was he without motives of his own, in light of the major new developments since the *Notebooks* were drafted: the emergence of armed resistance movements in many parts of Eastern, Western and Central Europe, the victory over fascism, widespread recognition of the decisive role of the Soviet Union in the war, the rise of powerful anti-colonial liberation movements, and the revolution in China. All this forced capitalism into a compromise and opened up spaces

3. Antonio Gramsci, *Selections from the Prison Notebooks*, London: Lawrence and Wishart, 1971, p. 238.

4. Karl Marx, *A Contribution to the Critique of Political Economy*, London: Lawrence and Wishart, 1971, p. 21.

for major social and political gains in the West too. However, the victories were obtained in alliance with a wide range of states and forces, including openly conservative governments and party leaderships in Europe. In contrast to the aftermath of the First World War, the armed resistance showed no sign of spilling over into radical popular insurgency. A new power, left intact rather than exhausted by war, was establishing its global economic and military supremacy on the ground, if not yet in policy terms, after the Yalta agreement that had enshrined certain constraints as well as guarantees.

Even those who, like Gramsci, had gone some way towards defining a new path, had been unable to predict either the headlong advance of Communism in the world, or the consolidation of capitalism in the West. Trotsky himself, who, lucid as ever, foresaw the Nazi attack on the Soviet Union and the aid it would receive to fight back, noted shortly before his assassination that if a new world war did not lead to revolution in Europe and the overthrow of bureaucratic rule in the USSR, everything would have to be rethought. Such a re-evaluation is also what Gramsci would have undertaken, I don't know in what way, if he had lived. He would have faced up to the new historical framework, recognized the limits imposed by the relationship of forces in Italy and the world, mobilized all the new resources to preserve and strengthen an autonomous Communist identity in a new 'war of position', and sought to transform a possible new 'passive revolution' into a new hegemony – which is what the followers of Mazzini had failed to do, indeed not even attempted, in the Risorgimento.

This reconstruction of the 'prior events' – which I neither took part in nor witnessed, but have tried to outline, book in hand, with benefit of hindsight – contains nothing original or previously unknown. Its purpose is to re-establish the truth, to counter strictures and judgements that have become today's 'idols of the marketplace'. This should be the starting point for a reflection on the history of Italian Communism.

2

A Founding Act: The Salerno Turn

THE LIBERATION

What would be the most fitting date to mark the birth of this new Communist party, whose particular identity enabled it to have a major influence on Italy's new, and also distinctive, postwar democratic state? I will choose one precise event: Togliatti's return to Italy and the line he proposed – or perhaps one could say imposed – for his party and the whole of the anti-fascist movement, with not only immediate repercussions but long-term importance for the future. It enabled the armed resistance to become a popular insurrection, but defined the limits beyond which it should not go; it attached wide sectors of the masses to Communism, and outlined a strategy for them. The new line thus remained an active element for decades, in successive periods of history, giving rise to close scrutiny, varied interpretations and bitter controversies; it was invoked in support of fruitful innovations and doomed compromises. In the end it hardened into a conventional framework that could be hung on the walls of a museum of national unity, allowing for new approaches as for the removal of embarrassing elements, so that successive ruling classes could pass by it with respect but without thinking or feeling anything. Something similar happened to that great icon of the early Risorgimento, the famous meeting at Teano between Vittorio Emanuele and Garibaldi, which adorned the cover of my school textbook as a child.

Now that the value, conflicts and decline of the First Republic,[1] with all their twists and turns, are past history, and now that the PCI itself is no longer with us, we should unhook the picture from the wall, dust it off and take a closer look at it in its original context. We are lucky that the Resistance, the aftermath of the war and the Salerno turn have for some time now been the object of serious, well-documented research by national as well as regional historians (Paolo Spriano, Aldo Agosti, Giorgio Bocca, Claudio Pavone and Roberto Battaglia are some of the names that spring to mind), and the memoirs of key protagonists are for once ample and forthright (Luigi Longo, Pietro Secchia, Giorgio Amendola, Pietro Nenni, Ferruccio Parri, to mention only those at a high level). The archives themselves are less niggardly, which makes it easier to check and cross-reference the facts. The political pressures today lean in quite a different direction: the First Republic is widely remembered as a time when kickbacks and rule by parties excluded the involvement of citizens in politics, while the PCI is thought of as a fifth column for the Soviet Union; anyone who disputes such crude notions finds himself forced to portray the Resistance as a spontaneous, undifferentiated popular epic, or to argue that the PCI, even in Togliatti's day, had little to do with Moscow. The task, then, is to reorder the wealth of historical material on that founding event and to arrive at a more accurate appraisal of its significance and eventual moorings.

In March 1944, when Togliatti returned to Italy after his long exile, it was no longer in doubt that the war would end with an Allied victory. What was completely uncertain was the future of the country. There was still a long, painful road ahead to win freedom and to safeguard national unity and independence, and the anti-fascist forces, partly divided among themselves, faced an obstruction in their path. This barrier consisted of rubble and moral debris from the many humiliating battles fought and lost on the national territory, and was further reinforced by older ramparts where armed men stood, determined to keep it in place.

Italy was not Yugoslavia, where a lengthy armed struggle had first helped to divert German troops from their Blitzkrieg on the

1. The period from 1947 to 1992 is known in Italy as the First Republic, while the institutional and party-political system that took shape after the crisis of 1992 is referred to as the Second Republic.

Russian front and then advanced to victory in a national and civil war. It was not even France, militarily crushed and occupied, partly ruled by a para-fascist government imposed by the invaders, but with a long democratic tradition. The French resistance movement had taken up arms in 1941, won recognition from the international alliance, and liaised with an exile government in London under the credible figure of de Gaulle. It was no accident that Italy was the first country where fascism had imposed itself by force, enjoying twenty years of power in which to remould the state and its bureaucracy, to drive opponents into prison or exile, and to sink roots into mass culture. Having joined the war on the German side, Italy was now a country more 'occupied by the victors' than liberated. When the regime fell on 25 July 1943, it was due not to a revolt in the country but to a crisis within the ruling group, of which the king[2] had prudently but reluctantly taken advantage. The people flocked into the streets to cheer their regained freedom and, above all, the promise of an end to the war. But those who took power were an oligarchy with scant interest in freedom. Political prisoners were released in dribs and drabs, while in the name of a 'continuing wartime emergency' the press was censored, demonstrations were banned, and anyone who refused to comply was courting arrest or a bullet.

The aim was clear: to negotiate a separate peace with the Allies that would keep a semi-authoritarian state in place, in such a way that the masses remained immobile and the social order was preserved. The talks dragged on for weeks behind closed doors, while the Germans had a free hand to occupy large parts of the country. The terms of the resulting Armistice of Cassibile were initially kept secret, not only because they amounted to unconditional surrender, but also because the victor was given full power – at least until the end of the war – over political developments in territories gradually recaptured from the Germans, and because Marshal Pietro Badoglio's government remained formally in charge of the day-to-day running of the state. The armistice included no pooling of military resources to drive out the Germans more quickly, since at the time the Allies thought the way was open for them to advance without incurring any obligations to Italian forces.

2. Vittorio Emanuele III, who remained King of Italy throughout the fascist period. The country finally became a republic in 1946 following a plebiscite.

The consequences were more disastrous than anyone had foreseen. On 8 September 1943 the king and Badoglio fled Rome, without leaving orders to oppose the Germans; the army dissolved, despite a few isolated acts of heroic resistance, and the soldiers hurried back to their homes; people were in a state of utter confusion, not knowing whether to hate fascism more, for taking them into the war, or the monarchy for leaving them in the lurch; there was no attempt to keep Mussolini in secure custody, lest he join his forces in the North. Was this the result of felonious or incompetent behaviour? Not entirely, in my view. It was also part of a preconceived plan, which if the Allies had rapidly occupied the country would have had some chance of success (as in Japan) – with the help of a pope, Pius XII, who did not conceal that his main concern was the Communist threat.

But it was not to be, because the front became stubbornly blocked at Monte Cassino, the Anzio landing failed to meet expectations, and the Americans and British had to move forces away in preparation for the Normandy landings. It was a tragic pause, but it gave both time and incentive for the political-military launching of a national liberation struggle. The first weeks were extremely difficult, as the Resistance set about collecting discarded or captured weapons and recruiting ex-soldiers and enthusiastic young people into uncoordinated groups in the mountains. But by the early months of 1944, the anti-fascist parties were already working effectively together in liberation committees, which were recognized as the leadership of the struggle. In the large cities of the North, workers' strikes were sparked around basic economic demands, gradually becoming openly political, flanking partisan action though not yet coordinated with it, responding to indiscriminate fascist repression and forced enlistment. In this way the Resistance managed to influence broad sections of public opinion, and by the spring its take-off period was complete. Key parts were played by the network of Communist cadres formed in prison or the Spanish Civil War. The Allies had to take them into account and to weigh up their usefulness.

When Togliatti arrived, his potential base was caught up in a pair of knotty problems that needed to be swiftly disentangled, concerning the character and aims of the liberation struggle and the alliances that would give it the greatest possible impetus. What was the right way to overcome wait-and-see attitudes and involve a majority of the population in its own deliverance? Which postwar outcomes were likely, and which should be fought for? Sharp divisions on these issues existed in both north and south, though to different degrees, and they threatened to paralyse, if not split, the anti-fascist forces as a whole. The first disagreement centred on relations with the monarchy and the Badoglio government, which the Allies had legitimated and were working with in the zones they occupied in their northward advance. All the anti-fascist parties, in both the south and the north, rejected more or less trenchantly the legitimacy of that regime, and refused to fight under its banner. But, whereas the parties of the Left (Partito d'Azione, Socialists, Communists) called for a republic and a government based on the National Liberation Committee that would put an end to equivocation and win the allegiance of the betrayed people, the moderate liberal forces wanted to compel or persuade Vittorio Emanuele to abdicate. They would then form a new government, which, though headed by a prime minister less compromised with the fascist regime, would maintain a line of continuity with the state that had existed before it. The Christian Democrat Party, only just reconstituted around the old leaders of the Partito Popolare, remained non-committal, although some young people who were formed in Catholic Action were already active in the Resistance. The Communist Party itself conducted a lively internal debate: any agreement with the Badoglio government was unanimously ruled out, but, whereas the leading group in Rome (headed by Mauro Scoccimarro) considered this a priority issue, the *milanesi* around Luigi Longo did not want to waste too much time on diatribes, thinking that matters would sort themselves out with the development of the armed resistance. The Allies too were divided: Roosevelt, partly swayed by US public opinion, was hostile to the king and his government, while Churchill remained firm in his support for them, mistrustful or even contemptuous of the anti-fascist forces; the British, however, were the main military force in the Italian theatre.

Togliatti cut through the knot in a few days. His proposal was that the question of the republic could remain open, pending a referendum at the end of the war, and that Badoglio could remain in office with a government that included all the anti-fascist forces, on condition that it waged war against the fascists and the Germans, without any more prevarication, so that part of the national territory could be liberated at least some time before the arrival of Allied troops. With greater or lesser conviction, everyone soon accepted this proposal because of its intrinsic strengths: it was a realistic compromise, dictated by the internal and international relationship of forces, but it also gave a new boost to the armed struggle and the perspective of a people's uprising. It called on everyone to make the maximum effort, while guaranteeing that all would have space to vie for their views in the future. This would probably not have carried the day, however, without the authority and determination of the man who proposed it. Palmiro Togliatti, the undisputed leader of a force whose prestige had been earned on the battlefield, had the courage to argue bluntly for his position as if there were no alternative. Besides, Joseph Stalin – who enjoyed huge popularity, and not only among Communists, after Stalingrad and the Red Army's advance – had already created a fait accompli by recognizing the Badoglio government.

Since then there has been much discussion about which of the two men instigated the policy, and which implemented it. But it is an artificial debate, since on this occasion at least the convergence was based on conviction, even if the two men's intentions were different. Stalin wanted to develop resistance in European countries still occupied by the Germans, to hasten the end of a war that was costing a huge loss of life; he did not wish to compromise the Yalta agreement, or be drawn into supporting a series of civil wars in Western Europe that had little chance of success. Togliatti, for his part, rightly believed that only a unified armed struggle and a genuine popular uprising would enable the PCI to become a major force commanding widespread recognition, and allow Italy to consolidate its independence and tear up at least some of the deep roots of fascism. His policy soon secured results: the Allies explicitly recognized Italy's role as a co-belligerent, and the right of Italians to decide democratically upon the shape of their future institutions; the national liberation committees spread more rapidly on the ground; and new regions, new social groups (especially farmers) and new political currents (especially Catholic ones) streamed into the operations of the partisans. Over the following months, these conditions proved vital in overcoming the disorientation caused by the ill-omened 'Alexander declaration'[3]

3. On 18 July 1943 General Alexander, supreme commander of Allied forces in Italy, had issued a proclamation that dissolved the fascist party but effectively maintained the personnel of the fascist regime in positions of authority:

and the block on supplies to the Resistance that it had threatened to entail, and thus in preparing for the terrible winter ahead and the insurrection that led to the epic victory of 25 April 1945.

But Togliatti had to face another problem, less immediate but more complex, after his return to Italy: the problem of tactics and strategy for the postwar period. This was already preying on the mind of the organizations, as well as the individuals, most deeply involved in the Resistance. Those who risked their lives fighting in the mountains, or risked deportation organizing strikes, were undoubtedly eager to drive out the Germans and liquidate their henchmen, to win freedom and redeem the nation. But they were also driven by more radical and ambitious objectives: they wanted the political, economic and military leaders who had supported fascism, and ultimately profited from it, to pay a just price for their actions; they wanted not only the restoration of pre-fascist institutions but a democracy open to control by the people, with worker participation in factory management. Many of them were also impatient to begin transforming society in a socialist direction. But how and when, and within what limits, could such ambitions be satisfied, given Italy's place in the international situation and the overall relationship of forces within Italian society itself?

Stalin, still believing in the possibility of a favourable development of international relations – he had found an interlocutor in Roosevelt – and fearing an incipient tendency to cold war that might turn hot, did not veto any new course in advance. But nor did he provide any active encouragement, since his military victory and enhanced status in world politics strengthened his original misconception of a self-sufficient Soviet Union that would serve as a political guide and model. He therefore suggested tactical prudence to the Western Communist parties, with an unchanged strategy and ideology. Togliatti used the space this offered him, as well as the new strength of the PCI (whose limits and contradictions he nevertheless recognized), and moved boldly to make the Salerno turn the strategic starting point for a refoundation of Italian Communism. In speeches at Naples, Rome and Florence,

'All administrative and judicial officials of provinces and communities and all other government municipal functionaries and employees, and all officers and employees of the state, municipal or other public services except such officials and political leaders as are removed by me are required to continue in performance of their duties subject to my direction.'

and again after the victory of 25 April, he put his cards on the table. It was neither possible nor desirable, he argued, to continue with ambiguous perspectives that failed to distinguish between the terms 'socialist democracy', 'people's democracy' and 'progressive democracy'. The objective should be a democratic, multi-party democracy, with full guarantees for the freedoms of speech, press and religion, but constitutionally committed to a programme of deep social reforms and to regular participation of the workers and their organizations, which would guarantee national independence and a rejection of war and power blocs. There was no contradiction or Chinese wall between democracy and socialism that would have to be broken down soon through a new armed uprising. The road ahead called for a new party, a mass party – not only in the sense that it would be large in size, but also because people would join it on the grounds of its programme rather than its ideology. It would be capable of political action, not only propaganda, and while basing itself on the working class it would seek alliances with other social layers and the political forces that represented them. It would be cohesive and disciplined in action but allow space for discussion, solidly rooted in a world Communist movement but not taking any other party as a model to be imitated.

Much remained to be fleshed out and clarified, but this was the first signal for the immediate construction and adoption of a new identity. This well-timed choice of perspectives and positioning claimed two major results in the decisive few years after the end of the war. First, a constitutional charter that was one of the most advanced in Europe in terms of values and guarantees, which, despite the intense political divisions of the time, was adopted by an overwhelming majority in 1948 and has continued to hold to this day, only slightly battered by numerous assaults; second, the birth of the largest Communist party in the West, whose simple presence stimulated the rise of other popular parties in Italy and ensured decades of active mass participation in politics.

It can scarcely be denied that, in the context of its time, the Salerno turn achieved its main objectives and paved the way for a number of possible sequels. But taking a longer view, and with regard to the hopes it aroused, the analysis and judgement have to be more nuanced.

THE NATIONAL UNITY GOVERNMENTS, 1944–7

The years from 1945 to 1948 were not only those of the Liberation, the Republic and the new constitutional charter. They were also a period of transition that saw the reshaping of society and the state, class relations and the conditions of life corresponding to them, economic reconstruction and Italy's place in the international order. This was the work of the national unity governments, whose scope gradually increased as the Allies relaxed their control, alongside an elected popular assembly that from 1946 also exercised legislative functions. The Left, particularly the Communists, carried major weight in both branches – all the more so given the mobilization of the masses and the general climate of enthusiasm created by the national insurrection, the 'wind from the North'.

The record of government action and early legislative measures was rather meagre, however, both in their objectives and, even more, in what they achieved. 'Progressive democracy' existed only on paper, quite remote from the scrutiny, interests and hopes of the individuals and classes who had risked death or deportation, and from the intentions of those who were writing it into the constitutional charter. Predictably, power was not even partially transferred to the national liberation committees. The partisans handed in their weapons, often without a grumble of protest; that too went as planned. Waves of unrest and isolated acts of violence were actively opposed by the Communists (and by none more than Longo): that was fair enough, at the end of a conflict that had also been a civil war. But it was neither just nor planned that the eradication of fascism, so often demanded and promised, showed no real sign of happening in everyday reality, and kept being postponed until better times. No doubt this moderation was due to weighty objective factors. First, the calamitous situation of the productive sector of the economy (and the services it needed in order to recover from dislocation), as well as of the basic state administrative functions. Second, a string of electoral tests in which the whole nation (now including women) had spoken for the first time in decades and shown the Left to be a strong force but still a minority, with a sharp division between the north and south. The monarchy only just lost the referendum on the future shape of the country's institutions. And the international situation revealed the first signs of crisis among the major powers of the wartime alliance.

But these were not yet insuperable barriers. The parlous condition of the economy and the state was the source of difficulties, but also of opportunities for reform, and served to delegitimize the classes that had brought it about. Moreover, the combined Left vote was over 40 per cent, and it was very difficult for a conservative bloc to be successfully put together, given that anti-fascism still outweighed anti-Communism in the popular mind.

There was still an interregnum on the international stage; not by chance was it between 1945 and 1949 that the Chinese revolution found the space to triumph without igniting a wider conflict.

So why, in that brief transition between Resistance and cold war, was it not possible to carry through at least a partial and provisional programme of reforms, similar to the drafting of the constitutional charter (which, though always at risk and largely unimplemented for fifteen years or more, left a marker to be taken up in the future)? Can it be said that the Communists and Togliatti himself did the best they could, as they had in relation to the liberation struggle and the Salerno turn? With the best will in the world, I honestly do not think it can. I have no intention of stirring up old polemics that were idle and unhealthy at the time, and are even more so today: for example regarding the disarming of the partisans, the failure to hand power to the national liberation committees, the amnesty law, the vote on Article 7,[4] or the lack of nationalization – all the paraphernalia of the 'blocked revolution' debate.

I would simply like to say something about what the Communists in the government could have refused to accept or tried to push through, in a reasonable manner, even at the risk of a governmental crisis. Let us take a few examples.

a) Economic policy. After the brief and rather inconclusive parenthesis of the Parri government,[5] its successor headed by De Gasperi[6] gave the effective leadership of economic policy to

4. Article 7 of the Constitution of the Italian Republic, which came into force on 1 January 1948, established that relations between the state and the Catholic Church would be governed by the Lateran Pacts of 1929.

5. Ferruccio Parri: leader of the Partito d'Azione, prime minister between June and December 1945.

6. Alcide De Gasperi: founder and leader of the Christian Democrat Party, prime minister of eight successive governments between December 1945 and August 1953.

ministers and governors who, though competent enough, were followers of the liberal school and somewhat antiquated in their approach: people like Epicarmo Corbino and Luigi Einaudi. Their main priorities were to reintroduce controls on incomes and pensions, to restore order and authority at the workplace, and to ensure monetary stability. But they also had ambitions for the future that included restructuring and redundancies, as well as incentives for investment and technological modernization, steering American aid towards large private corporations and gradually lowering customs barriers. The Left opposed this with a vision of rising consumption and rising employment – a gesture to Keynes (never read, never reflected upon), but without a clear-cut content. It was an approach that had garnered both successes and failures. It had worked in the 1930s, when budget deficits had offered a realistic way to tackle an underconsumption crisis in a context of large excess capacity. But the postwar Italian crisis was quite different, involving structural weaknesses, technological backwardness and galloping inflation, so that a bold programme to revive production would have had to include elements of planning and investment-steering from the outset, as well as income redistribution to balance the reconstruction sacrifices necessary to control inflation. Otherwise it would have been unfeasible and widely repudiated.

In fact, the economic programme of the Left remained at the level of generalities, useful only to back up trade union demands; wage struggles did take place, but they produced scant results and were undermined by redundancies and unemployment. Was anything else possible? Could there not immediately have been struggles and mobilizations around tax policy? Could workers not have been given a charter of rights in relation to layoffs and collective wage contracts, and a minimum of power over restructuring plans, new investments and the return of factories to their former owners? Was it not possible to propose, or perhaps impose, a first but significant batch of land reforms: not perhaps 'land to those who till it', but at least abolition of the archaic sharecropping system, expropriation of large absentee landowners, and greater stability of farm contracts? As for the sizeable public industrial and banking sector, which fascism had been forced to create amid the pressure of the 1930s crisis, could it not have been resolutely used as a lever for macro-economic planning, not merely as a support for private monopolies? Could currency reform and the expropriation of war profits not have helped to improve the state of the public finances and to boost the first stages of reconstruction, as in other European countries?

All these battles were postponed, owing to the lack of clear definition and rigorous leadership. Only when the national unity policy was on the brink of collapse did the PCI launch a campaign for a 'new course', albeit without the enthusiasm it showed for di Vittorio's Labour Plan when it was already too late to act on it.[7]

b) Reconstruction of the state. The state bureaucracy had hypertrophied in the fascist period, but its personnel had also been handpicked by the fascists, its powers redefined and the legislation covering it rewritten. The resulting problems could not be solved in draconian fashion: bureaucrats from the old regime could not simply be locked up or sent home en masse. But a purge at the top could have brought in a new personnel of intellectuals, non-political perhaps, but democratic. It would have been possible to tear up the repressive clauses in the Rocco code and elsewhere in criminal law,[8] and to guarantee the independence of the whole judiciary. It would have been possible, without entirely reforming the educational system established by Gentile, to eliminate the class barriers built into it, to revise syllabuses most blatantly in conflict with the new Republic, and to limit the powers of the academic barons. The autonomy and jurisdiction of local bureaucracies could have been broadened, and the power of prefects reduced. In short, it should have been possible to begin implementing what was written in the new Constitution. Yet this was not done, nor vigorously debated in parliament and the country.

c) Foreign policy. Italy's clout in international policy was very limited until the signing of the peace treaty. The cold war was already looming on the horizon, but this did not prevent the Italian or French Communists – while in government – from taking initiatives, not merely on the propaganda level, to improve the situation. From the beginning, Togliatti emphasized the theme of national independence and the rejection of new power blocs. But now it

7. Giuseppe di Vittorio: leader of the Italian General Confederation of Labour (CGIL), initially inclusive but after 1950 mainly supported by the PCI and PSI Socialists, until his death in 1957. The Labour Plan that he launched in 1949–50 mainly called for an anti-cyclical programme of large-scale public works.

8. Rocco Code: the revised penal code of 1930, so called after the justice minister of the time, Alfredo Rocco.

would have been possible to go further – which, come to think of it, would also have been in the interests of the Soviet Union as he understood them. That is, after two world wars that had left Europe disarmed and without imperial fantasies, the PCI could have argued for the old continent to take the lead in promoting dialogue between the great powers and building global institutions to guarantee peace and international legality, and to shake off its onerous historical responsibility for colonialism. A coalition of forces, still a minority but with some real substance, could have been built around this idea. It could have encompassed states such as Switzerland, Finland and Austria that were now stably committed to neutralism; large social-democratic parties (Kurt Schumacher's SPD or the more cautious British Labour Party); and a number of cultural and political currents or authoritative leaders (including, in France, the radical-democratic 'third force', sectors of Catholicism, Mendès-France or even, in one sense, de Gaulle), who, partly out of national pride, rejected the binary division of the world for moral and theoretical reasons. Dialogue among all these forces would not have been easy, but the initiative might have caught on; only a decade later, it would have been able to link up with the neutralism of the Bandung conference. But no moves were made at the most auspicious moment, when the tragedy of the war was fresh in people's minds and recent victories suggested that the anti-fascist unity between different social systems might be prolonged.

THE NEW PARTY

I have dwelled on particular criticisms of the immediate postwar governments, but there is also a wider problem that would re-emerge later, in various ways: the question of a 'new road to socialism'.

At the core of Togliatti's new strategy was the nexus between revolution and reforms, autonomy and unity, social conflict and institutional politics, involving a lengthy advance stage by stage, each tied to a historical period but inspired by a clear long-term purpose. As Togliatti freely acknowledged, it was not a completely new conception: it was present in Marx's thought, in the better period of the Second International, and still more in Gramsci. The novelty was its reintroduction into the reservoir of Communism, its integration with the October Revolution, and the prospect of strengthening and developing it in the future.

But a number of difficult conditions had to be met if this strategy was to be rigorously applied, for the first time, in practice; that is, if the programmatic nexus was not to end up in a minimalist reformism geared to compatibility with the system or, at the opposite extreme, to become a mere tactic for the accumulation of forces while awaiting a more favourable moment for the genuine revolutionary leap. To avoid these dangers, it was necessary to develop a clearer vision of the kind of society to be aimed at in the long term. The phase through which Italy was passing at the time and its scope for taking steps towards the ultimate goal, had also to be analysed. Wide and lasting social support had to be won, especially from the working classes, around a coherent programme; and a 'historic bloc' had to be constructed to pursue that programme as a real prospect. Finally, it was necessary to transform subaltern masses into an alternative leading class, capable of organizing social struggles and managing the spaces of power that were gradually captured. If, as Mao put it, a revolution is 'not a dinner party', a strong reformism is not the same as an intelligent pragmatism.

In the immediate aftermath of the war, such conditions were lacking not only in reality but even in people's consciousness – and especially in the 'new party' that was supposed to be the key vehicle for overcoming the country's difficulties. The vision of a mass party had come true, in an incredibly short time and with results far beyond expectations. In 1945 the PCI had a card-carrying membership of 1,100,000, the majority of whom were active; in 1946 it reached the figure of two million, larger than any other Communist party in the West (including France), and one of the largest in the world. Its strength was not ephemeral, not simply a byproduct of the emotions of the Liberation period or the myth of the USSR; its organization held up for many years, despite disappointing setbacks and the conditions of the cold war.

The social composition of the PCI was both a great resource and a major problem. It was a class party such as perhaps had never existed before. But what was that class, exactly? Longo, with customary curtness, once said after a tour of the country that it was not a party but a crowd. And I might add, basing myself both on statistics and on my own direct knowledge at the time: a crowd of manual workers in industry and agriculture, many of whom had not completed elementary school and had trouble reading or understanding the national language, who were poorly informed about the world, who had had no experience of trade unions or political struggle (even before fascism or in the years covered by the Vatican's *non expedit*),[9] and who had then been exposed to all the rhetoric of fascism. Now they were taking their first steps in local Party branches, learning to write, to read books and newspapers, to understand the essentials of national history; and in the evenings, fired by a new passion, they would spontaneously gather in squares up and down the country to discuss the issues and form ideas of their own. The Communist cadres, whose job it was to organize and educate them, numbered no more than a few thousand and sometimes had to be brought in from different parts of the country. They too were mostly workers, trained through clandestine activity, the partisan struggle and the war in Spain – or else in the special school of prison and internment, where they had learned the ABC of Marxism-Leninism as imparted by the Comintern in the 1930s, and strove to master the intricate reasoning of the charismatic Togliatti. There were also a number of young intellectuals or students, who had turned against fascism and been recruited in the years immediately before the war, or had come straight from the partisan ranks. They were often valuably well-read, but more knowledgeable about the arts, literature or cinema (which the regime let pass) than about history or economic and political theory.

The real leadership group, which discussed and adopted the decisions, was very small and of proven quality and loyalty. Only Togliatti (and, more marginally, Umberto Terraccini) had played any part in the founding experience of *L'Ordine Nuovo*.[10] The others, from very different backgrounds, had become Communists in the oscillating period of the Bordiga leadership,[11] and under-

9. *Non expedit* ('it is not expedient'): the policy of non-involvement in elections and political activity, enjoined on Catholics after the formation of the Kingdom of Italy in 1861.

10. *L'Ordine Nuovo*: the weekly, founded in Turin in 1919, which became a rallying point for the Communists who split away from the Italian Socialist Party.

11. Amadeo Bordiga's group fused with Gramsci's *L'Ordine Nuovo* group in 1921 to form the Communist Party of Italy, but after his arrest in 1923 his authority in the Party dwindled and he was expelled in 1930.

gone the loss of Angelo Tasca[12] and other dissidents. The group finally consolidated itself, with trouble but no repression, during the years of full Stalinist orthodoxy. Acting first out of discipline, but soon out of conviction (though not with full knowledge of the facts), this leadership group had accepted the choices made by Togliatti. Pietro Secchia continued to harbour doubts (which he later made explicit), believing that it might have been possible to obtain more from the partisan struggle, but also that it was necessary to prepare for a resurgence of reactionary forces. Longo, for his part, baldly admitted that 'you build socialism when you have power in your hands – and we don't yet have that'.

In 1947, then, for both material and cultural reasons, the mass party was still a long way from being the 'new party' advocated by Togliatti, and still further from Gramsci's 'collective intellectual' (capable of hegemony, generating the cultural and moral reform Italy had never had, gradually shaping the working class into the ruling class). Nor did it have the wealth of experience and capacity for debate that German Social Democracy had achieved by the end of the nineteenth century, or a leadership comparable to that of the Bolsheviks before the Russian Revolution, whose concentration of brilliant minds had been unique in Europe and rare in the whole history of politics.

The PCI's shortcomings should not be overemphasized. After all, none of the other political and social forces was more prepared for the task of government. The divided Socialist Party wavered between contradictory positions: the extremist contortions of Lelio Basso and (at times) Rodolfo Morandi, the *politique d'abord* of Pietro Nenni, the breakaway by Giuseppe Saragat. The Christian Democrats soon proved their ability to collect votes, but De Gasperi had trouble steering the party with the unreliable authority of the Vatican. The real power to guide the Catholic masses, including many workers and farmers, lay firmly with a Pope who had always been more wary of Communism than of fascism, and who ran a formidable network of obedient cadres covering every village parish, university and religious association. The productive industrial and agricultural bourgeoisie, politically delegitimized by its complicity with fascism but still bolstered by

12. Angelo Tasca, associated with Bukharin and his supporters in the Soviet Union, was expelled from the Party in 1929.

its economic power, remained largely – as Gramsci, Gobetti or Dorso had foreseen – not only conservative but illiberal, and often inept and parasitic; it showed nothing like the mixture of reaction and modernizing dynamism typical of its counterparts in Germany and Japan. The state apparatuses had been noted for their subservience and incompetence long before the fascist period. And the diffuse intelligentsia, even when non-fascist, had remained – indeed, chosen to remain – in the wings of the great iconoclastic yet innovative debates and controversies which, for better or worse, had enlivened the first half of the century in Europe and the United States. Gramsci was still unknown, but even Pareto and Michels, Sraffa and Fermi, had gone abroad to work. It was a little while since Machiavelli's death ...

In short, the mass parties were more advanced than the society they represented. They could reach a progressive agreement when it was a question of defining institutional principles or arrangements: the Communists were then dealing with a secular or Catholic intellectual elite strongly linked to the Resistance (the likes of Giuseppe Dossetti or Piero Calamandrei). But when it came to challenging deeply rooted attitudes or specific centres of power in society, the road ahead would be long and hard, and the Party's ideas, strength and skill were still wanting.

To educate and organize broad masses who had been downtrodden for centuries, to help them raise their heads and use them, was itself a great and lasting conquest – both for the PCI and for Italy. But it was not adequate to the task of dodging, or leaping, the new road block that lay just around the corner: the cold war, and the related political showdown among the founders of the First Republic.

3

On the Brink of the Third World War

At this point in the book, I faced an unexpected difficulty that was different from any other. For here I have to deal with a fifteen-year period of great risk (of a third world war), which nevertheless ended with a relatively peaceful agreement between two antagonistic systems. Everything seemed to be returning to how it had been before, yet the reality was a new world order destined to last for thirty years; everything in those times seemed frozen, yet they paved the way for huge changes that opened a new chapter of history. Here, not only individual or collective memory but also the 'benefit of hindsight' can obstruct critical reflection more than they assist it.

The memory is not lost, so much as stiff and fragmentary. After all, they were years in which politics played a primary role, as never before or since; it became a collective passion, driven by the conviction that it was necessary either to defend the civilization in which we lived or to change it root and branch. Millions of people, from every social layer and with all manner of beliefs, participated in this process, adopting a conscious identity and choosing an affiliation they considered permanent (and which did indeed last longer than one might have imagined). But they were also years of bitter conflict, when politics tended to be reduced to ideology, facts were conveniently selected or distorted, propaganda counted for more than argument and loyalty more than a critical spirit. Personal experience or oral testimonies endowed whole generations with indelible memories, which later doubts or choices made it easier to guard with pride than subject to critical analysis. Even today, in any discussion of the 1950s in Italy, the Right uses schemas and language from 1948; whereas those who reject them prefer to play down the conflict, considering it an episode imposed from abroad which the combined wisdom of De Gasperi and Togliatti – too often omitted from the picture – managed to keep under control and to close as soon as possible.

The same applies to the 'benefit of hindsight'. Since the Third World War did not happen and the competition between the two systems ended without bloodshed, that harsh period of the 1950s becomes so much water under the bridge, with nothing to tell us except the obvious fact of its outcome. The great events of the second half of the century – so often the subject of analysis and debate – then appear separate from what immediately preceded them and, for good or ill, left its mark on them.

Although it was then that I moved towards Communism, I too have tended to underestimate the significance of those harsh years, sticking to my convictions of the time and reacting with annoyance to belated, impromptu self-criticisms that actually deserved a longer, and better documented, reply. Forced now to draw up a balance sheet, I have been able to consult some recent, often little-known memoirs, as well as updated historical accounts and declassified archive material (to be handled with caution, but not lacking in fresh insights). This has made me realize how important the period was as a whole, how many misjudgements or prejudices cry out to be revised, and above all how many questions remain surprisingly elusive and in need of more convincing answers.

The first task must be to clear up a curious misunderstanding. No one would dispute that for those fifteen years international politics was the decisive and overriding element, including in the internal politics of each country. Yet, especially in Italy, the omissions in relation to the cold war are striking and numerous, and the actual course of events is seldom examined. In fact, the meaning of the term is so generic, its specific reference so uncertain, that any discussion of it appears confused.

THE LONGER COLD WAR

To speak seriously of cold war, we need to distinguish between two things: a historical phenomenon of considerable duration, and a shorter period when the likelihood of a third world war dictated certain preparations and was the reference point for everything else.

In the first sense, the cold war had a clear beginning and end and constant protagonists, but was intermittent in character and variable in its forms and intensity. It began at the moment when long-subaltern classes and nations developed an ideology, built an organization and took advantage of favourable conditions to become a state by means of a revolution – a state whose land surface, resources and energies potentially equipped it to become a great power alongside others. This ushered in social, economic and geopolitical competition between the two systems, which was also expressed at the level of ideas. Alliances, trade-offs and, above all, armed might and the economic capacity to sustain it became a factor in the rivalry, either as an instrument with which to attack or threaten the other side, or as a means to resist such threats. The opening scene goes back as far as 1918, when the major Western powers intervened informally but bloodily in the Russian civil war. This is worth emphasizing, because it occurred before the revolution acquired a stable form, when the idea of crushing it in infancy might have remained little more than a vicious Tsarist dream.

Shortly before the Germans surrendered in 1918, they managed to snatch a significant chunk of the former Russian empire at the Treaty of Brest-Litovsk – an excision that was essentially confirmed by the Treaty of Versailles, and became a bone of contention again at the end of the Second World War. The victors of the first war sponsored or supported a series of assaults from every side to bring down the Soviet republic: Kornilov's army from the Baltic region, Kolchak's from Siberia, Denikin's from Crimea, Georgia and Turkestan, and Piłsudski's from Poland. What is less known, or has been forgotten, is that the Western intervention was not limited to political solidarity, funding, the supply of weapons and advisers and logistical support (which Churchill, then British war minister, publicly listed in accurate detail), but also involved the sending of combat troops into battle. In 1919 the French foreign minister, Stéphen Pichon, estimated the number of regular troops and mercenaries fighting alongside the Whites at 140,000 for France, 190,000 for Romania, 140,000 for Britain and 140,000 for Serbia. The Americans and Japanese avoided direct involvement, but they provided loans and jointly occupied Vladivostock and other Far Eastern ports to ensure that communication routes remained trouble-free. Local satrapies made it difficult to coordinate attacks, while official corruption and savage plunder and abuses by the rag-tag-and-bobtail White armies alienated wavering populations and transformed early successes into costly retreats. Their enemy was poorly armed and had to organize on the hoof, but it knew what it was fighting for and had a solid leadership. In the end, the interventionist capitals aroused the hostility of a war-weary public opinion; the costs were too high, success too improbable.

The long cold war was not formally declared, nor was it by any means cold: millions died in battle or from starvation and disease. Unexpectedly, the Bolsheviks emerged victorious from a conflict that had been both domestic and international. This was one reason for the debate that divided them in the 1920s – the most candid and painful of their history. Should armed support be given to the revolutionary thrust in key countries that might pierce the isolation of devastated Russia? Should force be used to consolidate the Soviet state itself, and to embark on the 'impossible goal' of socialism in one country? It became clear that Stalin's support of that goal, which won through and was never revoked, did not entail an opening-up of the regime or a brake on economic planning. It did imply a cautious, realistic assessment of the international relationship of forces, which, with rare lapses, remained a permanent feature of Soviet external policy.

A period of more normal international relations ensued in the 1920s – for example, as a result of the Rapallo pact with Germany. But then the cold war tendency gathered momentum again, even if the Nazi menace complicated the picture in the 1930s. Thanks to the large number of data, documents, memoirs and private letters that have lately become available, it is easier to understand how the long period of sufferance in the West that enabled Hitler to build up to war, and to score early victories in it, was linked to the hope of turning his aggression against the Soviet Union. It was a crazy objective, because if it had worked it would have made it almost impossible for the Western democracies to beat Nazism on the battlefield; it would have forced them instead into unsustainable compromises, and opened the way to limitless use of force.

The broad anti-fascist alliance, partly imposed by necessity but crystallizing into a fervent hope for the future, cleared the field of that incubus but only for a short time, and not completely.

Worrying signs already appeared at the height of the Second World War, especially after Stalingrad and the Red Army advance, when victory seemed just a matter of time and thoughts began to turn to the future balance of power. One thinks of Churchill's proposal for spheres of influence in Eastern Europe, accepted by Stalin, or of the differences among the Allies over military strategy (the continual and costly postponement of a 'second front', then the question of whether to open it in Normandy, where it would be most effective, or in less practicable areas of the Mediterranean and Balkans, to keep the USSR at a distance).

In any event, the long cold war persisted for decades. After the danger of a third world war diminished, the rivalry shifted to non-military fields; but it was constantly interrupted by unruly regional crises and accompanied with a reckless arms race. It ran through the whole of the 'short twentieth century' and came to an end only when one of the contestants wound itself up, in 1989.

The intermittent siege of the Soviet Union cannot explain away the degenerate aspects that finally led to its collapse; these had other causes. Still less do I intend it to excuse the late and foot-dragging manner in which the PCI distanced itself from Moscow, when it was both necessary and possible for it to do so. But it seems equally dishonest to ignore the extent to which the external threat weighed on events, or to apportion the blame for them in a Solomonic spirit.

THE GREAT SURPRISE

The term cold war may also refer, more specifically, to the sudden and surprising shift in the international situation beginning in 1946, which conjured up the real danger of a third world war. A danger that rapidly grew, before gradually receding again.

How are we to explain the fact that only months after the end of a massive war that had cost millions of lives and immense destruction, in which each member of the victorious coalition had been necessary, governments and nations were speaking of another, even worse war to come – despite the fact that agreements had been signed and solemn undertakings given to cooperate for a lasting peace, and that great new institutions were being born to ensure a peaceful solution to future disputes? Who and what was responsible, in which degree, for this sudden devastating turnaround?

How did the new prospect take root in people's minds: through what specific acts, in which temporal sequence, by virtue of which arguments? How close did the world come to catastrophe? What price, both immediate and long term, was paid for depicting the conflict as a life-and-death struggle between civilizations, in which sooner or later force could not but have the final say?

Looking back almost afresh at these questions, as we are able to do today, I have formed a slightly changed view, which is a little clearer than the one I had at the beginning. The 'new cold war', especially at first, was a free, conscious and unilateral option embraced for various reasons by all the major (and many minor) Western capitalist powers, which also came to include the countries against which they had recently been fighting. This choice soon won the active support of many political forces on the Left, and gradually percolated through to a majority of the public, by means of a persuasive propaganda campaign largely based on manipulation. The fault of the Communists and their few Socialist allies was not that they provoked or fuelled the new cold war, but that they had not seen or wanted to see it coming, that their response to it served to encourage rather than obstruct its progress, and that, not by accident, they committed many mistakes that made the risks and the costs greater for themselves.

THE NEW COLD WAR

I would date the outbreak of the new cold war from the day of Franklin D. Roosevelt's death, since it is both too much and too little to present him in time-honoured fashion as the man of the New Deal and the wartime alliance.

Too much, because when he became president ten years earlier he had seen the necessity for action but had not been able to offer a clear vision, still less a solidly based theory, of the reforms that were necessary to address the great economic crisis afflicting the United States and the world. His new economic policy only gradually took shape (Keynes offered him a considered plan after 1935); it scored early successes, but then encountered intractable obstacles and was in danger of petering out by 1938. As to the war against fascism, American public opinion was so hostile to this idea that Japan's acts of aggression in Asia went unchecked for years, and Roosevelt could at first do no more than offer loans and weapons for the struggle against Hitler in Europe. Only in 1942 did Pearl Harbor give him the green light for intervention.

Too little, because Roosevelt inspired the process that brought a 'possible America' into the light of day, encouraging intellectual circles, a new trade union organization and a radical democratic impetus. Above all, these two experiences – the economic crisis and reforms, the international anti-fascist coalition – shaped a long-term horizon for his own thinking and action.

The crude attacks against Roosevelt after his death, accusing him of having divided the world and handed a large part of it over to the Soviet adversary, were completely unfounded. Roosevelt was neither a pushover nor a dreamer. He was a bourgeois strategist, as were Keynes and the late Schumpeter, persuaded that capitalism could and should spread through peaceful, constructive competition, so long as colonialism was gradually eliminated and a democratic system of government proved capable of regulating and steering the spontaneous appetites of the markets. He was further convinced that the United States possessed the strength and the ideas to achieve this. As a matter of fact, the world was not shared out at Yalta. Apart from negotiations on specific points, many of them unresolved, the discussion mainly focused on prospects and methods, and the solemn undertaking by both sides to rule out another world war in the decades ahead. Not by chance did it attach so much weight to a future international organization, underwritten by the great powers, which would not end in the laughable impotence of the League of Nations. In this connection – as we can see from the memoirs of Harry Hopkins, Cordell Hull and (indirectly) Sherwood Anderson – everyone agreed that a stable international organization would be necessary to preserve the peace, even when a new generation that had not experienced the horrors of the Second World War had taken the reins of power.

Those who put Roosevelt 'on trial' soon afterwards had to prove, however, that his vision was only one of the 'possible Americas'. The man he had chosen to succeed him, Harry Truman, did indeed have a vision of his own: he began by declaring that he had not read a single document from the Tehran and Yalta conferences, swiftly replaced the US foreign policy staff, promoted a conservative Republican (Arthur Vandenberg) to the Senate Foreign Relations Committee, and in July 1945 let slip at Potsdam his view that it was necessary to stop 'mollycoddling the Russians'.

The point was driven home in deeds as well as words, when the first atom bombs were dropped on Hiroshima and Nagasaki in August 1945 – a decision that served not only to finish off the tottering Japanese, but also, more or less deliberately, to display the new balance of forces to Russia and the world. Soon the American establishment was openly wondering whether the Soviet Union would be capable of acquiring the new weapon, and in what space of time. Could anything be done to stop them? The scientists who had developed atomic energy took the initiative in a lively international debate about how it could be controlled, but nothing came of this. However, the times were not yet ripe politically for a doctrine of pre-emptive war, and the threat to use the bomb was put on ice until MacArthur revived it a few years later during the Korean War. Meanwhile, the slide into a new cold war showed no sign of slowing. Everyone has heard of Winston Churchill's 'Iron Curtain' speech in Fulton in March 1946, but few know where Fulton is or why the speech made such an impact. At the time Churchill was no longer head of the UK government, since the Labour Party had won a resounding victory in the postwar elections. It might seem that he was expressing no more than his own opinion, however authoritative, at a small-town college in Missouri. But this was the state for which Truman had previously served as senator. Churchill had travelled to Washington for an interview with Truman, and the president in turn went down to Fulton to hear him. It was worth it. Churchill's analysis was fresh, and his proposals crystal clear.

The Fulton speech made a huge impact, both among those who warmed to it and among those who were alarmed by its tone. For the speaker did not appear as an old man defeated electorally in his own country, but rather as a senior statesman seated alongside the president of the world's greatest power; this setting gave his assertions the eloquence of a new long-term strategy. 'Nobody knows,' he argued, 'what Soviet Russia and its Communist international organization intend to do in the immediate future, or what are the limits, if any, to their expansive and proselytizing tendencies.' If a new tyranny was to be avoided, there could be no repeat of the appeasement of Hitler; the military and political supremacy of the West had to be reasserted at all costs.

The atom bombs on Hiroshima and Nagasaki had already sent a clear message. And bearing in mind that the British and Americans were jointly engaged in a new race for weapons of mass destruction, we can measure the new distance from their wartime ally, a nation ravaged like no other. Yet lending to the USSR was stopped, at the same time that Communists were driven out of government in the West. In breaking with Roosevelt's policy, the Fulton speech marked a sharp turn towards a completely different global order.

Churchill himself repeated his ideas in Europe, adding in 1947 that his aim was to achieve a continental unity; the 'whole purpose of a united democratic Europe was to give decisive guarantees against aggression.' But the Fulton speech also encountered hard-headed objections within the American and European ruling classes (and also among the Social Democratic parties 'behind the Iron Curtain'). For the conservative political commentator Walter Lippmann, it was obvious that the United States and the Soviet Union could never win a war with each other outright, but only embark on a conflict that would continue ad infinitum in a snarl of civil wars, famines, devastation and annihilation.

In 1947, first in a speech, then in a document agreed with the new Secretary of State, Dean Acheson, Truman officially endorsed Churchill's earlier analysis and proposal, adding a few touches of his own that sanctified the defence of private property. The whole thing was then dressed up as the 'Truman Doctrine' and the 'containment strategy', but the real idea behind it was to lay siege to the Soviet Union. Indeed the influential civil servant George Keenan, credited with formulating the idea of 'containment', soon changed his mind. Nor was it just a question of words: unambiguous actions were taken at the same time, although they have since been ignored or forgotten. Gradually a chain of American bases was put in place, while bombers equipped with nuclear weapons remained constantly airborne. Communists were driven out of every government in which they still participated.

We should also mention a few events linked to the running of particular territories, some of which would merit more detailed attention and might come as a surprise.

The American occupation of Japan, dispensing with any consultation, established the permanent right to a direct military presence (which continues to this day), virtually dictated Japan's new constitution, and confirmed the positions of Emperor Hirohito and the economic magnates who had bankrolled the Japanese war effort throughout Asia.

The French drive to restore their colony in Indochina, with the help of scattered Japanese forces, detached Vietnam from Cambodia and Laos and succeeded in confining the zone liberated by Ho Chi Minh's nationalists to a small area close to the Chinese frontier. The well-known sequel stretched over nearly thirty years.

In Indonesia, British and Dutch forces re-established colonial rule, overthrowing Sukarno's new independent government and provisionally severing the largest and richest islands from the rest.

The Iranian government was pressured into ending any Soviet presence in its country, and even to break off the commercial agreements that had allowed it to sell oil to the USSR at higher prices than those operated by Western companies.

The Turkish guarantee of free passage through the Dardanelles was revoked, with major implications for the Soviet Union in particular.

The French and British independently moved to redraw frontiers or to set up new satellite states in the Middle East, as a means of safeguarding their oil supplies.

Washington stubbornly resisted the entry of newly emerging states into the United Nations, in order to retain a majority in the General Assembly based on the bloc of South American countries; a special dispensation was granted to Perón's Argentina, despite its pro-Axis stance during the war. Later, Chiang Kai-shek was granted a seat on the Security Council almost as a hereditary right, although by then he controlled no more than the offshore island of Formosa (Taiwan).

Violent repression in Africa (from Madagascar to Kenya, Congo to Algeria, Mozambique to Angola) kept a lid on that continent.

I could go on, but this suffices for a brief look around a world in which Eastern Europe was for decades presented as the only instance of 'oppressed peoples'. More needs to be said, however, about two particularly important cases: Greece and China.

Greece rightly figured in Italian political debate as a warning of what could happen to the kind of abortive uprising that the Italian Communists had avoided. It was a convincing argument, and was borne out by later events, but it also helped to obscure memories of the time and to distort the judgement made of it. For the Greek situation did not come about as a result of armed insurrection by a minority, and the Communists did not initially play the major role. National resistance and a people's army had grown ever stronger during the war years, fighting fascist aggression and German occupation until they managed to liberate the country before the Allies arrived. This struggle produced a strong organization, the National Liberation Front (EAM), whose objective was a freely elected government that would prevent the return of the monarchy (which in its time had handed power to the para-fascist Metaxas regime) and exclude all who had openly collaborated with the Germans. The British wanted almost the exact opposite, and tried to impose it by bombing Athens and firing on peaceful demonstrators, using a pliant Papandreou as cover, then rejecting a compromise agreement even with the moderate liberal Sophoulis. This is what provoked the guerrilla campaign, which the Soviet Union could not be seen to support, and which only the Yugoslavs and Bulgarians assisted from across their frontiers. It was the first and crudest application of external force to shore up one of the new 'spheres of influence'. Greece's guerrilla war was a (failed) response to the violent subjugation of a sovereign nation.

Even more overlooked, though much more important, is what happened in China immediately after the war. For years Manchuria – then the industrial heartland – had been occupied by the Japanese, who gradually extended their control to the large cities (Beijing, Nanjing, Shanghai) through a series of horrific massacres. Two distinct armed resistance movements opposed this occupation: the official Chinese government in the south of the country, resting only on the legitimacy of an army organized by the Kuomintang and enjoying international recognition (somewhat by default); and Mao's peasant army, which gradually won control of large swathes of mainly agricultural territory, carried out a series of social reforms and established new institutions. These two forces not only acted independently of each other, but had repeatedly clashed since 1926, as Chiang's army attempted (at times with apparent success) to crush the Communists and the nascent peasant rebellion. The clashes continued during the Second World War, when Chiang tried on several occasions to reach a *modus vivendi* with the Japanese in order to free him to deal with an equally dangerous adversary. Meanwhile, the Allied powers knew little about what was going on in China and were unable to intervene directly. After Pearl Harbor they tried to help the anti-Japanese struggle, mainly by channelling aid to the government forces; the American general Joseph Stilwell, in his capacity as chief of staff in Chiang's army, tried to coordinate the various forces in the field but met with such hostility from Chiang that he was forced to leave the country.

Thus, with Japan on the brink of collapse, a huge and complex political problem arose as to how the world's most populous country would be ruled. The initial idea, of course, was a coalition government, and the Americans – the only Allied power represented in that sector – sent out two emissaries (Patrick Hurley and later General Marshall) to investigate whether such a solution was possible. Hurley first met Mao – the tougher nut to crack – and was soon reporting that he had found him encouragingly amenable to a deal, so long as it was a genuine compromise that respected the balance of forces on the ground. But Chiang imposed three prior conditions: that the Communists should withdraw from their liberated zones, cancel the reforms they had already implemented, and merge their forces into the Nationalist army. This put paid to any agreement, and soon afterwards Chiang marched north in an attempt to decide the issue by force. Marshall could not prevent this; the new administration in Washington was neither willing nor able to break its alliance with Chiang, and so it supported his recklessness with money, aircraft and pilots, while realizing that the Kuomintang was so divided, corrupt and unpopular that victory was impossible. The first, and certainly the most important, contest in the new cold war was gradually lost by those who had promoted it. Then Washington refused to recognize Mao's China diplomatically, unleashing a crisis in the UN and the Security Council.

Whatever one thinks of the social system and ideology of the two camps, this indisputable sequence of facts and accompanying discourses demonstrates that the initiative for the new cold war came almost entirely from the major Western powers, and that they had already marked Communism down as the new enemy.

THE INVENTION OF THE ATLANTIC PACT

The force that drove this sudden radical shift, and later gave it direction, was not only geopolitical and military. There were other factors more directly linked to the internal politics of each country, to the restoration or redefinition of its social system, and to the hierarchical relationship among the nations of the world.

First among these was the economic factor, symbolized by the Marshall Plan. Here our analysis needs to be more complex, and our judgement less clear-cut, than it has been hitherto. The American offer of economic aid to countries whose productive apparatus lay in ruins, and which lacked the financial means to rebuild it, was in itself an intelligent idea. It could be associated with a number of very different policies: removal of East European countries from the Soviet sphere of influence and isolation of their economies at a very difficult moment for them; gradual opening up of commercial and cultural relations between different economic systems, rewarding European capitalist countries for their full and rapid alignment with US foreign policy; or the weaning away of former empires from their remaining colonies, by reshaping their economic policies and overcoming their internecine conflicts (which had led to fascism and two world wars).

In the context of the new cold war, the first of these orientations prevailed over the others. In this sense, the Marshall Plan functioned as an accelerator of political change, since the offer of aid was selective and came with evident strings attached. Before it was proposed, the Soviet Union – which had suffered the gravest losses in the war – had requested not aid but a simple loan from the United States, as well as indemnities from the countries which had invaded it. Washington did not grant the loan – indeed, even before the war was over, the Senate blocked the Lend Lease legislation that it had supported until then. When the terms of the Marshall Plan were announced, the USSR suddenly found itself excluded from the list of beneficiaries. Various countries of Eastern Europe that still had multiparty systems expressed an interest in the Plan nonetheless, but they, and they alone, had to meet a number of stringent conditions, such as an end to their still very cautious economic reforms, and agreement with donors about how and where the aid would be invested. The talks therefore came to nothing. As to Western Europe, the political quid pro quo was already implicit and readily accepted: expulsion of Communists from government, and investment of Marshall aid above all in large-scale private industry. Preparations were already under way for the Atlantic Pact, as a permanent US-led military alliance. Economic aid and security in return for limited sovereignty: the trade-off was clear enough.

But it would be factious and misleading not to mention that, for good or ill, there was something more to the Marshall Plan that the Communists should have grasped as the years went by. For all his aggressive crudeness, Truman was not actually seeking to impose a return to either Hoover's free tradism or Taft's isolationism. The harsh lessons of the great economic crisis and the world war made a grander ambition both necessary and possible; the conflict with the Soviet Union was the primary issue, but it was also the means to a new global order based on American hegemony. So the aim of the Marshall Plan was not to restore an earlier economic policy in countries with a partly developed economy, nor to prevent the export of advanced technology, nor to breathe life back into old-style protectionism, but rather to stimulate a form of subaltern modernization and integration, in Germany, Japan and Italy first and foremost. In the underdeveloped world, American policy certainly helped to thwart liberation movements, but not to block decolonization processes. It paved the way for new forms of dependence at the level of lifestyle, mass culture and consumption patterns, attempting to spread the 'American way of life' shorn of the impurities of New Deal progressivism – all, of course, within the confines set by a hard-line, dyed-in-the-wool anti-Communism. Anything that stepped outside those limits would be inviting repression, support for reactionary regimes, military threats – hence rearmament and the spectre of a new war.

The new cold war involved one final component, the most surprising and revealing of all. How and why, especially in Europe, did the dangerous new policy find such broad support, among populations initially moved by different feelings and different fears, and even among political forces that had played an active role in the anti-fascist resistance and shared the hopes of peace and dialogue that had seemed inseparable from it? The surprise is not so much the persistence of anti-Communism – which had deep roots and respectable justifications and, once the danger was over, could revive around the theme of democracy – but the fact that the social, political and cultural contest served to legitimize an arms race and preparations for war against a new enemy. No doubt this can be explained – and was explained – by the growing fear, bordering on hysteria, of an imminent Soviet attack. But it was an utterly groundless fear, contradicted by the real shape of things and even by the words of many cold warriors in America.

However underhand the intentions and inordinate the ambitions that might be attributed to Stalin, the Soviet Union, especially in the early postwar years, was in no position to attack anyone beyond the often shaky territories it had acquired. It was exhausted by war. Twenty million of its citizens were dead (compare this with 450,000 British, 400,000 Americans, or even seven million Germans), and countless others wounded or crippled; it would take ten years for the population to return to its prewar level, even if the recaptured territories are included. The 'horseless soldier with calloused hands'[1] had more to live for than another war. Industry had been dispersed in various parts of the country, and needed to be reorganized. Fertile farmland had been laid waste by retreating and reconquering armies, 70,000 villages burned to the ground, whole cities demolished. People often went hungry, and in 1946 there was again a widespread famine. Per capita income stood well below the level of 1938. Twenty-five million people were homeless; manpower was in short supply for the first time, so that the size of the army had to be cut at a stroke from twelve to two million; most of the men made their way back home on foot or on horseback, because the railways were in bad repair and there was a shortage of motor vehicles. Productive capacity declined in 1945, and again in 1946 and 1947. Western Europe, by contrast, had few weapons but (even in Germany) an efficient industry to produce them; and the United States stood behind and above it, output up 40 per cent since the beginning of the war, productive capacity more than doubled, new technologies coming on stream, military bases and troops all around the world, often on the very borders of the cold-war adversary. And it had the atom bomb. Some congressmen and generals were speaking of a pre-emptive war, before America's overwhelming superiority was whittled down.

Which madman in Moscow would dream of sending anyone to occupy the Place de la Concorde or St Peter's Square? Yet not only bigots and illiterates, but even educated opinion in countries awash with world news became convinced that an attack from the East was imminent. Why? Manipulation certainly played a major role, cynically building on ancient fanaticism not yet laid to rest, and on the expediency of doing something to deserve American aid. Perhaps there was also some ideological investment for the

1. The allusion is to the opening lines of *La Guardia rossa*, the 'anthem' of the Communist Garibaldi brigades of the wartime resistance: 'Ecco s'avanza uno strano soldato/vien dall'Oriente non monta destrier/la man callosa ed il volto abbronzato/è il più glorioso di tutti i guerrier.'

future. In my view, however, something more tangible and less avowable contributed to the success of that mobilization. Several key European countries were apprehensive of the collapse of a colonial system that had for centuries been integral to the national identity, providing resources and markets, raw materials at knock-down prices, and unpaid labour, whose profits were at least to some extent shared with the subaltern classes.

Let us take the extreme example of Britain, for which there is ample documentation. In the 1930s, the Conservative government had been so worried about change in the world that it had led the country into protracted appeasement of Nazism. The Labour Party opposed this and, during the war, developed a sincere sympathy and tolerance towards the Soviet Union. After forming a government in 1945, it did more than other European Socialist party to reform the social-economic system, basing itself on the Keynesian-inspired Beveridge report and the dynamism of men like Aneurin Bevan. But the opposite happened in the sphere of foreign policy: Labour adopted the line put forward by Churchill at Fulton, and the foreign secretary, Ernest Bevin, became one of its most zealous practitioners. The explanation for this is simple, as Keynes spelled out in a confidential memorandum to the government: Britain could not bear the cost both of building the welfare state and of keeping or regaining its colonial empire; it had to be one or the other. Special economic, political and military support from the Americans was necessary to put off this choice (and doubtless not for long). The dream of saving the empire was 'worth a Mass' on the Atlantic altar, even for socialists, and much of their electorate was induced to accept the price.

Italy is another limiting case that deserves a mention. It did not have profitable colonies to regain, nor could it have recovered the few it had lost, but there too a special international factor entered the picture from the beginning. I am not referring so much to the question of Trieste, which caused such uproar but for which a solution was soon cobbled together, as to the polemics over Eastern Europe. I would not venture to say that this was a primordial factor, but I do believe its importance has been overlooked in the evolution of the country's largest party and public attitudes: I am speaking, of course, of the Catholic Church and the orientation of its hierarchy. The pope at the time, Pius XII, had always regarded the Communists as the main enemy – the 'godless ones', as he called them in a

Bull in 1949 that excommunicated Party members and active sympathizers. Roosevelt's first contact with him was in 1945, during the days commemorating the Fosse Ardeatine massacre[2] and the deportations of Italian Jews, when a shocked envoy reported that Pius's main preoccupation had been with the Communist partisans in the surrounding countryside. Two years later, the same pope found himself facing an even pricklier and more dramatic problem, since in Eastern Europe – especially Hungary, Slovakia and Croatia – the Catholic hierarchy had not only supported but actually served as ministers in fascist governments, accepting the deportation of Jews and retaining vast ecclesiastical estates. The situation was less fraught in Poland, where many Catholics had supported the anti-German resistance, but fired by equal hatred for the Russians had gone on to back an attempt at guerrilla warfare against the national unity government. The conflict therefore bore on material issues, and a crusading spirit was necessary to distract from the weakness of the pope's arguments. A quotation reported in the memoirs of Paolo Spriano will give some idea of what I mean. In an official speech to a gathering of 500,000 Catholics, the influential Jesuit Padre Lombardi evoked the Resistance as follows: 'Meanwhile, adventurers had come from evil faraway countries with lists of people to be brutally murdered. Thousands upon thousands of Italians were killed and their corpses torn to pieces. This horrific spectacle was repeated in all the cities of Italy. The murderers, who are still honoured, will one day be struck down by Justice.'

De Gasperi, a moderate, anti-fascist Catholic, was for a long time in a weak position vis-à-vis the Vatican, as Togliatti would be vis-à-vis Moscow at a different historical moment. The para-fascist right wing of political Catholicism already showed a tendency to autonomy at the 1947 elections, and the Church's trust in Christian Democracy was not at all firm, either at the top or at parish level, whose priests' role in giving guidance to the faithful was no less important than that of the bishops. The legitimacy provided by the Americans, as part of a worldwide bloc to stop 'the Reds', must have seemed a heaven-sent means to unite ordinary Catholics with a bourgeoisie long linked to fascism and a state apparatus still clinging to power.

2. On 24 March 1944 German troops carried out a mass execution at the Ardeatine caves in Rome, in reprisal for a partisan attack. The anniversary is the occasion of an important official commemoration held each year at the site.

Once it had been embarked on at a global level, as a free choice but also an unequivocal responsibility, the road to the new cold war was very difficult to block. Senseless and dangerous though it seems, the mechanisms underpinning it were fairly straightforward. However, in order to trace its evolution and assess its results, and to gauge how Togliatti's PCI operated within it, we also need to pause for a moment over the political response of the Soviet Union and the world Communist movement. Here it becomes easier, and more important, to grasp the difference between two phases of the fifteen-year period: 1946–52, and 1952–60.

4

The Communists and the New Cold War

STALIN'S RIPOSTE

Every war has two sides. Whoever starts it and keeps it going has to face the actions of someone else: the behaviour of the one influences, and is modified by, the behaviour of the other; the conflict finally ends, after various phases, in victory or compromise. In the case of the fifteen-year cold war, I therefore cannot avoid reconstructing and evaluating how the Communist movement and the Communist states acted in relation to it. My first point is to distinguish clearly between the period from 1945 to 1952 (which brought us to the brink of a third world war) and the period from 1952 until the beginning of the 1960s, when that danger gradually subsided and gave way to a different contest.

Regarding the first phase, just as I am firmly convinced that the aggressive initiative came mainly from the big Western powers, I am by now equally convinced that the Communists generally responded in an unintelligent and ineffectual manner. They made mistakes in nearly every department – forecasting, analysis, strategy, tactics – which often, instead of containing or countering the aggressive thrust, made matters worse by offering ammunition to the enemy. The mistakes should be laid at the door of Joseph Stalin, since at that time all decisions of worldwide import depended on him. Although I have consistently refused to demonize the whole of his record, I have to recognize that the last five years were the worst.

In the first two years after the war Stalin underestimated (or pretended to underestimate) the scope and severity of the change in American policy, remained confident (or tried to feign confidence) that the broad anti-fascist coalition might last or be rebuilt, and tailored his political actions to that confidence. He did not fret over the atom bomb, and had little time for those among its inventors who wanted to subject it to international control. He polemicized against Churchill's Fulton speech, without seeing that it heralded a general and permanent turn in American foreign policy. He was mild in his criticism of British actions in Greece. He advised the Chinese Communists to show caution, and went so far as to divide captured Japanese weapons equally between Mao and Chiang. He said nothing against the way in which the PCI and PCF had ended the partisan struggle and entered national unity governments. He acted with moderation in parts of Eastern Europe occupied by the Red Army. He pulled the few Soviet troops out of Iran, and did not interfere in the dramatic events in South-East Asia. He proposed the unification of Germany as a neutral, unarmed state. He advised Tito to be more flexible on Trieste, and recognized the right of the Israelis to form a state (while upholding the same right for the Palestinians). He argued that the construction of the United Nations should be speeded up, and that it should be given decision-making powers. In short, he showed willing to comply with the letter and the spirit of the wartime meetings in Tehran and Yalta.

But in 1947 such confidence was no longer sustainable; the new cold war was an obvious fact of life, and the Soviet Union and the world Communist movement had to adopt a general line to face up to it, at least for the medium term. They were not bound to choose the line they did. Without throwing everything up for debate, without abandoning the role the Soviet Union had won as a world power or the social model it had constructed, there were two roads open to them. One was to reject the ground chosen by the enemy – bloc against bloc, with an emphasis on ideology and military force – and to focus instead on peaceful competition and the terrain of politics and social struggle. The Communists already had such a strategy in their historical baggage; it had been endorsed by Stalin himself at the Seventh Congress of the Communist International, in 1935, too late (given its inadequate forces and makeshift programme) to avert the war but offering some of the conditions to win it, and to kindle a desire for social transformation among the masses resisting fascism. In my view, conditions after the war were at least initially favourable for the persuasive development of such a programme.

Togliatti's suggested course, though ineffectual within the limits of a small defeated nation, could really have come into its own in the fight against the senseless idea of another war, had it been adopted as an international strategy that allowed for adjustment to different historical and cultural contexts. Soviet society, though ground down by war, displayed an extraordinary energy for reconstruction in those early years. In Western Europe, the Communist parties put down new roots not only because of what they had done, but because the burden of reconstruction weighed especially dramatically on the living conditions of the poor. Some Social Democratic parties, even if anti-Communist, promoted experiments in reform that pointed in the direction of socialism (Britain, Scandinavia, Austria). In Italy, the Socialists took up position alongside the Communists and the Soviet Union. Economic thinking had been transformed by the shock of the 1929 crisis; the trade unions were building themselves up again, stronger than before; and the most authoritative voices in the intellectual world (the Frankfurt School, Einstein, Picasso, Sartre, Curie, Russell, and so on) counselled against a mere return to the past. In the United States, Roosevelt's New Deal might have been cancelled at the top, but it had left huge traces in the national culture and in one of the two large trade union federations; and even the conservative elite and some top military men (Eisenhower, Bradley) were urging caution in foreign policy. At the level of popular culture, in the films I saw as a child – at least until the McCarthyite early 1950s – the enemy always wore a German or Japanese, not a Russian, uniform, and Frank Capra's meek model of American man was still the main one going. Above all else, however, the third-world liberation movement was now seriously under way. The Chinese, after their peasant revolution, were building a great new state without Soviet intervention; India was conquering independence and taking up a neutral position internationally; Indonesia and Vietnam were putting colonialism under great pressure; and significant forces (civilian in North Africa, military in Egypt) were struggling for independence in the Arab world. Of course, in order to grasp these opportunities and to draw these forces together, in a way that brought out the internal contradictions in the new cold war, it was necessary to recognize national specificities, to raise the banner of bourgeois freedoms that Stalin himself had evoked, and to give some evidence of those freedoms.

Once the country that had had the strength to attempt 'revolution in one country' had become a world power, what was to stop it carrying out a modest reform of itself? As soon as a turn was made in that direction, not long after Stalin's death, the resources for the West to keep up the cold war began to fail and the world situation took a different course. It cannot be objected that such a road was blocked at first by America's atomic weapons superiority, since the kind of political and social initiative I have in mind was the best way to prevent the adversary from launching a 'preemptive' nuclear war, and offered more time to restore the military balance as well (which is what happened). The brains for doing it were there.

Stalin, however, chose quite a different road. To understand why, it may be useful to mention the paradox that, in the final years of his life, Stalin was one of the chief victims of the 'personality cult' for which he had been so voraciously enthusiastic. The enormous prestige of his image, the ritualistic but earnestly spoken eulogies, the stock gestures of obedience: all this not only stifled critical thinking, debate and research, in a world movement now so extensive and diverse that it badly needed them, but also paralysed the mind of the Leader himself, anulling the gifts of intelligence and political insight of which he had given many a proof in the past. The personality cult prevented him from seeing the new resources he had created, from assessing the situation as it was and foreseeing how it would develop. Instead of encouraging him to look for new answers to a new predicament, it led him to fall back on fossilized ideas and previous options. Chief among these, the idea that 'socialism in one country' offered a universally valid model to be followed in every particular, and justified the Soviet Union's long-term role as the leading party and state (hence, after the great Patriotic War of 1941–5, as the leading nation); or the idea that every advance of socialism produced greater polarization and a sharpening of the class struggle; or the idea that capitalism was in irreversible crisis and heading towards another inter-imperialist war. These assumptions already determined how Stalin would respond to the new cold war. The priorities were to be the unity of Communist forces, and the struggle of camp against camp in ideology and politics, without adventurism but also without cracks in the edifice, until the unstoppable growth of the Soviet economy and a more favourable military balance carried the movement towards global hegemony. The search for alliances, and the autonomy of individual Communist parties, could not and should not be allowed to clash with these goals. It was a high-risk strategy, however: 'bloc against bloc' could move from cold war to hot without a conscious decision on anyone's part. In any event, it often made the image of the Communists much more like the one their enemies tried to pin on them.

THE COMINFORM ERROR

This tragic prologue that dragged on for years is almost impossible to explain, except as a conditioned reflex on the part of apparatuses that had lost their powers of reason. In the hour of a great victory and broad consensus, and in an international context not yet torn down the middle from top to bottom, state repression struck again at a society now bubbling with the vitality of reconstruction, further from the spotlight than in the past, but even more random in its choice of victims. The 'Leningrad affair' – that is, the summary liquidation of the leadership of the greatest and most heroic resistance of the Second World War – eventually engulfed the best mind, and the man most loyal to Stalin, in the field of Soviet economics: Nikolai Voznesensky. Not a few survivors of German prison camps, or veterans of the Garibaldi brigade who had risked their lives in Spain and later in various European resistance movements, ended up in Siberia, on suspicion of having deserted or surrendered to the enemy. Then doctors were charged with plotting to kill political leaders in their care, and finally the former Jewish association, which had supported the Bolshevik revolution, was accused of Zionism – even though Moscow had by then officially recognized the Israeli state. It was a cruel and senseless blow, favoured by the climate resulting from Stalin's political turn of September 1947.

The turn became explicit at the meeting near Wroclaw that gave birth to the Communist Information Bureau (Cominform). This was not a replica of the Communist International: first, because only ultra-loyal Communist parties (plus a couple that would later be accused of betrayal, the French and the Italian) were invited to attend the meeting; and second, because in the course of its brief life it met only rarely to issue directives or judgements, after the decisions had been taken elsewhere. The meeting's lead player was unquestionably Andrei Zhdanov, whom Stalin then considered his spokesman, even though he often spoke his lines so emphatically that his 'Report' seemed to offer, in the crudest way, a new analysis of the situation and a new political line. His thinking is easy to summarize. The division of the world into two camps, hitherto presented as an enemy objective to be opposed, was now a fait accompli that Communists had to adapt to and even turn to advantage; there was no longer room for equivocation on either side, and the search for alliances was a secondary, or slippery, business. The Soviet Union was not only the natural political leader but the finished model, whose imitation was to be proposed to everyone everywhere. The capitalist camp was already entering a new economic crisis and the cold war would develop into an inter-imperialist war; its ruling groups were turning towards a new kind of authoritarianism. There was no point in fooling around any longer with the concept of 'progressive democracy', which was inevitably sinking into mere parliamentarism and obscuring the class struggle. Political unity should be based on the organic, codified ideology of Marxism-Leninism-Stalinism, of which the 'History of the CPSU, Short Course' was the finished synthesis. All sectors of culture (including science, literature and music) had to adopt an explicitly political viewpoint and express themselves in simple forms close to popular culture, avoiding any comparison with Western culture, including unorthodox Marxism and 'degenerate' avant-garde arts. This platform, conveyed in extreme terms that even Stalin would have avoided (and at one point slightly corrected), met with no resistance or objections at the Wroclaw meeting, only a few expressions of concern from Gomulka, Tito and Dimitrov, who subsequently became its targets of attack. The Chinese were not present, and anyway they were used to going their own way. Criticism and accusations – necessary, as always, to establish the limits of orthodoxy – were directed, as we shall see, against the French and the Italians.

At the level of foreign policy and inter-state relations with the West, the infant Cominform confined itself mainly to counter-productive propaganda. Especially in the early years, there was never any hint of expansionist intentions. Even the Berlin blockade, which caused a period of tension in 1948, was presented merely as a protest against the arbitrary and unilateral decision to unite West Germany into a permanent state entity. The blockade was soon lifted, because instead of re-launching the serious proposal for a united, neutral Germany it helped to fuel West German nationalism and to underline the powerlessness of the Soviet Union to do anything about it.

Two facts speak volumes about this. The first, more important than any other geopolitically, concerns the Chinese question, which entered its decisive phase in 1947. The Americans directly intervened and the Senate called for the effort to be stepped up, yet the Cominform did not have much to say on the matter and the USSR maintained its usual caution. The second concerns the situation in Italy, whose Communist party was present at Wroclaw but only to be hauled over the coals. We have some interesting, and entertaining, testimony in connection with this. During those weeks Pietro Secchia was sent to Moscow at the head of a delegation, with the task of finding out what the Russians thought should be done differently. At a confidential meeting with the top Soviet leaders, which he recalled twenty years later, he frankly expressed his doubts about what he regarded as Togliatti's excessive parliamentarism and moderation. In his view it was possible to raise the level of the mass struggle in Italy, and besides, in the event of repression, there were enough forces to oppose it successfully without going all the way to an insurrection. Stalin, who had been silent, then interrupted with a few eloquent words: but you *would* reach that point, he said, and now is not the moment. Chapter closed: there were to be no adventures.

The words of the Cominform had much greater force inside its own camp, where they were meant to produce a standardized way of thinking among the states and parties on whose obedience Zhdanov was counting. They certainly had a dramatic effect, although not always in the way he had intended. First, in 1948, came the attack on Tito, until then the Soviet Union's strongest and most solid partner. It was of a sharpness that was clearly meant to shake him.

The various confidential documents that the two sides published soon afterwards reveal no political differences that might have justified the break. The new model of socialist society, involving self-management, non-alignment and a rejection of blocs, did not feature at all in the text submitted by Tito and Kardelj. The issues in dispute thus appear studiously beside the point: the arrogance of Soviet technical advisers and the kind of economic aid given to Yugoslavia; secret approaches to some of the country's military leaders, and so on. The real problem was that Yugoslavia had been the only East European country capable of liberating itself, through a tremendous guerrilla war against enemies both external (Italian fascists and Germans) and internal (right-wing Chetniks, monarchist nationalists, Croatian Ustashe). The cause and result of this great epic struggle was the birth of a real nation, which united peoples, religions and ethnic groups who had been fighting one another for centuries, and the formation of a leadership that was very proud of its inter-ethnic composition. I love the Soviet Union – Tito wrote to Stalin – as I love my own fatherland, implying that he recognized the one as a guide, but claimed independence for the other. This was the heresy that gave him the strength to carry the people with him, but it was also a principle that might infect other countries. The stakes were now raised considerably, to include the very stability of the people's democracies. It was the weakest point in Stalin's strategy, and it cost him a price that would never be recovered.

Eastern Europe was both an essential and a highly complex issue; it was from there, after all, that Russia and then the USSR had twice been invaded. Having liberated the countries in the area, Stalin wanted at least to see 'friendly governments' there, but the fact was that the situation on the ground varied greatly. Some countries, such as Yugoslavia, the Czech lands and to some extent Bulgaria, had undergone a regeneration in the anti-fascist resistance; others, such as Poland, had fought the Germans but, being Catholic and nationalist, also hated the Russians and showed as much over months of small-scale armed struggle. Still others, such as Horthy's Hungary, monarchic-reactionary Romania and Monsignor Tiso's Slovakia, had been fascist or para-fascist before the war and fought openly on the side of the Germans. The secret deal between Stalin and Churchill, with its absurd percentages of influence in each country, did not guarantee much. Besides, Churchill soon violated its terms by his actions in Greece.

The only common factor in the area was that the Red Army had passed through on its way to Berlin. At first Stalin used wisely the moral and material status this had given him, taking into account the diversity of the countries in question. He was neither able nor willing to give in over the 'friendly countries' principle, but he accepted the idea of a new experiment which he called 'people's democracy'. This has been stupidly treated as a verbal trick to cover up straightforward occupation regimes, but that is not how things were. The national Communist parties tried to give the term a meaningful content, stressing that, rather than a variant of the dictatorship of the proletariat, people's democracy represented a new road to socialism. They could count on two sources of strength, apart from the evident guarantees provided by the Soviet presence. On the one hand, the social vitality and influx of ideas from the anti-fascist struggle had not only strengthened the Communists but also buoyed up other democratic forces more or less on the left (Social Democracy, parties representing rural smallholders). The principle of multiparty politics and electoral representation could not be erased at a stroke. On the other hand, the fact that Germans, or their agents and accomplices, had for a long time been largely in control of major landed, industrial and financial interests meant that it was now possible, after their flight or expulsion, to redistribute land among small farmers and to nationalize large industrial or banking corporations without provoking major conflicts. Countless fascists and collaborators had also left vacant posts in bureaucratic apparatuses that had never known a jot of democracy. François Fejtö, an anti-Communist but certainly a serious historian, grants that in most cases the changeover was conducted with conviction and in incremental steps, securing both popular consent and effective results; only the military and police apparatuses were suspect in principle, and kept under close scrutiny.

The conditions attached to the Marshall Plan proposals had caused some passing difficulties, but the new Cominform line totally changed the picture: the people's democracies now had to transform themselves into socialist societies, the multiparty systems, with all their virtues and defects, became no more than a façade, and the economy was statized (with some caution in regard to agricultural collectivization). As for foreign policy, there was only one of those – and everyone knew who would decide it. Commercial and cultural relations with the West were to be limited and tightly controlled. It was more like a chastity belt than an iron curtain.

But Zhdanov would not have done enough, even if he had not died suddenly in August 1948; Beria stepped in to finish the job. To quash any objections, to safeguard the future and to make Tito's excommunication seem more credible, there now followed a series of horrific trials on trumped-up charges and the sentencing (sometimes to death) of supposed Titoists at the top of various East European Communist parties: Rajk, Kostov, Gomulka, Kádár, Clementis and (soon afterwards) Slánský – in Hungary, Bulgaria, Poland and Czechoslovakia. In my view, this brutal 'normalization' was the most severe price paid for the Cominform turn, and the greatest favour handed to the cold warriors in the West. It set up a long-term spiral of repression and revolt, had the most negative impact on Western public opinion, and blocked or reversed the development of new ideas and organizational forms among the Communist parties.

It is more difficult to express a judgement on the last chapter of Stalin's leadership, the Korean War. For some time this has been cited as an example of the Soviet tendency to export Communism through armed invasion – one of many legends peddled by cold warriors in the West. The story of the war is long and complicated, however, and since the danger of world war peaked in those years it needs to be reconstructed on the basis of documentary evidence, not the propaganda of either side. Korea had been occupied and enslaved by the Japanese for many years, and during the war diverse centres of resistance developed with difficulty in all parts of the country (though more in the north than the south, because of the proximity of China and Manchuria). In the closing stage of the Second World War, the Russians reached the country first but, at the request of the Americans, stopped at the 38th Parallel. The Americans then arrived in August and occupied the south, but being unable to find reliable local forces they negotiated with the former Japanese governor and installed a government under Syngman Rhee, a friend of the Japanese fascists who was linked to the big landowners. In the north, meanwhile, the liberation committees launched a land reform under the direction of Kim Il Sung, who had fought in the resistance in Manchuria. The agreement reached among the Allies (unification and free elections within two years of peace) therefore became difficult to implement, especially as Syngman Rhee staged fake elections, with many deaths, and established a regime of his own that was swiftly recognized by the UN as well as by President Truman.

With unification and monitored elections now postponed *sine die*, frictions and minor border incursions began to erupt on both sides. After an attack by the South, the better-organized forces of the North decided to cut the knot and swept on down to Seoul. Stalin could have prevented this, but he underestimated the risks and let events take their course, until an American expeditionary corps intervened with the authority of the UN Security Council (from which the USSR had been temporarily absent in protest against the refusal to recognize the new China). Washington was not content to restore the status quo ante, but crossed the old border into the north, provoking the entry of Chinese 'volunteers' who broke through and established a new front line at Seoul. The Americans then doubled their forces and achieved a breakthrough of their own, with high casualties on both sides. A rational compromise seemed possible – and indeed one was eventually reached. But General MacArthur, the American commander-in-chief in Korea, thought it was necessary to cut the knot with a sword, by driving the Communists out of the whole peninsula and nearby areas of China. That required the atom bomb, and he openly asked for it to be used; things would then not have stopped short of a general war. Truman, however, now near the end of his second term, did not go for the nuclear option, after receiving advice from his Allies and the Pentagon. An armistice followed and has held ever since. The reader may judge this sequence of events – the recklessness of some, the aggressiveness of others. But one thing is clear: when the air becomes saturated with gas, an unintended explosion can occur; one spark is all it takes to start the chain of combustion. The world was on the brink of a precipice for more than two months. In retrospect, it was fortunate that two chance events occurred just in time to end the most acute phase of the new cold war: the death of Stalin and the election of Eisenhower. The consequences of both, but especially the first, could not have been foreseen.

THE HARD YEARS

The international situation in the hardest years of the new cold war had an inordinate influence on Italian politics. But since even then, in a country that had regained freedom and independence, where a major party had some scope for autonomous thinking and action, we should examine how Togliatti's PCI developed, what results it obtained, and what price it paid. The difficulties it went through will tell us a lot about its staying power and its resources for the future.

There can be no doubt that the turn in American policy, the threat of war against the Soviet Union and the Cominform response, together with the accompanying swing in Italian Christian Democracy, the incipient split in the Socialist Party and soon in the trade union movement, struck directly at the political line which Togliatti had begun to develop at Salerno.

The room for manoeuvre was really very tight. Togliatti was both unable and unwilling to make any dissenting gesture in his own camp: Stalin would not have tolerated it; and the base of the PCI, as well as its leadership, would have disowned him. Not even his Socialist ally Nenni thought it a good idea: he recorded in his diary a meeting with Gomulka, at which the Polish Communist leader had criticized Togliatti in confidence for his 'docility'. Many intellectuals who became fearless lions after 1956 demanded no less, and on the day of Stalin's death they mourned sincerely and declared that they had 'learned everything' from him. Togliatti's choice was therefore a question of 'damage limitation', willing to accept criticisms and promise corrections, but only to preserve the core of the political line he had charted until then: the 'democratic road', within the limits of the Constitution. It was an essentially correct decision, in my view – which does not mean it was applied as well as it could have been, with the proper audacity and the avoidance of avoidable mistakes.

Let us first consider the PCI's position in Italian politics during those years, which began in 1948 with a grave and not blameless defeat, and ended in 1953 with a major success. Togliatti, even more than Stalin, did not see or appreciate the scale of the 'new cold war', or else he did not want to recognize it publicly. When the Christian Democrats (DC – Democrazia Cristiana) announced in 1947 that they intended to drive the Communists from government, and even more when they actually achieved this objective, Togliatti expressed his conviction that the breach could soon be repaired. He could not turn it around and use it for propaganda purposes against De Gasperi, because the DC leader was actually flaunting it to the voters he sought to win over. Rationally, perhaps,

Togliatti's aim was to gain time before the inevitable showdown, so that the existing draft of a constitutional charter could be finally adopted by a large parliamentary majority. The game was worth the candle. For the principles and specific provisions of the Constitution made it one of the most advanced in Europe, forming a permanent barrier to reactionary temptations, and the vote in its favour consecrated a 'constitutional arc' that gave legitimacy to all the forces of the Resistance. These two outcomes would often be debated, or contradicted by real life, but they essentially held up for decades to come.

Nevertheless, when we reread Togliatti's speeches of the time, we can detect a misguided belief that the Italian Left was already socially and electorally too strong and united, and too likely to grow further, for the DC to govern in the long term without its support. Before the Cominform turn, this led to the huge political mistake – proposed by Nenni's Socialists, but accepted by the PCI – of presenting a joint list for the upcoming elections, and campaigning as if victory were assured in advance. The Christian Democrats were thus able to present themselves as the only bulwark capable of rallying Catholics and Liberals, big business, middle layers and small farmers, in defence of the West and freedom. The elections took on the character of a referendum: either you were for the 'Reds', controlled by the Communists and in thrall to Moscow, or you were for the 'democrats'. And, more than by the DC as a party, the show was run by Luigi Gedda's Catholic Action, Padre Lombardi and the parish priests, plus the 'independent' press (which at the time was unanimously pro-business). Defeat was predictable, yet the Communists experienced it as a bitter surprise. The size of it took them aback: the Left reduced to 31 per cent, and the DC up to 48.5 per cent, with an absolute majority in both houses of parliament. Clearly the democratic road was going to be a long haul, by no means easier than an insurrection. Neither a tactical error nor the money trickling in from Marshall Aid was enough to explain the scale of the defeat; something better was required, at least at the level of analysis. But it was not forthcoming, even when the space for the Left began to become narrower. On the other hand, it is to Togliatti's credit that some of the specific policies adopted after 1948 were as effective as they were.

The first choice was made at a tragic moment, when an assassination attempt left Togliatti at death's door. A popular wave of protest, on a scale never seen before or since, showed that the organizational strength and social roots of the PCI remained intact after the electoral setback. Togliatti's appeal from hospital, 'Keep calm!', was taken up by the leadership, while the government's disproportionately repressive response to the upsurge offered the PCI a chance to reaffirm its democratic credentials.

The second choice was the peace campaign. Togliatti's imaginative approach to this, especially in the second attempt, involved the collection of signatures against the suicidal use of atomic weapons: a total of sixteen million, twice as much as the vote for the Popular Front. Some of the people who signed were far from being Communists: for example, the Christian Democrats Giorgio La Pira and Giovanni Gronchi, or even the industrialist Vittorio Valletta.

The third choice was the out and out struggle against the *legge truffa* in 1952–3,[1] which, despite its importance, has faded from people's memory in recent years. To be sure, the law was seemingly less weighted than the one under which we are used to voting today (the premium applied only to a coalition that gained more than 50 per cent of votes cast), and De Gasperi's plan seemed not so much to avoid a coalition with the far Right as to avoid being forced by the Vatican into forming a joint list with it ('Operation Sturzo').[2] The real venom of the proposed change to the electoral system was that it would have allowed the centre parties – which could still be sure of gaining 50 per cent or more of the vote – to achieve the 65 per cent of parliamentary seats necessary to change the Constitution. For the Council of Ministers, under pressure from the American embassy, was discussing ways and means to outlaw the PCI, or to limit the right to strike and the freedom to hold public demonstrations. I emphasize this because no one without direct experience of it knows how widespread the repression in Italy was at that time. Strikes and peaceful demonstrations often ended in violent clashes with the police, and in a large number of cases (Melissa, Torre Maggiore, Fucino and Modena being only a

1. *Legge truffa*, or 'swindle law', was the name given by the Left to the electoral topping-up system introduced by the Christian Democrats in 1953, which assured them of a controlling majority in parliament.

2. 'Operation Sturzo': so called after Don Luigi Sturzo, the clerical leader of the prewar Italian People's Party (PPI), who formally took the initiative in proposing a joint list in 1952 between the Christian Democrats and the neo-fascist Movimento Sociale Italiano (MSI).

few examples) the police beat, shot at and killed peasants occupying uncultivated land or workers picketing factory gates. Inside the factories, workers were dismissed or isolated in special shops for nothing more than joining the FIOM metalworkers' union, while prestigious intellectuals such as Guido Aristarco and Renzo Renzi ended up in military prison for two years after writing a screenplay on the wartime invasion of Greece that was deemed insulting to the national honour. Others had their passport confiscated; a new job nearly always required the consent of the parish priest or the Carabinieri, and even the hire-purchase of Einaudi books (not only its pocket editions published jointly with the Communist daily *L'Unità*) would be recorded in files at the workplace.

If anyone thinks I am exaggerating this everyday repression, they should take a look at some police reports from the time, which can now be consulted in the State Archives. I will mention just two examples. One of the most grotesque is a Carabinieri report on sharecroppers:

> The main wish is to regulate the right to strike. The pretexts for lively peasant agitation have been the well-known economic demands, but also breaches of prefect's orders prohibiting the display of banners in farmyards at threshing time. It is right to take measures against this unacceptable abuse, which forces landowners to endure Communist violence in their own home by threatening that the harvest will not otherwise be completed. [1950]

And from an annual report by top police officials:

> Action by the forces of the state can no longer compensate for the inadequacy of current legislation, since this represents an insurmountable barrier. It is therefore urgently necessary to issue laws that will regulate strikes, hit at the organizers of acts of rebellion, curb the freedom of the press, place legal constraints on the trade unions, and allow greater freedom of action for the police. [1952]

As I can personally recall, the wind of the new cold war produced such trends in the life of the country, long after the danger of the 'Communists taking power' had disappeared with the elections of 1948. It is that wind which explains why and how politicians played fast and loose with the Constitution, and how they intended to revise it. To draw attention to this, Togliatti made the reasonable request that the majority premium should be set below the level at which the constitutional charter could be amended. De

Gasperi's flat refusal then triggered a full-scale electoral mobilization by the PCI, flanked by smaller lists including symbolic figures of the anti-fascist struggle (Parri and Calamandrei for the Democrats, Corbino for the Liberals). The result was quite extraordinary: on a turnout of 93.8 per cent, the *legge truffa* was 50,000 votes short of a majority; the Christian Democrats lost nearly 10 per cent of their vote, the Saragat Socialists nearly half,[3] while the Republicans and Liberals in the government coalition were virtually wiped out. From then on, the 'dual state' sank into behind-the-scenes conspiracies (although police abuses continued, at least until the DC government of Fernando Tambroni in 1960 and the deaths caused by violent police action in Reggio Emilia). The republican Constitution was now firmly rooted in the popular consciousness.

Togliatti's 'damage limitation' had therefore worked in internal policy, with some exceptions. Even today, for example, I cannot understand the indifference bordering on suspicion that Togliatti and the PCI maintained in that period, long before the papacy of John XXIII, towards the events shaking the political and ecclesiastical world of Catholicism: the jurist Giuseppe Dossetti, who withdrew from politics in 1951 despite the sizeable support for him in the DC, had voted against the Atlantic Pact and rejected the economic policy of Einaudi and Pella; while Carlo Carretto and Mario Rossi had been leading a struggle against Luigi Gedda in the leadership of the Catholic Youth, and ructions in the Christian Democrat youth were impelling some (like Giuseppe Chiarante and myself) to move towards the PCI and others to form a new left-wing current within the DC. It is also hard to explain Togliatti's persistent ill-feeling towards left reformists like Riccardo Lombardi and Vittorio Foa, or progressive liberals such as Ernesto Rossi.

In any event, 'damage limitation' proved more difficult in three other closely related areas that were very important at the time: international relations, the building and running of the Party, and the cultural-ideological training of its cadres and membership. On all these, the turn imposed by the Cominform left little scope for autonomy among individual parties. But it is also justifiable to ask

3. Giuseppe Saragat: leader of a faction that split away from the Socialist Party in 1947, on the grounds that it was too close to the PCI, and went on to found the Italian Democratic Socialist Party.

whether the PCI leadership made use of such scope as did exist, and to consider the price that it paid.

At the meeting in Wroclaw, where he stood 'in the dock', Luigi Longo responded with dignified prudence to the sharp criticisms levelled against the PCI. He admitted that it had made serious political errors, but did not specify what they had been. He declared himself willing to make corrections on non-fundamental issues, to highlight more the successes of socialist construction in the USSR, to give greater weight to class struggle than to parliamentary action, and to show greater vigilance within and over leadership groups. Upon his return to Italy, Longo minimized the event when referring to it at a meeting of the Party directorate; Togliatti did the same, adding that the basic line of the PCI had to be preserved; the other leaders – leaving aside some concerns on Terracini's part – agreed with this attitude and merely added a few self-criticisms of their own. Since the final motion in Wroclaw – the only one made public – had not emphasized the charges against the PCI, the shock in the Party was quite muted, and it died down still further after the attempt on Togliatti's life in July 1948, when Stalin criticized the leadership in a telegram for failing to protect him properly and thereby reaffirmed his confidence in him as leader.

But the first storm broke in 1949, when everyone was asked to endorse the condemnation of Tito. The PCI leadership did not hesitate to take sides – and, I repeat, it could not have avoided doing so – but there were, as always, different ways of taking sides, and in this case the one it chose was the worst. The Italian Communists could, in fact, have used strong arguments for taking Tito to task: the difficulties that his nationalism had caused over the fate of Trieste; his hasty and sweeping rejection of the very concept of people's democracy and a modicum of pluralism; his arrogant proposal of a Balkan Federation, which would effectively have meant the annexation of Bulgaria by Yugoslavia; his encouragement and support for the adventure of the Greek insurrection; his explicit and repeated criticisms of Togliatti's opportunism; perhaps even, exaggerating somewhat, his refusal to seek an agreement or compromise for the sake of national unity. In a cold-war climate, this was sufficient material for a condemnation of Tito that could be shared with others. Moreover, the Party was surprised at the turn of events more than opposed to them; a few here and there asked for explanations, but only the Reggio Emilia Secretary,

Valdo Magnani, disagreed so much that he resigned from his position along with Aldo Cucchi, without rebelling against Party discipline.

But did the PCI really need to claim that Tito was a spy in the pay of the Americans, or that Yugoslavia had crossed into the other camp (a charge that was immediately refuted by the facts)? Did it need to transform a resignation into the expulsion of 'two lice' with dishonour? Was it useful to blow up the 'betrayal' of the strongest among them, at a time when the key point was to strengthen the unity of Communist states and parties in opposition to the cold war? Was it to be feared that a more sober and truthful condemnation of Tito would have provoked the Cominform into new charges and a new excommunication, this time against or inside the PCI? I do not think so. Perhaps it was to be feared that there would be an acrimonious debate, a moment of tension, or even, if the leadership defected, that Togliatti would be replaced as Party secretary. But, in that extreme and unlikely event, he would have returned as leader a few years later, when Khrushchev made his journey of reconciliation to Belgrade, or after the Twentieth Congress of the CPSU; and his credibility, like Gomulka's, would have been all the stronger as a result. Instead, the PCI's crude way of handling the affair darkened the idea of the 'new party'.

Nor was that all. Equally serious was the PCI's failure to show the slightest doubt or scruple when many leading Communists in Eastern Europe were tried on wild and senseless charges and ruthlessly liquidated. What a miracle that socialism had scored such extraordinary successes under the leadership of spies and traitors! We are talking now of pointless and revealing mistakes on the PCI's part, beyond the limits of what might have been necessary.

When I thought back to the period from 1948 to 1950, I realized that these were not mere episodes but the first signs of a general threat to the PCI's original identity – a threat that Togliatti subsequently managed to avoid, with great skill, tenacity and courage, as well as considerable good fortune, but displaying a basic uncertainty and paying a high price in terms of future prospects. I am referring to the influence that Zhdanov's turn had on the organizational forms, ideology and cadre training of the Communist movement, as the myth of the Soviet Union and the worship of Stalin rose to a crescendo.

In his last, and in some respects most acute, work on the history of Italian Communism, Paolo Spriano devotes a whole chapter to this theme, starting with the undoubtedly extraordinary turmoil following the death of Stalin. The Stalin cult was not a myth – Spriano says – but a blind, absolute love that sought confirmation from the beloved. In trying to explain this, he relies both on a quotation from Gramsci – 'Among the masses as such, philosophy can only be experienced as a faith' – and on the indelible historical context of the victory over fascism, all the more necessary to preserve in a period of harsh defeats. However, not only does this seem to me an unconvincing explanation; it takes us off track and easily becomes a blanket justification or dismissal of a many-sided and contradictory process.

At a theoretical level, the Gramsci quotation is actually misplaced. Read correctly – that is, within his thought as a whole – it does not point at all to something that is necessarily the case, still less to a lever that can or should be made use of. On the contrary, it indicates a limitation to which the masses have been confined by age-old ignorance, but from which they should be liberated. For Gramsci, then, the party qua collective intellectual, in promoting a cultural and moral revolution that will transform the proletariat into the ruling class, must carry out the (now historically possible) task of emancipating the proletariat from faith and drawing it into the world of reason; that is why it bases itself on historical materialism, on 'scientific socialism'. To be sure, it does this at various levels of simplification, in accordance with an analysis of the facts of the situation, but always with a respect for reality and a sincere relationship to the truth. It may also hazard predictions that will fuel people's hopes, and provisionally buoy up their trust in difficult times, but without foisting on them beliefs that contradict or disguise reality; these can breed cynicism if they are too frequent or protracted, as the decay of the socialist societies illustrates. This is the difference between Leninism and Stalinism.

It is historically quite inaccurate to say that the myth of the Soviet Union rested entirely on spontaneous or irrepressible memories of victory in the Second World War. Objective elements did play a role – bloc rivalry, ideological virulence in the other camp, persecutions in everyday life – but there can be no doubt that the myth was also the result of a large-scale organizational and cultural operation imposed by the Cominform turn, which the PCI conducted intelligently and in a way that contained its effects, but too often out of conviction and in mistaken forms.

But why did the PCI pay a lesser price (in terms of membership and votes) than other Western parties and retain effective antibodies for the future? Why did it later expend so much time and effort in shaking off the ideological stereotypes and organizational forms that it had acquired during those years? In any event, the operation needs to be more carefully analysed. Those were the years when the Party organization acquired a more stable form, and when the cadres were trained who would lead it for decades to come. To put it a little schematically, my own memory tells me that it is possible to identify two lines of development. The first, truly original one stemmed from the choice made by Togliatti (but also by Secchia, then the chief person running the Party) to build a 'people's party' – unlike a vanguard partly, mainly restricted to the working class. I am thinking of the great effort that went into the recruitment and mobilization of new subjects and social strata, drawing on experiences of life that had previously been relegated to the margins of politics: above all women, both as Party members and in relation to issues of particular concern to them, which were taken up mainly, but not only, by the Italian Women's Union (UDI). I am also thinking of proselytism among family members, across generations, and in groups of friends and neighbours, which, in addition to increasing the Party's influence, established a permanent sense of belonging, a mutual commitment among individuals. And I am also thinking of organizational functions in areas distinct from politics proper: leisure activity, popular culture, entertainment, sport, the *case del popolo*, the many-sided ARCI,[4] the paperback libraries. No less important was the growth and differentiation of the Communist press: the Party daily, which volunteers helped to distribute in every village, sometimes achieved a circulation of more than a million; but there was also a large readership for weeklies and monthlies, both popular and intellectual, from *Vie Nuove* to *Noi Donne*, from *Calendario del Popolo* to *Rinascita* and *Società*. Not an army, then, but a real community linked by ideas, feelings and common experiences. I have recently come across Carabinieri reports that tell us a lot about this: some

4. ARCI: Associazione Ricreativa Culturale Italiana (Italian Cultural Recreational Association), first established in 1957, which greatly expanded its areas of activity over the following decades.

discuss the late time of the day set for meetings and conclude that they were intended to organize clandestine activity; others underline the danger that the Casa del Popolo will 'attract more than local orators, since they also have dancing there'. This model of a people's party clashes with the idea of a sect imbued with hatred or suspicion of 'non-believers'; it sometimes made it possible to live happily with a few cents in your pocket, to feel protected by a social web of solidarity, and to feel useful even if you had limited personal abilities. Given the hostile climate of the 1950s, it would have been impossible without all this to hold together a movement of two and a half million members (including 500,000 young and very young people), some living in the *zone bianche* of unplanned housing development. In the evening you went to a meeting on your bicycle or moped, where you would discuss newspaper articles or membership campaigns; then you came back late to eat a plate of tripe or have a drink or two at the café attached to the House of Labour (because the trade unions too were part of the alternative society). Anyone who thinks the old PCI was gloomy and militarized and contrasts it with today's 'new social movements' is either ignorant or stupid: if anything, the resemblance between them is too great. This type of 'people's party' was able to cultivate bonds with society: to both understand and reflect it. Yet there was a limit beyond which it could not go, since by necessity or by choice it reduced the scale of political organization at the workplace, leaving this as the domain of trade unions in their more immediate functions.

During these hard years up to and beyond 1954, a second, very different, reality was developing in tandem with the first. I am referring to the huge investment in the selection of leaders at every level – full-timers paid less than an average worker, without social protection but held to a rigid discipline, closely watched over at successive Party schools and even in their private lives, promoted only through co-opting from above, and trained not so much in the 'classics of Marxism' or other works (the main material in the 'prison schools') as in the 'History of the CPSU (Short Course)', from which no one ever deviated. The building of this 'second party' was largely entrusted to Secchia, the directly elected vice-secretary, who was responsible for the many tasks of the organization commission. Let us be clear. Secchia did not have an overbearing or authoritarian character: he surrounded himself with intelligent young people (Bufalini, Di Giulio, Pirani), retained a constant and humanly sympathetic rapport with other Party members, and agreed with the core of Togliatti's policy, though with quite a few reservations about his way of running the Party. Secchia was a cadre trained in the Third International of the early 1930s, before the period of its bureaucratic-repressive degeneration. The real priority for him was a disciplined vanguard party, mainly composed of cadres with a working-class background, indissolubly linked to the policies and destiny of the Soviet Union and its supreme leader, and therefore prepared to deal with any political climate that might develop. He was not a soldier, nor an aspiring member of parliament or mayor, but a professional revolutionary, intelligent and creative within the limits that had been laid down and accepted. He gave priority to the formation of that human type, and for the duration of this period the model functioned well.

The myth of the USSR, the Stalin cult and the tendency to ideological rigidity were together moderated, but also together fuelled, by a combination of naïve faith and Jesuitism. Intellectuals were less naïve but often more intransigent, and even when they excelled in the study of history they tended to engage in non-controversial specialist research, keeping within the limits of Italian history and culture so as not to have to measure themselves against modern (often Marxist but unorthodox) international thinking. Events such as the anti-Titoist campaign or the elimination of the people's democracies therefore intersected, as both cause and effect, with the twofold process of the PCI's development.

During the same period, this rich and contradictory process – and indeed international history generally – reached a juncture that could have had irreversible consequences. For in the late autumn of 1950 Longo, Secchia and D'Onofrio told the still convalescing Togliatti that Stalin was planning to transfer him out of Italy to lead and 're-launch' the Cominform. The origin of this proposal and the thinking behind it are not altogether clear, and we cannot be sure how definite or binding it was meant to be. Years later Togliatti himself confided to Barca[5] that he suspected the proposal had emanated from someone in Italy. It is doubtful whether it was

5. Luciano Barca: member of PCI leadership bodies in the 1960s and 1970s, and variously editor of the Party daily *L'Unità* and the cultural-theoretical weekly *Rinascita*; later editor of *Politica e Economia*, a review published by the economics department of the Central Committee, for which he was long responsible.

a direct order, however, given what we know of Stalin, and in the end he seems to have dropped the idea. As for its purpose, it may not have been intended only to remove Togliatti from the PCI leadership; it may have partly reflected a wish to adjust the orientation and functioning of the Cominform – the kind of shift that used to happen in the Comintern. Nevertheless, Togliatti's removal from the leadership would have followed, and it was in that light that he interpreted it. Before travelling to Moscow, he told Longo, Secchia and D'Onofrio that he had decided to reject the proposal. And when he was there, feeling sure of his ground, he requested the whole leadership of the PCI to first discuss it in his absence. In a memorandum he sent to Stalin before their final meeting, speaking in the third person to soften the impact, he clearly stated that he did not find the proposal convincing. His arguments were not rigid but pointed to objective circumstances: that he had not been long back in Italy, after many years in the Soviet Union; that he had started to build a major party, and taken on a public role; that he should therefore continue with his work, so as not to put everything in jeopardy; and that he would have personal difficulties in resuming his life in exile, since he wanted to build a family. Meanwhile, however, news came through that left him 'stupefied': the Party leadership in Italy had decided almost unanimously to accept Stalin's proposal (only Terracini voted no, and Longo abstained). It seemed impossible to escape the crossfire, but Togliatti acted firmly and skilfully in response. First and foremost he managed to persuade the PCI leadership, Secchia included, to postpone implementation of the decision for a few months, until after the forthcoming elections. In the final discussion, Stalin said that this amounted to killing it stone dead, but though visibly disappointed he accepted the postponement. Things ended well, then, and no one heard any more about it. The incident had demonstrated Togliatti's intelligence and tenacity, and given further proof of his courage, but his isolation could be gauged from the danger of finding himself in a complete minority within the Party leadership. A disciplined relationship to the Soviet Union now expressed more than mere love in the heart of the masses, and embraced layers well beyond the old cadres from the 'underground struggle' against fascism. 'Damage limitation' had enabled the PCI's identity to survive, but the hard years of the 'new cold war' had impeded its development and made its future course more difficult.

5

The Shock of the Twentieth Congress

In 1952 the 'new cold war' entered its second phase, changing character and direction and finally ending in a partial compromise. Although the new turn originated in Moscow, it did not have the improvised and disruptive quality of the previous one. It proceeded by small steps, starting and halting intermittently. It was perhaps not fully conscious in those who took part, and did not operate uniformly throughout the world; only at a certain point did it pick up speed and become noticeable to public opinion in general. But its scope is immediately evident at the level of the decade as a whole.

Although the danger of a third world war occasionally resurfaced, it had in reality been headed off. What remained were two structured blocs, which reopened certain channels of communication and agreement between each other, while new states that rejected the discipline of either entered the field. All this was not only the fruit of an international policy correction by the major powers and their ruling groups, but resulted from, and was driven on by, profound changes at the level of the economy, culture and social relations, which only became fully apparent at a later date but were already present and active.

The gradual shift to a bipolar balance of power, involving peaceful competition between two systems and a limitation of military conflict to regional frameworks, brought other factors to centre stage: ideological and cultural hegemony, economic development and social conflict, quality of life and efficiency of institutions. Before we look more closely at this process, we should recognize that a 'balance of terror' was both its prerequisite and a long-term encumbrance. This is another of the major omissions and hypocrisies that still mark political and cultural discussion today.

I chose 1952 as the date for the new turn because it was the 'year of the Bomb' – with a capital 'B' to emphasize its two-fold novelty. The dropping of the atom bomb on Hiroshima was a purely American decision: it demonstrated the military superiority of the United States, which could use it to threaten the Soviet Union or even defeat it in a possible war. But, even in the new plutonium version, the destructive capacity of the Bomb was still not great enough to prevent a long drawn-out war that might prove very costly to the state that unleashed it. On the other hand, the scientific information needed to develop it was fairly widely known: Soviet intelligence could obtain other details through espionage, and it had scientists and technicians capable of producing results; it was only a question of time before these were achieved. In 1949 Moscow succeeded in detonating an experimental device, so that all it had to do was build up an arsenal and develop the means to propel it over long distances; that too would not take long. This was one of the reasons for the early fervour of the new cold war, for MacArthur's rash proposal to use the bomb in Korea, and for the reluctance of European governments to accept it.

Washington, for its part, had for some years been looking to a much more effective means of establishing its supremacy on a long-term basis: namely, the thermonuclear hydrogen bomb, with a destructive power several thousand times greater than that of the Hiroshima weapon. But this required a solution to new theoretical problems and the deployment of much more advanced technological resources. As Oppenheimer and Fermi refused to be involved, and were anyway under a cloud, a new team under the trusted and enthusiastic Edward Teller was put in charge of the research. But then the unforeseen happened, as the physicist Zhores Medvedev (brother of Roy and, like him, all the more believable for being later persecuted as a dissident) has only recently revealed. While Teller banked on American technological supremacy rather than theoretical physics, Stalin – by good sense or by chance – gathered all the leading Soviet theoretical physicists and pure mathematicians of the time to work on the project. And while the Americans lost much time on contraptions that required rare and expensive materials, the Soviet team, coordinated by Sakharov, Tamm and

Landau, came up with highly advanced theoretical solutions that showed a way round the technological difficulties. The Russians made the breakthrough to a thermonuclear bomb in August 1952, a few months before the Americans. Meanwhile they had also been making rapid advances in missile research, which a few years later culminated in the launching of the first artificial satellite; this made up for their lack of forward bases for large bomber aircraft. After this dual qualitative leap, both powers had terrible bombs and the means to deliver them – so terrible, in fact, that to use them no longer meant victory but rather collective suicide. It was a true 'balance of terror', which held back anyone who was not crazy from launching total war. Like it or not, the effects could not fail to be colossal and long-lasting; my generation lived for decades under this shadow, and with this obstacle to the future. But the actual course of events, and the final denouement, would depend on politics, in all its forms and with all its players. For the whole scenario was suddenly about to change.

THE BEGINNING OF DE-STALINIZATION

Here I will concentrate on what happened in Soviet politics and society between 1952 and the early 1960s – on what goes by the approximate name of de-Stalinization. This period, which saw the Soviet Union assume a superpower role and express the 'forward thrust' of the Russian Revolution for the second and last time, would have a direct and major impact on developments in the PCI and the rest of the Italian Left.

The early signs of change, though much more episodic, are very important for an understanding of the great spurt that came in 1956. Paradoxically, some hints can be found before Stalin's death and were even advanced by him in an ambiguous kind of way. For it was he who called the first congress of the Communist Party of the Soviet Union in ten years; he too who, at the congress, imposed a leadership shake-up that strengthened his absolute power, making Politburo meetings irregular and superfluous, but also downgraded loyal old collaborators such as Beria or Molotov and promoted younger, less compromised men such as Khrushchev. In the last of his writings, *Economic Problems of Socialism*, the contradiction can be seen in full: on the one hand, no mention of the restoration of legality or economic reform; on the other hand, assertions that overturned the Cominform line by stressing the avoidability of war, the possibility of different roads to socialism (including peaceful ones), and the usefulness of allowing a role for the market in the exact determination of prices. Some of these positions were taken up and made official in Malenkov's opening report to the Nineteenth Party Congress.

When Stalin died without an appointed heir, power passed into the hands of an inevitably heterogeneous collegiate: Beria, Molotov, Kaganovich, Voroshilov (the four most authoritative but also the most leaden), alongside Malenkov, Khrushchev, Bulganin and Mikoyan (younger, and harder to pin down). Significantly, whether out of conviction or necessity, this whole group opted for renewal: it publicly affirmed the principle of collective leadership, recognized the need for economic reforms in favour of agriculture and mass consumption, began to release political prisoners (instead of just talking about it), and cancelled the judicial preparations against the 'Doctors' Plot' and the 'Jewish Alliance'.

The reasons for this new course were both the state of the economy (again in trouble, after a strong postwar revival) and the fear that each of the leaders had of succumbing to another power struggle. The once-omnipotent secret police was purged and partly dismantled, and the army, with Zhukov at its head, was given a new role as guarantor. A second sign of renewal came in agrarian policy. Khrushchev, who had responsibility for it, suddenly lifted the lid on the ongoing output crisis, for which the peasantry had been paying the price. He no longer blamed the war for everything: something had to be done, and done soon. A series of reforms, though uncoordinated, had an immediate effect: peasants were given the freedom to produce and sell what they wanted on the little plot of land individually assigned to them; the state raised the prices it paid to collective and state farms (to discourage hoarding) and lowered the prices they had to pay for industrial products (consumption goods, farm machinery). New virgin lands were brought under cultivation with the help of young volunteers, producing results that fell short of expectations in the first year, because of inexperience and lack of machinery and fertilizer, but were already more encouraging in the second year. Khrushchev won considerable prestige and popularity from these measures, eventually becoming number one in the Party secretariat. Malenkov was dismissed for incompetence after just one year at the head of the government; an investigation into the 'Leningrad affair' (the purge of the Leningrad Party organization in the last years of Stalin's life) revealed that he had been directly responsible for it. He kept his seat in the Politburo, but a hierarchy was already beginning to take shape in the collegial leadership.

In foreign policy, which the world was naturally watching closely after Stalin's death, the signs of change were at first more limited, perhaps because it was Molotov's area of responsibility. The proposal to unify Germany as a neutral country – not a new idea, in fact – was too ambitious to elicit a response in the West, at least until there was a turnaround in the international situation. A meeting of foreign ministers of the WWII victors had been no more than a goodwill gesture, without content and without results. And a peace treaty with Austria, locking it into neutrality and securing the departure of all foreign troops, had been scheduled for some time. But these small steps were contradicted by choices that displayed the worst kind of continuity with the past. Moscow showed great hostility to the Mossadegh government in Iran, which nationalized the country's oil resources, before being brought down in a CIA-staged coup d'état. The Iranian CP shared this hostility, in accordance with the Cominform principle that anything that moved without or against the Communists was to be suspected. I stress this because the (largely forgotten) position taken by the Communists at the time gave rise to the rapprochement between the Iranian masses and the fundamentalist clergy in the struggle against the Western-installed Shah, with the consequences we see today.

It was precisely in relation to foreign policy, however, that the first rift appeared in the top Soviet leadership. On 16 May 1955, Khrushchev flew to Belgrade to patch up relations with Yugoslavia and to reacknowledge the socialist character of its society. Back in Moscow, he openly declared that the excommunication of Tito had been an error. It was a highly symbolic act on his part, since it implied that even the model Soviet state could make the wrong decisions, and that not only different roads to socialism but also different ways of organizing society were possible (that is, in the Yugoslav case, workers' self-management guided by the Communist Party within the framework of a plan). The reconciliation with Belgrade was also important at the level of international relations, since Tito had recently returned from the great conference at Bandung, attended by representatives of twenty-five states and parties, which he had jointly sponsored with Zhou Enlai, Sukarno, Nehru and Nasser. It was the birth of the Non-Aligned Movement.

A careful if summary reconstruction of the early years of de-Stalinization makes it clear that the Twentieth Congress was not a brainwave that came to Khrushchev in the context of a power struggle, nor a mere flash in the pan lasting a few months between his Secret Report and the Soviet intervention in Hungary. Rather, it was the most dramatic event in a long and tortuous process, intertwined with changes in Soviet society and obstructed by established powers and deeply rooted sentiments. The process should be judged as a whole, within its historical context. Only then can we understand its value and limits, its lasting successes and the knots that it left entangled. Only then can we correctly analyse the particular events that make up the broader canvas.

THE TWENTIETH CONGRESS AND KHRUSHCHEV'S SECRET SPEECH

The Twentieth Congress of the CPSU took place over ten days in February 1956, but it fell into two parts that were widely disparate in form and content. The first, occupying nearly all the ten days, began with Khrushchev's report on the international situation and the state of Soviet society; it put forward a line on each, quoted Stalin only twice in passing, and was presented in the name of the whole leadership. After a debate in which everyone spoke in its support, albeit with differing emphases, it was adopted unanimously and immediately published. The second part, lasting just a few hours, consisted of a speech by Khrushchev, with no debate and no vote. It leaked out gradually, through many different channels and in a number of versions, and for this reason it is still known as the Secret Speech. It consisted entirely of an implacable denunciation of Stalin's faults and the personality cult he built up around himself.

Was it a good idea to divide the congress so sharply into two parts, and to denounce Stalinism in such a crude and personalized manner? Could a speech on the past, with a necessary element of self-criticism, not have been inserted into a more sober, rounded reflection on the history of the Soviet Union, so as to give a stronger basis for valuing what should be preserved and a clearer idea of the areas where innovation was possible and necessary? These questions were already asked at the time, by Communists and by people friendly to Communism, and even by those who considered the Twentieth Congress as a whole to be a historic step forward. In my view they did not become any deeper, and adequate answers have still not been given.

On the first question it has been said that, whereas the whole leadership backed the main congress report, the Secret Speech was a surprise initiative that Khrushchev took at his own risk, at a time when the whole matter was still under review. No doubt there is some truth in this, especially in light of the split in the leadership only a year later, but it does not really hold water. All the later research and memoirs agree that the text of the Speech was shown in advance to all but a few members of the Politburo, and that they accepted it with a greater or lesser degree of wholeheartedness. Still less convincing is the argument that it was a 'secret' speech, designed to circulate only within a closed group so that it would have limited impact on the masses at home and abroad. The fact is that the speech was soon being read out and distributed at rank-and-file Party meetings open to the public, that it was sent to foreign Communist parties (who were free to use it as they saw fit), and that it was eventually published in American papers, *Le Monde* and *L'Unità*. Never in the history of the Soviet Union had a text been so widely read and discussed by so many people around the world.

This tells us a few very interesting things. First, the painful jolt was inevitable; no one could oppose it head on, for the simple reason that the thousands or hundreds of thousands of people returning from the camps, plus countless families who had suffered an irreparable loss, would have become a dislocating force in the workplace and society if political amends had not been made to them. Second, unless something was done to shake up routine ways of thinking and to replace cadres and procedures that had become fossilized over the decades, any reform or new mass mobilization would soon have ground to a halt. To be sure, many workers and Party activists were unwilling to remove the portrait of Stalin from their wall, or from their heart; many intellectuals would have liked the self-criticism to extend to other compromised parties and leaders; and major figures such as Mao, Thorez and

Togliatti, each in his way, distrusted the bluntness of Khrushchev's speech. All these groups of people agreed on one thing at least: it was not possible to eradicate everything that Stalin had done and said, still less attribute the degeneration *in toto* to the personality cult. That was also my opinion. However – and here I must add my own little self-criticism – these attacks did not face up to one simple fact. Among the many things in the Secret Speech that I had long known and digested – for example, those relating to the assassination of Trotsky and Bukharin – there was one that even Togliatti, I think, had not known or been willing to recognize: that is, the mass scale and random nature of the terror, the prevalence of Communists (some of proven loyalty) among the victims. Perhaps this was the element that called for a stern denunciation and resisted rational explanation (why the terror was necessary, what its motives or purpose were).

When I reread Khrushchev's speech after all these years, I was struck by something which, as in Poe's *Purloined Letter*, had been so obvious that it had escaped my attention. The critique of Stalinism, however detailed and dramatic, was clearly subject to self-censorship, since it failed to reach back into the 1920s. It said nothing about how the construction of socialism in one country was radically redefined in terms of self-sufficiency; nor about the transformation of the regime inside the Party; nor about the use of force in the collectivization of the land, or the mistakes bound up with the theory of 'social fascism' (though these were later corrected by the Seventh Congress of the Comintern). In short, Khrushchev left out everything that lay at the origins of Stalinism, which could have thrown light on the objective conditions that had contributed to it and on the goals that it had set itself and achieved. This offered the key to my reading of the value and limits of the Twentieth Congress. For I was in for a number of surprises when I looked again at the main report, and the policy options that translated it into practice.

The first surprise was the boldly optimistic tone that permeates Khrushchev's opening report. Was this mannered propaganda designed to cushion the impact of the coming denunciation, which would certainly arouse passions among Communists and offer ammunition to their enemies? Such a view is contradicted by the facts, since the Twentieth Congress did in the end, after much soul-searching, achieve a consensus, imbuing Communists with a new sense of belief and rebuilding unity among their parties for some years at least. Paradoxically, the enemies of Communism saw it not as a sign that the movement was beginning to unravel, but as the prelude to a new period of expansion that would force them to seek dialogue, and to gird themselves for a new challenge. Isaac Deutscher, a historian of the Soviet Union noted for his seriousness and sharp insight, and author of Trotskyist-oriented biographies of Stalin and Trotsky, modified many of his judgements around this time, arguing that the Twentieth Congress revealed a Soviet Union which, after the terrible price it had paid, might be capable of reforming itself. Just as the cold war edifice was starting to crumble, partly because of the balance of terror, partly because of the turn in Soviet policy, a new world that had previously been hidden was eloquently emerging into the light of day. After years of 'containment' and attempted 'rollback', the Communists were governing a third of the world; the colonial empires were being swept away, and a broad group of new states, impoverished and fragile but 'non-aligned', entertained greater sympathy for socialism than for their former rulers. A new culture was coming into being: it was not 'orthodox Marxist', but focused mainly on the Third World (dependency theory) and on a conception of social rights as the necessary basis for democracy (Keynesianism). As for the economy, the situation in the Eastern Bloc countries did not correspond to the official propaganda, but their pace of development was generally remarkable, with some ups and downs, and their scientific research was excellent in parts, even if they found it hard to translate this into technological progress across the board. No major advances were yet apparent with regard to political democracy, but the restoration of legality and a more tolerant censorship were rightly considered significant. All this was not only a promise for the future but part of a 'de-Stalinization' process already under way. A faith was beginning to crack, but a hope might compensate for it. I remember scarcely any comrade at the time, however jealous of his past (or, like me, doubtful about the future), who did not think and say that we were moving forward. At least for the short to medium term, the hawks of the 'new cold war' had lost.

Yet in the prospects held out at the Twentieth Congress, and in the actual policies pursued by Khrushchev, one already glimpsed the lack of a full-scale reform of the state and society, since they made no mention of political democratization and failed to address the issue of the total statization and centralization of the economy. This is not to deny that Khrushchev had an innovative drive and introduced partial but courageous reforms with varying degrees of success, nor to suggest (as his opponents claimed) that he was merely improvising without a compass, or was just a bureaucrat who talked Communism without believing in it. He was an energetic, impetuous man of peasant stock, limited in his culture, who had fought as an ordinary soldier in the Civil War and earned his spurs running an agricultural region. He was curious about the outside world, and had a real desire to change things that were not working properly. He believed in peaceful coexistence in his way, and sought détente with the rival superpower (which he no longer regarded as an evil empire), seeking at least to establish contacts that would exclude a nuclear war 'by mistake', but capable of reacting to displays of arrogance such as the American U-2 spy flights over Soviet territory. He put forward some proposals for multilateral disarmament, and supported national liberation movements (in Palestine, Algeria and Cuba, for example), while accepting their independence and even their right to absorb or dissolve local Communist parties. He forged a substantial agreement with China, which had until then been 'distant', and which later became even more so, partly through his own fault; and he showed some interest in dialogue with European Social Democracy, which was never reciprocated. It was not a foreign policy that proceeded in a straight line, nor was it matched by complementary changes in internal policy, but it did help to limit the cold war and to build a number of important alliances (for example, with Nehru's India, with forces in the Middle East, and with the not yet clearly defined Cuban revolution).

Khrushchev also initiated reforms in economic and social policy. Industry was reorganized into a number of relatively autonomous regions, rather than centrally governed sectors – a change which, though meeting dogged resistance in the Gosplan apparatus, immediately had the effect of stimulating activity and reducing waste, but which after a few years generated a local corporatism that was countered with a de facto return to old-style ministries. As the director of one giant complex (Uralmas) put it: 'Organizational innovations are not much use if science does not give precise instruments to measure productivity and if firms do not have greater scope to implement them.' The reform left major traces only in a debate between different schools of economic thought, which was as heated as those of the 1920s, but unlike them left the political leadership and public opinion indifferent.

A new reform of agriculture had greater impact. It confirmed and extended the scope for whole kolkhozes (not just holders of small plots) to decide what should be produced beyond the fixed targets and how it should be sold; and it transferred the ownership of farm machinery, as well as responsibility for its upkeep and employment, from the state to the cooperatives. It was a bold and radical reform, which could have opened new horizons for productivity and income distribution. But it did nothing to put its prerequisites in place: that is, entrepreneurial competence at local level, an improved capacity to repair or replace broken-down machinery, greater availability of suitable fertilizer, an expanded long-distance transport network to deliver farm produce in time, and the development of markets and prices that encouraged its sale. Thus, the great hopes placed in this sector did not yield brilliant or lasting results.

The reform of the educational system was more innovative and also more successful. Funds were made available for greatly increased access to education and a campaign to achieve higher literacy levels (the number of pupils completing secondary school tripled in a few years, and the number of university students rose above two million). Above all, however, for the first time anywhere in the world, experiments were made with a combination of education and work, which was meant not only to help people in the most menial occupations, but also to promote equal opportunities and upward social mobility for all groups in society. But this advanced aspect of the reform was only ever partly implemented.

The policies that did more than anything to achieve popular consent and participation were those relating to what we would today call the 'social state': small but steady increases in real wages (which had been stagnating for some time); reductions in the income gap between workers and technicians; a widespread improvement of healthcare facilities, and a rise in pensions and in the number of those entitled to receive them. This remained the boast of the system over the next few decades.

On two points, though, innovation was minimal or even misleading. In the first place, the suffocating entanglement of Party and State meant that their pyramidal structure exercised direct and absolute power over the economy and in society. The restoration of legality heralded by the Twentieth Congress was not cancelled, even if there were still some limited areas of arbitrary power. But the boundaries that the law established between legality and illegality did not shift much; freedom of the press and freedom of speech were still restricted, as was the scope to have any real say in decisions; sometimes a bizarre concession came down from the top, only to be contradicted by an opposite one (for example, the publication of Solzhenitsyn's *One Day in the Life of Ivan Denisovich*, but the continued banning of Pasternak's *Doctor Zhivago* – and later the closure of the journal *Novyi Mir*). In the second place, the ideological crisis took the form of a pathological dissociation. Official Marxism-Leninism, not accidentally assigned to Mikhail Suslov, gradually became little more than a catechism by which to judge assorted heresies, incapable of arousing passions in the population and a barrier to the research work of intellectuals – no more than an empty shell. But the vacuum was filled by an idea that inspired Khrushchev and gradually became more explicit: the idea that the competition between socialism and capitalism was reducible to a contest over economic results, and that socialism would be fully accomplished and open the door to Communism when the Soviet Union had caught up with and overtaken the productive level of the United States. It was an implausible objective, even if many in the West took it seriously at the time. Above all, however, it cut off that belief in a qualitatively different society which is the driving force of Marxism, perpetuating Stalin's great misconception of the self-sufficiency of the Russian Revolution, and offering a new and poorer justification for the guiding role of the Soviet Union. Furthermore, the definition of the Soviet state as a state 'of all the people' – presumably intended as a milder alternative to the 'dictatorship of the proletariat', as well as to Stalin's theory (justifying any arbitrary action) that the class struggle intensifies with the advance of socialism – failed to recognize 'contradictions within the people', and therefore the possibility of social or cultural conflict in Soviet society itself. It corresponded to what Khrushchev, in a deliberately crude turn of phrase, called 'goulash socialism'. The way was being paved for the icy period of Brezhnevism, which replaced Stalinist hyper-subjectivism with political and ideological apathy among the masses, and fear of purges with bureaucratic cynicism among the Communist cadres.

The trajectory of Khrushchevism – from early successes to almost silent downfall in 1964 – was therefore written into its initial premises.

POLAND OR HUNGARY

An account of 'de-Stalinization' cannot conclude without some reference to what happened in Eastern Europe immediately after the Twentieth Congress. I use the term Eastern Europe here, because the crises in Poland and Hungary were the most dramatic manifestations of a problem that could quickly have spread elsewhere, in a much larger region with a major symbolic role in the cold war. In 1948, one stroke of the Cominform sword had put paid to any gradual attempt to build a socialist society in the form of a 'people's democracy', including a multiparty system and a two-sector economy, so that the differences with the Soviet model were suddenly annulled instead of being slowly reduced. All the countries of Eastern Europe were integrated into the Soviet system, in both their foreign policy and their economic structure.

It was clear that the Twentieth Congress would produce huge shock waves. The longing for deep reforms and a change of rulers was more than legitimate and impossible to control. Not only would it have been difficult to satisfy it by returning overnight to the status quo ante; in the specific conditions of the time, this would probably have led to the restoration of the prewar regimes and their integration into the Atlantic economic and military bloc. The Soviet leadership did not know how, and perhaps did not want, to look for a manageable intermediate solution; the local governments, realizing they would inevitably be targeted by any movement for renewal, were stunned by the Twentieth Congress. A political turn could only begin with spontaneous protests from below, without leaders or clearly defined programmes.

First came Poland, then Hungary. It would be wrong to conflate the two experiences, however: they differed not only in their outcomes but also in their premises, dynamics, leading players, objectives and international contexts. At the end of the war, Poland had been the country in which it was most difficult to put together a government, its heroic resistance to Hitler having been tragically repressed, as well as internally divided. Driven by intense patriotism, after centuries of being squeezed between two large, arrogant empires, the national movement detested the Russians (who had agreed to the country's partition before liberating it) more than it did the Communists, but reserved its fiercest hatred for the Germans, who had invaded and butchered it. Catholicism was an important element in national identity, caught as the country was between Protestantism and Eastern Orthodoxy. The Communist Party was therefore a minority force, but it too had incorporated a sense of national pride and made inroads among the workers and poor farmers, distributing lands confiscated from refugee Germans. It also had a strong and publicly recognized leader, who, not by chance, had spent time in prison during the Cominform years.

The Polish revolt began on 28 June 1956 in Poznan, in the form of a workers' strike for wage demands, but when this turned into a political demonstration the police attacked it, with the loss of dozens of lives. A week later, at the trial of its leaders, it filtered out that the government had not intended to use excessive force, and the judges, recognizing legitimate grounds for the strike, passed very light sentences. That was not the end of the story, however, because the protests spread to Warsaw shortly afterwards and became openly political. The regime rehabilitated Gomulka in the hope of establishing a dialogue, but the protest movement continued to gain momentum. Virtually the entire Soviet Politburo then left Moscow for Warsaw, with the intention of promising, or imposing, a Red Army intervention. But when it arrived it found that the Central Committee had unanimously elected Gomulka to the position of First Secretary. A long hard night of talks followed, during which Gomulka stood firm and convinced the Soviets to reach a compromise. Khrushchev recognized the full national independence of Poland, the autonomy of its Communist Party in following its own road to socialism, and the dismissal of Konstantin Rokossovsky (a Soviet general with Polish citizenship) from the command of the Polish army. Gomulka, for his part, committed himself to maintain the socialist character of society in Poland and to remain loyal to the Warsaw Pact. Economic measures including wage rises and a revision of investment plans in favour of consumption helped to restore order in the country. A further key element was the 'appeal for calm' issued by Cardinal Wyszynski, who had for some time been living a secluded life in a monastery, but who now returned to his post and negotiated a mini-concordat between the Polish state and the Vatican that recognized religious freedom and secular public education (with the possibility of religious education for those who wished it). The final touch was single-party elections with a plurality of candidates, which succeeded without compulsion – as everyone recognized – in bringing out 98 per cent of the electorate. It was a surprisingly positive outcome, within the limits of a compromise agreement.

The Polish crisis soon had an impact in Hungary, although there the starting point was very different. After an impromptu socialist revolution had been drowned in blood following the First World War, a fascist admiral had taken power and ruled the country until October 1944, flanked by Nazis during the war years. Historically, the aristocracy had channelled a strong current of nationalism to ensure it a place as partner in the Austro-Hungarian empire; the intelligentsia was a dazzling force, cosmopolitan and liberal-minded, while the landowning class was largely parasitical, partly consisting of farmers linked to a reactionary Catholic church that itself owned large estates. As for industry this had for a long time been in German hands. Of course, this picture changed massively with the postwar expropriations of large estates and the property of German refugees. But when the Red Army appeared on the scene, it came not as a liberating force but as a victorious army; the Communist Party was therefore weak (14 per cent of the vote in the first free elections), and its leadership was chronically divided. After the elimination of László Rajk, Mátyás Rákosi – a man linked to Beria – ruled the country by making brutal use of the secret police (AVO), of which he was the de facto head. Malenkov therefore had him replaced with Imre Nagy, a more open figure, but not hugely energetic or sharp-witted. Then in 1955, in the run-up to the Twentieth Congress, Khrushchev made the incomprehensible mistake of allowing Rákosi to return to power.

The Polish events therefore stirred up feelings in Hungary, without suggesting a course that the country should take or a leader to direct it. The first sign of opposition came from Budapest University, mainly from academics and intellectuals who roughly shared Gomulka's line. But within a day the students took the lead and considerably raised the stakes: immediate appointment of Nagy to the government, dismantling of the secret police, greater freedom of expression. Above all, they called a demonstration for 23 October and, at little street meetings and in makeshift leaflets, urged the workers to take part. A veritable mass revolt now quickly got under way, in a series of stages that are not easy to reconstruct objectively. There are numerous detailed accounts of what happened next, often contradicting one another. Fuller and more dependable information can maybe be gleaned from the American press, which could afford to be present in force from the beginning, or from the works of historians who have conducted systematic research into the events. Here I will mainly draw on this material, without neglecting reports by courageous and impassioned journalists who left Italy 'for the front'.

The demonstration of 23 October, first banned, then 'monitored', soon took on a mass character, mainly involving students and young people, but not yet industrial workers. Starting from the József Bem statue, it marched to parliament and the main radio station (which refused to broadcast its appeals), while Ernő Gerő, who had hurriedly replaced Rákosi as Party leader but was little more than his double, delivered an arrogant, intimidatory speech calculated to stoke up the anger. More than two hundred thousand people were in the streets. The first scuffles broke out, Stalin's statue was pulled down, rumours began to circulate about someone who had been killed, attempts were made to occupy the radio station. Then the order was given – no one knows how or by whom – for the police to use its weapons. The political police opened fire, causing the first casualties, but the army mostly refused to follow suit; indeed, some units handed over their guns to the young people. Real fighting took place in the streets, and workers began to arrive in trucks from the factories, especially the key Csepel iron and metal works. Little by little the revolt began to draw in the 'old reactionary belly' of the capital. During the night Gerő made two grave mistakes: he asked for help from the Soviet troops stationed in Hungary, and at the same time appointed Imre Nagy as prime minister, without announcing it to the country or allowing him to say that it was he, Gerő, who had called in the Russians. Soviet tanks appeared on the streets of the capital. Suslov and Mikoyan arrived from Moscow, unable to comprehend an intervention that had only made the situation worse; but they absolved Gerő and sent him off to Moscow. Meanwhile, the few Soviet tank drivers – whether ordered to do so, or voluntarily – remained inactive, often chatting from their turrets with the rebels. The violence and confusion ratcheted up on the morning of 25 October, when units of the political police fired down from the rooftops at groups of demonstrators milling around the Soviet tanks (some bedecked with Hungarian flags) on Parliament Square; hundreds of people were killed. The Soviet tank men, convinced they were under attack from counter-revolutionaries, fired back in the direction of the roofs. As the revolt spun out of control, many tanks were set on fire, the soldiers were unsure what to do, sporadic hunts for Communists broke out, and Party offices were besieged. Instead of taking firmer shape, the search for an agreement and the possibility of imposing one seemed to vanish. In a last-minute move on 30 October the Russians issued a formal communiqué from Moscow, backed by the Chinese to give it greater solemnity, in which they offered more concessions on the issue of independence than they had given to Gomulka. The text even envisaged the complete withdrawal of foreign troops from Hungary and from any other country that wished it; we now know that this was passed by a majority of the Soviet Politburo, though only thanks to the additional votes of Zhukov and Konev, respectively defence minister and commander-in-chief of the Warsaw Pact. But there was no longer anyone they could talk to in Budapest who was in a position to halt the spontaneous revolt. Its aims and leaders were gradually changing: there were widespread calls for Hungary to leave the Warsaw Pact, and for the immediate holding of elections and the drafting of a new constitution; Cardinal Mindszenty was calling for Communism to be overthrown everywhere and had decided to set up a Catholic political party without further ado; a general who had been part of Horthy's wartime general staff became commander of the 'national guard' and Nagy's military adviser; the Voice of America issued inflammatory calls for revolt in all the East European countries, promising a support that would never materialize. After much hesitation, Nagy acceded to many of the demands placed on the government, including the return to a multiparty system and a free choice of international alliances. This created a dramatic dilemma, taking things well beyond the point at which the revolt had started. Should Moscow leave Hungary to pursue its destiny, now turned towards the West, with a high probability that other states such as Slovakia or Romania would imitate it? Or should it launch an invasion and pay an even heavier price? The second option was gaining ground, but the fateful decision had still not been taken at 2:30 on 30 October. At four o'clock it was announced that British, French and Israeli forces had occupied the Suez Canal.

This changed the rules of the game. At stake now was not just Hungary but the whole global balance, victory or defeat in the 'new cold war', the survival of Khrushchev as Party secretary. Whether after consultation or on their own initiative, all the Communist countries – including China and Yugoslavia – called for a drastic solution to the Hungarian crisis. And drastic it was. A desperate resistance which the Americans abandoned to its fate, having previously egged it on, ended with a thousand or more dead, not all of them Hungarian. The British, French and Israelis were soon persuaded to back out of Suez.

Was this denouement unavoidable? Far from it: it was the conclusion to a series of colossal errors on the Communists' part, in both Budapest and Moscow, and to a clash of rival hypocrisies. My own view (which later events confirmed) is that the Hungarian crisis of 1956 was a tragic and costly setback, but did not mark the end of a tendency to the relaxation of tensions. Poland defined better the value and the limits of this tendency, since Kádár, who shouldered the harsh legacy in Budapest, acted in much the same way as Gomulka in the years ahead.

I remember once accompanying Emanuele Macaluso to a private meeting with Kádár.[1] What I recall most clearly is his fascinating face, at once composed and tragic, reflecting a life that had led him into prison at the hands of his comrades and later involved him in repairing the damage of a drama in which he had had no part. We went to talk with him because at the time, in 1963, we wanted to prevent a world meeting of Communist parties to excommunicate China (another trauma), and knew that he too was not in favour. He told us that while such a conference would be untimely, he could not simply reject the idea. When we asked why, his right-hand man, the editor of the Hungarian Party daily, replied: 'We have a saying here, that if you miss a buttonhole when you're doing up your waistcoat, the best thing is to start all over again. But we are not able to do that.'

1. Emanuele Macaluso: Sicilian trade union and Communist leader, who joined the PCI Central Committee in 1956 and its national leadership in 1960.

6

The PCI and De-Stalinization

The first signs of a turn in Soviet policy, and of lesser harshness in the cold war, came in 1952 and especially 1953, after Stalin's death. The PCI's victorious campaign against the *legge truffa* should have encouraged it to make use of its greater room for manoeuvre; the road on which it struck out with the Salerno turn could have been not only more openly affirmed, but further developed and clarified. It cannot be denied, however, that instead of actively taking the lead the Party and Togliatti himself followed a little passively, and sometimes uncertainly, a process whose importance they had already grasped. At least that was true until the wrenching year of 1956.

When I say 'uncertainly', I am mainly referring to the PCI's internal policy – that is, to its way of intervening in the confused but real crisis that had opened up in the government coalition. It wasted months playing up the 'Montesi affair',[1] made overtures to the appalling Pella[2] government and hurriedly withdrew them, behaved erratically in relation to a proposed 'opening to the Left', underestimated the election of Gronchi,[3] and remained indifferent to the emergence of a left wing in Christian Democracy (at first

1. Montesi affair: sex and drugs scandal that engulfed Roman high society and the DC establishment in 1953–4, following the discovery of the scantily clad corpse of Wilma Montesi on a beach in Ostia outside the capital.

2. Giuseppe Pella: Christian Democrat prime minister from August 1953 to January 1954.

3. Giovanni Gronchi: leading Christian Democrat, who served as third president of Italy between 1955 and 1962.

quite distinct from the pro-establishment current around Fanfani), as well as to the early initiatives of Mattei[4] and Saraceno[5] and to Catholic minority movements independent of the DC and the Church hierarchy that prefigured the papacy of John XXIII.

The Party's immobility and great caution were most striking in relation to three major opportunities for debate and renewal. First, Khrushchev's bridge-building towards Tito should have induced the PCI to make not only a self-criticism of its own concerning the excommunication (which it had fully endorsed at the time), but also a general critique of the Wroclaw meeting at which Longo himself had stood in the dock. Yet it avoided doing either. Second, the defeat of the major strike at Fiat in 1954 might also have encouraged new thinking and initiatives on technological innovations and the organization of work, but instead it was merely put down to the repression organized by company boss Vittorio Valletta. Third, the dismissal of Secchia from the PCI's organizational commission – which, being due to real disagreements, should have been explained in some degree – was simply lumped together with the sad 'Seniga affair',[6] so that any new leadership orientation was more or less blocked until the Eighth Congress in 1956, and the running of the Party became only a little more flexible and tolerant.

It would be ungenerous to overlook the objective factors involved in this impasse. For the new cold war dragged on in Italy, and even flared up again in 1954–5, when the Scelba-Saragat government rekindled police repression (four demonstrators were killed by the police at Mussomeli on its very first day in office). Communists were disbarred by law from important posts in public administration, politically motivated dismissals and punitive actions became more common in factories, and open or covert censorship did increasing damage to cultural activity. A first, still limited wave of recruitment for work in industry operated with political

4. Enrico Mattei: left-wing Christian Democrat and public administrator, closely identified with the activity of the powerful National Fuel Trust (ENI) until his death in a mysterious plane crash in 1962.

5. Pasquale Saraceno: Catholic founder in 1946 of the Association for the Industrial Development of the South (Svimez).

6. Giulio Seniga: active in the Resistance and the postwar organization of the PCI, he absconded from Rome in 1954, allegedly with Party funds and secret documents.

criteria, and bitter divisions among the trade union federations, together with the influence of Coldiretti[7] and the Federconsorzi,[8] underlined the difficulties in the way of social struggles. Moreover, the American embassy intervened even more directly during this period, expressing concern over a possible admission of the Socialist Party into government and demanding tighter discrimination against Communists.

Nevertheless, subjective factors also played a part in impeding any renewal. The hard years had turned the Party in on itself and fostered ideological rigidity, with the paradoxical result that it sought a way out in political manoeuvring at the top and in parliament, more than through an expansion of its social and cultural presence in society. Thus, the PCI was not in the best shape to face the stormy weather of 1956.

TOGLIATTI AND THE SECRET SPEECH

Yet Togliatti's 'new party' had prefigured much of the thinking of '56 and the Twentieth Congress. What I have called his 'damage limitation' policy had kept alive such vital elements as the avoidability of war, the existence of different roads to socialism (including the 'democratic road'), the need to move beyond the cold war and to seek broad alliances, and the necessity of greater autonomy in culture and the arts and of less rigid and less centralized planning of the economy. It was therefore a source of great satisfaction and hope to see these directions finally legitimated by the Soviet leadership and borne out in practice by such developments as the successful anti-colonial struggles. In the end, this was the side of things that meant most.

The same cannot be said of the response to Khrushchev's Secret Speech, which left the PCI feeling more exposed than its counterparts on every level. It was a mass party that faced another great mass party, Christian Democracy, which controlled all the means of communication. It also combined the features of a 'people's party' and a 'cadre party', bound together by a strong faith. It was

7. Coldiretti: organization representing small farmers, founded in 1944 and currently claiming a membership of more than one and a half million.

8. Federconsorzi: Italian Federation of Agricultural Consortia, the variously private and state-run agricultural funding agency founded in 1892 and overwhelmed by scandals in the 1990s.

this faith that had enabled it to withstand unrelenting pressure from its opponents, to step up recruitment even at times of downturn in the mass movement, to endure persecution and sacrifices, and to prioritize unity rather than competition in dealings with the Socialist Party (which was already showing some cracks) – a faith, moreover, that was based on memories of the anti-fascist struggle and belief in the Soviet Union and its leader, Joseph Stalin. The hasty dismantling of the Stalin cult therefore cut deep into the hearts and minds of Party activists – not only, or perhaps mainly, because of the revelations (some of which could be met with incredulity, or put down to historic necessity), but because the Soviet party itself had suddenly sprung them on the Communist movement without any explanation.

More than fear of being made to share responsibility, or annoyance at Khrushchev's crude language, it was concern for the pain and disorientation caused to the Party that accounted for Togliatti's thinly disguised hostility to the Secret Speech. But he was astonishingly naïve to imagine that he could avoid trouble by ignoring its existence, and then by questioning the reliability of versions of the text that gradually leaked out over a period of months.

He did not report anything about the Secret Speech to the PCI leadership, or even the secretariat; nor did he mention it in the report he gave on the Twentieth Congress to the Central Committee meeting of 13 March. After the first abridgements had appeared in the *New York Times*, unchallenged by Moscow, Togliatti described them as a 'pretty crude manoeuvre' on the part of 'shrieking apes'. At the National Council meeting of 3 April, held in preparation for upcoming regional elections, he spent little time on the 'hot potato' of the Twentieth Congress – which caused evident disquiet in the hall and led Amendola and Pajetta[9] to insist, in their different ways, on the need for profound renewal. Yet his concluding remarks, which referred to 'the good things that Stalin did, despite certain mistakes', brought the house down and reflected the turbulent state of mind in the Party.

Such reticence may well have kept the electoral losses to a minimum (-0.8 per cent, mainly accounted for by the big cities of the North and working-class districts); this suggested that most of

9. Giancarlo Pajetta: member of the National Secretariat from 1948 to 1985, and a leading figure in the *migliorista* current in the Party alongside Amendola and Napolitano.

the dissent and resignations from the Party were a protest against the assault on Stalin, rather than against its lack of severity. But, when the full text of Khrushchev's speech was published in early June in America and France, Togliatti, unlike Thorez, ceased to ignore it and, without prior discussion with the leadership, published a long interview in *Nuovi Argomenti*[10] on the whole issue of 'de-Stalinization'. If one reads this out of context today, forgetting that it mainly addressed the work of the Party and the attempts by its enemies to write off the whole Russian Revolution along with Stalin, then it is easy to underestimate its value. The points it made were by no means new (with one exception); it left out a number of delicate matters, despite its emphasis on the importance of historical depth; and its argument was often flawed in its inner logic or its relationship to the facts. Nevertheless, I consider it to have been a political masterstroke in the situation of the time.

Togliatti's postulate – which seemed too obvious to need demonstrating – was that however one judged or defined Stalin's errors, they had not prevented the Russian Revolution from laying the structural foundations of a new socialist society, or cancelled out its propulsive power. Despite the backwardness from which it had started out, despite the fact that it had spent eighteen of its forty years in the throes of war and reconstruction, despite the isolation and constant threats, Soviet society had created a modern and dynamic productive system in the space of just a few decades; it had conquered illiteracy, united diverse ethnic groups from the old empire, repelled a military onslaught from the West, trained a high-quality scientific elite, secured broad popular consent and passionate political involvement, and eventually spread its model to other countries and established a new global balance of forces. All this was plain for all to see. The mistakes, including crimes and arbitrary uses of power, might have slowed or in some cases deflected the process, but they did not halt or distort it. And even the self-criticism, itself debatable in some respects, was a symptom not of crisis but of a newly acquired strength, and would contribute to further development in the years to come.

The postulate reassured most Party activists as well as the Soviet leadership. Honest opponents might criticize it, but they could not

10. *Nuovi Argomenti*: literary magazine founded in 1953 by the writers Alberto Carocci and Alberto Moravia.

dismiss it *in toto*; it allowed for the possibility of serious discussion, instead of disorientation and squabbling. Togliatti's interview brought new arguments into the debate, trying to give it a direction without choking the life out of it. It may be useful to recall some of its main points, without passing over its weaknesses.

1) Togliatti finally took Khrushchev's speech on board. He did not try to minimize the gravity of the revelations it contained: not only major errors but cruel and arbitrary actions that were not due to objective necessities and had caused needless damage, for which Stalin bore the main personal responsibility. After all his initial reticence, Togliatti now went beyond mere admissions. 'One cannot blame everything on the "personality cult" and reproduce it in reverse, by attributing every fault to Stalin after attributing every merit.' Without softening the criticisms, it was necessary to examine how and where such deviations originated, and why they had lasted for so long; deeper and more level-headed historical research into the period was required. In this way Togliatti responded to the unease of Party activists, who did not want to ditch wholesale the faith for which they had given so much, and finally directed his criticism at Khrushchev too. Nor could the Soviet leader brush it aside, since Communists in the Soviet Union, and a fortiori in the Chinese and Yugoslav parties, had been demanding the same.

2) Togliatti himself initiated the process of historical reflection, violating the taboo that restricted criticism of Stalin to events in the second half of the 1930s. He pointed to the origins of Stalinism in the 1920s: for example, the top-down reorganization of the Party, or the hasty implementation of the (correct) policy of agricultural collectivization. He also drew a distinction between the illegal acts committed in 1937–8, in the context of a merciless struggle against real dangers of subversion and terrorism, and the abuses of the postwar period, which had lacked any justification or standards. At the same time, he mentioned some of the positive changes in policy that Stalin had promoted, as at the Seventh Congress of the Communist International, and great achievements under his leadership such as the war victory and the heroic mass mobilization that made it possible. There was no reference, however, to the Cominform turn and its repercussions in the PCI.

3) In another important section of the interview, dealing with the problem of democracy, Togliatti's omission amounted to a

contradiction. He brought out more effectively than he had done for years the limited, formal character of classical parliamentary institutions. And, in order to counterpose 'socialist democracy' to them in a way that was not too facile, he redefined the concept of 'dictatorship of the proletariat' by appealing to the Lenin of *State and Revolution* (democracy based on soviets), very different from the author of *The Proletarian Revolution and the Renegade Kautsky*. This innovation was hardly negligible, since it gave a more advanced meaning to the idea of a 'democratic road' and found positive echoes on both the left and the right of the Party. But was it credible to say that substantive power in the Soviet Union lay in the hands of the soviets?

4) A similar contradiction appears at a key later stage of Togliatti's argument, where he courageously asserts that the errors of the past were not solely political. They were also both cause and product of a partial 'degeneration' in certain phenomena of Soviet society (the bureaucratization of some sections of the administration, the humiliation of the masses in some areas of the economy). There can be no doubt that he convinced the Party and many others on this point, since he went beyond recrimination to express a genuine will for reform. But it was very difficult for the Soviets to accept this, and in fact their criticism of this part of the interview mainly focused on Togliatti's use of the vaguely Trotskyist-sounding term 'degeneration' (which, as matter of fact, did no harm). What should be stressed, rather, is that this message did not sit well with another statement that followed it: 'Our critical reflection concerns institutions and behaviour in politics (the superstructure), not the social system (which has been and is fully and consistently socialist).'

5) Another question posed itself, however. If Stalin's errors were spread over a long period of time, becoming more glaring and noxious towards the end, why were they not identified and rectified earlier? Togliatti's answer to this was sincere and effective. Before Stalin's death, not only would it have been personally dangerous to seek to undermine him; it would have been thoroughly counterproductive. For his authority and popular prestige were so great that such an attempt would have produced, not a correction, but open struggle and crisis in the whole society. Even after his death, then, the first imperative was to begin correcting certain elements in the situation and to achieve a solid convergence of effort

within the new collective leadership. Next, there had to be a shock in order to end a way of thinking and acting that had become endemic at every level of power. Togliatti himself could not help wondering: if the crux of the problem was the 'personality cult', would it not have been possible first to tone down the praise of Stalin and to curb some manifestations of the cult? But he left the burden of answering this 'to the Soviet leaders, who knew these things better'. On the other hand, he avoided asking himself and his own party why they had not shown moderation or expressed perplexity about the break with Tito, or about the summary trials that followed it in Eastern Europe.

6) The final part of the interview, which deals with relations among Communist parties and the leading role of the Soviet Union after the Twentieth Congress, contains perhaps the most advanced and fruitful innovation. Togliatti did not confine himself to reiterating the now-accepted principle of the independence of each national party, of 'unity in diversity' among multiple roads to socialism; he went on to provide a firmer basis and broader scope for this principle. The enlargement of the socialist camp to take in many new countries around the world had made autonomy an indispensable condition for future unity, but it also meant that diversity of history, tradition and social structure could actually be a resource for the enrichment and development of the whole movement. The national roads were not different ways of reaching a predefined goal, but a way of better defining and adjusting the goal itself. So, beyond 'national roads' and 'national parties', Togliatti introduced another new term: *polycentrism*.

Unfortunately, the historical situation and the current level of theoretical elaboration did not allow him to define the active subjects of polycentrism more precisely, still less to say how, when or why each of them – Communist countries, Third World, the West – might contribute to a greater polyphony. And the vision remained long term: no attempt was made to develop it until it was too late.

In short, the whole interview is an example of how to overcome a difficult, distressing situation, not by simply trying to mediate, but by taking a bold step forward. And, although the wounds were not yet healed, the whole PCI, from top to bottom, recognized itself in Togliatti's reflections. Khrushchev himself made only marginal criticisms, and even balanced them by recognizing the 'major' contribution Togliatti had made; various interlocutors or opponents objected, but with respect.

By the middle of the year, the situation had changed and discussion was no longer muffled but constructive; the focus of dissent, even for minority currents, had shifted from the Secret Speech to the more fertile ground of what the Italian Communist Party had done and should do to renew itself. Togliatti's merits must be recognized here. For on perusing the complete set of leadership minutes – and, based on experience, I do not have much faith in them – the mediocrity, reticence and exclusiveness of the collective discussion during those months are quite amazing.

THE SECOND STORM

But it turned out to be the calm between two storms. The second, no less violent, upset came with the events in Poland and Hungary, although this time it affected the Party's national and local leaderships, and relations with intellectuals and other parties, more than it did the broad popular masses.

(*Note*. To tell the truth, in my periodization I am not sure where to place the end of the unity in action between Communists and Socialists, which was unquestionably an important phenomenon for the PCI and Italian politics in general. If I mention it here, it is because, contrary to an almost universal perception, the break began before the Twentieth Congress of the CPSU and gradually deepened in subsequent years over issues of government. In 1956 it expressed itself noisily only at the meeting in Pralognan between Nenni and Saragat to decide on the unification of their two Socialist parties, which took ten years to seal and lasted for rather less. It is illuminating to add that that meeting took place before the Hungarian crisis and the Soviet invasion, not as a consequence of it.)

The Hungarian and Polish crises of autumn 1956 were of considerable importance for the PCI. They aroused heated debate in Italy, but entered and still remain in people's memory only in a dilated form, as if they were the central event of the second half of the century, marking the key moment when the PCI, refusing to break with the USSR, lost the opportunity to open up Italian democracy, to avoid its permanent *conventio ad excludendum*, and to form a great social-democratic force capable of breaking the Christian Democrat hold on government.

For my own part – although years later I was expelled from the PCI mainly, but not only, because of what I had written about the occupation of Czechoslovakia and the unreformability of Soviet autocracy – I am in complete disagreement with the position just outlined; I will give it short shrift in this reconstruction of the history of the PCI and Italian politics. I shall not deny, though, that the Italian Communists – especially their leaders, Togliatti included – understood little about the revolt in Eastern Europe and adopted wrong-headed, poorly motivated positions that soon had important negative consequences. Here it is appropriate to quote the famous words of Joseph Fouché, a cynical man but a sharp-sighted politician: 'It's worse than a crime; it's an error.'

What was the error? I believe its roots stretch back a long way, to the habit of playing things by ear on the basis of highly abstract principles and a disciplined acceptance of superior authority on all major decisions. This meant that it was difficult for the PCI to exercise the autonomy it had only just conquered. Many said breezily at the time, 'We're on one side of the barricades and there we stay, even when mistakes are made'. Turati said as much long ago: I side with the party, even when it's wrong. But which was the side to be supported in this case? Obviously the Communist movement, in a difficult moment of transition, still hemmed in by the cold war. But what if that side was in a crisis of confusion and uncertainty, in faraway places of great strategic importance? How then should I defend the barricade, shore up my side and help to solve the crisis? There are many ways of manning a barricade, even if you're there to shoot it out, with no idea of flight: you can replace your leaders, you can move the barricade back or make a sortie to the front, you can seek a truce, you can appeal for reinforcements. Especially if you are a long way away, you can send help, or argue for a favourable compromise, or simply concentrate on holding the rest of the front. But, in choosing among all the options, declarations of solidarity or hasty condemnations are not enough. It is essential to know and say, at least to oneself, what the reality is on the ground, to foresee its probable dynamic, to assess the likely consequences, taking into account the context in which the conflict is taking place, and to communicate all this to the masses whose support you seek, and in relation to whom you assume the responsibility of leadership. Perhaps this is the greatest difference that separates Lenin from Stalin and so many other politicians before and after him.

In those critical weeks, however, the PCI proved unable to do this: it committed a series of blunders and drew a number of conclusions that erred in both content and timing. The first blunder was to conflate the origins, evolution and to some extent even the outcome of the Polish and Hungarian events, viewing them both as unacceptable revolts against a socialist government, quite apart from any particular mistakes. The strike and demonstration in Poznan were workers' actions in support of a demand for more equal wages, the right to strike, and a mitigation of the heavy sacrifices required by the economic plan. The police repression was therefore unjust, just like the police repression in Italy ordered by interior minister Scelba, and Di Vittorio and the CGIL union federation were right to point this out. But the Polish Communists understood the lessons and drew the right practical conclusions, so that when the insurgency spread to Warsaw and took on a more explicitly political character they appointed a man who had spent the early 1950s in prison, but who knew how to wrest an effective compromise from the Soviets – regaining the support of the workers, and winning the backing of the Catholic primate. It was a compromise that could have spread to other countries in the area, and the PCI could and should have actively wagered on that possibility, essentially in line with the Twentieth Congress. It did not do so.

The Hungarian crisis had quite a different background. The Communist Party there was shaky and divided from the outset; the dynamic of the revolt developed in stages, and it was much more difficult to find a solution that did not entail full-scale dissolution, at a moment of Western aggression against Egypt. This is the key point. If there was a minimal possibility of reaching a solution by political rather than military means, this still required external assistance, for which both sides would have to pay a price, although it would avert a revival of the cold war or worse. The Soviets were not against the idea of political 'aid': their first military intervention was decided on locally for demonstrative purposes, and they subsequently got rid of Gerő and put Nagy at the head of the government. The document they finally proposed as a compromise offered even more concessions than the agreement they had reached with the Poles. But everything happened too late, so that it did not prevent but maintained the evolution from protest to revolt, from revolt to armed confrontation, from demands for greater democracy to a struggle to topple the regime – in a country that was experiencing not so much plots as a bubbling up of reactionary sediments from the past.

The PCI, and the Italian Left generally, neither understood this dynamic nor followed its unfolding, still less intervened to offer a solution. Di Vittorio was wrong on 25 October to interpret the first Soviet intervention in Budapest as a repressive move, or to see nothing but a democratic political protest in a movement that was beginning to assume the features of an irreconcilable *jacquerie*. And Togliatti was wrong to lump everything together, writing off the protest from the start as a counter-revolution in the making. When the options finally ran out and Khrushchev, egged on by all the Communist parties, decided on a real invasion, the PCI gave him its support.

So, was that the moment to break with the USSR and desert the degenerate camp of world Communism? I did not think so then, and I remain of the same view today – for a number of reasons, including three whose importance I realized only later.

Point number one. To have broken a link that was central in the formation of the PCI, and to have done so at a time when the USSR had begun a process of renewal and the camp associated with it was displaying major successes, would not have been understood or accepted by the great majority of Communist cadres, activists and voters. A struggle would certainly have ensued, leading to the break-up of the PCI. Perhaps what would have emerged would have been a more hardline party on one side, consisting of a minority tied to the USSR, and a small splinter party to the right, geared to convergence with the Socialist Party. The outcome would surely not have been a great force such as Swedish Social Democracy – rather, something along the lines of French Social Democracy, perpetually forced to govern alongside the DC in a subaltern role. Proof of this is that the PSI did not move to occupy the space that the situation seemed to offer it. Indeed, it soon suffered a split to the left, and the progressive democratic minorities, which included some valuable intellectuals, remained as politically dispersed and irrelevant as ever.

Point number two. By early 1957 the Soviet leadership itself was split – not only as an after-effect of Khruschchev's Secret Speech, but as an expression of general policy disagreement over reforms, the events in Eastern Europe, and the meaning of peaceful coexistence with the West. As we later discovered, these were not just disagreements but irreconcilable differences. A majority of the Politburo – the body from which power radiated outward – was now determined to remove Khrushchev. And in early 1957 Khrushchev took an unprecedented risk: he assembled enough Central Committee members on a military aircraft to form a quorum for an emergency session, then prevailed on them to accept the expulsion of the so-called anti-Party group. We have only to recall the names – Molotov, Voroshilov, Kaganovich, Malenkov – to appreciate the kind of policy turnaround they would have imposed on the Soviet Union, which was already a great power and had the weapons necessary to ensure that it remained one. Had Hungary been left to drift the previous October, had it even provoked similar crises in neighbouring countries, the showdown in Moscow would almost certainly have gone the other way. What effect would all that have had on relations with China, which was developing in quite a different direction after the elimination of Liu Shaoqi? Nor should it be forgotten that the war in Suez seemed to point towards a relaunch of the cold war.

Point number three. Granting that a change in Moscow might have resulted in a new compromise (something like the Brezhnev/Suslov takeover eight years later), would that have been good news for Communists and everyone else? For all the limitations of Khrushchevism, and the path it was destined to take, I think the answer is definitely no.

We may now calmly consider the argument that the PCI's real function in Italy was to consolidate democracy, gradually evolving into a social-democratic and then liberal-democratic party, and that it would have done better to complete the evolution more consciously and rapidly than it did (even if recent developments make this open to question). Be that as it may, the idea that such a wrenching change of camp and identity should have been carried out in 1956 seems to me utterly senseless – an ill-thought-out self-criticism, dictated by a need to shed the burden of a delusory hope, or of a past responsibility now considered to be a stain on one's character. I shall not even speak of the possibility of an American intervention in 1956 – a solution that many today consider almost right and proper – since it would simply have led to mutual nuclear destruction.

The errors the PCI made in those months of crisis did, however, have a number of significant consequences. They opened the way for, or anyway speeded up, the PSI's shift to participation in a DC-run government and, above all, its acceptance of a moderate policy that split the Party and pushed it further towards subaltern integration. They alienated important intellectuals from the Communist Party – men and women who were priceless bearers of various cultures – although it must be added that these not only voiced their dissent loudly and in unusual ways, but used it as a lever to remove Togliatti and shake up the rest of the leadership, trying to involve an unwilling Di Vittorio in their efforts and thereby weakening the authority of a major resource for renewal in the labour movement. Finally, the PCI's errors over Hungary handed the enemy an argument it could use obsessively, over and over again, to accuse the Party of duplicity and lock it into permanent opposition – and to sanction its own total complicity with the United States, even at times of its most ferocious involvement in plots, coups d'état, terrorist outrages and direct aggression in various parts of the world: from Guatemala to Brazil, Chile to Indonesia, Vietnam to the Middle East, to mention only a few.

THE EIGHTH CONGRESS

As in June, so too in December 1956, Togliatti had the intelligence and ability to propose his own platform for renewal, instead of resisting change or being swept away by it. His Report to the Eighth Congress of the PCI contained much that was new, while refraining, as always, from substantial self-criticism.

The report clearly separated the Polish crisis and the Hungarian tragedy from each other, while recognizing that the roots of both lay in the original fragility of socialism throughout the region; it admitted that it had been an unforgivable error to impose a 'servile and accelerated' imitation of the Soviet model, and that the stubborn resistance of their leaders to the new impulse of the Twentieth Congress had given reactionary forces the space for a revolt (and, in Hungary, the possibility of carrying one through), at the very moment when the Western powers were seeking to re-launch the cold war. As for the question of the leading role of the USSR, the report recognized past errors but also pointed out that the Soviets had had to build socialism amid tremendous difficulties, which had left their mark on them; their success against the odds provided an ever sturdier pillar for the world Communist movement.

On the 'Italian road to socialism', Togliatti's report went beyond his earlier positions, playing down the 'national' aspect and focusing more on the historic changes in the world that had made it possible. Above all, he tried to define it better as a strategy, rather than a tactic: no longer the classical 'intermediate goals' to accumulate strength for a future revolutionary break, but 'structural reforms' prefiguring a socialist perspective, achieved through social struggles and written into the legal system on the basis of the advanced principles of the Republic's Constitution. Not yet socialism, but a step closer to it. This marked a clear distance from social-democratic parliamentarism but also from strategies that implied waiting for the Big Day; the revolution was a process, which at a certain point could and should express itself in the peaceful conquest and democratic management of state power, already resting on subjective and objective supports within society.

Of course, this did not solve the problem but only shifted it. For it remained unclear how the leap would be made to a new principle of social organization, if and when the anti-capitalist reforms produced by class struggle, and guided by a Communist party, opened up a crisis of the system. It was neither necessary nor possible for Togliatti to give an answer, because this could take shape only in the concrete situation in which the question was posed. That was still a long way off in Italy and the West, and for the time being it was only possible to keep advancing along the thin line he had traced between gradualist reformism and socialist revolution.

The main weakness in the Report to the Eighth Congress lay elsewhere – in its inability to see the profound transformation looming in Western society, to envisage its likely course and to encourage research into ways of facing up to it and exploiting its contradictions. I do not wish to reduce the critique of the PCI to banalities (as many of us have done at times), by suggesting that it was fixated on the idea of Italian capitalism as a 'lumpen' capitalism. At the Eighth Congress Togliatti, unlike the French Communists, refused stereotypical visions of a decadent capitalism incapable of further development, and the idea that the bulk of workers were experiencing absolute impoverishment. He recognized the important changes taking place in technology and the organization of work, and was in favour of bringing the PCI's platform of demands up to date. But in essence he repeated the image of a monopoly capitalism closed in on itself, skimming off the profits from technological progress and imposing classical forms of social inequality and exclusion. This image still had some basis in reality, but only if one focused on the back of the moving train, not on the power and direction of the locomotive pulling it. It was an image that failed to engage with the general social and cultural ferment already in the offing – almost the opposite of Gramsci's theoretical effort in 'Americanism and Fordism', written in his prison cell, whose bold, if risky, prognoses long remained in the archives. All this was the Eighth Congress, the valuable but limited outcome of a battle between conservatives and modernizers.

Much as the first tangible results of the Twentieth Congress of the CPSU had been a change of cadres, a restoration of legality, the release of political prisoners and a relaxation of censorship, the PCI's Eighth Congress produced a generational change, a definitive commitment to the 'democratic road' (with no clear idea yet of how to travel it), and a more open climate inside the Party, allowing greater freedom of discussion and research, but still respecting the code of 'democratic centralism'.

An entertaining personal anecdote may serve to illustrate this. In late 1958, not having been a member for long, I returned from Rome to Bergamo as the local PCI secretary. At the same time, front-ranking leaders of the Catholic Youth were joining the Party and being co-opted onto the Federal Committee. In the run-up to the Ninth National Congress, Michelangelo Notarianni and I published an article in *Rinascita* – nothing special, just a piece emphasizing the necessary link between democracy and socialism. At the provincial congress, Luciano Lama came to preside on behalf of Party headquarters, and the provincial secretary, Eliseo Milani, and myself followed custom by inviting our illustrious guest to lunch in a good restaurant. After a while, evidently not remembering my name, Lama turned to me and asked whether I had read the *Rinascita* piece by a couple of Trotskyists. My blood immediately began to boil: who, me a Trotskyist? But I calmly replied: 'I don't need to read it, because I'm the one who wrote it.' A few years before, such a suspicion would have been the prelude to an inexorable freezing-out, but now we laughed about his gaffe and went on chatting amicably. This gives a good idea of the new limits to dissent, but also of the growth in tolerance. The following year I was even promoted to the position of regional secretary.

Innovation did not advance easily in these early years, however. The Ninth Congress was essentially a repeat of the Eighth, one central focus being the interesting but inconclusive 'Operation Milazzo' in Sicily.[11] Political discussion concerning the centre-left was confused and vacillating; the elections of 1958 pointed to stability more than new advances for the PCI, and optimistic hopes centred on the Soviet sputniks, one of them captained by a small dog. There is no reason to feel either surprised or regretful about that. Real innovation in a major organization does not occur through parthenogenesis: it comes on the crest of great social and cultural waves, and there were not many of those in 1950s Italy. The economic miracle, still in its early stages, allowed the bosses to make a few concessions without being forced to do so by mass struggles; the Christian Democrats were moving towards subtler forms of rule, without a clear sense of direction; the Socialists were gearing themselves up to participate in government, but faced much resistance and internal strife; peaceful coexistence was running into the ground. The Algerian war was hotting up, but its first consequence was the rise of de Gaulle and the exhaustion of parliament in France.

To be frank, it should be added that Togliatti himself was pressing on the brake a little. I shall give three examples. First, his report to a special conference on Gramsci emphasized the genius of the historic leader, but also his perfect consistency with Lenin's thinking. Second, a speech in Moscow (where he sensed a certain distrust, on top of open criticisms directed at him by Paris and Beijing) revived the language of triumphalism regarding the Soviet Union and its exceptional economic results, even endorsing Khrushchev's idea that it would overtake the American economy within ten to fifteen years. Third, he shared the almost unanimous reading of de Gaulle's rise to power as a classical conservative-authoritarian restoration, not a modernization from above that would include independence for Algeria. (On this point I put a different view in

11. Operation Milazzo: so called after Silvio Milazzo, who was elected first minister of Sicily in 1958 with the votes of assembly members of both the Right and the Left, and was promptly expelled from Christian Democracy. Communists, among others, participated in his first government.

a long article for *Nuovi Argomenti*, but was not censured in any way for doing so.)

In some channels, however, and on the margins of the Party, research and debate were already beginning to show results. I am thinking of the zeal with which certain trade unionists (Trentin[12] and his research department, Garavini in Turin,[13] Leonardi in Milan[14]), but also a few organizations on the periphery of the Party (Minucci and the Turin *Unità*), were examining the new organization of factory work; or the introduction of cultural 'sources', the new attention to the reading of *Capital*, the discussion among young intellectuals for and against Della Volpe, the influence of non-orthodox Marxist writings (early Lukács, Korsch) and the debate in France (Sartre and Merleau-Ponty, Hippolyte, Kojève) or the interpretation of Husserl put forward by Antonio Banfi and his students. The Party's Youth Federation and its weekly *Nuova Generazione* managed to stir things up a little by dabbling in all these unorthodox currents.

But to give all this a major political value, to treat the 'democratic road' as an open-ended problem rather than a stable formula, was something very different. It meant addressing the revival of workers' struggles (first electricians in Milan, then auto workers in Turin, then textile workers); the anti-fascist movement that started in Genoa and spread rapidly to involve surprising numbers of young people (the 'striped vest streetfighters'), followed as always by repression (deaths in Reggio Emilia), only this time not passively accepted; the mass migration from the South to the North of the country, debilitating the areas of origin but pouring new political lifeblood into the urban destinations. It meant facing the impromptu emergence of new lifestyles and needs which economic growth would eventually satisfy (but first stimulated and summoned up). Lastly, it meant grappling with a newly mature, albeit fitful and hazily defined, government majority – and with the election of Pope John XXIII and John F. Kennedy.

---

12. Bruno Trentin: Communist head of the engineering workers' union from 1962 to 1977, later secretary of the CGIL.

13. Sergio Garavini: Piemontese labour leader and later secretary of the CGIL; one of the leading inspirers in 1989 of Rifondazione Comunista, which he left in 2004 together with Magri and others.

14. Silvio Leonardi: an engineer by background, Communist deputy in the Italian parliament from 1963 and in the European Parliament from 1969 to 1984.

7

The Italian Case

The PCI entered the 1960s in promising conditions. Representing a quarter of the electorate, it still had nearly two million members, many of them active. It was part of an international movement that governed a third of the world, within which it had finally achieved autonomy. It commanded sympathy, or at least attention, in countries and movements that were shaking off colonialism; it had major influence in the trade unions, without thinking of them any longer as a 'transmission belt'. It found encouragement in, and gave encouragement to, an expanding working class that showed new signs of combativeness; it faced a politicized younger generation and an intelligentsia that was at last absorbing a non-dogmatic, non-canonical Marxism. It was in dialogue with minority Catholic currents that had gradually freed themselves from Pope Pacelli's intransigent anti-Communism; and it governed important regions of Italy, not only correctly but with good results. Above all, it was united behind a strategy that had been defined, at least in principle, by the Eighth Congress as the 'Italian road'. The alliance to which Italy had signed up kept the Party in permanent opposition, but the new global relationship of forces protected it from American military intervention in the event that it did manage to win a role in government by peaceful and legal means. All this obliged it, and permitted it, to verify whether the 'democratic road to socialism' was feasible, at least in the medium term, and whether it led where it actually wanted to go, instead of down one or another false path.

It was a new game for the PCI, then, in which its carefully constructed identity and its future existence were on the line. Indeed, the stakes were even higher: if no change came about in the West, if the confrontation between the blocs remained only a 'war fought with different weapons', then other parts of the world (the USSR or the non-aligned countries) might soon fall prey to the retreat and division that was already visible on the horizon. Perhaps only in Italy did some of the conditions – the strength and the will – exist to begin such a change.

But was the game ever really on? Fifty years later we know how it ended: the PCI gave up the ghost as an organized force and a body of thought. And almost no one claims its legacy. It did not die from a sudden stroke; it had for some time distanced itself from the Soviet Union and was not swept away when that collapsed. Nor did it succumb to exhaustion, since it retained a sizeable electorate (28 per cent) and a major cultural-political presence right to the end. It wrote itself out of history, with the aim of making a 'fresh start'. The fresh start failed to happen, and it is now clear that, even if the experiment had been more successful, it would have been the start of something completely different. That is a fact, so obvious and already long-established that it cannot be dismissed. But it does need to be explained. Why did a force that reached maturity in the 1960s, continuing to grow and throwing itself into an original and ambitious project, begin to decline after years of success, and finally dissolve?

Those who consider that project to have been a mere illusion, or a necessary manoeuvre to ferry the bulk of the army to firmer shores, will obviously have little interest in the PCI's discussions and activity during that long decade. If anything, they will focus instead on its later turn to national unity as the necessary prelude to a politics more solidly grounded in reality – that is, to a politics in which the goal of developing an alternative to the system was gradually discarded, in favour of a model in which two rival forces competed within the general limits of the world as it was.

The few like myself, however, who think that the project had a viable foundation and, without succeeding in full, could have developed differently with valuable results, will pay special attention to that long decade when so many things were in flux, and when the contest between an ailing capitalism and a communism looking for ways to redefine itself seemed to be – perhaps was – open-ended. This view today finds some support in the fact that, although the PCI has been defunct for some time, Italy is not exactly flourishing. This is not a sufficient argument, however. Other political projects, and the social players associated with them, proved disappointingly incapable of giving the stress on innovation a more definite shape, and it was not long before updated versions of an even shakier past, or mediocre schemes for running things as they are, ended by generating more gloom than hope. But this is not enough to demonstrate that the distant ambitions of the 1960s were plausible or correct. Of them too we can ask whether they did not, from the first, involve profound errors and face insurmountable obstacles.

The first point to be demonstrated, then, is that there really was an open-ended contest. Only if we grasp the reality of the time will we able to understand and judge the lively discussions in the PCI at the beginning of the 1960s and the choices that resulted. At the risk of harping on familiar points, it may be useful to review what was then so exceptional about the 'Italian case', in a long decade that in some respects may be said to have started earlier and to have finished later. We may identify two key periods within it (1960–5 and 1968–74), although they had many common or convergent threads. In fact, two distinct tremors were profoundly shaking Italian politics and society: the 'economic miracle' and the trade union offensive, which the projects for a centre-left government sought to use as the lever for a 'reformism from above'; and the student revolt and workers' struggles seeking to produce a new social order 'from below'. Both these perspectives failed in terms of their main objectives, but they left deep and lasting marks on the country, as well as opening up something like a systemic crisis in the short term. The PCI was unable, and in part unwilling, to take a direct role in promoting or leading either process, such as it had played in the Resistance and the foundation of the Republic. But it did help to initiate, support or shape them, and they in turn affected and crisscrossed the Communist movement. Only at the end did the Party gather the fruits, while having to shoulder the responsibility for an acceptable outcome to the social conflict. It also had to define and impose or reject a role in government that the evolution of events offered it, without having sufficient strength or ideas to meet the challenge.

We must now look more closely at each of these two tremors that were shaking Italian society, before finally considering what united them.

THE ECONOMIC MIRACLE

Between 1953 and 1964, Italy's gross national product (in constant prices) rose from 17 billion to 30 billion lire; per capita annual income from 350,000 to 571,000 lire. The growth rate, which began at 5 per cent, rose above 6 per cent and stayed there until the seventies, with the single exception of 1964. Nothing comparable has been seen before or since. Other capitalist countries were also expanding during this period, but it is still surprising that the more backward Italy, short of natural, financial and technological resources, not only succeeded in jumping on the train but found a place near the front: a little slower than Japan, equal to Germany, a little faster than France, and much faster than Britain or the United States. The term 'economic miracle' was imported from abroad to describe this, but neither word really does it justice. There are no miracles in economics – if we leave aside the one of the bread and fishes, as exceptional as the nature of the man who performed it. And, in the Italian case, the 'miracle' was not only economic; it went hand in hand with a number of major social, political and institutional transformations, whose guiding thread we must try to identify.

The process was set in motion by two political events – the anti-fascist revolution and the cold war – which together permitted the rapid dismantling of protectionism (an old legacy of Italian capitalism, rendered even more burdensome by fascist autarky). This forced Italy to look to trade with more advanced countries which had become politically close to it, and which were themselves in the throes of postwar reconstruction. It could have been a leap in the dark, since sections of both the employers (fearing competition) and the workers (fearing redundancies) were reluctant to go along with it. But the United States had good economic reasons to seek market outlets, and good political reasons to integrate high-risk Italy into its bloc of client states. It therefore called for the new turn and promised to support it (as it did in the case of Japan and, later, South-East Asia). This early option for free trade marked the new Europe as a subaltern ally in the Atlantic bloc.

It certainly offered high-priced export markets, but it could not alone guarantee that Italy would be competitive on them, given that Italy's real expansion was late starting and encountered many difficulties along the way. American aid in the early years covered little more than the food emergency and the costs of the occupation army, and then was geared to plugging the public deficit (a currency reform being excluded) and to halting runaway inflation. The true engine of the 'miracle' – in the 1950s and for a long time after – lay in what I would call, in slightly Maoist-sounding language, 'using backwardness as a development resource'. Or, a little more pompously, an original version of 'primitive accumulation'; or, more prosaically, a combination of technological leap and very low wages.

Technological leap did not mean only the application of better equipment and better work organization to a productive apparatus partly out of use (as in Germany or France). It meant revolutionizing both the one and the other and involving large areas previously excluded from modernity: that is, moving quickly from a narrow, and sometimes craft-based, industrial base to a Fordist industry that was already (at its most advanced) on the threshold of automation, and then extending it to new sectors and new types of production and consumption. It meant leaping over the intermediate stages that other countries had previously crossed with difficulty. This and only this could enable a number of companies to achieve the large and rapid productivity increases that would give them access to foreign markets. The United States, with its industrial equipment and its technological, organizational and management know-how, could offer this opportunity (plus a little direct investment) to those who were capable of buying and using them and were prepared to accept American leadership. But it was a very difficult leap to execute, especially at the start; many underdeveloped countries (not even in the Third World) were able to attempt it only much later. The countries that had a 'major revolution' carried it out unaided, but they were successful only in certain sectors and paid a heavy price, isolating themselves from the world economy. First they had to obtain the initial funding, then devote nearly all the increased output to financing new investments and building the necessary infrastructure. Only much later, after much pinching and scraping, was consumption given a share, in accordance with a development model imposed by foreign markets. A business sense was also required, as were a sizeable number of skilled workers and flexible technicians, and the support of public authorities capable of stepping in where the private sector was incapable of, or uninterested in, getting things done.

Postwar Italian capitalism benefited from some of these conditions. History had made of Italy a mostly backward but uneven country: ancient excellence slumbered in the 'city centres'; a number of major industrial concentrations went back a long way; and the still predominant agricultural sector, though on the whole very poor, was also quite differentiated, with large absentee landowners, smallholdings that were not uniformly wretched, rapacious sharecropping systems that had sometimes been given a more civilized form by advanced farmers, and large estates that Enlightenment despotism had once transformed from afar. Much of the population was only semi-literate, but a minority had access to high-quality traditional education, and prestigious islands of research existed in fields such as physics. Fascist provincialism had insulated some but not all areas of culture, and the country did, after all, have a great cosmopolitan tradition. The family was still strongly patriarchal, but in many cases it was an extended family that functioned as a labour unit (including the women) and a savings and social welfare centre, even continuing to operate as such over long distances during the painful transition to something new. A repressive moral code, especially in sexual matters, had been shaped by the Counter-Reformation and imposed by various traditions and conventions, but not everyone had internalized it, and society was therefore amenable to secularization.

In this diverse archipelago of modernity and backwardness, two elements had a decisive synergic effect in launching a particular model of expansion. The first, paradoxically, stemmed from a legacy of fascism: an anomalous economic form devised by the regime to confront the 1930s slump, involving the public ownership, but autonomous management, of large industrial corporations and nearly all major banks. This constituted a 'third pole', a real 'mixed economy'. At first perhaps by chance, but after the Liberation certainly because of the political climate, the variously minded men (Beneduce, Menichella, Mattioli, Senigallia, Saraceno, Mattei) who ran these entities showed great entrepreneurial flair and were suitably honest and conscious of their role, committed to investing public funds to give the country a modern industrial base (for example, a steel industry that used mineral ore instead of scrap metal, or oil exploration geared to the production of petrochemicals and synthetic fibres). On a more slippery slope, and to make up for the country's stunted and speculative stock exchange, Enrico Cuccia's Mediobanca used the savings collected by the semi-public banks to reorganize a private financial sector and to forge links with large industrial groups. Later, both the public entities and the Mediobanca system became the instrument of a perverse private-public network – a growth-inhibiting resource that enabled the government to run a pliant clientelism and to control information. But this should not obscure the fact that, in the take-off period, this idiosyncratic mixed economy was a powerful propulsive force.

The second and decisive growth factor, however, was the permanent wage freeze and the capacity of the proletariat for both sacrifice and initiative. This aspect of the 'miracle', though often noted, has not been sufficiently analysed. In 1946 real wages in Italy were 40 per cent lower than in 1938, and inflation was eating up almost any rise won through hard struggle. Only in 1950, with the tasks of reconstruction complete, did incomes return to their prewar level. In 1959 they were up on average by approximately 6 to 7 per cent, while labour productivity had soared by more than 50 per cent. These figures already speak volumes. But everyone had to pay for accumulation, and the powers-that-be decided that workers and farmers should be the first to pay and the last to profit. This option did not even need to be discussed in public: it was imposed by unemployment, redundancies and the closure of obsolete factories. The state merely helped out by brutally enforcing 'public order' and by keeping public expenditure low and selective. Furthermore, as everyone knows, unemployment can act powerfully to hold down wage levels and to stimulate labour intensity, thereby fuelling profits and investment; but once it rises above a certain limit it constricts the internal market, pushes down the level of savings and forces the state to feed an inactive population, resulting in stagnation and depression. That limit was being reached precisely at the time in question, mainly because there was no longer enough work in the countryside to guarantee even a subsistence level. But, contrary to what happens in the model, the extreme surplus of labour in the cities actually became a resource – thanks to three great migratory flows, which, despite their differences, were as invaluable for the development of the economy as they were momentous for those caught up in them.

The first flow poured into foreign countries in need of manpower. One to two million workers emigrated overseas (particularly to

Australia and Argentina), shortly followed by another wave to northern Europe (France, Belgium and, once it had absorbed German exiles from the East, the Federal Republic of Germany). These migrants were forced to live in shacks and to perform back-breaking work for exceptionally long hours, depriving themselves to maintain their families back home or to save up for the day when they could escape their hostile and uncomfortable environment and return to build a little house of their own. Their hard work and scrimping helped Italy's balance of payments or slowly added to the bottom line in savings books. It was a fine example of 'popular stakeholding'.

A second migratory flow was more local – that is, from the country to nearby cities, with the intention of remaining there, but keeping an active link with the family and the land. It began in central Italy, but then became more widespread. Young sharecroppers with little or no land of their own, but already accustomed to labour and to a slightly greater share of the produce than in the past, found employment in small firms, in the nooks and crannies of the market, for a third less than the minimum earned by regular workers. Or else they worked at home with their wives and children from dawn to dusk, on jobbing contracts from firms that provided them with old machinery, paying a share to agents who set up little businesses of their own. Alternatively the urbanized workers branched out into some petty commercial activity, and paid through the nose in rent. In all of these cases, the workers often supplemented their income with produce from the little family plot, on which they worked seasonally. Something similar, but not identical, happened in the better irrigated areas of the South, where day-labourers working seasonally for various employers might wrest some benefits through local struggles and agreements. We are talking, then, of a 'grey area' between country and town, agricultural labour and a thousand other activities: a distinctive model of primitive accumulation based on self-exploitation, which in the short term contributed to development and urbanization, and from which the Third Italy of tiny firms and 'zones' was born. With it also came a new kind of middle layer, the ultimate cross and delight of the 'Italian model'.

The third and most impulsive migratory flow moved from the south to the north of Italy, first to the big metropolises, then to the areas bordering on them. Many of its hardships resembled those of the first wave: separation from family amid a hostile local population, added to either accommodation in makeshift huts with few amenities, popularly known as 'Koreas' because of their unhomeliness and ugliness, or hours of commuting to and from a job on an unregulated building site. But, as in the second wave, the workers planned to settle down in the new place, bringing their relatives to join them as soon as possible, with hopes of finding a permanent job and a brighter future in one of the expanding industries. Careful recruitment, combined with anti-strike clauses and threats to dismiss anyone who stepped out of line, were very effective for a few years in controlling the new additions to the workforce. But the real novelty of the third wave was the economic circumstances in which it took place, towards the end of the 1950s cycle of 'primitive accumulation', as a new and original model of development was taking final shape.

The construction of a modern, largely state-owned, industrial base was already completed, or nearly: the steel works at Conegliano and Bagnoli were up and running, and another one was under construction at Taranto. Enrico Mattei, soon to die in a mysterious plane crash, had signed or was negotiating oil deals with Algeria and the Middle East, which brought him and ENI into conflict with the world's top seven oil corporations (the 'Seven Sisters', as he called them); in petrochemicals, work was progressing on ANIC in Ravenna and the refinery in Gela. As to the private sector, Fiat had forged ahead with the launch of the 600 model at its gigantic, ultramodern plant at Mirafiori, where an adequate infrastructure was indispensable. Thousands of plastic products were pouring out of the petrochemical plants. The textile industry was introducing automated machinery and switching to synthetic fibres. The modern agricultural sector required fertilizer and farm machinery, which the Federconsorzi was helping to market, and to transfer, with public assistance, to farmers grouped in the Coldiretti organization. And, very recently, new medium-sized and even large firms had sprung up from virtually nowhere, in a leap from semi-artisanal industry to the large-scale production of household electrical appliances. All these developments called for workers with few skills or pretensions, who would have to wait before they could be offered decent living conditions.

This expansion of manufacturing had two major social and cultural consequences. First, it redrew the map of real power in Italy, beyond the palace walls of the Montecitorio parliament in Rome, penetrating deep into society, regulating its conflicts and steering the consensus. The large industrial and financial bourgeoisie, having emerged from the war politically delegitimized and economically shaky, unable to face international competition, express political or cultural hegemony, or dominate the latest outbreaks of social struggle, thus came back as an autonomous organized player. It was once more in control of the factories, resting on a coalition organized and dominated by the Christian Democrats. Yet, as we have seen, the economic take-off owed much to public industry and to the support of the state and its apparatuses.

From the mid 1950s on, big capital found itself in a position to take the lead with explicit policies of its own. Public industry had served its purpose, and was not to claim any guiding role for the future; the fiscal system was not to stifle profits by changing the balance between direct and indirect taxation; trade union demands must continue to be resisted, and public spending to be channelled in ways that benefited corporate competitiveness. In advancing this programme, big capital could rely for support on the privately owned press (with the exception of *Il Giorno*, during Gaetano Baldacci's short-lived editorship), and had no scruples about threatening to mobilize all of Italy's surviving reactionary forces behind it. De Gasperi himself already referred to this as the 'fourth party' with which he had to deal.

A second consequence of the industrial boom concerned the relationship between production and consumption. We might speak here of 'early consumerism': not a conjunctural but a structural phenomenon. Industrial development, and future investment, were now strongly geared to the European Common Market, which for a long time remained little more than a customs union (apart from some residual agricultural protectionism in favour of the strongest countries), so that Italy, still a medium-poor country, was exporting consumer durables (cars, televisions, household appliances, furniture) to a region that was on the whole more advanced than itself. The rise of the televisual medium pointed the choices and aspirations of Italian consumers in the same direction, even for those who still lacked basic individual, not to speak of collective, goods. The word consumerism should be used with caution, however, since consumption was still largely a matter of satisfying primary needs in the particular social context of the time: a little vehicle of one's own to drive to work or on holiday, for lack of decent public transport; a TV set as a first window on the world after centuries of isolation. But this cultivated a new lifestyle tendency, already present in the American model, to give the individual priority over the collective, to raise status symbols above real needs. Public spending itself helped to reinforce this trend, both for the sake of the economy and for reasons of social integration. In 1959, for instance, the government allocated 36 billion lire to the ailing railways, compared with 2,000 billion to highway (above all motorway) construction. For a long time the health insurance system excluded much of the population, and was funded not out of general taxation but by the workers themselves. 'Consumerism' therefore preceded 'affluence', and a fortiori a more even distribution of income.

I could go on listing the social and cultural upheavals induced or anticipated by the Italian economic miracle. But enough has been said to illuminate its novel interlinking of modernity and backwardness, and how it fuelled imbalances and regional or class conflict between North and South, capital and labour, and old and new middle layers. To complete the picture, however, we should add another element that is often overlooked. The economic upheaval did not altogether bypass the political and social bloc upon which Christian Democracy had built its undisputed supremacy – a bloc that it presented as an emergency coalition to block the 'Communist threat', and which was fully backed by the Americans, by middle classes not immune from para-fascist influences, and above all by the mostly rural Catholic masses, loyal to Pius XII but still mindful of traditional peasant solidarity and recent involvement in the Resistance. De Gasperi had successfully united this bloc with the support of Cardinal Montini and the state apparatus. A right wing had broken from it as early as 1953, only to be pulled back on board as the economy picked up steam. But the very results of the 1950s – migration, urbanization, depopulation of the countryside, increasing bourgeois autonomy of a state bureaucracy that lagged in terms of income and social recognition – created a number of cracks and divergences of interest. As the cold war waned, the 'Communist threat' lost some of its bonding power. Even the Vatican, suspicious of secularization, was now headed by a prudent conservative more concerned to keep the Catholic world intact than to intervene in Italian politics.

The supremacy of Christian Democracy was therefore in danger, and the regime had to redefine the bases of its strength.

I hate to recognize it, because my sympathies lie more with Moro, but Amintore Fanfani was the only establishment politician, Christian Democrat or otherwise, who quickly understood the problem and had the wits and nerve to confront it (if not actually to resolve it). First, instead of seeking new political alliances, he did all he could to construct a new social bloc. He was an unlikeable, and in my view dangerous, figure, but he was a high-calibre politician, not a man given to politicking or restraint. He concentrated on society and the interests that ran through it, seeking to build a real political party. The compromise he tried to achieve was far from historic, but it was not insignificant, and had some lasting aspects. Or perhaps it would be more accurate to speak of several compromises, pointing in different directions. Fanfani reduced and consolidated the public presence in the economy, bringing it under a single ministry, appointing men who would do his bidding, and providing for autonomous bargaining with the unions through the Intersind organization. At the same time, rather than allow the most efficient public enterprises to take the lead in economic planning, he encouraged their gradual integration with mainstream private industry, while others became reserves of clientelism and welfarism that 'socialized' losses by means of imprecisely calculated government deficits.

In the mushrooming cities, the postwar promise of popular affordable housing under the auspices of INA-Casa[1] had given way to profit-driven construction free of planning controls, the demand from private individuals and pseudo-cooperatives being ensured by tax breaks and long-term bank loans. This gave rise to a 'housing bloc' that tied part of the middle layers, especially public employees, to the general defence of property rights.

Higher incomes, as well as better pensions and educational provision, were offered to public employees and dynamic small to medium-sized farms. As for the general regulation of wages, repression and unemployment lost much of their effectiveness, and for some years apparent downsizing served as a cover for separate local agreements and company unions.

1. INA-Casa: the planned state-led housing programme, associated with the Istituto Nazionale delle Assicurazioni.

Particularly clever use was made of a totally controlled public television network, which had a clerical slant but was of good quality and well run.

Last, and most important, there arose a peculiar kind of 'welfare state' mainly based on monetary transfers to sections of society left out of the economic boom – not as a universal entitlement, but in the form of subsidies to particular regions or a quid pro quo for political assent: for example, agricultural price support for notional products, often unsubstantiated invalidity benefits, or dubious loans to non-existent small firms.

So, the party-state and the perverse nexus of public and private had sunk roots in society before it began to shape alliances or even coalition governments: the iron centralism of Mario Scelba, shifting alliances with minor parties, so-called 'summertime governments' (which kept things ticking over and left the serious business for later), or occasional agreements with forces further to the right. The hegemony of Fanfani's style of politics persisted even when his own authoritarian centralism impelled the majority of the DC to clip his wings, for it was an expression of the economic miracle and a preventive response to the problems that arose from it. Another example of the intermingling of modernity and backwardness.

THE LABOUR REVIVAL

The whole edifice could last only as long as its supporting pillar: that is, the acquiescence of a class that had borne the costs of development and made the principal contribution to it.

If we look for the guiding thread of the 1960s, the key to its various twists and turns, then I think we will find it in the long and distinctive process of 'labour revival'. The term is appropriate, because it evokes older roots, but it may lead one to underestimate the many novel features. The distant roots lay in a powerful nexus of economic struggles, class consciousness and political struggle; and it was initiatives from below, overflowing institutional channels and bypassing leaderships, which played the main part in events. Each of these aspects was in keeping with the spirit of the times. Similar things were happening in a number of other European countries – Britain and Germany, for example – although there, one aspect did not mingle with and fortify the other but tended to exclude it; the fragmentation of the British shop stewards was very different from German-style harmonization and participation in management.

In Italy, the Resistance had begun with the strikes of 1943 and 1944, which, though launched on bread-and-butter issues, offered mass support to the anti-fascist movement; economic and political struggles merged with each other and moulded a new class consciousness. Armed workers defended their industrial complexes from sabotage by the fleeing Germans and, in the space vacated by collaborators and expatriate bosses, created a short-lived factory council experience that remained long after in their memory. Following the end of the war, social struggles against a backdrop of poverty achieved only limited results in terms of pay, but won rights that would never be reversed, such as contractual bargaining over redundancies, a sliding scale of wages or recognition of workplace committees. This led to a particular kind of trade union organization, which in the early postwar years, resting on a pact that spanned all the anti-fascist forces, took the lasting form of a confederation, at both central and regional level, in order to obstruct corporatist tendencies by sector or trade, and to unite struggles on issues to do with social protection and the defence of constitutional democracy.

At its first congress, in 1947, this movement had 5,700,000 members, which meant that more than half the industrial workforce was unionized. A total of 4,900,000 votes were cast: 2,600,000 for the Communist current, 1,100,000 for the Socialist current, 650,000 for the Christian and 200,000 for smaller secular currents. The split in the union movement that ensued in 1948 was almost entirely a reflection of the breakdown in the ruling coalition and the onset of the cold war; the Americans intervened directly and put their money behind it. However, the unity between Socialists and Communists allowed the Confederazione Generale Italiano del Lavoro (CGIL) to maintain its organizational strength and to take some lively initiatives, such as the proposal of a national Labour Plan; it also enabled groups of workers to stage a number of exemplary actions, such as the occupation and running of Reggiane, the long-established aircraft manufacturer, with the support of the whole population of Reggio Emilia. It was not sufficient, however, to prevent the complete collapse of central wage-bargaining and action in support of grievances. This collapse was due to several overwhelming factors: a new wave of redundancies associated with the restructuring or closure of whole factories; concerted moves by the state and the employers to put a lid on social conflict; and, somewhat later, social differentiation within the working class, linked to new technology and great disparities in the size of companies. The near-elimination of previous vanguards from the factories completed the process of erasing collective experience. Even when visible economic growth began to offer some margin for improvement, the 'silence' of the workers remained a feature of the situation almost until 1960. The 'new unions' resulting from the split of 1948 contributed to this, since for a number of years they actively collaborated with the employers by signing separate agreements and breaking strikes. One little-known sequence of events is enough to gauge the orientation of Catholic trade unionism during those years, and the correction that was subsequently made to it. I will reconstruct these events from memory and from meticulous documentation.

Everyone remembers FIOM's[2] dramatic defeat at Fiat in 1955. Having always won an absolute majority in elections to the works committee, it suddenly fell to 35 per cent of the vote, against 51 per cent for CISL[3] and 25 per cent for the even more pliant UIL.[4] A debate immediately began in the CGIL and the PCI, to consider how much the results owed to repressive actions by the employers, how much to the new organization of work, and how much to the CGIL's own slowness in understanding and confronting it. It was a difficult question to answer, because everything had played a role. But, three years later, fresh elections at Fiat offered a key. The CISL national secretary, Giulio Pastore, supported by the Christian Democrat Carlo Donat-Cattin,[5] declared his unwillingness to present candidates in rigged elections and managed to get them cleaned up. But the results were surprising. While FIOM regained some percentage points, the CISL vote collapsed from 20,000 to

2. FIOM: Federazione Impiegati Operai Metallurgici, the largest metalworkers' union, affiliated to the CGIL.

3. CISL: Confederazione Italiana Sindacati Lavoratori, the rival trade union confederation linked to Christian Democracy.

4. UIL: Unione Italiana del Lavoro, the trade union confederation oriented towards the PSDI (Saragat Socialist).

5. Carlo Donat-Cattin: one of the founders of the CISL, leader of the Forze Nuove current in the DC, and later vice-secretary of the party.

7000, and its membership in Turin fell from 18,000 to little more than 1000; its place was taken by a proper 'yellow union', SIDA. This simple fact said it all: CISL owed its previous success at Fiat to its role as mere figleaf, which was now giving way to a different arrangement; and the workers' acquiescence was not only due to blackmail, but had become a form of passive consent, an ideology beneath which individual rage was lurking. It could be broken only by developing a more adequate programme, in which rank-and-file initiatives based on memory would foster a new class consciousness and motivate ideas. To put it in Gramscian terms, the 'Catholic question' no longer concerned only the peasantry; it was now also a 'working-class question'.

As Italy moved into the 1960s, this passivity suddenly seemed to give way to a quite unforeseen combativeness. A first wave began in 1960 – not by chance in Milan, where the threads of memory had not been entirely broken – when the electrical engineers, though cautious on the wages front, raised demands for supplementary benefits in a way that implied they should be subject to collective bargaining at company level. The employers tried to stonewall, insisting that 'in the end only one person can decide in the factory'; national agreements were supposed to cover everything during the period of their validity. The dispute went on for months, from September until the following February, and the rank-and-file gradually had its say as the more militant company workforces carried the others along with them. December witnessed a new and moving Christmas celebration, when two processions a hundred thousand strong, one CGIL, the other CISL, marched towards the Piazza del Duomo and merged together. Other people in the square expressed their solidarity. For the first time, students also took part in an organized manner. Cardinal Montini came down to bless the workers. At that point the Intersind signed a preliminary agreement with the workers, and one private company after another bowed to its terms. It was the first trade union and political victory for many years; unity had found its feet again.

In 1961 and the first few months of 1962, a new round of national bargaining secured pay increases of between 7 and 13 per cent. Disputes then broke out at Alfa, Siemens and CGE, whose employers continued to resist the principle of supplementary collective bargaining at company level. Fiat tried to head this off by concluding a separate agreement with the yellow union.

Then the metalworkers' unions decided to move before their national agreement came up for renewal and called a strike for 7, 9 and 10 July. The first day was a complete success in all the companies in Turin, except at Fiat. But there too militant workers immediately launched a vigorous campaign against strike-breaking, both at the factory gates and door-to-door, and on the second day Fiat joined the strike action. Young people, students and social marginals, demonstrated and clashed with the police wherever the workers involved were inexperienced southerners. On 29 December, Intersind signed an accord recognizing the right to workplace collective bargaining over bonus payments and assembly-line speeds. The national agreement was signed in February, but only after an industry-wide general strike; it made a number of economic concessions, amounting to an increase of 32 per cent over the previous agreement. At the same time, a new contractual arrangement went beyond the old quarrel between 'generalist' and 'company-oriented' trade unionism: the agreement covering each trade continued to provide guarantees for everyone working in it, especially with regard to minimum pay levels, but it could now be combined with local agreements on working conditions or higher pay linked to company performance. It was important that these results were achieved partly through strike action by the 'new working class', and that rank-and-file involvement had often gone beyond the levels seen in previous disputes. In 1963 struggles were more widespread at company level, while the national total of strike hours reached a new peak.

This bare account already helps to explain the scale and suddenness of the labour revival. For, in addition to the long wage freeze, the heavy sacrifices of migration and new stresses associated with Taylorist work organization had led to a huge accumulation of pent-up anger. It was an explosive mixture, and, once full employment created the right labour market conditions (at least in some regions), it took on the radical character of a 'liberation struggle'. The workers' rights might be questioned; they could no longer be rejected out of hand. But that would not have been enough if other factors had not also been present. First of all, social conflict was re-emerging in a country which, unlike others, had a strong union movement and a strong party that kept alive class attitudes and genuine hostility to the dominant social system. At the same time, despite the difficulties and the lateness of their breakthrough, the workers now had the capacity to see – and the will to take on board – the new characteristics of class conflict. Second, trade unionists and politicians – whether Communist (Di Vittorio, Trentin, Minucci) or Socialist (Foa, Santi) – and intellectuals such as Panzieri or Leonardi made a frontline contribution to this. Changes in the Catholic world also proved deeper and more lasting than they had initially seemed: the openness discernible in John XXIII's *Mater et Magistra* encyclical offered new scope within CISL and later in the Italian Christian Workers Associations (ACLI). Soon *Pacem in terra* and the build-up to the Second Vatican Council indicated that something more was in the offing. Third, there was the generational changeover. Young people in the 1960s, in Italy and elsewhere, were ever less willing to accept the chains of established authority, felt the attraction of new lifestyles, and conformed to them even if they did not yet have the means to live them to the full. Nor was this just a question of music and personal behaviour. Another element was the memory of anti-fascism and a still-unresolved ideological conflict, so that the new lifestyles tended to encompass politics, albeit instinctually and often outside any organization. In July 1960, a popular revolt in Genoa caused by Tambroni's overtures to the fascists[6] spread to the whole country, resulting in a number of deaths but eventually forcing him from office; again, it was the 'young people in striped vests' who played the leading role.

In the short term, all this found expression in the electoral growth of the PCI. But it proved to be the prelude to a broader and more diverse upheaval in society, which in the long decade of the Sixties would bring not only students but also young workers to centre stage, and over the years carry even wider strata along with it. If one ignores or underestimates this thread, one will understand nothing of the 'Italian case' – still less of the PCI's debates and the role it played (and could have played better) amid the turmoil.

6. During his brief period in office in 1960, the Christian Democrat politician Fernando Tambroni mooted the possibility of an alliance with the neo-fascist MSI against the parliamentary Left.

8

The Centre-Left

The Centre Left – that is, a government coalition mainly between Christian Democrats and Socialists – was the political expression of the economic and social upheavals we have been describing, and an attempted response to them. The Socialist Party, which took the lead in advancing the idea, was also the chief victim of its collapse.

I confess that, a few years ago, I would have found it difficult to avoid a critique that was not only harsh but hasty and somewhat factious. I do not think the critique should be abandoned, because little by little it has been fully borne out by events. The negative consequences of that policy have also become more evident and entrenched. But I now think I should approach it in a different spirit and ask myself some new questions – for a reason linked to the present that is not at all obvious, and might even seem to point in a different direction, towards the kind of blanket demolition of a complex history that I accuse many others of performing in relation to Italian Communism. Today, whereas the word 'communist' has generally been written off as too compromising, the word 'socialist' has become overworked. A host of people fight over the term in order to cloak themselves in its mantle of legitimate tradition, or, more simply, to link up with European parties that still count for something. On closer consideration, however, fate has not treated the two terms so differently. For 'socialist' is now used with multiple meanings – or, more often, with none – in complete indifference to the long and complex history behind it. Kautsky, Luxemburg and Bernstein, Palme, Mollet and Blair, Nenni, Turati and Saragat, Lombardi, Basso and Craxi: all merge into an indiscriminate hotchpotch. Italian Socialism does have an interesting and original history, made up of mighty struggles, just defeats, successful initiatives and failures; and it all came to a humiliating end. One of the key episodes was precisely the experience of the Centre Left, whose short-term and long-term consequences therefore require serious assessment.

First mooted early on, the project went through a variety of phases and versions. The proposal came in 1955 from Rodolfo Morandi, who conceived of it as the first step towards a political turn that could not yet include the Communists but ruled out a break with them. The Christian Democrats, apart from a small minority, did not take it seriously. The Vatican and the Americans sensed a trap and vetoed it without a second thought. The events of '56 and the meeting in Pralognan (see p.127) put it onto the agenda, but when Saragat explained that it would only involve an expansion of the Centre majority and take the PSI into the Atlantic camp, a majority of Socialists opposed the whole idea. Meanwhile, Fanfani had lost all power in Christian Democracy, and the hard-line Dorotea current,[1] which had no intention of surrendering DC supremacy, was on the lookout for ad hoc alliances with subaltern forces. None other than Aldo Moro put it clearly in 1959: 'Anyone who is not against Communism is necessarily with Communism. The Honourable Nenni must therefore choose, in the knowledge that half-measures are not enough. Until then the PSI cannot be used for the defence of Italian democracy.'

Between 1957 and 1959, the Zoli and Segni governments, and then the Scelba government, were kept in power by the votes of the far Right. And early in 1960 *L'Osservatore Romano* wrote: 'Even in its most moderate forms, even if it repudiates Marx and the class struggle, socialism cannot be reconciled with the profession of Catholicism.' However, the dramatic and grotesque events that bedevilled the Tambroni government made it clear to everyone that Christian Democracy could not continue navigating by guesswork. Major new economic developments and social contradictions, together with the new international context and the turn then under way in the Church, made it urgently necessary to

1. Dorotea current: so called after the Convent of St Dorotea in Rome, where the majority of the current decided to accept Fanfani's resignation from the party secretariat and to block any opening to the Left.

chart a new course for the government. But which course, and in alliance with whom? By 1961 the 'Centre Left' was becoming an urgent political issue, to be confronted without delay. Inevitably, it could be confronted for different political purposes and with different agendas. Would the choice fall on Morandi's proposal of 1955, or on the line that emerged from Pralognan (and Saragat's explanatory follow-up)?

The most interesting aspect was precisely this initial ambiguity, which could be resolved in more ways than one. In the preliminary discussions, before all the actual forces had been mobilized, the Centre Left was quite an advanced project, floated by people who were both intelligent and influential. I am referring to a couple of national meetings: one called by the DC at San Pellegrino (where Ardigò[2] and Saraceno gave the main reports), and one called in Rome by the 'Friends of *Il Mondo*',[3] and by *Mondo Operaio*,[4] where notable speakers were Scalfari,[5] Lombardi,[6] Manlio Rossi Doria[7] and Ernesto Rossi.[8] At both meetings, the discussion downplayed directly political (especially international) issues and focused on the economic and social situation in Italy, so as to clarify an economic policy programme. It was forthright in this respect, denouncing the negative results of completely market-centred growth while advancing proposals to correct them. Beneath a sincerely reformist discourse – nationalization of electrical energy and war on corruption; prioritization of the Mezzogiorno as a national

2. Achille Ardigò: wartime anti-fascist Catholic, later prominent in the 'Bologna Left' of Christian Democracy.

3. *Il Mondo*: influential economic, political and cultural weekly, independent and secular, founded in 1949 and instrumental in the evolution of political life until 1966.

4. *Mondo Operaio*: cultural-political periodical founded in 1948 on the initiative of Pietro Nenni and, from 1953, the fortnightly organ of the PSI.

5. Eugenio Scalfari: an influential journalist, founder in 1955 of the weekly *L'Espresso*, PSI deputy in the 1960s, and founder and editor of the influential daily *La Repubblica* from 1975.

6. Riccardo Lombardi: then a leading figure in the PSI, who had sided with Nenni in 1956; in 1964 the current associated with his name criticized the evolution of the Centre-Left project and withheld its support from the second Moro government.

7. Manlio Rossi Doria: former leader of the Partito d'Azione, who in 1959 had founded the Economic-Agrarian Research Centre for the Mezzogiorno.

8. Ernesto Rossi: politician and journalist, one of the founders of the Partito d'Azione, and a contributor to the foundation of the Radical Party.

problem; critique of primitive consumerism; a new deal for Italian farmers; urban development reforms – the underlying idea was that public companies should play a vanguard role, coordinated by a 'plan' but without abandoning efficiency. The two meetings reached substantive agreement on this platform. It was therefore not unthinkable that Moro, Nenni, Vanoni and to some extent La Malfa[9] might give it the thumbs-up.

I followed the two meetings with genuine interest, but also with mistrust. The mistrust, I admit, was partly due to my ideological prejudice against generic use of the term 'reformism', which opened the way to a pragmatism that might serve any number of purposes. But it was not without reason: I could not see how that policy direction could take hold without breaking the existing political equilibrium, or how it could overcome the intransigence of Confindustria if it shunned in principle any support from the PCI and trade union or other forces close to it, and if it did nothing to alter its international choices. I remember reciting to my old friend Luigi Granelli, as we came away from San Pellegrino, the proverb that Giorgio Amendola had taught me: those with the most yarn will weave the most cloth. But mistrust did not stifle my interest. In fact, I confidently involved myself in the field of town planning, where the PCI carried considerable weight thanks to the presence of many intellectuals, and where I had a definite task – to support the attempts of Antonio Giolitti and his right-hand man Michele Giannotta to get Sullo's draft legislation adopted.[10] But short and happy was the life of Francis Macomber! After the fall of Tambroni, the Socialists were again left standing on the doormat. Fanfani and Saragat formed a government coalition, and the PSI supported it only with an unrecognized and unnegotiated abstention, which Moro, apparently without irony, called 'parallel convergences'.

The first overt attempt to reach a political accord between the DC and PSI finally occurred in 1962; the PSI still remained outside government, but it committed itself to some of the reforms mooted at San Pellegrino. This too was guided by Fanfani, who, no longer

9. Ugo La Malfa: leader of the Italian Republican Party (PRI), a minister in successive governments in the 1950s and in the Centre-Left government formed in 1962.

10. Fiorentino Sullo: one of the leaders of the Christian Democrat Left, whose proposals for urban reform were eventually disowned by the party secretariat.

being secretary of the DC, had moved to the Left and was accustomed by temperament to wrapping things up quickly. The budget minister, La Malfa, helped out with a note of his own proposing an economic planning committee, which was in fact entrusted to Saraceno.[11] Thus, nationalization of the electrical industry, a withholding tax on dividends to prevent evasion, and the establishment of a unified secondary-school system followed one another in quick succession. Paradoxically, the Centre Left appeared most forceful and resolute during the period before the deal had been signed and sealed.

Yet it was already possible to measure the obstacles and opponents standing in the way of the project. Nationalization of the hydroelectric industry was a historical objective of the whole Left, and it was difficult to mobilize opinion openly against it: for Edison and its satellite companies controlled a natural (and therefore objectively public) resource, owning plant that had long been amortized and acting essentially as financial groups. Nevertheless, pressure from the Bank of Italy and the Christian Democrat Right ensured not only that the blow was softened but that its purposes were distorted by means of huge compensation awards – not in the form of bonds distributed to the mass of small shareholders (and therefore in the service of a long-term public investment plan with fixed priorities), but directly to the narrow groups controlling the electrical energy industry. These groups then blew the money in a variety of ways for their own benefit, accelerating the formation of Chinese-box finance that combined the public and the private. The violent death of Enrico Mattei, the rise of Eugenio Cefis to the top of the ENI and then his move to the Montecatini chemicals combine, symbolized this drift towards a permanent economic oligarchy, powerful and often corrupt. As to the withholding tax on dividends – the first measure in a never to be completed fiscal reform – this was soon amended in a way that encouraged the secret export of capital, which was then reintroduced into the country with the usual tax breaks.

The pre-emptive war of the Right did not stop there. It turned into a full-scale political mobilization, especially targeting the reform that was supposed to end the massive circumvention of

11. Pasquale Saraceno: leading Christian Democrat economist and specialist in the Southern question.

town planning regulations and to separate land ownership and construction rights (so that local authorities would be able to buy up development land at the price usually paid for farmland and give approval for construction at a price that included the costs of urbanization). This would have eliminated the profit that landowners or builders made from converting farmland into building land – which often involved corruption, and saddled the local authority with all the costs of urbanization. The rationality of such a reform was indisputable: it would have ensured honest and civilized practices at a time of turbulent migration to the cities, and protected a country so rich in artistic wealth and natural beauty. But the Right managed to convince not only speculators and businessmen but even numerous smallholders that the reform threatened wholesale confiscation of land, and to scare homeowners into thinking that the state wanted to evict them. It was also implied that the reform was part of a general trend to eliminate the market and private property. The immediate result of this campaign was to block every point in the agreed programme: the creation of regional authorities, the adoption of an economic plan, and, of course, any review of international policy options at a time when the issue of installing nuclear weapons in Germany was being considered.

The Centre Left was therefore already in crisis by the time of the general elections of 1963. The Communists increased their vote, a little ahead of the Socialists, while the Christian Democrats lost huge ground among their conservative electorate. But the most important novelty was that Moro felt compelled to clarify his policy perspective; he was sympathetic to what Saraceno or Ardigò represented, but he was not willing to endanger the unity or supremacy of Christian Democracy. As was his wont, he did not dwell on any disputed areas of the programme, since these could be settled or deferred as the need arose. But he did speak of the principles from which the Centre Left could not depart: no uncertainty could be tolerated on relations with the Communists; the regions would be created if and when the Socialists undertook not to ally with the PCI in them; and the Centre Left meant amplifying, not abandoning, the political centre and Atlanticism. To show he meant business, Moro supported Segni's[12] nomination for the presidency

12. Antonio Segni: twice prime minister in the 1950s, and president of the Republic from 1962 to 1964. He represented forces in Christian Democracy opposed to an opening to the PSI.

of the Republic. In June 1963, however, on the celebrated 'St. Gregory's Night', the PSI Central Committee refused to participate directly in a government headed by Moro. This was the position of the left of the Party, but Lombardi and Giolitti also supported it, with more reservations than Santi.[13] De Martino[14] sided with Nenni, but he hesitated because both of them feared that a split would make it difficult to patch up the dialogue with the DC. The matter was referred to a special congress of the PSI, which met in November and changed the policy again to one of negotiating with Moro for a coalition government. Lombardi accepted this, in the belief that the key thing was to discuss the programme. In the talks that followed, Moro was as adroit as ever. He confirmed his previous undertakings on urban reform and a five-year plan (without specifying dates or instruments), knowing that Lombardi would fight to his last breath for them; he again set rigid conditions for the activation of regional authorities, but without saying when and how they would be introduced; he shelved the issue of nuclear weapons deployment until there was greater clarity, and so on. As for the allocation of government posts, the idea was that the Socialists would be in charge of areas where it would be difficult to keep to their commitments (for example, Giolitti in the budget ministry without any real power over planning, Mancini in public works to promote a town planning reform that would not actually happen). This is how the Moro government got off the ground, in an atmosphere of reticence and suspicion. A third of the Socialist deputies voted against it and had to face disciplinary proceedings; the result was a split which in itself did little to change the political landscape.

Togliatti was against this split, on the reasonable grounds that it might drive the Socialist Party even further away. But, at a confidential meeting with the PSI Left, he failed to convince it to hold back. At an even more private meeting, Lelio Basso explained the thinking of the Left: 'If all we faced was a step towards truly social-democratic positions, we could remain inside and try to influence and correct it. But what is actually going on is a race into government that will quickly lead the PSI to change its nature and social

13. Fernando Santi: historic leader of the PSI, joint secretary of the CGIL, and a parliamentary deputy from 1948 to 1968.

14. Francesco De Martino: a supporter of Nenni's position, who became secretary of the PSI when Nenni joined Moro's first Centre-Left government in 1963.

base, and it is not possible to take part in that without becoming caught up in it and transformed.' From today's distance, one might describe the split in those conditions in the words that Gramsci used in 1921: 'unfortunate but necessary.'

A few months later, the state of play emerged more clearly. A supposedly private (but in fact highly public) letter from the DC treasury minister, Emilio Colombo, stated that the economic situation was so grave, and the reaction of the markets so threatening, that it was necessary to suspend a number of ambitious programmes and to adopt at once a deflationary pay squeeze. Guido Carli was calling for the same on behalf of the Banca d'Italia. The government sank into crisis, and the DC imposed the umpteenth 'policy review', more drastic than the ones before. Lombardi and Giolitti again called the agreement into question and refused to accept ministerial posts; rumours fuelled by meetings between the President and top military brass, together with Confindustria blackmail, persuaded Nenni to soldier on and broke down resistance at both the top and the bottom of a confused party. The *coup de grâce* came the following year, when a foolish attempt to rush a fusion with the PSDI[15] turned into a power struggle and soon ended in failure, leaving the Socialists decimated and without perspectives for the future.

The Socialist Party began to be reborn ten years later, but from different loins and with altered chromosomes. After an attempted left turn led by De Martino, Bettino Craxi was elected leader with the support of Signorile and De Michelis. Everything about this seems perfectly clear: the aims and the results, and the responsibilities of each player. In fact, it was by no means a foregone conclusion that things would work out precisely as they did.

I do not wish to be misunderstood. The notion that the PSI could or should have marched in step with the PCI at the end of the 1950s and renounced any claim to independent thinking or a distinctive political role, including a possible agreement with the DC on a coalition government, is an unhelpful scholastic abstraction. Right or wrong, dangerous or not, the idea of a Centre-Left opening came up in the course of events and was already implanted in the heads of those who had to decide whether to pursue it. A more

15. PSDI: Partito Socialista Democratico Italiano, the social-democratic party that had split away from the PSI in January 1947.

likely sequel would have been the formation of weak governments of the Centre, with the unreliable and compromising support of the far Right in parliament and the backing of a hesitant Confindustria outside. The PCI would have been more on its guard, and would have responded more boldly to the events in Prague. The PSI would not have suffered a split and would have reopened internal discussion. And one can certainly wonder how things would have turned out three years later, if the great wave of struggles involving workers, students and other democratic forces had been in a position to aim at bringing down a weak conservative government that lacked popular support. It is reasonable to think that Italian history could have taken a different road, less rocky and more alive with opportunities for reform. If, in the changed international situation, the DC had been forced into a compromise, or if the PSI had sought to reach one, the underlying relationship of forces would have been much more favourable, and the leading actors would have been different. The PCI would not have found itself having to choose between the premature forcing of a government crisis, and abstention in the face of a monochrome Christian Democracy presided by Andreotti.

If, however, we accept that the PSI could realistically have taken a different road in the 1960s, we must ask ourselves why it followed one that took it round and round in a vicious circle. Let us leave aside one marginal factor: the influence that a subtle, repressed and not always unjustified streak of anti-Communism might have had at certain moments on some leaders of the PSI. It is probable that such a streak had always been there, especially among those with a background in the Partito d'Azione; the ideological reasons for it were respectable enough, and the PCI had unwittingly fuelled it with its air of self-importance. Paradoxically, its later policy of seeking broad agreements with the DC may have done more to kindle than to douse it, but it is hardly possible to argue that those who had stood beside the Communists at the toughest moments of the cold war and the Cominform would have let themselves be carried away by such sentiments at a time when anti-Communism was on the wane, peaceful coexistence was making headway, and the Soviet Union, though open to criticism, was again on the rise.

The momentum to stick with the Centre Left, at a growing price to itself, therefore came from elsewhere and is deserving of serious analysis. It was a period in postwar history when the two main Socialist forces in Europe – the Labour Party and the SPD, both with a class base and some link to Marxism – had recently executed a major turn. Neither Anthony Crosland's writings and Hugh Gaitskell's policies in Britain, nor the new SPD programme adopted at Bad Godesberg, contained any reference to Marxism or a specifically socialist end goal. This reorientation was not just implicit: it was openly stated as necessary in order to operate within a new social structure, to win the support of broad middle layers, and to aim at a role in government from which Socialists had too long been excluded. Each of these great parties held that its task was to redistribute the benefits of economic growth that neo-capitalism had provided and would continue to provide; it would achieve something in this respect after much time and effort, but only once it had obtained a majority and only if it actively placed itself within the Atlantic camp. Nothing conveys what this meant better than a passage in Kissinger's memoirs, where the former US national security adviser remarks that he does not recall any criticism of the Vietnam war from a European leader. Both Brandt and Wilson voluntarily decided not to comment on it.

Ideologically, during the Centre-Left period, the PSI was much more cautious in speaking about a radical turn, although it could not fail to be influenced by the analysis that accompanied it. Politically, however, it feared that any proposal which lost it American support would lead to its removal from the 'nerve centre'. East–West détente was in the air, but strict Atlantic discipline was necessary to participate in government – and that was now the number one priority for the PSI. What unified and drove the 'go it alone' majority was the idea that, without a place in government, there could be no hope of changing anything in society and gaining the people's support. Nenni was totally convinced of this, and Lombardi, for all his stubbornness regarding the programme, could not bring himself to disagree. Some tried to put their foot down over interpretation of the agreements, while others placed too much faith in promises on paper: but all concealed, even from themselves, the way things were actually going. Moro was a past master at tightening the rope and dragging them along: the time's not yet ripe but soon will be, so let's press on patiently together, overcoming resistance and clearing the obstacles in our path.

My aim here has been to stress the implacable mechanism in those distant events, since it would return in the 1970s to operate within the national unity governments. Craxi learned to use it again in the 1980s, with controlled, retractable gestures, as things went steadily downhill. Today it has become the default reasoning. First you try to win elections with a catch-all programme. Then, if successful, you decide on what you will actually do and work to convince people that this is the right, or unavoidable, thing. We have seen this over and over again.

9

The PCI Facing Neocapitalism

I am now entering a minefield. Records and historians offer only rough and ready maps, while the signs left by travellers are often cryptic and tendentious. To reconstruct and evaluate this period, I shall therefore also have to rely on my own memory, which is not failing me, but which it is only proper to distrust. After all, I was then not only an informed observer but also a party to the disputes: not in a lead role, but as an irregular soldier or a behind-the-scenes instigator. In retrospect, therefore, I am less marked by responsibilities but quite prone to bias. I have three means of avoiding this risk.

The first is to insert things that I myself said and did, whenever these were of at least minimal importance, and to apply to them the same critical standards that I use for others' positions, both recognizing the mistakes and asserting the merits. No false modesty, then, and no touching-up for the sake of comfort. The second resource against any *parti pris* is to use the conceit of one who claims to be still intelligent – or, anyway, intelligent enough to identify the reasons for the errors I shared and the important elements of truth mixed in with them, whether recognized or repressed. The third resource, obvious but crucial, is a commitment to draw as much as possible upon facts that can be documented.

RIGHT AND LEFT

The panorama of the Italian situation in the first half of the 1960s should already make clear both the opportunities and the difficulties that the PCI then faced. New space was opening up for it to act as a social and cultural opposition, even to achieve a degree of cultural hegemony. And it was well equipped to occupy that space, both because of its long tradition and by virtue of recent updating. Instead of relying on well-aimed propaganda to confront the new *cordon sanitaire* that the myth of affluence sought to build around it, the Party attacked it in society itself – through united and victorious workers' struggles, a re-launch of militant anti-fascism and anti-imperialism, campaigns among young people for world peace, and a new interest in, and understanding of, what was happening in the Catholic world beyond Christian Democracy. In the specifically political domain, Togliatti did not decry the 'betrayal' of the Socialists, but pointed up the risks and misguided ambitions involved in their Centre-Left operation, while expressing interest in their reform proposals and leaving it to the future to pass judgement. The PCI's strong advance in the 1963 elections (unmatched by any other Communist party in Europe, and accompanied with a drop in the Socialist vote and a sharp decline for the Christian Democrats) was the reward for its strong and effective opposition. It seemed to have won the first hand in the game.

So what was there to discuss and argue over? A great deal, in fact. To say that there was an unresolved and inescapable problem of strategy would be more than excessive: it would be imprecise. The 'democratic road', already charted by the Salerno turn, had survived the difficult stretch of the Cominform and the cold war, before being confirmed and clarified at the Eighth Congress. Yet it had left a vacuum in the PCI, since the Salerno turn owed its value to the fact that it was not only a statement of principle but a policy that accepted the risks, and recognized the limits, of a particular historical situation. It therefore involved precise choices or objectives, and workable alliances: the encouragement of armed resistance, unity in the anti-fascist struggle, a new Constitution and Republic, and a certain international role.

But much had changed since then – the economy, the global order, the main social actors – and the political equilibrium was in the grip of a general crisis. It was no longer enough to reaffirm principles, or to build up strength on a wave of social conflict, or to gain new voters by profiting from the difficulties of one's opponents. Indeed, the more assertive the Party became in opposition, the more it needed to make a correct evaluation of the new period, and to work out programmes, political and social alliances and organizational forms that offered a solution. Activate the Constitution? Sure, but that was a trifle vague.

The Italian Left was not alone in feeling the need for a fundamental rethink. For good or ill, a heated debate was under way all over Europe. It was agitating some of the major social-democratic parties: Willy Brandt and the new Bad Godesberg programme in the SPD; Crosland and Gaitskell ('New Labour' Mark One) in Britain; the rise of Olof Palme in Sweden and Bruno Kreisky in Austria. But something was also stirring in a number of Communist parties: in France, the clash between the PCF leadership and young dissidents and intellectuals (known as 'Italianizers') which ended in multiple expulsions or resignations, yet forced the Party to again pick up the thread of L'Unité de la Gauche; in Spain, Santiago Carrillo's break with Claudín and Semprún. Even more was this true of the intellectual Left, on both sides of the Atlantic: witness Sweezy, Baran, Galbraith, Marcuse, Wright-Mills, Friedman, Braverman, Strachey, Thompson and the 'New Left', Mallet, Touraine, Sartre, Gorz, and so many others. There was also analysis and discussion of and in the Third World: from Fanon to the theorists of neo-colonialism, dependency and polarization (Samir Amin, Andre Gunder Frank). The answers they came up with were very different, often opposite, but the question at issue was the same: how should neocapitalism be interpreted, and what should be the response to it?

So, when I speak of 'the Italian case', what I have in mind is not at all an anomaly – since Italy was more than ever part of a global process – but a specific case of enormous interest for everyone. For it was especially there that neocapitalism displayed such a tight nexus of modernization and backwardness, which had become even more complex and explosive in the latter part of the 1950s. A causal contemporaneity of phenomena that had occurred elsewhere in a temporal sequence permitted Italy's initial take-off, later facilitated a perverse modernization and dreary Americanization, and eventually ended in destabilization and crisis. More than anywhere else, it was necessary – and perhaps possible – to define a new medium-term perspective that did not involve subaltern conformity to the course of events. That was the issue to be discussed in the PCI. And, whatever the results, it was discussed with great passion and animation.

The first counsel that my memory gives me is one of prudence. It is a delicate task to reconstruct that discussion, to clarify its content, to identify the various forces that took part, to assess its conclusion and consequences. Simplistic schemas and abbreviated timelines cannot do justice to a complex and lengthy process involving so many leading figures and so many thousands of activists – on the contrary, they amputate all the things that emerged confusedly yet proved over time to have been valuable and prescient.

I used the word 'process' for several reasons. The discussion, which eventually turned into a political battle, developed in a number of phases over a critical five-year period. It did not start out from predefined schemas, but involved the gradual, never completed, coming together of multiple experiences and cultures. It took place on the terrain of research and analysis, more than of conscious political disagreement. On many key issues, individual positions evolved over time, groupings changed their composition, and the leaders were mere points of reference that did not command any loyalty. The debate inside the Party was linked with what was taking place on its margins or outside, in a wider Left that ran from *Quaderni Rossi* to the *Rivista Trimestriale*. And finally, the unity of the party was not merely an obligation to be respected but a value that was largely internalized by its members.

Two important moments, which date the beginning and end of the five-year period, may give some idea of the initially open and shifting character of the debate, and of its candidness. The Central Committee meeting of 1961 discussed Togliatti's report on the Twenty-Second Congress of the CPSU, where Khrushchev – probably in a bid to block a creeping restoration of old ways of thinking and exercising power – had further sharpened his criticisms of Stalinism. Togliatti was against Khrushchev's démarche, not because he was unaware of the need for renewal in both the USSR and the PCI, but because he considered it pointless and misleading to start with a repeat of the Secret Speech. However, instead of proposing a different way forward, he again avoided all mention of the most delicate part of the congress, at which he had been present, and about which everyone was talking. Many members of the Central Committee soon showed their unease and irritation: they did not want to start poring over Stalin's guilt again, but they would no longer put up with the old method of self-censorship; they wanted to discuss the Soviet model more frankly, and above all they wanted a bolder approach to renewal of the PCI. For the first time the unease expressed itself in an explicit critique, to which some members of the leadership contributed. Aldo Natoli, an isolated but authoritative figure, straightforwardly called for a special congress to be held. But it was Giorgio Amendola who spearheaded the dissent, supported by Giancarlo Pajetta and Mario Alicata. Togliatti grew more rigid and threatened an open confrontation. His polemical conclusions were neither voted on nor made public, and were later replaced with a collective document whose tone was altogether different. Togliatti not only acquiesced in this, but accepted the impulse behind it; indeed, he now began to take an active and conspicuous part in innovatory thinking, wrote a piece on the formation of the PCI leadership in the 1920s that broke with many mystifications, and published in *Rinascita* the whole polemical exchange of letters from 1926 between Gramsci and himself, which had never before been recognized as genuine. The right to engage in this kind of uninhibited reflection on Party traditions was not reserved for Togliatti and other top leaders. An open clash followed in the PCI journal *Critica Marxista* over the Popular Front experience (whether it should be taken as a model or understood to have been limited), between Emilio Sereni and a mere nobody like myself. And later, in an official volume on the theory of the Party, I took the liberty of arguing that Leninism had incorporated a shade too much of Jacobinism – a position that drew many reproofs but also many words of praise. (Not long ago, as I was happily moseying through the texts, I came across another detail from that stormy session of the Central Committee in 1961. In a section of his speech, which was later published, Amendola asked that everyone should have the right to voice their dissent, and stressed that it would useful to form, not organized tendencies, but majorities and minorities on the most important issues in question. He used words almost identical to those for which Ingrao would be crucified four years later, at the Eleventh Congress.)

A second example of sharp but not yet brittle debate comes from an important labour movement congress in 1965, at which Luciano Barca had to give the introductory report on behalf of a committee. In order to structure the session, a small group consisting of Amendola, Reichlin, Trentin, Garavini, Minucci, Scheda, Pugno, Barca and a few others, including myself, met at

Frattocchie near Rome. The agenda was binding, since what had to be discussed was not the situation in the trade unions but the weight and significance that should be given to the working class and its new struggles, in relation to the impending economic crisis and Party strategy in general. Many issues were connected to this, and a heated debate had already developed around them. Some considered that, because of their scale and the nature of their objectives, the new struggles should be the main axis for the building of political and social hegemony, as well as the starting point for a more participatory democracy inside and outside the workplace. Others took the more traditional view that such struggles were one of many movements emerging to confront Italy's backwardness, which together might produce a new balance of forces at an institutional and political level. The emphases and priorities were different and, so to speak, transversal to one another: for example, some attached greater importance to direct action in the factory, others to the link between workplace struggle and a turn in economic policy (thus accenting the role of the Party), and others to the extension of new forms of struggle to backward but evolving regions and social subjects, particularly in the Mezzogiorno.

Amendola, though sensing he was in a minority, did not mince his words at that meeting. His chief worry was the general drift towards a policy excessively centred on class struggle – which in his view might take the Party away from the 'Italian road' by narrowing the scope for alliances, diverting attention from immediate demands and, at the same time, setting too little store by parliamentary action and relations among different political forces. If I understand him correctly, he saw the main danger in a revival of 'Ordine Nuovo' politics and a doctrinal rigidity that would make the Party's programmes interesting but abstract. He therefore sharply criticized the meeting as a whole and referred the matter to the Party leadership, where he succeeded in convening the Central Committee not simply to address the usual 'struggle on two fronts', but to clamp down on a dangerous 'left tendency'. Longo was given the task of introducing the session. But, in accordance with custom, he asked comrades in the central apparatus to supply him with materials for the preparation of his report. I did my duty and set out my convictions in a more closely argued manner than before, focusing especially on the question of an economic policy consistent with the mass struggle. It was only a contribution, thirteen pages in all, but Longo, open-minded as ever, found it persuasive and put much of it into his own Report. This was nothing special, except that it meant the 'struggle on a single front' was suspended for the time being. Those who knew about the meeting at Frattocchie were surprised, others were not. Amendola stopped me outside the Central Committee and said: 'Don't think I'm not aware of what you've done; I won't forget it.' So, Barca was confirmed as reporter to the Genoa conference on the labour movement; he toned down some of what he had to say but basically stuck to his guns; Amendola criticized him in his concluding remarks, but was in turn criticized in the leadership by Ingrao, Reichlin and others. It was a Pyrrhic victory, however, since at that very moment the political discussion turned into open warfare between two orientations.

Using both familiar and forgotten examples, I have insisted on the open and shifting character that the debate inside the Party maintained for a long time – not to put a 'good face' on its internal life (which is nowadays so often depicted as an army barracks), but because I think it useful to raise a question that I have always avoided asking myself. Was it inevitable that, instead of blossoming into a responsible (non-factional) pluralism, those disagreements should harden into an intolerant confrontation, sometimes involving petty personal hostility? Here I had better clarify the exact issues over which differences emerged at this point. They were issues that had been lying beneath the surface, not only at official meetings and events, but also in articles, conferences and journals, and in personal squabbles and conversations unknown to, or neglected by, historians and writers of memoirs. The summary and selective material contained in the archives is not sufficient to explain what had been going on. I shall try to do this by tracing as clearly as I can the thread that links my own and other people's memories, as well as some of the texts that they enabled me to select.

TENDENCIES IN NEOCAPITALISM

In a Communist party, the political line at key moments is always based on a prior definition of the period. This was true in the early and late 1920s, in the mid 1930s, in 1944, in 1948, in 1956, and also to some extent after 1960. Thus, the debate inside the PCI first got going around an analysis of the capitalist tendencies of the time. It cannot be said that it began suddenly, because there had already been many telling hints, but it really drew attention to itself at a well-attended conference at the Gramsci Institute in 1962. This had wide resonance, especially but not only inside the Party, and it has remained engraved in people's memory, albeit in very distorted versions. To appreciate this point, it is enough to consult the two thick published volumes containing the record of its proceedings.

It is not true, for example, that Giorgio Amendola, the effective organizer and main reporter at the conference, put forward the traditional vision of a 'lumpen' capitalism incapable of keeping up the expansion of the productive forces. Indeed, the truly novel idea at the conference, shared by everyone there, was that Italy had completed a qualitative leap from an agrarian-industrial to an industrialized country. And Trentin's report, which commanded unanimous approval, rounded off the picture with a critical analysis of the tools that American sociology had offered, and was still testing out, to control social conflict in the factory and to gain the support of new middle layers – with particular attention to the ambiguous reflections of this in Catholic trade unionism in Italy. The disagreement that Foa, Libertini, Parlato, myself and others expressed in varying tones during the course of the discussion centred on two important points.

1) In Amendola's report, and even more in his polemical conclusions, the development of the Italian economy and the industrialization that had been its driving force and result coexisted with regional imbalances and areas of backwardness so oppressive that they could not continue for much longer without provoking attempts to correct them, and bringing about a political turn that included the Communist movement. It was therefore both possible and necessary to keep pursuing the Centre Left as it proved incapable of accomplishing what it had promised; to challenge the ruling class in the name of a more extensive development and a fairer distribution of income. This would require vigorous social struggles for achievable immediate objectives, not chasing after will-o'-the-wisps in a still distant future but seeking to consolidate democracy within its classical limits.

2) Industrialization and the development associated with it were undoubtedly the most conspicuous and immediate aspect of the

changes under way. But were they all that was new? Or was Italy part of a much deeper and more general change in the capitalist system? In the first case, the task was obviously to reaffirm and keep updating the line the PCI had defined some time ago, with the finishing post now finally in sight. In the second case, however, the task was to focus on longer-term trends, to identify the contradictions in them that might provide some leverage, to analyse the difficulties that needed to be overcome, and to define the corresponding new alliances, programmes, social subjects and organizational forms: in short, to hold certain principles steady, while developing theoretical and practical innovations. Right from the start, a 'left' critique inside and outside the Party homed in on this second hypothesis. In his concluding remarks, Amendola by no means ignored the scale and substance of the dissent, and he met it with a firm but skilful response. Actually he chose me as his 'whipping boy' – as Luciano Barca put it in his journal – not only for the obvious reason that I carried the least weight among the dissidents, but also because he did not have much time, and my recent written contribution, despite having won some acceptance, offered ample scope for his criticism. For my analysis had emphasized individual consumerism as a characteristic feature of neocapitalism, leaving itself open to the charge of abstractness and 'ideologism' in a country where prosperity was still far off and many vital needs remained unfulfilled. I soon realized the misunderstanding I had helped to create, which perhaps also partly existed in my head, and I took the opportunity of a commissioned article for Sartre's *Les Temps Modernes* to amplify and correct what I had written. I tried to clarify my view that, on the one hand, consumerism resulted from tendencies not in the culture but in the mode of production, from the capitalist use of major new means of mass communication and, above all, from the fragmentation and alienation of labour; and, on the other hand, that right from the start the phenomenon had been opening up a contradiction in the Catholic world that was of directly political significance. This clarification served to save my soul and to develop my own thinking at the time, which I now recognize to have had a premonitory character. But it had no bearing upon the basic assumption of the Gramsci conference: the emergence of a number of more advanced issues, and of a Left that was doing work on them, even though it was still incapable of moving beyond analysis to offer a definite political line. On the contrary, it was the Right that had the capacity to express one of the new themes clearly, if not adequately.

DEVELOPMENT MODEL AND STRUCTURAL REFORMS

Between 1963 and 1964, the discussion in the PCI on the above points began to assume the features of an openly political contest, as two currents of opinion took shape. One of these was the current identified with Pietro Ingrao, who was then in the course of working out his positions. Here too, the memory that has come down is not only sparse but confused and approximate. It therefore has to be supplemented and corrected. Has there ever been such a thing as 'Ingraoism'? And, in so far as there has, what positions actually characterized it?

My answer to the first of these questions – indeed, my sworn testimony – is precise and verifiable. Ingraoism, understood as a minimally organized or consciously cohesive group, never existed; it was invented posthumously, even unwittingly, by Ingrao's opponents, and stemmed from a journalistic need for simplification. Over long years of debate, even in the final period when debate became a sharp political contest, there was never a single meeting to decide on a common course of conduct, still less to create a binding discipline. Ingrao told his closest friends that Ingraoism neither could nor should exist – not out of prudence, but because that was what he believed. In the leadership he bluntly expressed the ideas of which he gradually became convinced, and more rarely, in a less clear-cut form, he published articles or intervened in public debates in the Party press, but he never wove these together into a platform. Many recognized themselves in these ideas, and helped to give them clearer shape; others shared them, while sometimes taking a distance, depending on what they considered opportune to say at a particular time and place. It is therefore legitimate to speak of Ingraoism as a diffuse current that gradually came together around important political-cultural questions and embodied a certain political inspiration. It is practically impossible to define its boundaries or to list its adherents: this or that person would draw closer or move away at particular moments and in relation to particular issues. Yet it was an important political fact, because it meant that a 'non-dogmatic, non-Stalinist' Left was present for the first time within a Communist party. A figure of great authority and popularity did not lead the current, but one did inspire it and bond it together. That is all.

The themes and proposals that were becoming characteristic of the 'Ingrao Left', and which eventually led it to clash with Amendola and a majority of the leadership, have passed into the collective memory in a similarly distorted and confused version that makes little or no sense. Perhaps the greatest misunderstanding arises from conflating that particular controversy with the later, much more radical, conflicts that followed the havoc of 1968 and the purging of *Il Manifesto*.

So, Ingraoism was written off as a high-minded utopian deviation that envisaged an anti-capitalist and radical-democratic alternative, denied the importance of intermediate objectives, counterposed direct democracy and social struggle to parliamentary action, and rejected the possibility of forging new alliances with the Socialists on the grounds that they had become incorporated into the dominant system. In short, Ingraoism was alleged to be undermining, perhaps without realizing it, the Togliatti road to socialism. This was the version put around by the victors: both the victors in the internal Party struggle, who congratulated themselves on having rescued Ingrao and many others from a passing fancy; and the external victors, who ceaselessly called upon the PCI to turn itself more quickly into the robust force of thoroughgoing reformism that Italy needed so badly and the PSI had failed to become. Ingrao? A noble, visionary spirit: the image became so much part of the canon that even he sometimes indulged in it. The truth of the matter was very different. In the mid 1960s Ingrao was much less subversive, and his battle inside the PCI much more down to earth, than people believed. It was a battle over definitions of the period. The strictly political confrontation later developed around three highly practical and interrelated issues: an 'alternative growth model', structural reforms, and judgements of the Centre Left.

The concept of an alternative growth model was by no means an abstraction, nor did it imply that we underestimated the importance of reforms. In fact, it showed that we took them all too seriously. The economic crisis in Italy – the system's response to the first wave of union struggles and the announcement of a few reforms that hit at profits and unearned income – posed a burning problem. If each reform did not act as a spur to production, if the whole package did not have the impact and coherence to offer a new market-compatible framework, if it was not supported by social pressure and flanked with direct public intervention and effective planning, then it would soon lead to deadlock and offer the basis for a right-wing counteroffensive. We therefore criticized Pajetta's talk of 'opposition in thousands of rivulets' and Amendola's thesis that 'mass struggles are measured mainly in sums of money'. At the time Lombardi was saying more or less the same as we were: it was a pity he supported a government that did the opposite.

A plan, then? Yes, an organic, binding plan, but not 'in the Soviet style'. It should be one that made use of the mixed economy. Public corporations should be bound and supported by democratically defined priorities, but measured by their efficiency on the market; any losses they made should be covered only if they demonstrably resulted from objectives that did not pay in the short run. Public expenditure should be geared to collective consumption and vital needs. A private sector should be free to compete, but steered by demand and no longer hampered by excessive unearned income that diverted resources away from production. The whole economy should rest upon worker participation and supervision, and working conditions should be of a different quality.

These were not tasks for a single day or a single year. But was this not the horizon of a democratic road to socialism? Was it not a phased objective on which a government could set its sights? Perhaps it was exaggerated; perhaps it had to take the stages more slowly. But it was not off-track: it called for structural, not corrective, reforms; a new growth mechanism, not just faster growth; a different modernity, not just a continuation of that which was given. On the eve of the Centre Left experiment, it was precisely the Communist Left which supported Sullo's proposals for town planning reform; which criticized the vast, ultra-modern but wasteful 'cathedrals in the desert',[1] floated the idea of universal welfare against corporate privilege, and highlighted the urgent need for fiscal reforms to allow productive public investment to proceed without running up excessive debt. (Napolitano may remember a document on the pensions system that he asked me to write, analysing the sobriety and coherence of the Swedish experience.)

1. 'Cathedrals in the desert': the term used by the Left to refer to the vast infrastructural and industrial complexes then being built in remote areas of southern Italy.

Of course, when it became clear that the Centre Left was drifting off course, we did not merely denounce it but drew the conclusion that, although the political reform project had failed, the same was not true of the Christian Democrat project to pull the PSI into the opposite camp – and that it would be very difficult to make it turn back. On this point, the discussion in the PCI assumed a directly political character and resulted in a clash of views between Amendola and Ingrao. In October 1966, Amendola believed that the economic and political situation made a major new initiative both necessary and possible. In a series of articles in *Rinascita* he argued as follows. The 'economic miracle', and the victorious workers' struggles that had accompanied it, found themselves in a tight corner. They would exhaust themselves unless there was a political turn, and the PSI was incapable of imposing one alone. This threatened a counteroffensive by the Right in society and the political arena. Therefore the PCI could not afford to temporize or to close itself away in defensive positions; it needed to intervene decisively, and propose a single party of the Left to the Socialists. This idea rather disconcerted the leadership and the rest of the Party. And it brought forth a series of (mostly critical) replies. Norberto Bobbio showed himself appreciative of Amendola's intentions, while arguing that unification was possible only on a clearly social-democratic basis; it could not be linked to a political emergency, but must have a strategic bearing on both the past and the future, involving a change of heart by the Communists regarding the Livorno split from the PSI in 1921. Amendola took up the gauntlet and raised his sights in a second article. The very difficulties mentioned by Bobbio, he wrote, showed the value of his proposal. Since the past fifty years had shown that neither Communists nor social democrats were in a position to build socialism in a European country, the time had come for them to think again about their respective options and strategies. This unleashed a critical chain reaction, from which I now pick a few quotes to indicate its diversity. Lelio Basso: 'The ideological and political gulf between social democracy and revolutionary Marxism has widened, not narrowed.' Romano Ledda: 'In the history of the twentieth century, we cannot put the responsibilities of the Communists and social democrats on the same plane, either in Europe or elsewhere, either for the past or for the present.' And I myself, moderate for once in my polemic: 'The problem posed by

Amendola is real: reflection on revolution in the West is necessary, and it requires everyone to be innovative. But the renewal in which we are involved is certainly not moving in the same direction as the renewal that the Socialists have in mind, and an eclectic top-down operation would fail to provide a solution.' When the question came before the Party leadership, Amendola did not seem to change his view but remained in a minority. A commission was then set up to consider the differences. It concluded that Amendola's proposal had been mistaken because the time was not ripe for it, but that it was still necessary to come to a new agreement with the Socialists. Ingrao stated clearly more than once that he thought this a banal and purely verbal formula, and he therefore dissented from it. At the next meeting of the Central Committee, more than one voted against, while a number of others abstained.

This came on top of the conference in Genoa to which I referred above, so that it was clear by now that the discussion in the Party had turned into a visible clash between two different lines. And that is how it was seen. The debate had been so long, heated and public, and the sensitivities had become so intense, that the slightest allusion, tone or turn of phrase was enough for someone to be included or excluded from a list. That is the truth, and I say it without acrimony. Those who were smart enough not to give anything away were regarded as cunning little devils. The tension seemed to slacken on the eve of the Party congress, when the theses for it were being drafted, and in the course of its proceedings the sorest points in the long discussion were handled with perhaps excessive caution, or simply omitted. The confrontation, when it came, erupted suddenly over a question which, for the past five years at least, had been only hinted at by various participants in the debate, and which the Party's practice seemed to have partly defused.

10

The Eleventh Congress

THE LEGITIMACY OF DISSENT

One sentence and one round of applause were enough. A few days before the congress opened, Longo and Ingrao came to a kind of gentlemen's agreement – at least that is what Barca, who acted as a go-between, tells us in his journal. Longo, as Party secretary, was worried there would be an attack on the policy of peaceful coexistence; Ingrao assured him that for his part, out of conviction rather than prudence, he would do nothing of the kind. (Today he confirms that he never had any sympathy for 'guerrilla' impatience.) To remove any doubts on the matter, he had the text of his speech read out in advance to the secretary (I knew this at the time first-hand), who showed no sign of dismay and did not ask for any changes. The most authoritative *ingraini* (Reichlin, Rossanda, Pintor, Natoli, Trentin) gave very measured speeches, mainly addressing areas within their own field of competence. On the third day, Ingrao went to the rostrum and – contrary to what was said afterwards – reaffirmed frankly and effectively, without heat or demagogy, his position on matters that had already been widely debated in the Party. But, at the end, he threw in a sentence that we must quote precisely: 'I would be insincere if I did not say that Comrade Longo failed to convince me by refusing to introduce into our party the new custom of public debate, so that every comrade understands clearly not only the orientations and decisions that prevail and have binding effect, but also the dialectical process of which they are the result.' Almost everyone in the hall reacted with prolonged applause, and this turned into an ovation when Ingrao, in the grip of emotion, raised his clenched fist high in the air. On the tribune, however, nearly everyone kept their arms stiffly crossed. From that point on, the atmosphere in the congress changed totally. One harsh attack followed another in the hall, and even more in the political committee, denouncing factionalism or pointing to the danger of division. In a Communist party, that kind of disinhibited criticism of a leader used to mean almost automatic excommunication – or at least a closing of ranks around the secretary.

Today it seems scarcely credible that measured words and mere applause – itself partly a display of affection, far more than a vote – should have called down such a fierce reaction and opened wounds that took so many years to heal. Or, more specifically, that the ensuing leadership selection process should have been so strict as a result. Moreover, after years in which dissent had been largely tolerated on much more important issues – and precisely for that reason – the open display of disagreement was read as the occasion and instrument of a power struggle. I do not think it was, however. The sudden tightening of control, which I consider to have been a mistake that had negative consequences all round, obeyed a certain logic and had an important political and theoretical motivation. It happened when the delicate issue of reforming the Party itself was added to the many questions that had been under discussion and still remained open. To understand it, then, we need more than a simple reconstruction of events; we need to venture an overall interpretation.

In the history of the Marxist-inspired workers' movement, the role and organizational form of the party has always been a decisive question, a pillar of revolutionary theory, tightly bound up with the question of democracy in general. This was the case long before the October Revolution and the historic split between Social Democrats and Communists; it divided Kautsky and Bernstein, Bernstein and Luxemburg, Bolsheviks and Mensheviks, Luxemburg and Lenin. It divided Lenin and Trotsky, Lenin and Stalin, Gramsci and Togliatti, Togliatti and Secchia, Stalinism and Khrushchevism, Khrushchev and Mao, Mao and his comrades of old. I might add that it was also a bone of contention between parliamentary Labour and the trade union movement in Britain, or among Nenni, Morandi and Basso in Italy. Nor was this fortuitous. Whereas the bourgeoisie constituted and asserted itself as a class through its economic power and cultural supremacy, only expressing itself last of all through political institutions that had no need of parties in the strong sense of the term, the proletariat could not take shape as a ruling class, still less actually aim for power and exercise it, without a permanent political organization. But what guarantee was there that such an organization would be sufficiently independent and compact to avoid being swallowed up by the existing ruling class, and at the same time sufficiently democratic not to become the locus of a new bureaucratic power and privilege?

Today this question is being posed again, not only openly but in a more acute form. More than ever, we can see how democracy without genuine parties degenerates and lays itself open to manipulation, and how what call themselves parties have degenerated into professional apparatuses competing with money and spectacle. For the moment, it is enough to stress the importance that the question of the party form used to have for a political force like the PCI, which joined together millions of members and voters in a complex society, and walked a tightrope between social struggles and parliamentary institutions. And it is enough if I show that, in that transitional period of the 1960s, the party form was a factor that could not be disregarded in any forward movement, and perhaps made it possible for such movement to take place.

The PCI had empirically come up with partial solutions to the problem: its choice of a mass party had survived Cominform pressure through the invention of 'two parties' (a people's party and a cadre party), cemented by a shared faith, high levels of activism, ideology and pedagogy, and a high-quality leadership enjoying the legitimacy of a great past. After the Eighth Congress, this party had absorbed new blood from the Resistance and gradually allowed greater space for debate and research, as well as local experiences. But it had retained a Constitution that protected the unity of the leadership and gave it the first and last word on important choices; the party line was handed down from top to bottom and, although each level was free to discuss it, it was also obliged to pass it on in a collegial manner; the selection of cadres (and, to a slightly lesser extent, of parliamentary deputies) took place by co-option, albeit with reference to individual capacity and proven talent. Especially in the final years of the period, there was extensive freedom of speech together with limited possibilities for influencing decisions: in short, a regime of 'protected democracy'. This is not to say that the democracy was a façade. I will give three examples to illustrate its value and its limitation.

The first concerns me personally. In 1961, when I was a member of the regional secretariat in Lombardy, I was asked to prepare the theses for a regional Party conference. I wrote a text which, I admit, offered much food for thought but was hasty and inaccurate. No one opposed it locally, but when Amendola came to read it one evening to give the green light, he threw it in the waste-paper basket instead. Understandably I found no one to back me up, and so I conscientiously resigned my position. That was not the end of the story, however. Togliatti invited both myself and the Milan leadership to his office in Rome and gave me a whole morning to explain my way of thinking. Interesting ideas, but questionable, he concluded. And, instead of purging me, he appointed me to the *commissione di massa* in Rome headed by Napolitano, where I was made to feel welcome and gradually put to good use.

The second example concerns Rossana Rossanda. Long-time director of the Casa di Cultura in Milan, she had been making it a lively centre for contacts with the most advanced sections of the intellectual world, without concealing her own propensity to prioritize scientific research or new Marxist thinking at the outer limits of orthodoxy, in contrast to the classical Communist emphasis on established intellectuals, history, cinema and the 'fine arts'. But, although Alicata's[1] inclinations were very different from Rossanda's, this did not prevent him or others from giving her national responsibility for the sector in 1962.[2] In her new post, she recalls, she encountered quite a few obstacles and ran up against limits beyond which she was not expected to go. In essence, though, someone who had something useful to say, and the pen and office to do it, met with not only tolerance but – and this is what counts – genuine interest.

The third example concerns the scope offered to local Party organizations, especially where they were part of local government.

---

1. Mario Alicata: top PCI leader with special responsibility for cultural policy; national editor of *L'Unità* from 1962 until his sudden death in 1966.

2. It was in 1962 that Rossana Rossanda moved to Rome, having been appointed head of the Central Committee's cultural policy department.

The town planning policy in Dozza's Bologna,[3] stimulated by such architects as Giuseppe Campos-Venuti or Pier Luigi Cervellati, was quite different from that of the coastal communities, which, though also 'red', were more attracted to the facilities of brick, rich in short-term results but extremely poor in longer-term prospects. Party headquarters let them both get on with it.

During those years, then, the Party did not function badly. Frankly, I myself had no time for the view that organized currents were the way to expand internal democracy.

However, 'protected democracy' was not adequate to tackle the new problems, the general lines that needed to be revised, the multiplicity of positions within the leadership. Even more important was the general state of the Party: not everything was rosy, as the changes within society were having an impact here too. Although the PCI vote was rising, although the workers had turned to struggle and many students to political activity, Party membership had declined in a few years from 2,100,000 to 1,600,000 and that of the FGCI[4] from 358,000 to 170,000, while the factory cells were declining in both numbers and importance. None of this could be attributed to disillusionment or the outbreak of dissent, or to the shock of 1956 (which the Party had come to terms with by now); nor was it a criticism of moderation, since the PCI had animated the struggles of 1960, and 1968 was still a long way off. Still less did it reflect competition from the parties in government, whose decline was even more pronounced.

Especially at that point in time, the main reason for the Party's organizational decline should be sought in its existential and operational characteristics – that is, in how it linked what it was demanding from, and offering on a daily basis to, the new subjects active in society. Young people in particular were not attracted to political activity that mainly consisted of internal meetings, election campaigns and recruitment drives; what they needed was not basic education (now provided by the school system) so much as greater information and more specialized training. They wanted to understand and play a real role in policy formation, bringing their own experiences to bear on it, and they

3. Giuseppe Dozza: highly respected Communist mayor of Bologna from 1945 until 1966.

4. FGCI: Communist youth organization, the Federazione Giovanile Comunista Italiana.

wanted leaders at all levels who could guide their struggles and share their feelings and forms of expression, instead of going on about their glory days in the mountains or the best way to run a local council.

The Party ducked most of these issues. We had often argued about the functioning of the Soviet Party, but had taken the real state of the Italian Party for granted. We were all leaders or clerics. We all spoke of the centrality of the working class, but we did not see that fewer and fewer workers were becoming leaders in their trade union or the Party.

Ingrao alone, perhaps not fully consciously or with adequate arguments, had the courage to face up to the problem. And he suggested a first step towards tackling it. Nothing earth-shaking, in appearance at least – because he did not question democratic centralism (that is, the duty not only to accept but to support and apply the 'current line' in a disciplined manner, without continually challenging it). But nor did he stop at calling for the freedom to express dissent. He wanted the 'current line' to result from a process of argument intelligible to all, and for everyone to be able to contribute to its verification, clarification or correction in the light of events. In essence, then, he proposed a return to democratic centralism as Lenin had conceived and practised it, before the emergency brought on by civil war and scarcity that persisted through much of the 1920s, with Stalin already in power. More specifically, this had meant not only congresses but also 'discussion periods between congresses', involving collective platforms that were put to the vote and a norm that everyone should abide by the decisions and take part in the bodies that implemented them. This 'constitution' was changed in the 1920s, and the CPSU at its Twentieth Congress, like all other Communist parties, had ridded it of arbitrary abuses but had not returned to the original model. Ingrao himself now proposed a limited restoration. It was possible at that time, because the Party had a strong shared culture; its leading group had won recognition and held firm through stormy seas. Its cadre had been trained in the spirit of unity, was not moved by careerist ambition and still freely endured hard work and sacrifice. For these reasons, the expression of disagreement at the top had not caused upheaval. There was a risk that this might happen, however, as in any reform, especially since Togliatti was no longer alive.

Here we see the importance of the general and persistent applause that Ingrao received – a 'deluge', as it were. The simple fact that it was not organized by a faction, or associated with a definite political platform, meant that 'Ingraoism' had spread in the Party like a virus, and that what Ingrao had was not strength but charisma. There could be no half-measures: either the virus was stamped out or it was accepted as a stimulus with which it was possible to live. It was not a question of a power struggle, but of a diffusion of power in the Party; there was a need for mutual trust. But the Party leadership did not trust itself. The mistrust was directed not at Ingrao's ambitions (which were by nature not great) but at the virus and the danger it represented. Not so much Amendola, who remained in the background, but the so-called centrists (Pajetta, Alicati and the secretaries of the large regions) called for the Party to rally around the secretariat and, as I later found out, persuaded the secretariat that an attack was being mounted against it.

A selectively targeted purge then ensued, striking at the most extreme and exposed figures (Rossanda, Pintor, Coppola, Milani, et al.) and isolating Ingrao within the Party's institutions. Berlinguer, until then head of the national secretariat, was accused of excessive tolerance, sent to run the Lazio region and replaced with Napolitano in the key position. A number of others moved on without leaving a forwarding address. I was not removed because there was nothing to remove me from; nor demoted, because I had no rank I could be stripped of. But, viewed as a bad influence who had the ear of others, I was simply confined to my office and given nothing to do. After a few months I went to Amendola and told him I couldn't retire at the age of thirty-two, and asked to be sent to work in one of the smaller regions of the country. He replied without smiling: 'You've got to stay in quarantine, because you're an intelligent young man and we've worked well together, but you still have to learn some Bolshevik discipline.' I picked up my cards and walked away from Botteghe Oscure,[5] to reflect and study by myself. I do not think this was vanity on my part.

The fact that Ingraoism was not a faction is confirmed by the fact that no one protested against their 'punishment', nor did anyone defend anyone else. We simply did not see one another for a long

5. Via delle Botteghe oscure (literally, street of the dark workshops): the site of the PCI headquarters in Rome from 1950 until its dissolution in 1990.

time, while remaining on the friendliest of terms. Perhaps I may be allowed, for emotional reasons, one strictly personal memory. In August of that year I went on a camping trip to the still wild island of Sardinia, where Luigi Pintor was serving his confinement: not to hatch any plots, but to regain my strength with some wonderful sea-bathing.

USSR AND CHINA

In politics, as in each person's life, it is not only the conscious problems and choices that are important, but also what is evaded or disregarded. I therefore cannot omit the fact that, in the intense debate of those years, there was a lack of analysis, reflection and initiative about one great problem. It was a failure shared with the rest of the Italian and European Left, but the Italian Communists paid a higher price for it, even though they were better placed to fill the void. I am referring to what was happening in the world, or rather one part of it.

This sounds paradoxical, because some aspects of world events were not only dramatically evident but produced a great revival of internationalism that formed and oriented whole generations: the Algerian war of independence, the victorious Cuban revolution and the threats that soon rained down on it, the repression in the Congo and, even more ferocious, in Indonesia, and especially the Vietnam war. On all this the PCI campaigned more than any other party, freely discussing such issues as the nature and role of 'national bourgeoisies' or the dangers of neocolonialism as an exit strategy from certain liberation struggles. But it did this without ever denying the importance of coexistence, and therefore of the struggle for peace and disarmament.

The void of which I speak concerns the incipient crisis of the world Communist movement, the break between the Soviet Union and the People's Republic of China, and particularly the two developments that symbolized it and made it irreparable: the collapse of Khrushchevism and the rise to power of Brezhnev and Suslov in the USSR, and the Cultural Revolution in China. It is true that the import of these events became clearer with time, and perhaps it is only today that we can fully grasp the weight they had in shaping the world in which we live. But it is equally true that the crisis of the world Communist movement was only just beginning in the early 1960s, and that it was still possible to contain or correct, if not reverse, the drift of events. The PCI had an influence that would have allowed it to intervene, or at least to take up a more solid and original position amid the global tumult. But it did not properly understand or act upon the opportunity. Togliatti had some responsibility for this at first, but he then had the great merit of trying to find a remedy.

His responsibility was that between the late 1950s and early 1960s, when the disagreement between Khrushchev and Mao was latent but not total, the PCI mainly concerned itself with defending the autonomy of the 'Italian road', while discouraging discussion of the general value this road might have elsewhere. Although Togliatti often said that 'advanced democracy' (beyond the mere form of a multiparty parliamentary system) was a problem that also concerned the socialist societies – and indeed, that only they were in a better position to solve it – he avoided bringing this question into the international debate. Tito did try to do this again, by introducing the experience of self-management in Yugoslavia. But Tito was under suspicion because of the past, Yugoslavia was too small to carry real weight, and the self-management experience had itself been too half-hearted. On the other hand, the 'Italian road' had too little to show for itself, and was too identified with gradualism and parliamentarism, to be accepted as a stimulating model; both the Soviets and the Chinese tended to view it as dangerously 'revisionist', a Trojan horse of social democracy.

Togliatti's merit attaches to the 'Yalta memorandum', the notes he sent to Khrushchev in preparation for a meeting of clarification with the Soviet leadership. When I reread these recently, long after the event, I realized for the first time what was really new in them. While reaffirming the key elements of PCI strategy in Italy, Togliatti also offered a survey of the European situation that made its application to other countries seem plausible. But, above all, he expressed the kind of illuminating premonition that great figures are often capable of formulating on the eve of their death. He who for years had been the object of crude polemic from the Chinese was now saying to Moscow: be careful. If the disagreement between the USSR and China continues to deepen, if a way is not found to reopen dialogue, to improve mutual understanding and, above all, to cooperate at an international level, then everything will be in jeopardy. This is what he wanted to discuss, but by then it was too late. The Soviets were unable and unwilling to understand him, and did not publish his memorandum. Neither did his comrades in Italy understand: although they immediately published the text and gave it great prominence, they did not put its most salient point on the agenda of their forthcoming congress.

In fact, the rift between the USSR and China had been gradually widening between 1958 and 1962, at first in a veiled manner, with botched attempts at reconciliation, then publicly and with increasing acrimony. It was not easy to discuss the issues, because the terms used were intentionally distorted and misleading, often at variance with the actual choices. Was the attempt to rehabilitate Stalin really credible, on the part of those who had always disobeyed him on both tactical and strategic questions? Was it possible to distinguish between those who believed in coexistence (USSR) and those who rejected it, given that the Chinese needed the 'balance of terror' more than ever to protect themselves from attack by the Americans? Was it possible to denounce Moscow's claim to be the guiding state of the world movement, if at the same time any party seeking a 'new road to socialism' was taken to task for 'deviating from Leninism'? Or, conversely, was it reasonable to accuse the Chinese of using language that betrayed their wish for a split? After all, the split was already under way following the withdrawal of Soviet technicians from China, causing huge difficulties, and Moscow had made things worse by suddenly refusing to cover China with its nuclear umbrella. In short, the PCI could have let the facts speak for themselves as it tried to contain an artificial polemic and to express an active and not ineffectual position of its own, in the hope of carrying along many other parties that did not assume that the wrongs were all on one side or the other. Things would have become clearer, and there would have been more point in soberly taking part in the underlying debate.

Khrushchev was removed in the middle of 1964, fortunately without bloodshed, but through the usual palace coup. By way of explanation, Moscow accused him of a personalized style of leadership and of overhasty reforms in agriculture and Party organization – which had indeed been broadly unsuccessful, though no one had objected before. The PCI criticized the methods, but did not ask why Khrushchev had failed and what the new leadership wanted to achieve; a reassurance that the line of the Twentieth Congress would not be changed was all it took to end the matter.

Yet the Twentieth Congress had also been important because of its promise of substantial reforms, as well as its dream of a strong economic growth that would ensure victory in the peaceful competition with capitalism. The defeat of that perspective surely required some analysis. Besides, the replacement of Khrushchev with a new leadership, more sensible perhaps but clearly more grey and bureaucratic, promised nothing more than a period of stability – two decades that led the Soviet Union to the brink of its final decline. This could not have been predicted or evoked aloud, but a certain note of alarm should have been sounded.

A year later the Cultural Revolution began in China. It was possible either to criticize this and express fears about its outcome, or to value it as a new source of hope. But, in the end, the political and strategic content of the Sino-Soviet split was clear enough, and there should have been serious discussion of it. It was always out of order to believe that Mao had recklessly converted to extremism, when in reality he had started from a simple and well-founded observation. The class struggle could reproduce itself even after the conquest of state power – not because, as Stalin said, the old classes became more aggressive and dangerous, but because a new, arrogant and privileged social stratum could emerge within the regime itself (that is, within the party), separated from the broad mass of the population that had long been mired in poverty and cultural backwardness. This could not be prevented by a factional struggle within the party, nor by a multiparty system for which the objective bases did not in any case exist. Nor could it be expected that economic development would gradually solve the problem, since in reality it made it worse. It was therefore necessary to encourage a mass challenge to privilege, and to create a tendency towards equality and democratic participation among younger people who had not experienced the revolutionary war. New revolutionary waves would have to be launched at cyclical intervals, at the level of both ideas and practice. This was the true lesson to be drawn from the glories and the involution of the Russian Revolution. Hence the watchword: 'It is right to rebel!' There was, of course, much truth in this argument.

But there were also reasons to criticize it. Two of them were especially strong. First, if rebellion was not to degenerate into violent and destructive anarchy, there had to be a reference point to guide and stabilize it. That reference point could not be the

Party, which was being made the scapegoat for everything, but had to come from a charismatic leader, Mao himself. However, charisma produces a cult, and a cult produces an even more questionable kind of regime. It also gives rebellion the character of a faith, or rather of a mysticism of which many different forces, competing with one another, consider themselves the legitimate interpreter. This pointed towards increasingly violent confrontation among the 'rebels'.

The second question was the material basis for this revolutionary re-launch. Mao was more aware than anyone of China's economic backwardness, and of the fundamental role that the vast peasant masses played in the economy, but he neither could nor would place the main burden of primitive accumulation on their backs. It was with them that he had carried out a revolution and unified a great country devastated by colonialism and warlordism – not through one big *jacquerie*, but through a war proceeding outward from liberated zones, in which he had introduced such reforms as the emancipation of women from servile status, the expropriation of large landholdings, the distribution of land to the peasantry (who were helped and encouraged to combine into cooperatives), and the building of a disciplined army without privileges. He had educated the masses in egalitarianism by force of example, organized a party with a close-knit but consciously creative ideology, and inserted his guerrilla campaign into the framework of the anti-fascist alliance, supporting himself on the achievements of the Soviet Union, but not subordinating himself to it. Once in power, however, he had had to confront the task of building an industrial base – which the peasantry itself needed, and which the country required to achieve real unity – and of developing an educational system that would both spread mass literacy and produce the skills for economic development. The failure of the 'Great Leap Forward' in 1958 had shown that a subjectivist forcing of the pace was not enough to solve these problems. The point was to modernize the country by spreading the costs, without abandoning the goal of a new society or postponing it to a distant future. The Cultural Revolution was intended to solve this problem: to create anti-bureaucratic antibodies in the people's consciousness, and eradicate the individualism and privilege that were the natural concomitants of modernization. But was a rebellion of the youth, especially students, enough for this purpose? No. And Mao knew it. For he preached that, although the majority of cadres should be subjected to criticism, they were mostly good and redeemable; the rebellion should therefore not turn into summary justice. Leading figures should become workers, without harming production, and an attempt should be made to draw peasants into the revolution, while respecting their convictions and learning austerity from them. Nevertheless, the student rebellion all too easily took the form of humiliating summary trials. When the movement laid siege to factories and fields, it mobilized consciousness but disrupted production; and, although it might abolish formal ranks, the army remained in place, with its own discipline and leadership. The ideology could not, at one and the same time, lay claim to orthodox Marxism and chime with the radical revisionist insistence that communism is born of the materiality of the productive processes. An attempt might be made to force those processes and to avoid 'passing through capitalism', but it was not possible to avoid reckoning with it altogether. In fact, Mao himself stepped on the brake in 1968: the Cultural Revolution had produced hugely important results and its inspiration should not be erased, but it had now to be wound up, without being dispersed. For a time this gradual return to normal was managed in a cautious and balanced manner (leaving aside the jolt of Lin Biao's mysterious liquidation) – first by Mao himself and then, after his death, by Zhou Enlai and Hua Guofeng. But we know today that what followed was a Thermidor. And Chinese history took a quite different road.

There was much to discuss here between 1966 and 1968. Yet the PCI understood little and discussed little. It exorcised the Sino-Soviet conflict by remaining on the outside. We woke up to it only after the Soviet occupation of Czechoslovakia, when the Chinese Cultural Revolution was already ending – and ending badly, as a fait accompli. Everyone at the Eleventh Congress shared the responsibility for this. And the hurried purge that followed it led to a delayed discussion full of blunders. Although the 'tankist' majority criticized some individual decisions, it continued to stand shoulder to shoulder with the Soviet Union, nourishing the implausible hope (in which it did not really believe) that the CPSU would gradually reform itself; it continued to speak of a 'new world government', heedless of the camp in which the PCI had been born and on which it could still exert some influence. Only a small minority set any store by the Cultural Revolution and the possible contagion from it in the world, but it did so only once the Revolution had completed its cycle, in the fond but baseless hope that another would soon follow. This delay and this neglect were bound to weigh heavily in the future.

11

Italy's Long Sixty-Eight

In the 1960s, a second and greater upheaval shook Italy. This time it came from below.

I am referring, of course, to Italy's long sixty-eight. Let us be clear: 1968 was a worldwide phenomenon. In rapid succession, a great anti-establishment movement erupted in nearly all the major Western countries and went down to defeat – a radical, confused and variegated movement, like the one in the middle of the previous century, in 1848. This time, students were the driving force almost everywhere; the university was their headquarters. But the revolt did not hinge on a *cahier de doléances*, drawn up to obtain this or that reform in the educational system or students' living conditions. It struck at the roots of the institutions: teaching methods, forms and criteria of selection, the scale of priorities (manufacturing of consensus, formation of skills required on the labour market). In all these respects, the movement mounted a common challenge to the authoritarian perpetuation of the established social order, which thwarted the freedom to imagine and to help build a different society. The revolt therefore encompassed a whole generation, rejecting values, rules, lifestyles and institutions that had governed society for centuries but had been exhausted by capitalist development itself, and already demystified by a new culture. It was something less than a critique of capitalism as the structure underlying the system, but also something more. In claiming to overcome 'in one leap' the bondage that afflicted collective existence and penetrated into the everyday life of each individual, it seemed to chime with (a mythical version of) the Chinese Cultural Revolution.

Anti-authoritarianism was a great resource, since it made it possible to unite different demands and motives in a non-corporate manner and to sustain other conflicts then at their height (such as the movement against the senseless and bloody war in Vietnam). Moreover, its forms of struggle (university occupations, communal living) could go beyond mere demands to become a collective everyday practice, which left an indelible mark on ways of thinking, on family and interpersonal relations, on attitudes to representative political institutions, and partly too on a new and more radical feminism. On the other hand, anti-authoritarianism was too restrictive when it came to tackling the mode of economic production and the state – two much tougher nuts to crack, involving powers and mechanisms that could not be simply dismantled but had to be controlled and modified, to guarantee better living conditions and greater rights for the majority of the population. It was restrictive also because youth is a temporary state, and students rejecting a particular form of society were destined (if it survived) to form part of its privileged layers. Thus, although the youth revolt of '68 rapidly spread around the world and left its marks everywhere, it soon became isolated and divided, without any repeat performance.

But there is an even more contradictory, though no less important, aspect that we have tended to overlook. The worldwide '68 began with the Tet Offensive, which ushered in the phase of victorious humiliation of the Americans in Vietnam; attempts were still under way in Latin America to imitate the Cuban revolution; Mao reined back the Cultural Revolution in China, without denying its merits and significance; the student revolt shook the whole of France for a time, and although de Gaulle soon got the upper hand he paid a price for it; Arab nationalism had been militarily defeated by the Israeli attack but was politically stronger than before; the 'economic miracle' was running out of steam and would soon be followed by monetary crisis and prolonged stagnation. All this encouraged hope, but more oppressive new realities were already coming into view. The invasion of Czechoslovakia stifled any optimism about the capacity for economic and political reform in the Soviet Union; developments in China pointed to a new course in internal policy, while the now irreversible rift between Beijing and Moscow was altering the whole global balance; the death of Che Guevara founded a myth, but also sealed the defeat of a whole continent; social-democratic governments in Germany and Britain showed no sign of reconsidering the discipline of Atlanticism. In short, a world in turmoil, but crisis in each of the camps. This was enough to spark new thinking about the character and importance of revolution in the West, but certainly not enough to make one think that it was around the corner.

All of us – the New Left, but also the PCI – left these aspects out of the picture, or underestimated their importance. But, if we continue to do this, any discussion of '68 will remain not only incomplete but thoroughly distorted.

THE CENTRALITY OF THE WORKING CLASS

It is useful to dwell for a moment on the specificity of the Italian '68, in terms of length, quality, protagonists and results. Perhaps for the last time, and more than ever before, it was justifiable to speak of an 'Italian case', which, though not as 'spectacular' as the French May, drew attention from abroad. This specificity consisted, shall we say, in a 'happy encounter', largely explicable by previous history but partly accidental.

As capitalism changed, many social conflicts, many forms and subjects of revolt and many cultural rifts had emerged in other countries at various times, or anyway not in synchrony with one another; the system had been able to confront and neutralize them separately, sometimes even deriving a boost from them. Above all, the system had managed to minimize, or marginalize, the presence of trade unions and political organizations that might offer the protest movement some representation, or at least a solid support.

In Italy, by contrast, many rebellious impulses peaked simultaneously for a number of years around 1968, with the capacity not only to come together but to interact with one another – when the material base in which they had originated still had body, when the masses recognized good reasons for their existence, when working-class unions and parties with an anti-capitalist inspiration were still strong and rising, and when the governments in office were shaky and discredited. Before venturing a judgement on that still quite controversial upsurge, we need to reconstruct the character and trajectory of the various movements that made it up, and the way in which the mass organizations reacted to it.

I shall begin with the workers' struggles, since the schema later fixed in popular memory is not the truth, or only partly. It is not true that the student revolt preceded the social conflict and radicalized it, only to be then held back by wise trade union leaders, and repressed by Communist apparatuses. It might be possible to read the French May in that way. But events in Italy were much more complex, mainly because the workplace conflict between capital and labour was at the heart of them, and because their protagonist was the working class in flesh and blood. I know the risk I am taking when I use the expression 'centrality of the working class' today. Too often it has been invoked to indicate a faith in something still to come or already on the wane, or presented in so many different ways that its meaning has been lost. I should like therefore to make it clear that, when I speak of the working class in the Italian '68, I am being damn specific. I mean a population of wage-earners mostly engaged in fragmented manual labour within an ever more rigidly organized production cycle, concentrated in medium-to-large companies where everyone felt part of a collective and, gradually, of a class – mostly industrial workers, then, at a time when industry in general employed a majority of the labour force and was the engine pulling the country's economy. An ideological conviction inside me, having nothing to do with myth, always impelled me to recognize the birthright of that class; its primacy found corroboration at that time, although in today's society I grant that it must at least be reconsidered. What I am referring to now, however, is a specific, indisputable fact: a cycle of workers' struggles that lasted more than a decade and, by virtue of its scale and quality, spoke to many other movements and profoundly shook the balance of economics and politics in Italy.

Its origins go back to the labour revival of 1960–3, which, as we have seen, went beyond wage issues to raise demands connected with the organization of work, engaging in forms of struggle that tended to undercut not only the despotism of the bosses but also the vertical structure of the trade unions, in a constant interplay between national and company-level bargaining. In every respect, those struggles achieved significant results, during a period that also saw the rebirth of militant anti-fascism and the politicization of young people. Social movement, union and party marched together and broke new ground together. And that experience, led by the PCI, directly resulted in major changes in the culture and practice of Catholic social organizations (CISL, ACLI).

In 1964–6 the bosses and the government responded with a deflationary squeeze, export of capital and limited but telling technological innovations, mainly designed to boost productivity, which had the effect of reducing employment and intensifying the labour process. In the space of one year, for example, Pirelli increased its total output by 28 per cent; Fiat almost doubled it at Mirafiori, with the same workforce and wage bill. Other companies that were unable or unwilling to follow suit started to lay workers off. All this temporarily served to dampen down disputes, but it also intensified the workers' anger and belied the reformist promises of the Centre Left at a political level.

No sooner did the economy start to recover than local disputes flared up over piecework and line speeds. But now, since the labour of white-collar workers and technicians was also subject to fragmentation and intensification, militancy often extended to occupational categories that had hitherto remained aloof. The year 1967 witnessed struggles in the steel, auto and clothing industries (Italsider, Rex, Zanussi, Dalmine, Lebole, Magnetti Marelli, Tosi, Autobianchi) and, more unexpectedly, at the textile giant Marzotto. In the course of the year, 3,878 supplementary agreements were successfully reached. Fiat as usual was a special case, only this time for the better. In March 1968 the company tried to head off a dispute by making a deal with the union itself; but FIM and FIOM rejected this, 100,000 workers went on strike and won more, for the first time in fourteen years.

Other things are now almost forgotten. Between 1967 and 1968 two broad struggles broke out: one against the pensions system, which had always been vague, stingy and unfair, the other against the wage gap that left workers in the South 20 per cent worse off. The victories were important: a pension totalling 80 per cent of final salary after forty years of employment, the right to a pension after thirty-five years, and complete abolition of regional pay differentials by the year 1975. No less significant was the way in which these results were achieved, for the three union federations initially signed a draft agreement that was challenged by the rank-and-file organizations, so that the CGIL called another general strike alone and carried everyone with it until the successful conclusion.

This brings us to the next round of national wage-bargaining, the 'hot autumn' which marked a real qualitative leap. The platform of demands, with engineering workers in the lead, was unusually ambitious: sizeable wage rises, equal for all; a cut in the working week from forty-eight to forty hours; the same regulations for office and shopfloor workers; a right to hold factory meetings in company time. Even more novel were the forms of struggle and the composition of decision-making bodies. Strikes were accompanied with impressive demonstrations to win public support; action continued during negotiations; a number of strike hours were assigned to individual factories and departments, supported by improvised demonstrations to win over waverers and to interrupt the production cycle; the workers themselves spontaneously slowed the speed of production and organized on-off stoppages. This was not Luddism: it was a way of making strikes more costly for the bosses and less costly for the workers. As to the decisions, they were not left up to inconclusive general meetings of the workforce, but proceeded through prior consultation on the set of demands, then the election of delegates from each section, in which every worker had a vote, then delegate meetings in the form of a factory council. Full delegations from these councils could attend national negotiations with the employers, and often influenced them with applause or booing.

Some facts speak for themselves. In 1965 there were thousands of workplace committees in the engineering industry, somewhat ossified and controlled from above, representing 500,000 workers; in 1972, just 4,300 factory councils represented a million workers and were controlled from below. Another two figures testify to the contagious effect and political shifts that gradually occurred outside industry: whereas in 1968 the CGIL had 4000 members among public employees, it had increased this to 90,000 by the early 1970s. Membership grew rapidly when the rank and file raised its sights and the quality of its demands, and when the union accepted initiatives from below to give them effective representation. Were these trade union struggles? Certainly, and that social subject could not do without them. But it is impossible to deny their political value when one looks at their aims and results, at their forms and general spirit, at the level of rank-and-file involvement, and at the cadre that rapidly took shape within them.

The strength of the movement lay in this mingling, or let us say ambiguity, between trade union bargaining and radical inspiration or behaviour. This persisted after the movement passed its peak, leading to important conquests (for example, the Statuto dei Lavoratori,[1] the 150 paid hours for further education, an integrated salary scheme for office and shopfloor workers) and to the consolidation of trade union unity (the FLM, the unity pact among the federations). More important, it hinted at a general political strategy adumbrated by Gramsci in his time: the idea that, especially in the West, the revolution had first to progress as a social movement before there could be any question of taking power. The working class had to acquire the capacity of a ruling class, to capture fortifications, field intermediate objectives, and establish not only alliances but a hegemonic historical bloc.

But this ambiguousness of trade unionism and politics in workers' struggles involved a contradiction. The more a struggle grew and asserted itself, eroding the power of the bosses in the factory and the associated organization of work, and the more it became necessary to improve the workers' living conditions outside the factory (along with those of broad sectors also being sacrificed), the more did two huge interconnected obstacles emerge in the path of the movement. On the one hand, talk of economic crisis was used to blackmail the workers, especially at a time when capitalist development was facing difficulties and industry was becoming integrated into, and having to compete in, international markets. On the other hand it was necessary to find resources for the 'social state', and to develop a normative framework and managerial capacities to tilt those resources toward the satisfaction of collective needs, in accordance with a precise scale of priorities. In both cases, the problem of a profound turn in politics was bound to come up – especially with regard to economic policy, the key support for the capacity and development of the movement.

In the short term, the problem appeared and was insoluble. The government's forces were in full-scale decline as they entered 1968: the Socialists had foolishly attempted unification with the Social Democrats and exited from it in a comatose state, while the Christian Democrats were more than ever obsessed with clinging onto power and divided by internal brawls. There was no scope

1. Statuto dei Lavoratori: the term commonly used to refer to the Law on the Protection of the Freedom and Dignity of Workers and of Trade Union Freedom in the Workplace, and on Norms of Employment, passed in May 1970.

for serious dialogue with them. In the abstract this might have been to the advantage of the Left opposition, but worrying signs were simultaneously beginning to come from Italian society.

I am referring not to the 'strategy of tension' (of which more later), but to the subversive revolts that broke out in Reggio di Calabria and L'Aquila, which showed how upsurges in rundown areas rife with clientelism and organized crime can push people towards a reactionary localism. Less theatrical, but perhaps even more alarming, was what happened in Battipaglia, in the Campania region, because the fascists did not have much of a hand in it, and the impetus for rebellion was neither localism nor mass marginalization. It was one of the few areas in the South where development was clearly in evidence, albeit with the concomitants of low pay, job insecurity, clientelism and *caporalato*.[2] When redundancies were announced in the tobacco industry, the whole town rose up and occupied the railway station to make its voice heard; the police intervened violently, and the population responded by burning the town hall, as the centre of all vices. It was a *jacquerie* in a modernized society, directed against everything and everybody, mirroring the reality in an important part of the country where trade unions and labour disputes did not suffice to express and channel an uncontrollable and legitimate rage.

The elections of 1972 provided a snapshot of the real relationship of forces in Italy: the PCI's advance was halted, the total Left vote shrank (collapse of the PSI, humiliating results for *Il Manifesto* and the Livio Labor list[3]), the DC retained its vote but shifted to the right, and the MSI made a leap forward. The situation had evidently not stabilized, but an Andreotti-Malagodi government was formed with the support of the MSI. The working class did not give in, however: it soon won an integrated salary scheme for office and shopfloor workers, and supplementary bargaining and disputes at company level did not stop (strike hours in 1973 were down only on the peak of 1969). We know what the PCI came up with in 1972 as a political outlet for the movement: National Unity.

2. *Caporalato*: the system, once prevalent in the South, whereby charge hands hired labour at designated points in the street for a day's work at a time.

3. In the previous year, 1971, Livio Labor and others had founded a small left-wing Catholic party, the Movimento Politico dei Lavoratori (MPL). After its failure in the 1972 elections (0.36% of the vote), the great majority of its members joined the Socialist Party.

Could not something different have been done, in terms of political content and protagonists; something that reflected the enormous changes in the world and Italian society – but with a reasoning and orientation similar to Togliatti's at the end of the anti-fascist war, when conditions had been so much more difficult? Could the PCI not have remained within the mass struggle, gaining credibility and guiding it with its consent, not towards an early 'revolution' but to a stage on the approach road, whose distant objective would be clearly stated and evident? Before we discard this possibility – assuming that it can be discarded with serious arguments – we need to complete our survey of the long '68.

STUDENTS AND OTHERS AROUND THEM

The other protagonist of the Italian '68 was, of course, the student movement, which exploded suddenly and impulsively – a little later than in the United States or Germany, but in time with the French May. The different experiences displayed the same aspect of a cultural, above all ethical, generational revolt, with a strong anti-imperialist component, although the specific material conditions and historical backgrounds of each country also gradually asserted themselves.

In Italy's war of liberation, as well as in the ensuing two decades, a large number of young and very young people participated, together or on opposite sides, in harsh political struggles that involved a high degree of ideological conviction and class differentiation: first, anti-fascists against fascists, then Communists against Catholics. This gave rise to large and extremely militant youth organizations. The 'Green Berets', guided by Luigi Gedda's Catholic Youth movement (GIAC), had a presence everywhere, from St Peter's Square to individual parishes; the Communist FGCI had half a million members all through the 1950s. Students, particularly university students, had remained a minority on the margins, for the simple reason that the children of workers and peasants usually went straight into work after elementary school, or stayed behind to work in the family; only the children of the bourgeoisie went to university. At least after 1948, young Catholic students no longer felt the need to involve themselves in day-to-day political struggle, and Communist students were thin on the ground. When I was at school, the few small demonstrations were organized by a para-fascist minority in favour of Italian rule in Trieste.

By 1960, however, as we have seen, a new batch of young people had joined the front line of workers' struggles, driven by militant anti-fascism and early anti-imperialist sentiments (before Vietnam there was Congo, Palestine and Cuba). Students were still a minority in the streets and squares, but they were not there as students. The conclusion is simple: a highly politicized, left-oriented new generation was taking shape in Italy; even part of the Catholic Youth, after its break with the Gedda leadership, was beginning to gravitate towards the workers' movement. But all demanded that the Left parties renew themselves, meanwhile tending to support them rather than actually join. In the absence of renewal, an intellectually capable minority looked for new masters or formed dissident cliques (workerist, Marxist-Leninist, Trotskyist); the 'groups' of 1968 already had their future leaders. The FGCI tried to relate to them and open a dialogue, until it was 'normalized' at the Eleventh Party Congress. An even more important factor, though, was the material situation in education and among the students who spearheaded the anti-establishment challenge. In addition to explaining the strength and character of the student movement at that time, this was a national issue that has never actually been resolved.

Mass education in Italy suffered from the same problems as elsewhere, though here they were more acute and widespread. Like the new industrialization, it sprang up in the course of a few years, without any reform and without adequate funding. Rossana Rossanda's book on students in 1968 draws an effective picture of the situation.[4] In Italy, the uniform and compulsory secondary education that had long existed in other advanced countries was not introduced until 1960, but the only measures to make it more accessible were the elimination of Latin from the syllabus and the hiring of more traditionally-trained teachers. The middle classes, a little better off and as hungry as ever, anticipated the growing demand for skilled employees by making every effort to send their children to university, access to which was being gradually opened up. Even those who could not afford full-time study found some little job that enabled them to stay in the race for a career that required at least a symbolic qualification (the worker-students).

4. Rossana Rossanda, *L'anno degli studenti*, Bari: De Donato, 1968.

So, by 1967 university students numbered approximately half a million, concentrated in twenty-three cities (almost the same number as at the beginning of the century). Ordinary professors, the so-called *baroni*, who had numbered 2000 for every 43,000 students in 1923, had jumped to 3000 for 450,000 students, required to perform teaching duties for fifty hours a year (exams included). The lecture theatres could not hold even the minority of students who regularly attended courses, and laboratories and libraries were difficult to access. As a result, only one student in four actually obtained a degree, the other three having wasted their time or become tied to extracurricular activity. The parliamentary Left demanded action and funding to remedy this intolerable state of affairs, but it ran up against budgetary constraints as well as resistance from the *baroni*, many of whom were themselves Centre Right deputies, and who had no wish to give up their dual responsibilities for a less powerful, full-time position. In any case, the modernization proposals would have made the problems worse, since the labour market could not absorb a growing number of graduates – especially graduates who lacked the professional capacities for the work they would be required to do. Less well-known but even more scandalous was the de facto social discrimination which meant that out of 100 graduates, only one came from a working-class or peasant family. Workers ended up financing a university education for the children of the bourgeoisie, who by the same token claimed a much higher grant. This sheds light on the social role not only of the university but of the whole educational system. Who went to university, and why was the drop-out rate so high? The disaster can also be traced back to lower levels of schooling.

By its nature, secondary education has a dual function: to develop a general intellectual capacity and a view of the world, and to provide the knowledge base for later professional specialization. The traditional school, associated with the name of Gentile,[5] had contents, methods and structures (the *liceo*) that took seriously the task of training an elite and passing on reasonably up-to-date knowledge. It was assisted in this by well-to-do families who not only gave their offspring an early training in intellectual effort, but nearly always made culture a part of their lives. Mass

5. Giovanni Gentile: self-proclaimed 'philosopher of fascism'. In 1923, as minister of education in the Mussolini government, he was responsible for a major and long-lasting reform of the secondary school system.

education undercut all that. First, the ceaseless transformation of culture and social relations, as well as of productive technologies, made it impossible simply to pass on fixed knowledge and occupational profiles. On the contrary, these now required the critical capacity to confront ethical problems and new technological issues. Second, knowledge bound up with traditions could no longer be handed down, still less assimilated, by people who did not have a ruling-class background. And third, the pillar even of well-to-do families had collapsed: if the older generation tried to impose its way of seeing things it was not even listened to. Besides, it had little to say, since professional specialization and cultural change were gradually alienating even adults from the exercise of their intellect. It has been statistically demonstrated that people forget all they learn at school (except for things that enter narrowly into their everyday practice) within ten years of leaving it. The new illiteracy of the elderly compounds an earlier lack of education and the effects of ultra-fragmented labour or even research. Traditional education, crammed in raw, actually excludes the subaltern classes; a wish to avoid overload and to make things easy for everyone ends up creating a cultural and behavioural 'grand casino', in which higher training is delegated to 'centres of excellence', while lower levels are left to the mass media. The half-baked result is a shapeless mass, destined for repetitive tasks, and perpetual confusion. Such was the mass education that emerged in Italy, without the corrective measures that other countries had been applying to limit the damage at least from the point of view of the system (expensive elite universities and selective brain imports in the United States, *Grandes Ecoles* and *instituts* in France, high-quality Institutes of Technology in Germany). This material plight helps to explain why the student protest movement was so radical in Italy, and highlights the irresponsible blindness of the government (as well as the Left) to a problem that was so fundamental for the future of the country. It should have been tackled at that time, precisely when a revolt in society made that possible, and when people were searching for new lifestyles and the country was on the eve of a new technological revolution (computers, biogenetics).

Let us now return to the student movement and try to identify its different phases, without forgetting that they sometimes overlapped with, or retained traces of, one another. The first phase (1967–9) was marked by the spontaneous mass character of the revolt, which in a few months spread with varying degrees of intensity to all parts of the country, specifically as a student movement. In its ideas it owed a great deal to the Germans, in its practice to the Americans, and in both to the short but dazzling May events in France. The unifying element was anti-authoritarianism, soon evident from the fact that the main form of struggle was to occupy the university, as permanently as possible. It was there that the students held their frequent assemblies, and even interrupted lectures; they camped out there to discuss and decide on tactics, to meet new people and have fun; sometimes the rector would call in the police to chase them out, but it was never long before they were back. In Italy, more than in other countries, there was initially a precise focus of attack: the teaching methods and content, and the material and moral condition of the students. Indeed, in the pilot experiences (Trento, Venice, the Milan architecture faculty), the first step was linked to the specific reality of a discipline or a situation (what is sociology? what should architecture aim at? what should a sociologist or architect be like?). Nor was it by chance that the first national coordination took place around the occupation of the Campana Palace in Turin, which resulted in the drafting of the document *Contro l'università, potere studentesco*. It soon took on the character of a broader protest movement, however: that is, starting from a specific situation, it identified the main sources of student discontent, mobilized the mass of students, and produced not only a critique but a victorious struggle, above all against the arrogance and negligence of the academic establishment and the stifling regulations and organizational structures that testified to rot and decay. Occupations, and the expression of criticism or ridicule during lectures, were enough to make the point that 'the emperor had no clothes'. But, little by little, the movement was also able to grasp the logic underlying the whole institution and the wider role it played in the social system – and would continue to play even if, or when, it was modernized.

It was possible to see an analogy with the trajectory of workers' struggles, from immediate demands through rank-and-file insubordination to demands for power. There was also a profound distrust of any kind of organized structure, any kind of delegation, even of the very idea of an 'intermediate objective' – hence the refusal to analyse the overall framework that the students rightly sought to subvert, but which could not be subverted in a single blow. This refusal, natural enough in a spontaneous student movement, served to protect it from the corporatism of a privileged layer and to make of it a social subject in its own right. This was particularly fruitful in the early stages. In fact, something similar had happened in the partisan war, becoming almost a norm for young people – the idea of fighting for freedom, but also the idea that, in taking up arms and risking one's life, one would carry the whole country along and change society. The PCI could have, now as then, taken such aspirations to heart and, by operating as a recognized part of the movement, given it an orientation that corresponded to the limits of the historical situation. After all, would the workers' upsurge have acquired the scale and character that it did without a trade union prepared to transform itself in order to represent and lead it? But the PCI, by contrast, was incapable of grasping the dimensions of the student revolt in its early stages. Left to itself, the movement did as much as it could. But it was not enough – in fact, the experience was full of traps.

The second period, from 1969 to 1971, began on a note of high danger (largely avoided) and continued with a great opportunity that was sadly wasted. The danger was conjured up by the forces of reaction and the state apparatuses. I am referring to the terrorist bombing of the National Agricultural Bank on Piazza Fontana in Milan – an incident on which it is as well to linger for a moment, since it would affect the history of the whole country. The 'strategy of tension' that it inaugurated would last for years, with occasional spikes; bombs and often savage acts of terrorism (from Peteano to Brescia and Bologna) both preceded and followed the Milan outrage of 12 December 1969. We know that all these incidents were fascist provocations, and that rogue elements within the state also had a hand in them. In fact, minus the terrorist aspect, the dark side of the regime had made itself felt throughout the 1960s and before: from SIFAR's Piano Solo[6] to Miceli, Borghese and Propaganda Due.[7] But Piazza Fontana was of a

6. Piano Solo: the plan for military intervention to restore public order, drawn up by the military intelligence service (SIFAR).

7. General Vito Miceli, then head of the SID (Military Intelligence and Security Service) and a member of the secret masonic Propaganda Due (P-2) lodge, was arrested on charges of conspiracy in 1974 in connection with the failed coup d'état planned in 1970 by Junio Valerio Borghese, a notorious army commander from the fascist period. Miceli was eventually acquitted in 1978.

different order. Not so much because the secret services were directly involved (we are still not quite sure how) in planning the operation and shifting the blame, but because people right at the top took the opportunity to mount a precisely targeted attack against the student and workers' movement (the coincidence between the two dates is all too revealing). I am not interested here in establishing whether Pinelli was pushed or not,[8] nor in reconstructing the clumsy, scandalous attempt to frame the 'anarchist dancer'. What interests me is that, a few hours after the bombing, none other than the minister of the interior leaked that the police had reason to focus their enquiries on the Left, and a frenzied press campaign got under way, with daily updates from the 'investigation', to make this idea stick. And it interests me that the onslaught of disinformation was directed against the far Left and a small section of the democratic intelligentsia. The operation was too crude and amateurish to succeed, but for a long time the PCI did no more than say 'let there be light' – and when there was light it did not invoke the plot to mount a full-scale attack on the dark face of the regime. This opened an unbridgeable gap with the student movement; worse, the Party gave up one of its classical weapons, democratic mobilization. The movement came out of the episode invigorated rather than discredited, but more convinced than ever that all institutions were rotten and capable of anything: the PCI itself was, if not an enemy, an adversary, or at the very least an untrustworthy interlocutor. Part of the movement believed that state violence had to be countered with defensive violence. The idea of armed struggle was still some way off, or the object of mere chatter, but the general view was now that any demonstration that did not end in a little skirmish with the police was just a 'stroll'. This struck me as foolish, yet I feel a little embarrassed at how I rushed to distance myself from it! Was this wisdom, or incurable moderation?

As to the missed opportunity, it came with the 'hot autumn' of the workers. Hard facts convinced the students – and not only those who had long been expecting a workers' revolt – that it was necessary to 'go to the workers' (as the Russian Narodniks had gone to the peasantry), and to build with them the new political

8. Giuseppe Pinelli: anarchist railwayman who was seen falling to his death from the window of a Milan police station in December 1969, after three days of interrogation ostensibly in connection with the Piazza Fontana bombing.

organization that both groups lacked. This turn expressed a real necessity, not a false ideological contrivance. If it was true – and it was, or so people believed – that the educational system could not be really changed without changing society as a whole, then it was natural that the students should seek to join up with the workers, precisely at that 'magical' time for both. And if it was true that they shared aspirations and experiences which the traditional political forces were unable or unwilling to represent, it was natural that they should seek to fill the vacuum together. Of course, not everyone followed this through in practice; it was a terribly difficult choice to make, because what it involved was not 'joy and revolution' but the sacrifice of constant hard work to break down a wall of stubborn mistrust, to find a common language, to work out what to say about new problems in an unfamiliar environment. But an exodus there was. Thousands of young students spent more than a year at the factory gates and in workers' bars, adopting their ways and stoking their sense of pride. The students transmitted some of their own enthusiasm and rejection of established authority, and managed to recruit several thousand workers into political collectives, soon giving them the leading role. In some places (Pirelli, Montefiori, Porto Maghera in Venice, Bologna), students helped to build labour organizations independent of the trade unions and political parties, if not in open conflict with them. To dismiss such activity as an irrelevant or even harmful fantasy, to deny its formative ethical value, is both foolish and ungenerous – even if some of those who lived through it often contributed to that impression. A critical balance sheet is certainly desirable, but for that period at least the experience should be worn as a medal, not borne as a cross.

When we turn to the practical application and results of that turn, our judgement has to be more severe – and, in my case too (for the little I contributed), self-critical. The students went to the factories sincerely proclaiming that 'the working class must be in charge'. But in reality, without meaning to, they seemed to be telling the workers what to do. And what they told them was more than a little mistaken. First of all, they poured scorn on the trade union struggle, which, of its very nature, however advanced, must always end in an agreement and, if it is a good one, be resumed later when the relationship of forces permits, or if the employer tries to renege. 'Permanent revolution', always running, always forging ahead, is a foolish idea, reserved for those who can do without a job and have no children to support. To refuse to accept this meant clashing head-on with the union and denying its importance for the workers, at a time when it was becoming more open to rank-and-file initiatives and ensuring that the most advanced struggles did not remain isolated at the apex of the industrial apparatus. Second, by putting all existing political organizations into the same bag and disregarding their different histories, the students reduced the possibility of a political turn to a timeless abstraction; they did not bother to ask themselves how, despite all the challenges from below, the PCI could maintain its strength and even increase it among popular layers. To keep repeating that the PCI had been in the wrong camp for decades, while noting that it still had widespread support among the workers, was like saying that the workers were too stupid to see what was before their eyes. It was also a way of reaffirming that any intermediate objective, any partial change in the regime and the workers' living conditions, was an idle fancy.

A number of small, though not too small, political groups took shape around this experience and these diffuse convictions, mostly with a background in the student movement. They were sustained by selfless, untiring activism and often guided by valuable leaders, but their distorted view of reality, and their mistaken belief that a revolutionary break was on the horizon, meant that they lacked incentives for more complex analyses and strategic innovation. Paradoxically, therefore, a sizeable movement born out of the new contradictions of modernity, eager to propose or speed up a clearer alternative to the existing political strategies, adopted a political-ideological approach and organizational forms that drew upon the old arsenal of the far Left (spontaneist, workerist or Trotskyist), or else upon mythical versions of evocative but recently defeated game plans, such as the multiplication of guerrilla campaigns ('one, two, a hundred Vietnams') or a repeat of the Cultural Revolution outside its Chinese context. None of these ideologies stood up, especially since they had to cope with sectarianism and growing conflict among the individual groups. A long cycle of social struggles and cultural upheaval thus left the student movement weaker, not stronger, in both extent and intensity. Enfeebled, but not yet extinguished. University occupations flared up sporadically in places. Demonstrations against fascism or in support of Vietnam brought out tens of thousands of young people. Even the secondary schools showed signs of agitation.

The third period (1970–2) was therefore also important, in that it witnessed new experiments, however belated and unsuccessful, that offer food for thought. The small minority who were beginning to gear up for armed struggle will be considered at a later point, when they become significant. The bulk of the movement ramified in two directions. One branch, mainly consisting of the 'groups' and those recruited into them from popular layers, tried to re-launch the social struggle outside the factory around the theme of collective needs, particularly the housing shortage and exorbitant rents. (The union federations had been doing the same, in fact, with quite different methods but equally disappointing results.) The watchword was 'Let us take back our city!', the methods included squatting empty property (sometimes before construction was completed) and rent strikes. Various buildings in the big cities (Milan, Rome, Turin) were occupied and held for a time against police attempts to clear them, and in some districts a number of tenants stopped paying rent. But the weak points of both actions were that they never grew to become anything more than exemplary, and that they concentrated on municipal housing in popular districts – in the hope that the local authority would ratify the occupation and refrain from evictions. Consequently, other needy families who were on the waiting list justifiably protested against the squatting. Tensions rose when someone occasionally tried to make money out of it, creating conflict with poor people in the neighbourhood and fierce arguments among the squatters themselves. It was then that the police would arrive to restore order. On the other hand, the union-led protest actions did not mobilize large numbers and obtained only crumbs from the increasingly conservative governments of the day; sometimes the upshot would even be a loosening of planning regulations that gave a further boost to property speculation.

Another branch of the movement, centred on Milan, returned to the university with a plan for 'partial alternative use of the institution': no longer just occupations and protests, but the organization of seminars, even whole courses, to redefine the content of teaching and focus it more on the analysis of society, critique of intellectual roles and professions, and the development of a new political culture, keeping the lecture theatres open in the evening for the benefit of worker-students. This new initiative never really took off, however, and did not last long. In many cases it lapsed into something much more modest and questionable: collective examinations, guaranteed grades. Probably because it came so late in the day, without an adequate level of participation, it was overwhelmed by the logic of the 'political group'.

And yet had the experiment begun earlier, on a larger scale and with greater conviction, some of the conditions present at the time would have favoured its success; it is also worth remembering that these 'favourable conditions' were valuable in themselves. I am referring above all to the movement that '68 unleashed in intellectual circles, both inside and outside academia. Workers' struggles, student struggles, democratic and internationalist struggles: these all had an impact on intellectuals and the institutions in which they worked and were organized. It was not only at the margins that individuals and collectives were critically reflecting on the role they were required to play, and on the underlying culture in which they played it.

I will simply mention a few examples of a broader phenomenon: the Medicina Democratica movement, headed by Giulio Maccacaro, which mainly concerned itself with industrial environments and the need for preventive medicine, but whose concept of a general right to health resonated among thousands of young doctors not seeking a highly paid niche in the private sector; Psichiatria Democratica, headed by Franco Basaglia and the Trieste group, which campaigned against the institution of the lunatic asylum and argued for new thinking about the relationship between mental illness and health; the 'scandalous' initiatives of certain industrial tribunals, later leading to Magistratura Democratica, which challenged the rigid hierarchy of magistrates and the limited independence of the judiciary; the editorial committees of journalists demanding greater freedom from the press magnates (not so much publishers as industrial groups), or from the Christian Democrat fiefdom in television; the protest by film directors against the commercialization of festivals, or the discussion among top scientists about the perversion of scientific neutrality; the police pressure for demilitarization of the force and the creation of an independent trade union; or even the 'stealthy' formation of a Left in the diplomatic corps. All this was reflected by an unprecedented split in the academic world: not only a more democratic attitude on the part of lecturers to the student challenge, but also a frequent readiness to take part in renewing their own discipline and re-examining its relationship with other disciplines. In short, there were new resources for the development of the university's educational role and the orientation of its research, without neglecting its function of reproducing the skills necessary for society and the economy.

There was, and still is, much to discuss about how the educational system should be equipped to deal with these new tasks. Lifelong education, the relationship between schooling and work, the training of lecturers, the quality and quantity of funding: these are some of the areas to be considered. After all, legislation and bureaucracy cannot give birth to a new system: it can only arise out of a great cultural movement related to new hegemonies in society. Today, forty years later, we finally have the educational system designed by Mrs Moratti,[9] a late import from America, like the hamburger that is also on the decline over there. The reformers in our country are serious, down-to-earth people, who need time to think and still more to act.

So, you can find as many defects as you like in the student movement and 1968 in general, and you may wish – though I never go that far – to wash your hands of the whole business. But to deny that Italy's long '68 offered extraordinary resources and forward-looking ideas, would in my view be culpable and obtuse.

THE VATICAN COUNCIL

To complete the picture of Italy's '68, we need at least to mention another event: the Second Vatican Council. If I only say 'mention', it is not because I underestimate its importance and complexity, but, on the contrary, because it was a key moment in a 'parallel history' – that of the Church and religion in general, of its evolution and later involution. The world of secular politics and culture was wrong to consider it irrelevant, to think that the formula 'a free church in a free state'[10] was the last word on the matter, or

9. Letizia Brichetto-Arnaboldi Moratti: businesswoman, wife of oil magnate Gianmarco Moratti, and Berlusconi's education minister from 2001 to 2006.

10. 'A free church in a free state': first used in France in the early nineteenth century, the phrase is mainly associated in Italy with Cavour's speech of March 1861, proclaiming Rome the capital of the Kingdom of Italy.

to conclude that the rise of science and technology had doomed the Church to a culturally marginal position. The fact is that, for good or ill, it has continued to interact with the history of Italy and the world, right up to the present conflicts among various fundamentalisms. From Pius XII through John XXIII to Wojtyla and Ratzinger (not to speak of Islam, or the spread of new sects and superstitions), we are talking of a special history. And those who, like myself, do not believe that its stages are inspired by the Holy Spirit, or even that the ideas it throws up take account of the reality in which pastoral activity has to take place, cannot avoid investigating how it relates to history in general. As far as postwar Italy is concerned, the religious question continued to have a directly political significance, because a party was founded there on the principle of the unity of Catholics, and a powerful and vital network of Catholic mass organizations developed throughout the country. Moreover, the Catholic religion has always linked faith with good works, seeking to give the latter a basis in 'natural law' (that is, to demonstrate that faith and reason, each with its own history, are consistent with each other).

For now I shall focus on certain tendencies that specifically relate to the 1960s and the upsurge of '68. These were years when a profound religious and political reorientation in the Church, together with an equally profound turn to the transformation of society, favoured dialogue and even degrees of convergence with other forces, although there were obstacles on both sides that it was not able to overcome. On the side of the Church, a first new direction partly opened up with John XXIII's two encyclicals (*Mater et Magistra* and *Pacem in Terris*), which affirmed peace as a value of the highest importance and drew a distinction between error and those who err. On the Communist side, Togliatti reciprocated by offering a redefinition of the Catholic question. This first new opening encouraged a change in the behaviour, if not the culture, of large sections of the two great social organizations (the CISL and the ACLI) which played a part, not without hesitations, in the labour revival of 1960. This did not prevent the Christian Democrats – for political advantage, not for religious reasons – from using the opening to the Socialists to shut the Communists even more firmly out of the picture; nor from watering down the proposed reforms so much that the whole operation ended in failure.

The real turn came with the calling of the Vatican Council, decided on and pushed through by John XXIII, then followed up more cautiously by Paul VI. It was even more radical at the religious than at the political level, but once again it is possible to use worldly instruments to interpret the course of events, without dragging in the Holy Spirit. Two new features of the historical situation were inciting and enabling the Church to engage in a bold reform. The first and most evident, and also the most inescapable, was the following. The Catholic Church had always considered itself a 'universal Church' and had indeed long been one, but essentially because of the (often atrocious) imperial role of Western Europe in carrying its civilization to the rest of the world. The Church's claim to universality, evident in the Middle Ages, suffered deep cracks as a result of heresies and schisms, but these all involved fellow-Christians, divided from Rome and among themselves. The Church was able to expand into continents which, though still dominated by various other religions, could be considered 'missionary lands'. For some time, however, Catholic universality had been more apparent than real – and even appearances had crumbled once the colonial peoples began to throw off colonial rule and to claim autonomy for their own history and culture. If the Church of Rome continued to present itself as a religious projection of the civilization that had oppressed them, it was destined not to convert but to lose souls. Even where it had sunk deep roots, it could preserve them only by recognizing the identity and autonomy of the national churches. And that meant not only moderating the more and more centralized authority of the Primate, but also facing up to national realities dominated by absolute poverty and local wars.

The second new feature was still only partly recognized. In the 'Christian' countries too, even those in which the Church had always retained hegemony and sometimes controlled the government, the fact was that the number of vocations was falling, religious observance was on the wane, and the gap was widening between people's declared faith and their actual lifestyle. All these phenomena were, of course, linked to changes in society (collapse of the peasant world, spread of new means of communication, migratory trends, decline of the family and its educative capacity, and so on). If the ruling party itself continued to describe itself as Catholic, it did so more for its own political advantage than out of any deep conviction; it was Catholic because it was conservative, not conservative because it was Catholic. Americanism was no longer the questionable guarantor of religious observance, but rather the vehicle of 'secularization'. In order to resist this decline, it was therefore no longer enough to invoke an obsolete orthodoxy: even those – the majority – who balked at coming to terms with 'deviant' behaviour and the objective processes in which it originated, or rethinking the values that formed the dividing line between good and evil, were unable to disagree that the Church should prioritize pastoral work again and mobilize the laity for a new evangelization drive.

This was the starting point and the purpose of the Council, which produced an imposing raft of reforms: to modernize the liturgy and language of the Church, to make its local communities more autonomous, to change the relationship between lay Catholics and the hierarchy, to lay greater emphasis on issues such as equality, solidarity, non-violence, and the 'People of God'; to criticize consumerism and hedonism, and to combat atheism, less as a doctrine than as a practice. It was no accident that Cardinal Lercaro,[11] and through him Giuseppe Dossetti,[12] provided the stimulus for such a large part of the Council. This explains why, for some years at least, certain Catholic trade unionists were the most radical in the new workers' struggles, why so many Catholics were (often extreme) leaders of the student movement, why many local churches became hotbeds of dissent, and why Father Milani's *Lettera a una professoressa*,[13] published in 1967, had a greater impact than the writings of Marcuse.

But, in this great and undervalued reform movement, there was also an unresolved contradiction that would later weigh heavily in the balance. A twofold contradiction, in fact: one between '68 extremism and the ineradicable tendency to moderation present in every Catholic, which asserted itself when extremism turned violent and claimed to overturn the world without knowing what else to do, to change the world without first changing

11. Giacomo Lercaro: Archbishop of Bologna until 1968, popularizer of the 'Church of the Poor' and a proponent of dialogue with the Communist Party.

12. Giuseppe Dossetti: early vice-secretary of Christian Democracy and later priest, favoured an orientation to the poor in opposition to De Gasperi.

13. Lorenzo Milani: priest and pedagogue, and a prominent figure in social Catholicism.

consciousness; a contradiction that appeared when the changing of the world directly and radically affected centuries-old strongholds of Catholic culture (for example, the immutable value of the family, however reformed or redefined, or the rejection of libertinism and permissiveness as a dimension of freedom). These contradictions were destined to explode, and eventually to foster a new Catholic integralism, in the absence of a culture and politics capable of carrying things forward. Not only were Left culture and politics incapable; the Left did not even realize what was at stake. The value and limits of Vatican II were not discussed, and paradoxically it was like water off a duck's back in the party that governed in the name of Catholics. Dossetti had left, saying that to change politics it was first necessary to change the Church. But, when he seemed to be succeeding, he could not find anyone to handle the political part of the agenda. Its very scale and radical character made it an extremely arduous and urgent undertaking. Let me explain. The protest movement had grown on a wave of rapid and distorted economic development and social change, exposing both old injustices and new contradictions, alienations and subjections that it produced or heralded. The anti-establishment challenge threw this underlying development into crisis: it created disorder and uncertainty at key points of the country's productive apparatus, paralysed the university that was meant to train new cadres and build a consensus, and undermined or destabilized the functioning of public institutions. Yet it still needed development: not only to make further material gains and to consolidate those it had already achieved, not to speak of extending them to the large numbers of people who had a right to demand them; but, above all, to attain at least a few of the ambitious goals that drove it forward.

The movement had postponed or laid aside such problems during the period of its spontaneous rise, thinking that they would slow it down and open the way to parliamentarism and delegation, and hoping that the revolt would spread by contagion until it broke the back of the system and created a new political order. By 1970, however, this hope had gone, and rival groups within the movement were aiming to build an alternative political party, in the belief that a revolutionary breakthrough was on the agenda. It was a groundless belief, but the problem of making a sharp political turn, with an advanced programme, was real and inescapable.

The fact that it remained unresolved for years, becoming more and more difficult as a result, was therefore another, much more general, factor whose importance many took a long time to appreciate. In fact, at the beginning of the 1970s, a deep structural crisis of the whole capitalist order (to which the movement made a small contribution) was beginning to rage. The period of rapid, uninterrupted expansion was coming to an end.

This crisis was more gradual and less dramatic than others, but like all crises in the history of capitalism it had two faces, two rhythms. It exposed the system to risk and conflict, but also forced it to develop new technologies, a modified class structure, and new hierarchies of power. This could lead either to a compromise on a more advanced basis, or to restoration of the original matrix in a harsher form. A political way forward for the '68 movement therefore meant changing course in troubled and dangerous seas; but not to change course meant being swept along by the new wind that was starting to blow.

At this point I think we have the elements to return to my main focus: the Communist Party.

12

The PCI in 1968

The specificity of the Italian '68 was also that it unfolded within and in relation to a major political organization that acted as stimulus and support, and as a conditioning factor – a party with influence in the institutions but even more in society, not declining but rising, with more than one and a half million members, mostly working-class, built over a period of decades amid great victorious struggles, waves of persecution and bruising defeats, and confined to opposition because it had opted for Communism and stuck with that choice. It was easy to ignore it in the head, but not so easy to remove it from the scene. More important still was the fact that it had assumed, defended and gradually developed a particular identity within the world Communist movement in which it had been born and still participated.

I have repeatedly spoken of this identity in relation to various testing situations. But it may be useful to summarize its founding principles one last time, in the kind of plain language that might have been used at a local branch meeting.

1) The goal, which we consider achievable, is a major turn in human history: that is, an advance beyond capitalist society, not only to distribute income more equally and to improve the living conditions of the masses, but to socialize the principal means of production now in private hands and to gear them towards common aims. This will gradually overcome wage labour, the class division in society, the general opposition between (purely implemental) manual and (creative) intellectual labour, and the division between rulers and ruled. It will create a community of free and

equal individuals in solidarity with one another: a new human type. Therefore we are a class party, but of a class that seeks to abolish all classes, itself included. That is why our goal is socialism, but as a transitional phase to a still higher form of society. In this sense we are a revolutionary party.

2) In countries where the force of domination blocked development, the revolution had to take violent forms and to avail itself of authoritarian political institutions. But it successfully achieved economic progress, greater equality and a higher cultural level, as well as helping to defeat fascist barbarism; we are confident that this will enable it to develop a broader democracy and to combat bureaucratic forms, and what happens in more advanced regions like our own may offer it support and encouragement along that road. The precondition for all this is peace and independence for all nations. There are no models to be imitated. Rather, it is a question of international solidarity against imperialism, and mutual exchange of diverse and ever more advanced experiences on the road to socialism.

3) In the West, where society is more complex and the economy at a higher level, it will be easier to achieve pluralist socialist institutions and unrestricted freedom from the beginning, but the conquest of state power cannot and should not have the character of a sudden violent break; it will be the culmination of a long process of political and social struggle, through which the working class will progressively acquire the capacity to rule, to capture fortified positions, to forge alliances, and thus to gain lasting consensus among the majority of the population. This will require a number of stages and intermediate objectives. Reforms are not the same as reformism, provided there is a clear plan and perspective, democracy is not made identical with parliamentarism, and the winning of votes merges with mass struggles to ensure all the material conditions for free and conscious expression – and provided this whole process goes hand in hand with the construction of a stable and organized political force.

This set of logically interconnected principles, based on real experiences and fixed in the heads of millions of men and women, was more than a moon-gazing statement of values. It was the framework for a strategy, a collective way of thinking, which strengthened unity and nurtured hopes based on solidarity. It had many gaps and unresolved problems, and more than once it was contradicted by particular decisions (not all justifiable), by events that dented confidence, and by incomplete and belated self-criticisms. Yet in the 1960s it was the most plausible thing around, with points of support in the real world. The long '68 would both disprove and confirm this.

The difficulty lay in translating general principles into actual policy: that is, inserting them into a historically determinate situation and avoiding adventurism, while having the courage to take some risks and the patience not to chase after premature compromises or to enter into dubious alliances. In the situation I have described, the possibility of error was even greater than the opportunities. For the PCI the problem was one of content, organization and timing.

PROLOGUE

We need to step back and look again, in the light of '68, at what had been happening in the PCI immediately before it. First of all, it is not true that the PCI had stood outside the movement, unprepared for its focal issues and therefore lacking the authority to influence it or the capacity to learn something new from its ideas and experiences. There would certainly have been no hot autumn, with all its advanced characteristics, if the labour revival had not occurred in the early 1960s; a comparison with the May wave of factory occupations in France, and with the way in which they ended, is enough to convince us of this.

It is even possible that the student revolt would not have turned left and become so rapidly politicized, nor shown such a keen interest in Marxism, had it not been for the anti-fascist mobilization and constant anti-colonial struggles of those years, and the gradual revival of an unorthodox or at least non-dogmatic Marxism, partly imported from abroad, which had by then found a warm reception in the PCI. On the other hand, that long process of implantation, and the resulting influence within the movement, was not as effective as it might have been – partly by choice, partly through sheer ineptitude and bad luck. When I say 'by choice', I am referring to the conclusion of the Eleventh Congress and the needless suppression of dissent. I confess that when I was still a member of the PCI, not too disciplined but harmless enough, and even more after I had been driven out, a tendency to recrimination may sometimes have blinded me to the reasons for things that seemed to me, and were, mistaken. And, when the great victories gave way to a slow decline, the lines from Molière sometimes went through my head: 'Vous l'avez voulu, vous l'avez voulu, Georges Dandin, vous l'avez voulu ...'

Today is no longer the time for recrimination, and I suspect that its object was anyway not as important as I once thought. But the fact remains, and I recall it to help me understand how things shaped up as they did. The so-called *ingraini*, or followers of Ingrao, were for a long time accused of overestimating the political and trade union value of the new workers' struggles, and thus of downplaying the question of alliances with other sectors of society. Three years later, in 1969, such a criticism would have appeared absurd; if anything, the Party made the mistake of not speaking up and establishing a presence of its own in the factory, instead of leaving everything to the unions in the name of their autonomy. The *ingraini* were also accused of abstract, long-sighted vision, of chasing after new contradictions of neocapitalism, of seeking a different growth model when there were still major areas of backwardness to combat, traditional forces to mobilize, and traditional middle layers to keep from defection. These charges too were disproved by the facts three years later. The real *casus belli*, as we have seen, remained the question of reforming the Party. When '68 was at its height, was it really possible to think that the party form might regain credit among a new generation without undergoing any change? My concern is not to dwell wistfully on who was right. Perhaps no one was, entirely. What matters is that the Party was bereft of ideas, inspiration and energy to establish dialogue with the new movement, and to put forward convincing criticisms of it when necessary. Perhaps the clearest case in point was the Communist Youth, which did try to thrust forward, making some mistakes, and found itself intimidated and herded back into line, not long before the time when, in order to intervene in student meetings without appearing an outsider, it was essential to be young.

One little episode struck me at the time, as a measure of the Party's indifference more than hostility. When we were still in our corner, neither protesting nor plotting, Rossana and I – though she was a parliamentary deputy and involved in education – closely followed the May events in France and the university occupations in Italy. After working for months on an interpretation of them, we each published a little book: she *L'anno degli studenti*, I *Considerazioni sui fatti di maggio*. Both sold more than 20,000 copies, and we were invited to speak in a number of towns. Yet not one Party leader called us to find out any more, or to have a chat about things.

No less, indeed more, important as a resource for '68 were the thoughts of Togliatti, although they were hardly applied. Fate had it that he died in 1964, at a crucial moment when the break was about to happen. There has been much discussion over the years about the role of personality in history, some exaggerating, some nullifying its importance; but no conclusions have ever been reached, for the obvious reason that the role varies in accordance with the historical moment and the individual in question. In the present case, I think it was important. Togliatti was a combination of a great intellectual and a great politician (a combination that has since become rare); he lived through extraordinary, fast-changing events in his formative years (Gramsci and *Ordine Nuovo*, the Russian Revolution, the final years of Lenin's leadership), then experienced the birth of the fascist regime, the Seventh Comintern Congress and his own role in the leadership, the Spanish Civil War, the Terror in the Soviet Union, the great victory over fascism and the construction of the new party; and finally the Cominform clampdown, de-Stalinization and the laborious gaining of autonomy for an 'Italian road to socialism'. Through all those years he had an authority that enabled him to keep the Party united, mediating in, without suppressing, the many tensions that surfaced within it. That alone would have been enough to set a different stamp on the Eleventh Party Congress. But there was more. Some time before his death, Togliatti asked to be released from his active functions as Party secretary – not, I think, because he was tired, but because he needed to think more freely and on a 'grander' scale. And he did begin to do that. In little more than a year, he drew up an agenda of outstanding problems, and suggested some ideas on where the Party should be heading. They were like messages in a bottle, which he sent out to sea in the hope that they would be read by his successors. I have already mentioned two of these: the need to restore some understanding between China and the Soviet Union; and the need to recover the things in Gramsci's thought that 'went very far'.

But there was something else in that bottle. First of all, a rereading of the Catholic question, which involved a redefinition of the Communist question. Having matured rather slowly, this now emerged as if by chance, in a rather curious way that may not be known to anyone. It had been a constant theme in the elaboration of Communist strategy, passing through a number of versions at various moments. There had been the interpretation of the Catholic question as the peasant question, at the Lyons Congress in January 1926; the understanding with Christian Democracy on a very advanced draft constitution (at the price of voting for Article 7[1]), protecting its anti-fascist character from the Vatican's virulent anti-Communism; the struggle against clericalism during the harshest period of the cold war; recognition in the Party statutes of a right to membership for all who accepted its political programme, even if they were not Marxists or atheists; and an urgent attempt to establish cooperation on peace at a time when war threatened to destroy the human species.

After Roncalli's election as Pope John XXIII, his two encyclicals and the launching of Vatican II made it possible to go further. Togliatti decided to go much further and to raise the level of discourse, the occasion being a proposed amendment that resulted from an innocent plot of which I was the instigator. At the Tenth Congress, Romano Leddo and myself had been assigned the painstaking work of sifting through the hundreds of minor amendments to the theses put forward by Party branches or individual members, so that those of any interest would make it to the congress floor. It was generally considered a pointless task, since there was never time to discuss the amendments, and nothing of importance would be passed. Partly out of conviction, partly to relieve the boredom of the work, I slipped in an amendment of my own above some signature or other: 'An anguished religious consciousness can make a contribution to the socialist revolution.' However, realizing it was not exactly kosher, we went to Togliatti and asked him whether we should send it on with the others. He thought for a moment and said: 'Don't discuss it too much, just put it into the theses that will be approved.' It could have been a way of letting it through as irrelevant, and indeed it did not attract notice. But that was not his intention.

1. See note 4 on p.53.

A few months later, when Eliseo Milani and I asked him to come and speak in Bergamo, as he had promised to do many times, he finally accepted and suggested the topic: 'The New Catholic Question.' His speech there, in a packed theatre, became famous, but only as an opening of dialogue; there was little awareness of its implications. Starting from the few words of mine inserted in the theses, he gave them a much greater significance and added an analysis that was altogether new. This is worth quoting at some length:

> The destiny of man in a developed capitalist society, where technological uniformity creates a superficial uniformity of life, debases human beings and estranges them from themselves, limits and suppresses their initiative and their real scope for choice and self-development. It brings the loneliness of modern man, who, even when able to enjoy all the goods of the earth, does not manage to communicate with other men and feels shut up in a prison from which there is no exit.

From this he inferred

> the necessity of a socialist society, which for the first time takes on a new and richer aspect. Man is no longer alone, and humanity truly becomes a living community, only through the many-sided development of the individual, of all human beings, and through their organic participation in a common endeavour ... Therefore the Catholic world cannot be insensitive to this new dimension of the problems of the world. Not only can the aspiration to a socialist society be felt by people with a genuine religious faith; it can find in them a stimulus, faced as they are with the dramatic problems of the contemporary world. This is reflected in the conception of socialism itself, as a society that calls on all men and women to work together and calls on all to contribute equally with their labour to decide the fate of the whole of humanity.

This presents us with a critique of capitalist modernity ('no' to chasing after it), points to the contradiction between a non-clerical church and the capitalist West (such as emerged at the Vatican Council), and raises some of the more radical themes that would emerge in the '68 revolt – although it resolutely rejects the anarchistic individualist response contained within that revolt.

A final prescient message in the bottle, both synthetic and surprising, concerned the youth question. In 1964, well before the revolt erupted, in a message to the Communist Youth Federation Togliatti did not hesitate to write:

> Today we should consider the new generations all around the world as a revolutionary force. For we may speak of a new generation when the ideas and practice of men and women with their life ahead of them display homogenous elements that have built up over time, when new problems and experiences concerning their lives today and tomorrow mature within those elements, when new answers start to be given to those problems and a process of development appears that begins from certain fundamental positions. On the basis of these, we must work to arrive at struggles of a fundamental character.

This is similar to the language he used about the spontaneous emergence of the partisan war; it shows the same will to participate in the struggle, and the same confidence of being able to guide it, aware of its limits and risks, but also conscious that it is the necessary pillar for a more complex and less exciting political operation in the immediate future.

Instead of rehearsing an established canon, all of these messages, individually and together, look ahead to the future and offer stimulating suggestions on how to confront it. But little was done about them, and still less was their value understood or their content deepened. That goes for everyone. So the PCI reached '68 less well equipped than it might otherwise have been.

PRAGUE REMAINS ALONE

The first and thorniest question that the PCI faced in '68 was posed by the Prague Spring and the invasion of Czechoslovakia by Warsaw Pact troops. Prague was not Budapest, nor was Dubček either Gerő or Nagy. The reform programme was decided by the majority of the Communist Party leadership and supported by a majority of its activists and the Czechoslovak people. Its stated objective was not to undermine the socialist system, still less to break off international alliances and links with the Soviet Union, but rather to make socialism politically less intolerant of dissent and less highly centralized in its management of the economy (a more extreme minority also wanted to allow some space for the market, without giving up planning, and to trade with foreign countries where possible, without becoming subordinate to them). Was this a re-launch of the revolution? Clearly not. Only a correction of the Cominform version imposed in 1947, a resumption of the 'people's democracy' that Dimitrov had designed, with Stalin's tolerance, and which had had good results. Czechoslovakia had the economic capacity and a sufficient degree of political consensus to attempt it, while avoiding being pushed beyond the limits of its stated intentions. Dubček had good arguments for his claim to be operating in the direction indicated by the Twentieth Congress. And indeed, at his meeting with Brezhnev, everything seemed to point to an agreement.

Were there risks? Certainly – above all if the new course was isolated, or even opposed by its allies. But what led Brezhnev and Suslov's USSR to make its hasty military intervention was not a fear that the Czech experiment might fail, but precisely a fear that it might succeed and encourage other countries, perhaps even the Soviet Union itself, to proceed in their own way and at their own pace to carry out much-needed and long-promised reforms. The invasion was therefore not a 'mistake', nor only a limit on national sovereignty; it was a resounding rejection of 'unity in diversity', of the possibility of 'various roads to socialism' that remained in dialogue with one another and stood together against imperialism. It was a violent reaffirmation of the leading role of the CPSU, and of the doctrine of 'limited sovereignty'. For this reason the reactions it triggered in Communist parties around the world were quite different from those aroused by the Hungarian crisis in 1956. Apart from the parties directly involved, the ones that approved of it were those of Syria, Chile and, with some hesitation, Cuba and Vietnam (which could not do without Soviet aid). Manifesting open disagreement, only later toned down, were the Communist parties of France, Switzerland, Norway, Finland, Spain, Austria, Belgium, Romania, India, Belgium, Morocco, Australia and, above all, Yugoslavia and China.

Longo's PCI was the clearest in its condemnation and the most openly appreciative of Dubček's project, repeating its stance at the Moscow Conference of Communist parties in 1969 and abstaining on part of the final motion. From the beginning, however, some of its authoritative leaders (Amendola, Pajetta) were not convinced that this was the right course, and to limit its impact the theory that the invasion had all been a 'mistake' was gradually introduced; it was particularly stressed that the 'mistake' should not impair the PCI's solidarity with the Soviet Union and confidence in its future. A deluded belief set in that the split between Czechoslovak dissidents and Moscow would soon be healed and that Dubček had not really been purged: in 1969, much credit was given to Husák's conciliatory positions in this respect. But things took quite a different direction – towards total restoration. And not much fuss was made about it.

This was to have major consequences, especially at the international level. For it was the PCI's last opportunity to intervene as an active force in the international Communist movement, starting an urgent ongoing debate on the real areas of disagreement and seeking to rebuild a 'unity in diversity' that was not based only on opposition to a common enemy.

The Americans, embroiled in a war they were beginning to lose, were bracing themselves to absorb the shock waves that would result. The Chinese had curbed the excesses of the Cultural Revolution without disowning it altogether, and were in the throes of a debate on where they should go from there; it would last for a period of years, from the liquidation of Lin Biao to the difficult cohabitation between the Gang of Four and Zhou Enlai, then to the liquidation of the 'Gang' and a more harmonic cohabitation between Zhou Enlai and Hua Guofeng, and culminating in the gradual rehabilitation of Deng Xiaoping.

The illusion of 'guerrilla foci' was dissipating in Latin America after the death of Che Guevara, but with nothing to withstand the military coups that were being prepared and supported by the United States. In Cuba, Soviet aid had become indispensable, but there was a debate about the type of economic development and political forms the country should adopt. Nasser was not yet dead (poisoned?) – indeed, the aftermath of the Six-Day War had fuelled an anti-colonialist, non-Islamic Arab nationalism. Even in the USSR things were not standing still: the freeze was not total, as we can tell from the published discussion in the Academy of Sciences, the planned debate among economists in Novosibirsk on the general policy of peaceful competition, and the recurrent difficulties evident in the country's economic performance. These were all symptoms of malaise. Was it not the moment to use the real prestige enjoyed by the PCI to open a full and frank debate, without clamorous rifts but also without prior reservations?

In Italy, too, it was not the reticence so much as the downgrading of the 'Prague case' that had major consequences. To be sure, the youth movement did not pay it much attention, since it anyway had no trust in 'actually existing socialism' and felt more drawn to the anti-authoritarian message of the Cultural Revolution, separating it off from the historical events in China that were now coming to an end. But intellectuals, Catholic figures, even the Socialists (though busy with the shambles of the unification with Saragat) were not insensitive to the issue, and the Christian Democrats, in a state of confusion, seized on it as cover for their dyed-in-the-wool anti-Communism. For Communist activists, from top to bottom of the Party, the 'half measures' in relation to Czechoslovakia were not unsatisfactory in the short run, but in the longer term, and in their inner consciousness, the issue was destined to create a new type of 'duplicity' between what they said and what they thought. After years of hopes that 'Communism was sweeping the world', they continued to believe that the movement was advancing in Italy, but were less sure that it was winning the world as they had once dreamed. Fortunately there was Vietnam and the long '68 to cloak the duplicity, but precisely after the victory in Vietnam the 'old mole' seemed to be burrowing his way backwards. I therefore continue to believe that the events in Prague were particularly important.

PARTY AND MOVEMENTS

The second question the PCI had to face was its relationship with the new conflicts in society. It dominated the period from 1967 to 1970, and the analysis and judgements must here be more finely structured: the role the Party played in workers' struggles cannot be lumped together with its role in the student revolt.

As far as the workers' struggles are concerned, it is true some leaders were worried and sceptical. Amendola, for instance, denied that the right to hold meetings in the workplace could ever be achieved, let alone enforced, when in fact it had already been won. Fernando di Giulio presented a report to the Seventh Labour Congress in Turin which, though effective in terms of complaints, could have been written ten years previously. The two general disputes on pensions and pay grids were highlighted, but nothing was said about the wretched agreement signed by the union confederations, or about the rank-and-file revolt (including in the Party) that tore it up or the CGIL's go-it-alone strike that led to its revocation. Although factory struggles had become sharper and more widespread well before the hot autumn, the PCI did not concentrate its energies on building and mobilizing its own workplace organizations, and these continued to decline. Other signs of concern or caution were more understandable and deserved serious discussion. Trentin himself had doubts about the idea of equal pay rises for all, fearing that the flattening of wage bands might have dangerous effects over time (although he wisely went along with what the movement was demanding). There was initial resistance to the replacement of internal committees with direct election of section delegates to a factory council from an approved list, but it was not long before this was accepted.

On the whole, the PCI was present and active in the workers' struggles through its own activists, giving them extra strength without holding back their initiative. But in effect it gave unions a completely free hand. In the short term this was all to the good, since the aim was to mobilize the large factories and certain groups such as the engineering workers, and because at the time organizations such as the FIM were encouraging the struggle more than reining it in. But the delegation of responsibility would also prove to have limitations. First, when it was a question of drawing in workers from smaller companies or extending the list of demands to other areas of life (housing, health), the Party had an essential role to play. Second, delegation (not autonomy) impeded the growth of political subjectivity in the strict sense among the workers. The Party did eventually criticize *pansindacalismo*, the idea that the union was everything, but after all this had been a way of compensating for the Party's lack of direct involvement in the workplace. The Party was being driven to concern itself mainly with elections and future governments, while in the factory it had wide support but no real hegemony or strong organization. Among the workers a discourse that was both radical and down to earth might have worked best, and the workers themselves had a natural authority to speak to all the social movements.

There were many signs of what all this cost the Party: difficulty in putting a left stamp on social protests in the South (Reggio di Calabria, L'Aquila, Battipaglia), a low level of mobilization and poor results of struggles over collective needs, difficulty in converting the social combativity of Catholic organizations into new choices for the 1972 elections, lack of clarity about trade union unity at central level (which was limited to an agreement on united action, dependent on a parity commission in which forces linked to the ruling party were still in a majority and the Communists plus PSIUP[2] had 20 per cent in all). Nevertheless, with all its contradictions and ambiguities, the social conflict of '68–'69 gave rise to one of the most influential unions in Europe, with one of the largest memberships.

The balance sheet of the PCI's relationship with the student movement is much less satisfactory. Here the Party was not only inadequate and uncertain but sorely lacking in analysis, proposals and achievements. It therefore lost what I would not hesitate to describe as a historic opportunity.

In the initial phase the PCI, unlike the PCF, did not show hostility to the student movement or discount its importance. Longo met with Roman students after the clashes at Valle Giulia, in an attempt to understand their thinking, and wrote a long article whose importance I realized only recently, as I was rereading it in the light of what has since become of the educational system. For Longo did not confine himself to words of encouragement and analysis of the underlying reasons for the movement, but said that he considered it to be a positive development politically (apart from a few points of which he was critical). Indeed, he inserted a kind of self-criticism of the Ninth Congress into the article, saying that, in the face of such new phenomena, the Party should boldly discuss and change some things in its own house: 'We often think that our meetings will be less solemn if they display differences or even sharp disagreements, but the truth is that these are part of their richness.' Many were amazed by his audacity. Two weeks later, however, Amendola and then Bufalini[3] expressed a very different, if not opposite, point of view: namely, that the student movement was certainly the product of real grievances and a progressive impulse, but, in keeping with its social base, it involved a rebellious ideology with a number of irrationalist features. The Party therefore had to distinguish between the mass of students and dangerous vanguardist elements that had taken over leadership of the movement, and thus to conduct a struggle 'on two fronts' – persisting with its calls for adequately funded modernization of the educational system and student involvement in the

2. PSIUP: Partito Socialista Italiano di Unità Proletaria, a left split from the PSI that was active between 1964 and 1972. Its leaders included Tullio Vechietti, Lelio Basso and Vittorio Foa.

3. Paolo Bufalini: responsible in the PCI for foreign relations (including with the USSR), and a senator from 1963 to 1992.

running of universities, but having no truck with positions that challenged the institution as such, or claimed that students should play a strictly political role. Despite some resistance, this was the line that eventually prevailed. But it was definitely mistaken and ineffectual.

The analysis was wrong. First of all, although the movement reflected discontent with the material circumstances of students, these were not solely due to the rudimentary or inadequate nature of the existing structures. The revolt involved a much broader challenge to the educational establishment and its links with professions that promised much, but failed to satisfy students either quantitatively or qualitatively. In fact, the revolt broke out first in countries where there were proper facilities and the educational system had been modernized for some time. Second, the radical character of the movement was a spontaneous mass phenomenon, not attributable to various *groupuscules*; it took up issues concerning the family and traditional behaviour and values, spreading around the world and picking up any 'rebellious' suggestion. It was absurd to imagine that it could be simply bypassed – as if, once it had cleared a few obstacles and opened up new areas of individual freedom, it would just sit back, content with the small privileges it had been destined to attain. On the other hand, the PCI could have played an invaluable role if it had grasped the radical character of the movement and related to it accordingly. Only then would a broad social group, mainly originating in well-off, *bien-pensant* layers of society, have avoided the risk of corporate defence of privilege and, in attempting to hook up with the needs and struggles of subaltern classes, have translated its own material and moral discontent into a general critique of society.

Here too, perhaps, was the greatest resource that the movement offered to the PCI. For a party that considered itself revolutionary but conceived of revolution as a lengthy process, the problem was not how it might increase its vote or recruit new members from an incidental wave of youthful protest, but how it might convert that wave into a permanent conquest of 'fortified positions'. Any student movement is provisional by nature: those who initiate or join it will soon find a place in society, and perform various roles in keeping with their class origin. To preserve the best of the critical legacy of '68 and the political disposition resulting from the protest movement, it was therefore necessary to bring about profound changes in the educational system – its methods, content and purpose – instead of simply modernizing it and making it more accessible: in short, a 'structural reform' geared to building a new society, and capable of transferring the same inspiration to ever higher levels. At that moment in time, and perhaps only then, the conditions were favourable for this. Workers and technicians were demanding changes in the organization of work and rejecting the ghetto of low-quality housing; many intellectuals were looking at their role in new ways; many young lecturers felt unhappy with what they were expected to teach. Moreover, knowledge was becoming more important in production, in people's lifestyles and in the exercise of citizenship. Science was in the throes of a new leap forward, but also becoming ever less neutral.

Am I saying that the radical character of the student movement should have been accepted and encouraged just as it was, and used as a battering-ram for a general revolutionary breakthrough? Quite the opposite. What I mean is that a 'revolution' in education could have been aligned with the workers' struggle and brought in still other social subjects. Combination of study and work, production of a positive alternative culture, lifelong education both job-related and for its own sake: such goals were extraordinarily far-sighted but also open to practical experiment, subjectively ripe but also materially feasible.

On these matters the PCI had the resources to compete within the movement, and proposals for definite actions, not just words, might paradoxically have placed it on the left. Perhaps Togliatti had foreseen this a few years earlier, when he attributed a revolutionary role not to 'this new generation' but to 'new generations', which – I would add – could not have transmitted experiences to one another without a material base to sustain them.

The PCI's failure even to attempt this, at a time when the mass revolt was seeking a way forward, prevented it from acquiring an important role in the student movement. And, when the movement began to wane, a deep gulf opened up subjectively between frustrated radicalism and sermonizing moderation. Communists were scarcely able to speak at meetings, or were treated as 'His Majesty's Opposition': allowed to vote, but lacking all authority.

So, the education system we now have is easier but unchanged, more accessible but even less capable of offering opportunities, less authoritarian but more fragmented and bereft of genuinely educative power. It is not a captured 'fortification' defended by new troops, but a bombed one subjected to makeshift restoration.

LONGO, BERLINGUER

Before we move on, we need to consider why, at the most favourable moment, the PCI acted skilfully but with so much delay and wavering.

Everything was not predetermined by the past, or by the future. There were time lags that could have been made up, errors that could have been avoided, real difficulties that could have been confronted better. I will take just two examples, which, though perhaps not decisive, were certainly significant, and which are worth pondering from a distance, with more information at hand, in a calmer manner and with a greater openness to doubt. The first is the succession to Longo as Party leader. In a mass Communist party, the question of who led it was fundamental at moments of upheaval; the 'secretary' was then the expression of a history, who had the last say on key decisions and was changed only if he died or there was some great trauma. The PCI had always been the party of Togliatti, and he had left an indelible stamp on it. But he had died a few years before, old but not worn out, in a new period of creativity. His sudden disappearance had therefore been a far from minor blow. Nevertheless, there had been no difficulty in electing Longo to take over from him: not only because he had long been vice-secretary, but because his record in the Party and his gifts of balance, firmness and tolerance had won him huge popularity and general trust. He did not possess Togliatti's stature, nor did he claim to. His age meant that he was destined to be a transitional secretary, but that did not make him a mere administrator. Indeed, he was a special kind of 'Togliattian', as Amendola and Ingrao were too, in a rather less prudent way. The story of his life had defined this specificity. He was one of the 'youngsters' who, in the early 1930s, stood out by arguing for the return of exiles to Italy to organize the underground struggle, which soon led to their arrest and imprisonment. He subsequently served as inspector-general of the International Brigades in Spain and became effective leader of the partisan war in Italy. Even in the postwar context of the 'democratic road', his attention was focused more on the mass movement than on parliamentary subtleties; he supported the policy of broad alliances, but put unity of the Left before it. Thus, it was no accident that he reacted to the student revolt in the way I have described; nor that in 1969 and until the end of his life he opposed operations in the governmental arena, and refused to give much credence to Christian Democracy as a progressive force.

At the end of 1968, however, he was struck by an illness that prevented him from effectively leading the Party. He was advised against taking positions that differed from those of the rest of the leadership, and he was forced quickly to resolve the problem of his eventual successor. In fact, his choice had already been maturing, since he had pushed a reluctant Berlinguer to enter parliament in preparation for his gradual takeover when the time came. That time came soon, and his choice was not set aside.

Berlinguer's huge popularity over the years has convinced many that it was obvious from the beginning that he would become Party secretary. But that is not at all the case, since he did not have a long *cursus honorum* behind him; he often moved up the ladder of hierarchy and recognition, only to slip down again. Not long before Longo's resignation, he lost his position as coordinator of the secretariat, accused of being too 'conciliatory', and was sent off to head the regional committee in Lazio. He was replaced by Napolitano, a man closer to Amendola.

But Amendola proved to be a sharp politician; he was impetuous in wielding power, but he was not vain. His realistic idea was to refrain from standing as a candidate for secretary – at the same time ruling out everyone else from his generation, and keeping Napolitano out of the running – and to call on everyone to 'rally round Enrico', without upsetting the balance that had emerged from the Ninth Congress. The real leadership that would flank Berlinguer would therefore consist of Chiaromonte,[4] Bufalini, Pajetta, Napolitano and Di Giulio, some of whom were his own men or were moving closer to him. It remains a mystery to me, however, why those who had been genuinely close to Longo (the Nattas, Tortorellas and many '*ex-ingraini*') avoided pushing themselves forward at the time, and for nearly the whole of the next decade.

4. Gerardo Chiaromonte: Communist senator from 1968 to 1993, part of the so-called *migliorista* current in the Party.

Under these circumstances, even if he had wanted to, Berlinguer would have had little scope to patch things up quickly with the left of the Party, or to correct the prevailing orientation.

THE PURGE OF *IL MANIFESTO*

In all honesty, however, it is impossible to ignore another sharer of the blame. How could a Communist Left have exerted political influence, when although equipped with the best of arguments, it showed neither the strength nor the will to assert itself?

Recently, in his memoirs and a number of interviews and contributions, Pietro Ingrao has been lavish with self-criticism in relation to the past. Many of the points he makes do not convince me at all, as the reader of this book can see; others are ungenerous towards himself because they make out that, for all his good intentions, he was nearly always on the wrong side. One does seem to me important, however, and another I consider fair enough, though somewhat incomplete. They will allow me to speak of the birth of *Il Manifesto*, the purge of its initiators from the Party, and the consequences of all this. And I will speak without holding anything back, even as I express my recurrent doubts.

The important point that Ingrao makes today is that it was not only an act of disloyalty but a political error on his part to abruptly call off the battle he had started before and during the Ninth Congress. His giving up was a momentous decision, for himself and many who supported him, and for the whole Party. Let us therefore look at it more closely.

Following his heavy defeat at the congress, Ingrao personally agreed to say nothing about the undeserved marginalization of a number of comrades (I do not include myself), and submitted to a long period of silence, even when events took place that might have led him to break it. The so-called *ingraini* evidently went their separate ways. Only the trade unionists, who quite rightly had not exposed themselves too much, had the possibility of taking their ideas and experiences further, in the free zone of trade union autonomy. Trentin, Garavini and Pugno, for example, together with Foa and his friends, had a major influence in workers' struggles. They succeeded in building a new kind of union, particularly among engineering workers, and trained valuable cadres in Turin, Bologna, Brescia and elsewhere.

Others did not have so much scope, but they did not surrender or repent (I am thinking of places like Puglia, Venice, Bergamo, Naples and Rome, and of many intellectuals). At the first seriously encouraging sign, they would be able to return to the discussion within the Party's official structures. Only a few – who can be counted on the fingers of two hands – kept up friendly relations among themselves and considered the battle to be merely suspended, perhaps because they held more radical views and were more severely marginalized, or perhaps because they were anyway marginalized in their radical views: in particular, Luigi Pintor, Rossana Rossanda, myself and a few friends. In any event, the experience had not left any of us, Ingrao included, harbouring a grudge: we simply parted 'just like that, without rancour'.

In August 1967, driving to Bari for a few days by the sea, Reichlin and I made a little side-trip to Scilla to say hello to Ingrao (he was on holiday there) and to probe his future intentions. He did not strike us as particularly combative. The next year, the French May and the university occupations in Italy stirred the waters. Rossana and I took off. Later I went back to Paris for three months to collect people's accounts of the events for my essay; Rossana made a tour of the liveliest universities. We were fired up and excited by it all, but it is enough to read what we wrote to see that our heads were clear, without any revolutionary raptures; we realized the problems and limitations of 'self-declared revolutions', not only the mistakes of the French Communist Party. The bases existed for a constructive discussion in the PCI, and in this connection I asked Ingrao if we could meet privately and confidentially, but as a group. The gathering, which took place at Rossanda's, consisted of Ingrao, Reichlin, Trentin, Garavini, Castellina, Pintor, Rossana and myself. It was the first meeting of a 'faction' that never came into being, which dissolved before it was born. The idea was to find out everyone's answer to a simple preliminary question: 'With everything that's bubbling up inside the Party, doesn't it make sense to start a new general discussion in the run-up to the Twelfth Congress, like the one that was aborted in 1966?' The picture soon became clear. The most authoritative of the people there, the ones who might have carried some weight, thought that an initiative of that kind – even on an individual basis, without joint platforms and in individually chosen tones – would immediately create tensions and suspicions, and instead of helping matters would be an obstacle to the movements already under way; it might make the latter even more unpopular with the Party and its leaders. Others, including myself, objected that a dull congress without any new thinking would create a gulf between the Party and the movement, and would not provide the Party with the strength, language and analysis it needed to gain weight and authority in the movement and to correct its errors.

Of course, if the outcome of that meeting had been less clear, *Il Manifesto* would not have been born and there would have been an interesting, not necessarily polarized, discussion at the Twelfth Congress. Perhaps a middle way might have been found between the sung masses of monolithism and the call to 'Bombard headquarters!' The criticism which, in my view, could be made of Ingrao or others is that they did not try – although I know that, if they had tried, the results would have been uncertain and would have greatly influenced what some of us were then thinking or intending to say. When no agreement was reached, the only remaining course was to express a radical dissent that would put us in a tiny minority. And it may be that, if no one else had joined our two men and a dog – which was how we looked on ourselves – we would have thought it not worth the trouble.

But there was a surprise in store. Spontaneously, without any warning, positions and demands consistent with our own began to emerge from various provincial congresses, in some cases gaining the support of a sizeable percentage of the membership (Cagliari, Bergamo, Venice, Rome, Naples). To be sure, the trained eye of the apparatus would have allowed only a small part of this discontent to reach the national congress, but it could not erase it altogether. It included a lot of old-time *ingraini*, but also young activists, figures in the Party who no longer felt themselves to be *ingraini* (Aldo Natoli, Massimo Caprara), and scattered but high-quality intellectuals (Luigi Nono, Cesare Luporini and others). The speeches of Natoli, Pintor and Rossanda at the national congress in Bologna, though all delivered 'at the crack of dawn', as the papers noted, found a favourable hearing and had considerable resonance outside. When I read the congress records today, they give an impression of complete inadequacy to the situation then facing the Party. Report, debate and summing up did little more than repeat one another, and echo what had been said at previous congresses. The leadership formed an even more tightly-knit group than usual. Discordant elements were present only in our scanty contributions, and even those do not seem today the best we were capable of producing: some interesting analytic points, but political and programmatic proposals that could be summed up in the statement that we were facing a crisis in the West, and now also in the East, which we needed to counter with a systemic alternative. The critical response contained in Berlinguer's summing up was measured in tone, but showed not the slightest interest in a genuine discussion. He mainly directed his remarks to Rossana, using a mordant quotation from Machiavelli about 'those who speak of non-existent realms' – not realizing that, especially when he spoke of the Soviet Union, China or the youth revolt, he was the one who avoided facing up to reality.

On the day after the congress, we therefore found ourselves with a very difficult choice to make. Whatever else, there had been a clear expression of disagreement, and a small but cohesive group had been formed. We could have simply returned to silence and waited for a better opportunity, or we could have worked in semi-secrecy to build a little faction. But we ruled out both options: the first because now seemed the moment for urgent policy decisions, and both party and movement required, and made possible, an open clash on the fundamental issues; the second because we had always been sincerely convinced that mini-factions led to rivalry over little positions of power inside the Party or to mini-splits, both of which undercut serious thinking and were damaging to everyone concerned. Our (probably fanciful) aim was to contribute by various means, even by breaking established codes, to a renewal of the whole PCI, because we believed that the development of the 'Italian case' depended on it. Our third way, then, was to publish a journal that would not organize forces but produce ideas, to offer a channel of communication between insurgent movements and a priceless tradition by reflecting critically on both. The original plan was for a monthly that would be sold in bookshops, in a few thousand copies. We looked for a prestigious publisher close to the Left (Einaudi, Feltrinelli, Laterza), but each politely turned us down because it did not wish to damage relations with the PCI as a whole. All we found was an enterprising printer in Bari who was trying to break into publishing: Coga. Paradoxically it was he who founded *Il Manifesto*, offering us a leonine but original deal whereby we handed over the print-ready layout free of charge, produced with voluntary labour and an office paid for from subscriptions, while he printed and distributed the copies, even risking news stands, and kept all the receipts for himself. His estimates proved to be better than ours, because the first issue of *Il Manifesto* was reprinted twice and sold more than 50,000 copies.

Success changed its character, rather like the applause from the floor that Ingrao had received at the Ninth Congress. *Il Manifesto* became a political fact, in Italy and abroad, beyond our intentions and perhaps beyond our merits. The Party leadership first tried privately to persuade us to give up, then banned the initiative in the name of the rules against factions; and, since a journal as such was not a faction, they explained that we had become one through the collecting of subscriptions, the establishment of a permanent group of helpers and contributors, and regular interventions on topical political issues. Two successive meetings of the Central Committee were convened, to add weight to the ban. At that point, realizing that we risked expulsion, we all had a moment of hesitation. If we nevertheless pressed ahead, it was not out of pride or light-mindedness, but for reasons of method and substance. The Party press was publishing authoritative articles (by Bufalini, for instance) that not only denounced the danger of factionalism and criticized individual pieces in *Il Manifesto*, but contemptuously dismissed everything we wrote as mere nonsense that was not worth discussing. Substantively, moreover, it was becoming clear – though not in public – that the real reason for the hard line was the Prague question, and our judgements of the Soviet Union. But those were precisely the issues over which we hoped, not to bring everyone around to our point of view (of course not), but to stimulate a discussion that recognized them to be real problems. So we continued on our way, and it was not long before Natoli, Pintor, Rossanda and myself (as director of the paper) were expelled from the Party. The Central Committee voted in favour of the decision, with only two votes against and five abstentions. Shortly afterwards, Luciana Castellina, Massimo Caprara and Liberato Bronzuto were publicly expelled at branch level, and a few others were vigorously 'advised' to leave quietly (Parlato, Barra, Zandegiacomi, Milani). We avoided asking others to follow suit, partly because it was not clear what form our enterprise was going to take.

Not only Ingrao but many others who voted for our expulsion have since made a self-criticism, on the grounds that the PCI should have been capable of holding off a small group of dissidents without resorting to administrative measures, and that this would have underlined its own democratic character. This belated change of heart pleased me, especially as I know that we did not mean to harm the Party by sowing discord but, on the contrary, thought we were assisting the renewal that it actually needed. Nevertheless, at this distance in time, the self-criticisms seem to me a little misleading. In reality, the expulsions had only a limited and short-lived effect on the PCI's image and its relations with other parties and public opinion, since, however reproachable the methods, many found it reassuring that it had rid itself of a far-Left group. Other 'New Left' groups, competing with one another but all 'communist', had little sympathy for us, since our expulsion meant that another possible rival had appeared on the scene and that one source of ambiguity, previously useful to the PCI, no longer existed. Overall, however, it made little difference to anyone whether we were expelled or shunted off to an Indian-style reservation. That was indeed the truth of the matter.

The really negative consequences were to be found elsewhere. Overstepping its original intentions, the PCI conducted a huge and oppressive campaign to make life difficult for anyone who even partly shared our views, and to mobilize the entire apparatus for a struggle 'on a single front'. It was a very harsh and long-drawn-out campaign. For a long time, much of the leadership stopped personally greeting us, and *L'Unità* came out with headlines such as: 'Who Is Paying Them?' It did not seem enough to answer 'Confindustria', so they ended up suspecting 'Confagricoltura': the dregs of the dregs, for many ordinary rank-and-file members.

This *cordon sanitaire* of hostility encouraged us to draft an ambitious document that would define our identity in a less ad hoc manner, and provide a more structured analysis. The resulting 'Theses of *Il Manifesto*', which filled a whole issue of the paper, sold 75,000 copies and even today strike me with their foresight. But they also led us to make some hasty and harmful political choices. For example, our proposal for rapid unification of the various New Left groups was not only impracticable but pulled us into a simple-minded extremism that was not part of our nature, and then induced us to stand in elections without a chance of success. These decisions pinned on us the deformed image that the PCI leadership had been polemicizing against.

Trying to regain our bearings, we gradually returned to our conception of ourselves as a hinge between the traditional Left and the social movements. Honesty compels me to admit that, while playing an important role in the enterprise, I personally rushed into those errors and then energetically tried to correct them. But doubts still linger within me: perhaps Natoli was right to suggest that we should resist the temptation to give the review an immediate organizational projection. For the moment my main concern has been to explain that the negative impact of the expulsions – the reason why they were a major error – had to do not only, or mainly, with the toleration of dissent, but with the substantive issue of whether our dissent expressed something true and useful, and should therefore have been treated as a genuine contribution to PCI policy. That alone would have served to change things a little and to help the Party through the difficult 1970s, a period so rich in successes at the beginning and so full of bitterness by the end. If only at the level of image, it would have been good for the PCI to allow a space within its ranks for left-wing dissent that was culturally undogmatic, and not politically tied to Moscow.

13

Towards the Endgame

The trickiest and most demanding moment in chess is the one that separates the middle game – when many pieces are still on the board, forces still appear level in positions not codified in theory, and each player has a plan of action – from the approach to the endgame. This is when a skilful player needs to be boldest in attack, but also most alert to the weaknesses of his position and the strengths of his opponent's, foreseeing likely moves ahead and showing sufficient flexibility to adjust his own plans when necessary. The strange-sounding title of this chapter is meant to indicate that the problem I must now face is the politics of the PCI in the 1970s – a decade in which early successes soon gave way to great difficulties in seeing them through to the end. The Party persevered, head down, on its chosen course and three years later suffered a sharp defeat, both external and internal, at the polls and in its relationship with the masses, not just temporary but long-lasting. Still at its peak, when it had the resources for a correction, it was unwilling or unable to execute it in time, in a way that might have limited the damage and allowed it to recover. That is part of the price one pays for an extreme lack of internal dialectic.

The salient facts that shaped everything else are well known, or at least available to anyone interested. An abundant literature – history, memoirs, diaries – covers the finest details and behind-the-scenes events, but what was missing then, and is still missing today, is a general and not too partisan overview of what actually happened; one which, however open to debate, is consistent and capable of being documented. What we lack, then, is: 1) a realistic appraisal of all the major events, and of the one-way or two-way cause and effect relationship among them (for example, the widespread view that Moro's killing dictated the end of the national unity governments strikes me as implausible); 2) a precise identification of the main cause, overarching other lesser ones, for both the early successes and the swift collapse of the political project (for example, it does not seem convincing that the latter was due only to tactical mistakes in handling a correct policy); 3) a consideration of the new impact of international events (without which we end up with a false picture of reality); and consequently 4) a full realization that, far from being a parenthesis, the decade laid the basis for a really historic break, which is what then came to pass.

None of these points is discussed today. But reflection on them is necessary: not only to understand the past, but to grapple with the world of unipolar neoliberal globalization in which we live, and to offer some suggestions for the future. If it is true – and it is – that the decline and dissolution of the PCI cleared the way not for a stronger, more intelligent Left but for one that is weaker and less rich in ideas, and if it is true that Italy itself has degenerated as an economy, as a society and as a participatory democracy, then we can say that the Italy of those years is still interesting as a case study – only now in a negative sense.

THE ECONOMIC CRISIS

One of the major new developments in the 1970s was the economic 'crisis' that hit the whole of Western capitalism, as sudden, general and lasting as the 'miracle' of headlong growth had been. I put the word crisis between inverted commas because it can have several meanings. Economists are aware of this and actually employ a number of different terms (negative conjuncture, stagnation, recession, depression), nearly always keeping 'crisis' for use in combination with 'restructuring'. But in practice they have considerable difficulty in choosing the right term, or hesitate a long time before they decide. For the whole history of capitalism is punctuated with an alternation between successes and difficulties, including moments of crisis. Each of these is unique in its causes, duration and conclusion, but a dividing line may be drawn between two types of crisis.

Some squeezes, usually involving one or few countries, can be quickly resolved with appropriate measures, while longer periods of stagnation can sometimes be unblocked more gradually through energetic intervention, without touching the basic structures of the system. There has been a lot of theoretical work and practical experience in these matters, and they have often come up with satisfactory answers in favourable situations, but not everywhere or all the time. For example, in the 1930s Keynesian policies assisted the US recovery between 1934 and 1938, but failed in the France of the Popular Front and were most effective in Nazi Germany (where, however, they served the purposes of war); after 1945 they successfully stabilized and prolonged economic growth where it was under way, but blocked it instead of producing it in Britain. Therefore Keynes, who had written a brilliant work on the necessity of public intervention to counter the recurrent tendency in capitalism to put liquidity before investment, suddenly turned on those who thought that demand management was a magical panacea for all time.

Crises have been very different in their scale and nature. At least three epochal ones are recognizable in the history of 'actually existing capitalism': 1) the crisis that followed a lengthy incubation period (colonialism, land enclosures, sharp conflicts between bourgeoisie and aristocracy, the Napoleonic wars) and established British world hegemony on a foundation of the textile industry, the railways and free trade; 2) the crisis from 1870 to 1890 which spurred, and then accompanied, the irruption of science into industry (chemicals, electricity), the integration of industry and banks, a final division of the world, and the clash of nationalisms that ended in the First World War; and 3) the post-1929 Great Depression, born of Fordist overproduction, which spread around the world, aided the breakthrough of fascism and was overcome only after a second global conflict. Different situations, different sequences, and above all different outcomes: but in each case, a severe and contagious economic crisis accompanied, and ended with, profound changes in the social structure, the hierarchy of states and the social division of labour, often involving the threat or reality of war and victorious or defeated revolutions. Capitalism sometimes gained the space for a re-launch, sometimes had to accept a compromise, but it always had to transform itself.

The most acute theorists of this type of crisis have passionately tried to identify a historical tendency hidden within it. But none has ever fully succeeded, as all have had the honesty to admit. Marx, who searched hardest for a tendency that would support his revolutionary expectations, found one countervailing factor after another; he repeatedly asserted his confidence in revolution, but did not exclude the possibility that everything would end in common ruin. Keynes predicted the euthanasia of capitalism, without going into the whys or wherefores. Schumpeter, who was really a conservative, and who assigned to crises the task of salutary destruction, ended up thinking that capitalism and socialism had reached a positive convergence with each other.

I am not going to join the absurd chase for a key to the secret. What I do think we are now in a position to say with certainty, as we were not able to do at the time, is that a transformative crisis of this type began in 1970. And we might add that, until 1982, the crisis fulfilled its particular role of disorganizing and destroying obstacles to capitalist restructuring – a role that could be either overplayed or underplayed. To adapt an expression I generally abhor: it was possible to see through provincial and political excesses and decipher something in the 'plan of capital' of which capital had as yet no inkling, but of whose future course the world economy already offered a number of signs (some noted above). The first rumblings of crisis were audible everywhere in the late 1960s, as profits and investment entered a long decline and productivity growth slowed. Governments and bosses did not attach too much importance to this; it was attributed to various factors in each country, but tolerance thresholds were still high and recovery did not seem difficult. In France, where wages were not inflation-proofed, pay rises were won and absorbed in a couple of years with a small devaluation; in Britain the Labour government reduced taxes a little and cut social spending a little; in Italy, the shopfloor rights won by workers were more of an issue than wage rises, which, as the lessons of 1964 showed, could be successfully handled through a mixture of speed-up, a little deflation and the threat of job losses. The preoccupations of young people were more political than economic.

The game started in earnest in 1971, when Nixon suddenly announced the end of the gold-dollar standard and brought on the collapse of the postwar Bretton Woods system that had ensured stable exchange rates in a context of rapidly growing international trade. It was a hugely important decision, not taken lightly, which a number of factors had made necessary. The United States was overburdened with spending related to the Vietnam war (of which other countries, especially a booming Japan, took advantage), and with a balance of payments deficit connected to the 'Great Society' programme, through which Johnson hoped to win over disaffected workers, social minorities and young people. Falling rates of productivity growth (from four to three and then one per cent) were also a worry, as was the effective competition from countries whose development Washington had supported over a quarter of a century for political and economic reasons of its own.

In Italy, not much importance was given to what the new announcement revealed. Employers and the government felt released from a cage, freer to control the value of the currency as it suited them best; besides, the dollar retained its de facto role as the benchmark currency, and confidence in the American economy remained unshaken. Only a few isolated voices detected a turnaround in the economic situation. I remember with some pride an editorial in *Il Manifesto*, 'The Short, Happy Life of Lord Keynes' – a Hemingwayesque title that was perhaps unfair, because Keynes had actually foreseen the fragility of the Bretton Woods agreement, although it highlighted the end of a golden age of policies that had taken his name in vain and sown the illusion that they could deliver permanent growth.

Soon a second alarm bell was heard by everyone, even with exaggerated emotion, and then dismissed. In 1973, and again in 1979, the oil-producing countries concluded that the international balance was in their favour and jointly imposed huge price increases. This was a heavy blow for the whole capitalist economy, which had been guzzling oil at knock-down prices, but it did not affect everyone equally. Third World countries, in particular, found themselves unable to pay for essential oil supplies, whereas the United States, which already covered part of its needs from internal production, had unused reserves which the new prices enabled it to exploit. For two countries, Britain and Norway, it was actually a stroke of good fortune, since it spurred them on to discover highly advantageous oil reserves in their territorial waters. The price rises were certainly a problem for countries like Italy that relied heavily on exports, with important chemicals and plastics industries and high levels of automobile production and consumption. But they also triggered another serious, if less widely noticed, process. The oil-exporting countries did not have the capacity to deploy the new influx of capital efficiently for their internal development, nor the will to use it to improve the conditions of life for poorer sections of their population – still less either the will or the capacity to invest it productively elsewhere, in underdeveloped countries. What they mainly did instead was direct it towards secure financial assets in the West that offered high rates of return. But, since there were still barriers in the United States to the movement of capital, huge quantities of footloose 'petrodollars' piled up, mostly in the City of London, on the lookout for speculative returns. In the end, in order to regain some control over the dollar, Washington had to give way and allow free circulation of these sums. So began the 'financialization' that later became the guiding feature of the real economy, whose costs and results we are able to measure today.

All this had two ominous short-term effects. One part of this capital, unable to find productive outlets in a world economy hungry for investment, threw itself into currency speculation that magnified the impact of any (deliberately chosen or externally imposed) exchange-rate variations. Meanwhile, under the auspices of the major international organizations (IMF, World Bank), another part was offered in the form of loans to underdeveloped countries, at rates of interest that started low but later crept up. This tended to replace import-substitutionist industries with export industries, so that the countries in question, with economic and political systems incapable of competing internationally, accumulated huge levels of debt and had to use a large part of their export revenue to pay off the interest, in a vicious circle of poverty and underdevelopment. A similar vicious circle developed in Eastern Europe and the USSR, which tried to use loans and imported turnkey factories to make up for their own modernization deficit.

This set of factors, and others I shall mention later, did not cause a general collapse, but they did lead to a downward trend of ever more frequent conjunctural crises and a new, uncontrolled situation that no one knew quite what to make of: its name was stagflation. Deflation, or lay-offs, were tried as a way of fighting double-digit inflation, raising profit levels and lowering wage costs. But it was soon realized that working-class resistance was a tough nut to crack. Unemployment in a fragmented labour market, where social protection could not be easily eliminated, had little effect on wage costs and welfare expenditure; above all, in an integrated market, deflation in one economy could combine with deflation in others to precipitate a depression instead of recovery. Attempts were then made to boost public spending, to revive consensual politics, and to give cautious Keynesian-style support to companies, but it was soon realized that, in an open market, rising demand sucks in imports and generates inflation rather than new investment. In short, the outcome was a vicious circle between and within the two fronts. The final experiment, then, was competitive devaluation. This brought some relief for a while, but only until other countries reacted in the same way. The inflationary effects then kicked in, further accentuated by international speculation, especially in countries where, for good or ill, wages and the interest on public debt were index-linked.

The economic crisis was not equally serious or out of control in all the affected countries; it is useful to keep this in mind, because the differences were replicated in the later restructuring. Japan, for instance, was actually able to contain imports without explicitly protectionist measures, while its companies boosted exports through overseas subsidiaries that assembled their products within the final market (mainly the United States). Germany managed to remain industrially competitive because it focused on the quality of its goods rather than price differentials, or because it could more easily shed a surplus of foreign labour; it was therefore under less pressure to vary the Deutschmark exchange rate, and indeed it began to export capital. Other economies closed their eyes and accepted the plentiful loans on offer that gave an illusion of wealth, but the resulting debt burden eventually saddled them with an even deeper depression, plus runaway inflation.

By the end of the decade, unemployment had reached levels reminiscent of the 1930s, public debt was higher than ever before in peacetime, growth rates in the West had fallen by half in a seesaw movement, real wages were stagnating or even falling, and the social state faced rising costs and the first round of significant attacks. Meanwhile, neoliberal theories were unexpectedly staging a gradual but strong comeback in the academic world. International financial institutions, seemingly autonomous but effectively governed by Washington and finance capital, were increasing their power, and national governments (whether headed by conservatives or social democrats) had more or less lined up with them. The only recognizable exceptions were two little countries, Sweden and Austria, whose strong prime ministers (Palme and Kreisky) were responding in ways that greatly cushioned the impact of the crisis and saved the basic framework of an alternative model, prioritizing full employment and even extending social protection. But, we should note, it was an exception based on international neutrality, deep popular trust and a perfectly functioning social state. And they were two small countries on the margins of Western Europe.

We may now draw a few conclusions that will help us assess the developments in Italy.

1) It is by no means evident that a major disturbance to the economy should have necessarily entailed the defeat of the Left, nor that capitalism started out with all the instruments to solve the crisis rapidly to its own advantage and to impose the kind of restructuring it thought best. The crisis of 1929 led to the New Deal and gave Roosevelt three presidential terms, but it also led to Nazi rule in Germany, to a second world war, and eventually to a constructive compromise between the two rival systems. What is clear is that such a crisis always requires difficult choices, bold and consistent alternative programmes, a strong and stable basis of support in society, high-quality leadership capable of taking sharp knocks or making real compromises, and a capacity to look ahead to the future. All that is very difficult for anyone to have all the time – and particularly so in the period of which we are speaking. For the economic crisis hit a group of countries to which Italy, a relatively minor country, was now linked, at a time when Europe was only a common market, and politically subaltern to boot. We had to, and wanted to, keep within the limits of a fragile parliamentary democracy which functioned well enough when it was a question of maintaining prosperity, or redistributing its fruits, but much less well when it came to paying here and now for future projects, replacing key powers with others that worked better, or building compromises that would convince and benefit one's supporters, while needing to be imposed on those disinclined to accept anything more than petty verbal compromises. Above all, we were not aware of the reality in which we operated, and still less had we made the masses aware of it; we therefore did not know the minimum that we could achieve without capitulating,

nor the maximum that we could rationally propose. In retrospect – and keeping to our chess metaphor – the conditions did not exist for a transition to socialism (since this could no longer take place only at a national level), but at the same time any limited corrective reforms were inadequate. The task was to avoid defeat and to use the strength we had already acquired to achieve a 'pact', which would consolidate the gains, avoid decline and leave a way ahead open, both preserving an identity as a lever and moving on to face the next encounter over a period of years. Togliatti succeeded in doing this in 1944. Berlinguer did not succeed in the 1970s, because of mistakes that were not only his (of which he was later aware), but about which it is not possible to remain silent.

2) In that crisis period, as in any other, elements of a new structure began to take shape amid the chaos of the 'destruction' of the old. Towards the end of the anti-fascist war or immediately afterwards, for example, the conditions had already been ripe for the coming cold war, American hegemony in the West and unification of the European market – in short, for a new capitalist order and a bipolar world. About that future, even Togliatti (unlike Gramsci) had lacked a lucid vision. Now, however, the signs of a new order were beginning to emerge: a speeding up of globalization to integrate a series of new countries, a technological leap, a different class composition, and so on. Before that took shape, it was necessary to analyse these incipient tendencies, so that we could equip ourselves to confront them.

AN UNCONSUMMATED MARRIAGE

So, the PCI found itself face to face with two very difficult problems – distinct from each other, and not exactly contemporaneous, but more and more intertwined and interactive. Both required prompt answers, and clarity about long-term objectives. The first problem was to offer a political outlet for a social conflict in which many of the PCI's old and new voters had played a part, but to do so while avoiding a slump in production and a victorious reactionary counteroffensive. The second problem was how to cope with the economic recession and the long international financial crisis. De facto this task fell almost entirely to the PCI, since, partly through its own fault, it was the only party with the strength to take it on and some intellectual resources to bring to bear on it. To accuse the PCI, and particularly Berlinguer, of assuming this task only to break down the prejudice that barred its entry into government therefore seems to me unjust and misleading. It would be equally unjust to read in his choices an undeclared intention to discard any Communist identity.

But this does not preclude – indeed, it makes more trenchant – a critique of Berlinguer's policy in the 1970s, both as a whole and in nearly all its phases. I myself, for example, recognized from the beginning that it dealt with real problems, even contained partial truths, but I also argued that the answers it offered were fundamentally mistaken. There were a series of tactical or operational errors and unforeseeable difficulties, and things were undoubtedly aggravated by attempts from elsewhere to sabotage the policy. But even these are indicative of an error and an underlying fragility, which continued to mark the stubborn pursuit of the policy over nearly ten years, and doomed it to failure.

THE FIRST STEPS

The political line that Berlinguer developed to confront these complex problems, and which he applied in stages, without ever recoiling, took shape long before it came to be known as the 'historic compromise'. The first steps came as early as 1970: they were cautious and concerned a number of areas, but it is not impossible to pick out a guiding thread and to assess its importance.

The guiding thread of the first stage, though only implicit, involved an objective that was reached sooner than expected. The reasoning was simple and had all the force of common sense: in order to compel the government to change direction soon, as the situation demanded, while remaining on the democratic road and avoiding the risk of abortive confrontation, it was necessary, though not sufficient, for the PCI to become so strong electorally that Italy could not be governed without it. That was the priority. To achieve it, Berlinguer thought it was not enough to restart the social struggle, even with legitimate and widely heard demands, since these were mainly of concern to proletarian layers and vanguards already won to the Left. The aim had to be to change the allegiance of disaffected middle layers entrenched in their petty privileges and traditional ideology, and to neutralize the growing hostility of a modern bourgeoisie alarmed by workers' struggles.

The Party leadership discussed this frankly and heatedly on more than one occasion. The minutes, useful for once, show that Berlinguer directly proposed a new line of thinking, first expressed in greater worries than before about the economic situation and the rightward shifts in society that it was producing. To contain this danger, he argued, the Party should not encourage but restrain demands and disputes related to the social state, which the trade unions had recently been launching. When Lama[1] retorted that such disputes were not demanding wages for workers but rights for all, Berlinguer made himself even clearer: 'But you're still talking about an indirect wage.' It was not a good time to communicate such a clear policy choice to the membership; it would also have encountered criticism among trade unionists still engaged in national bargaining. Nevertheless, well-disposed individuals would certainly have got to hear about it. Meanwhile, a more general signal was given in a document that appeared in *L'Unità*, which stated that the PCI was a national force ready to help the country in its hour of need. A number of employers picked up on the signal appreciatively. Confindustria was divided between an obtuse section that could not abide trade unions and was shifting its capital abroad, and the more powerful large corporations, which understood that it was necessary to keep the door open for dialogue. These corporations were even then making new investments in labour-saving technology, but they could not secure wage cuts only through higher unemployment; they were beginning to try out a new strategy, slowly at first, but with a bright future. The idea was to farm out parts of production to satellites whose workforce did not enjoy social protection, and at the same time to spread the company's own investment through the formation of financial holding companies. None of this would be helped by confrontation, and so there was a need for some kind of political protection. The major newspapers, owned by the same corporations, but also the foreign press suddenly began to speak of the PCI as a 'responsible' force.

A second step, also designed to win over moderate opinion, was taken in 1971 and again in 1972. It concerned relations with other parties and with the government. I have already said that

1. Luciano Lama: leading Communist and national secretary of the CGIL from 1970 to 1986.

the latter was like a bear garden at the time: there was certainly more scope to push something through it. The PCI therefore gave up trying to put pressure on the Socialists – who were wavering just then because they had decided to put an end to the Centre Left governments – and adopted a wait-and-see attitude, prepared to judge their actions on a case by case basis. It toned down its criticisms of the famous 'Decretone',[2] which in fact was a deflationary manoeuvre to rein in public expenditure. In exchange, it obtained shortly afterwards a number of important agreements on legislation that it had been demanding for decades: implementation of the constitutional provision for regional authorities, a progressive income tax, allocation of a trillion lire for the construction of public housing on land compulsorily purchased at farmland prices. These were not insignificant measures, which could be presented as proof of the PCI's effectiveness in opposition. But, if we look at them a little more closely, we can already see how half-reforms could remain on paper, or contain a hidden sting, if they were entrusted to inefficient or hostile civil servants and their workings were left deliberately unclear.

For example, the initiative on a progressive income tax left inflation out of account in the setting of higher bands, exempted financial profits, lacked norms and structures for combating avoidance or evasion, and ended up punishing dependent labour (on which companies acted as tax collectors) and favouring various forms of autonomous labour (grant recipients, moonlighters, freelancers). As for the regional authorities, there was to be no matching reduction in the central apparatuses, nor any redefinition of areas of competence or recognition of fiscal autonomy and responsibility. This meant that they were likely in the end to repeat the past experience of autonomous regions: that is, offer new opportunities for clientelism and burn a hole in the public budget – which is what did happen in many cases.

In any event, the immediate effect on the Party's image was positive. By the time we became aware of the damage, it was very difficult to repair (in fact, some of it we still carry on our backs).

Another example is the important government directive that required public corporations to allocate 40 per cent of their

2. 'Decretone': packet of direct taxes on items of working-class consumption, issued in a decree of August 1970, which triggered a wave of struggles in opposition to it.

investment to the Mezzogiorno. This was supposed to be the industrialization fund for depressed areas. But in reality, since there was no plan to steer it, the investment went into the creation of giant factories unconnected to their surrounding areas, in declining sectors of the economy. They created short-term employment in the building industry, but were 'desert skyscrapers' that dug a bottomless pit of public debt amid pockets of parasitism.

The third step in the evolution of PCI policy, by necessity more than choice, was the long, mishandled but eventually successful saga of the divorce law and the referendum that attempted to cancel it. This prefigured the still more delicate issue of abortion. Meanwhile, a late but priceless fruit of '68 burst onto the scene: the new women's movement, concerned not only with emancipation but with gender difference, which it regarded as a value to be recognized, not an inequality to be rectified. The referendum thus provided the occasion for one of those great mass debates that shape the profile of a whole people – a debate on the relationship between individual and collective morality. The starting point of the women's movement was explosive, and only superficially methodological: 'The personal is political.' In that historical period, this was a revolutionary idea. For neocapitalism was beginning to invade and remould – indeed, it was compelled to remould – every dimension of life: culture, mentalities, lifestyles and consumption behaviour, interpersonal relations, family structures and places of residence. It thereby threw into crisis structures and institutions that had existed for centuries. If it was true that the personal was political, then politics and especially economics must in turn be capable of directly shaping the personal. The question was how to take on board the liberating aspects of the crisis (the crumbling of intolerable hierarchies and chain-like restrictions), while moving beyond it in the direction of freedom, solidarity and responsibility.

The PCI sidestepped this debate, and today it confronts us only in impoverished, histrionic and degenerate forms – that is, as a clash of religious or ethnic fundamentalisms driven by a common struggle against 'moral relativism', value-free liberty and ephemeral culture. This is too complex a theme to be tackled here. I shall simply consider how the PCI approached the battle over divorce, which is not uninteresting in itself.

Togliatti had always been reluctant to take up issues regarding marriage and divorce. But in the early 1960s a number of women in the Party and the women's union (UDI) broke the embargo, focusing on scandalous elements in the existing family law and challenging the absolute power given to the husband. Today the points they made seem self-evident, but in those days it was a key battle that required much courage to wage. It is enough to see the film *Divorce Italian-Style* again, or to read about Coppi and the 'lady in white',[3] to realize that patriarchy was not an insignificant relic of defunct legislation but enjoyed the full protection of the law. Pius XII expressed the Church's view with solemn eloquence: 'Each family is a common life, each well-ordered common life needs a head, and each head comes from God. Therefore the family you have founded has a head that God has invested with authority.' This conception was present not only in the unequal law that regulated and punished sexual behaviour, but also in property law, choice of residence and the education of children. It was therefore the first bastion to fall. The PCI leadership fell into line on this point, and a new bill was presented in parliament, only to be opposed and blocked by the ruling majority. But the bill also contained a proposal allowing for divorce – and here Togliatti put his foot down. He obviously feared a confrontation with the Catholic world, at the very moment when it was moving away from the rigid positions of Pius XII. But there was also another, more respectable reason for his veto: a fear that the proposal would be opposed in the country by women themselves, or at least that it would expose them to blackmail and other risks, since the relationship of forces and the material position of women – a million had just been made redundant, and many worked 'on and off' for a pittance – made them the weaker and more exposed partner in a marriage.

But society was changing: '68 had left indelible traces in people's conduct, full employment had spread to many regions, and girls too had been brought into the educational system. The divorce issue was ripe for the agenda and could well end in victory. When Liberals and Socialists took up the banner in parliament – Pannella was particularly effective[4] – the PCI could hardly withhold

3. Fausto Coppi was a famous racing cyclist who, in the early 1950s, began an adulterous cohabitation with Giulia Occhini, first referred to in the press as 'the lady in white' after she was seen waiting for him in a white outfit. The 'scandal' of their relationship prompted highly public interventions by the police and the Church.

4. Marco Pannella: founder-member and leader of the Radical Party.

its support, and so the new legislation was passed. But the Vatican remained intransigent, and Fanfani saw a referendum to scrap the law as a means of rebuilding unity in Christian Democracy and scoring a victory nationwide.

Berlinguer knew he had to commit the Party, but he was afraid of hindering dialogue with the DC and – above all – he felt sure of losing. He therefore tried various ways of reaching an agreement (with the Vatican through Bufalini, with the DC through Moro and Andreotti, and finally Cossiga). Bufalini and Barca – Berlinguer's *hommes de confiance* – were taken on as secret agents. But the negotiations were murky, intermittent and doomed to failure. In the end, the PCI marched its troops to the referendum, carrying 'Catholic dissidents' with it, and Berlinguer's fears proved to be unfounded: the victory was greater than anyone had foreseen. The PCI enjoyed the rewards of being on the winning side, having at the same time convinced its adversary that it was much less secularist than the others. But the price of success was not inconsiderable. Its way of handling the divorce issue gave the hegemony to Liberals and Radicals, in a battle in which individual liberty was at stake; and it implanted the idea, in various sections of the public, that the PCI saw the Vatican and Christian Democracy as its main interlocutors when it wished to speak to the Catholic masses. This was also its first step in a new kind of politics, based on a network of permanent (and often secret) contacts with apparatuses and individuals. It was the modus operandi that has always characterized diplomatic relations between states.

14

Historic Compromise as a Strategy

Encouraged by these first successes, Berlinguer decided that he could and should propose a long-term organic political formula to the Party and the country. In a three-part series of articles in *Rinascita* he offered what he saw as a strategic platform, to which he would stick throughout the 1970s. This essay won over and committed the entire PCI leadership, Longo being the only one to voice any objections. And, after some bewilderment, the rank and file too accepted it and tried hard to stand by it.

Even those who later expressed puzzlement about what they were implementing (Ingrao and Natta, for instance) did not challenge the proposal. Only after some years, courageously noting the poor results and the impossibility of taking it further, did Berlinguer himself take responsibility for a profound change of course, at which point he ran into not a little resistance.

Careful analysis is therefore in order here. Recently I have reread and thought some more about Berlinguer's articles, prepared, if necessary, to change my mind about the clear criticism I expressed of them at the time. But I have found no reason to correct it, and in fact it seems to me more justified than ever. What followed was not a result of unforeseen events, tactical errors or hostile actions, and it helped to accelerate and worsen both the defeat and the consequences of defeat. But the weakness and contradictions of the project are even more visible today in the initial outline. I shall now try to demonstrate this.

The first part of Berlinguer's essay was almost entirely devoted to the lessons of the tragic events in Chile, which were then weighing heavily on the mind of every comrade. The choice of this as his starting point was questionable, and, consciously or not, his reconstruction of the events was improperly inflected by support for a political decision. There was no doubt that weakness or naïvety on the part of Allende and his comrades had played a role in the disaster. Allende had become president – and in Chile that meant having full responsibility for governing the country – in a constitutionally unacceptable manner, with a sizeable but only relative majority of 39 per cent of the popular vote. He faced a parliament in which he had an occasional majority, but which created obstacles more than it gave him support. Moreover, his aims and dispositions by no means had a revolutionary character, concentrating their fire against long-standing predatory foreign monopolies and unsustainable agrarian oligarchies. These were powerful forces, but other international ones, even more powerful, stood behind them, and Chile belonged to a region of the semi-colonial world in which all the elements of stability were then under threat. The army had re-pledged its loyalty to the Constitution, but this did not change the fact that it was a separate caste, trained in the United States. The dangers of a reactionary counter-attack were therefore real. Probably Allende underestimated them, but some of his left-wing supporters were also pushing him to press ahead at a faster pace. He certainly did not lack popular support, and intellectuals and technical experts were arriving from all over Latin America to help him; the opposition parties were divided and lacked a mass base, although the other side of the coin was that a large part of the population was depoliticized and wavering. In the end, Allende was overthrown neither by a parliamentary coalition nor by popular mobilizations. First he was worn down by economic chaos and corporate revolt – both consciously directed from abroad. And then, when this did not suffice, a military coup, suggested and funded by the United States, unleashed a wave of bloody repression and installed a despotic government that would last many years. In his essay, Berlinguer recognized this dynamic in a somewhat leaden sentence: 'The characteristics of imperialism, especially North American imperialism, remain those of bullying, a spirit of aggression and conquest, a tendency to oppress other peoples, whenever circumstances suggest it.' But, in that case, how would it have been enough to develop a 'better relationship', as he put it, with part of Chilean Christian Democracy, an impotent and often complicit element? And did the conditions really exist, or could they be created, for the same danger to strike Italy and Europe, at a time when at least formal democratic institutions were returning in Greece and Portugal, and when Washington was losing the war in Vietnam and sinking into paralysis? Certainly there was an economic and political crisis in Italy too, but it was of quite a different kind and much more controllable. To take Chile as a typical case, as Greece had been taken before, was not only forced but misleading. It blurred other real difficulties with which it was necessary to come to grips, as well as the possibilities of change offered by the situation. It indicated an uncertainty of analysis, which, in the end, was reflected in uncertain proposals.

In the second part of his essay, in which he dealt with the Italian situation and the PCI's objectives in the period ahead, Berlinguer changed his tone and raised his sights. Here his argument is well put together, and we can summarize it without risk of distortion. Italy was passing through a crisis period of utmost importance: a crisis of the economic system, unable to guarantee a continuation of the long boom; a crisis of social equilibrium, such that there was no longer any guarantee that prosperity could be maintained, or spread more evenly through trade union pressure alone; a crisis of the institutions, paralysed by corporatism and often riddled with corruption and hidden power networks; and a crisis of the political system, no longer capable of delivering stable majorities and functioning governments. Amid all this, old dimensions of backwardness were reasserting themselves in society, together with new contradictions arising from a certain kind of capitalist modernization. Also visible, however, were the results of major defensive and offensive struggles that had challenged the system, conquered new rights, affirmed new values, new social subjects and newly independent states – in essence, new relationships of forces in Italy and the world. If such a crisis spiralled in on itself, left up to a ruling class bent on restoration, it would put democracy itself at risk. To prevent this, it was necessary and possible to bring about a profound turn in the government of the country, in its programme and in the structure of power. Berlinguer added two further points to clarify what he meant by 'turn'. First, 'structural reforms geared to socialism' were necessary, that is, a higher stage of progressive democracy. Second (quoting Togliatti and Longo), it was 'wrong to equate the democratic road with parliamentarism: parliament can fulfil its role only if the parliamentary initiative of labour-movement parties is linked to mass struggles and the growth of democratic power in society and all the branches of the state.' And, even when he underlined the need to gain majority support in the population and to bring together the Communist, Socialist and Catholic masses, he mentioned in order: working-class unity respecting the diversity of roles and cultural traditions; alliance with progressive middle layers free from corporatism (though not otherwise differentiated socially); and women, young people and intellectuals, that is, the new social subjects that had emerged in the struggle.

Up to this point, not only was his analysis consistent with the historical identity of Italian Communism; it also more clearly took the offensive. The only criticism one could make – and I did make it at the time – concerned its perfunctory analysis of the crisis and the world situation (especially in the internal Communist movement), its failure to assess the state of the mass movement, and its lack of programmatic priorities with which to measure the turn. These were not insignificant points, since they left too much leeway in the relationship between tactics and strategy, alliances and objectives.

In the third part of his essay, Berlinguer tried to round things off by giving a clearer idea of how and where to begin. But it was precisely here that contradictions appeared which changed the character of the project, undermining both its logic and its realism. The main thrust was summarized in a sentence that later became famous: 'It is not possible to govern and transform the country with a majority of 51 per cent.' On the whole, and in light of the preceding argument, this was an incontrovertible statement. It is indeed impossible to 'govern and transform' a socially, regionally and culturally complex country while respecting the Constitution, unless one has sufficient strength, in parliament and elsewhere, to decide on and implement deep reforms affecting diffuse interests and ingrained habits, and sufficient time for the reforms to have the desired effects. This was incontrovertible but ambiguous. For what happens if one does not yet have that strength, and there is a vacuum of government and a dangerously heated crisis? Does one remain in opposition, waiting for the crisis to produce the conditions for a real turn, and trying to help it along? Or does one separate the two parts of 'govern and transform', and at least initially take part in a heterogeneous majority with a minimum programme and uncertain prospects, putting off until later a real turn, in the hope that the very dynamic of cooperation, and the resulting advances in mass consciousness, will combine with the greater legitimacy that comes from government office to make a more ambitious set of objectives possible? Clearly it was not an abstract choice based on principle, but nor was it only a question of tactics to be adapted step by step with a view to the likely advantages. There was a strategic choice to be made, on the basis of an analysis of a particular historical situation.

Togliatti opted in advance for participation in national unity governments, and was prepared to accept a version that was perhaps more moderate than necessary. But he did so after an assessment of the relationship of forces in a country emerging from fascism, which had lost the war and had Western armies on its soil – although it may be that he hoped the unity among the victorious powers would last a little longer than it did. Above all, he thought that immediate involvement in government – to which all the forces in the Resistance were open – was not the key thing. What was key was to win the Republic and an advanced, commonly agreed, constitutional charter. And that is what he achieved, with the support of Dossetti, Lazzati, La Pira and other Catholic intellectuals and politicians. It was a 'historic compromise', and we would defend it today against any attempts to dismantle it.

In the 1970s, however, neither the economic crisis nor the social conflict could be solved by separating government and transformation 'in advance'. In fact, scarcely was the ink dry on Berlinguer's last article when he himself was proposing a 'new turn in society and the state'. But even if we accept, as he was inclined to do, the idea of a transitional period that would pave the way for more ambitious advances, was such a separation into stages really possible, and on what conditions? The central issue here became that of the political forces available for the project. And Berlinguer did turn his attention to this, in a final section that had a lot in common with those 'imaginary realms' of which he was so scornful. For it really was 'imaginary' on his part to take the unity of the Left for granted: unity with the PSI had broken down ten years earlier on the political level, and had been several times in danger within the trade unions and local authorities; it could have been rebuilt in the 1970s, but only with patient work and without any certainty of success; the PCI had to avoid giving the impression that, in prioritizing its relations with Christian Democracy, it wanted to reduce the PSI to a marginal or subaltern role. No less imaginary was the notion that the far Left had no influence and would be easy to control. It was, to be sure, disoriented and scattered, but its very crisis made it more likely to mount challenges: for example, the interesting formation of the Party of Proletarian Unity (PdUP) and the rethinking in Avanguardia Operaia and the Workers' Movement for Socialism (MLS). Moreover, the vast youth arena that had developed between 1968 and 1970 was still a large-scale, if disorganized, presence, and although it was often prepared to vote for the PCI as the only parliamentary opposition it had by no means thrown in the towel; its reaction to the PCI's low-profile support for a broad government coalition was unpredictable, but it would certainly not be sympathetic.

A coalition government that would include the PCI in the near future therefore depended mainly on a direct agreement with the DC, but here too flights of the imagination ran up against hard facts. Just a month previously *Rinascita* had published a special supplement on Christian Democracy, which had contained analyses by Chiaromonte and Natta, and by experts on the DC such as Chiarante[1] and Accornero.[2] One is struck today by the way in which they all agreed, from their different angles, that the DC had become very different from its original self: less clerical but also less religious; deeply rooted in society, but through multiple channels of clientelism, social protection, shrewd use of power and support for companies; projecting itself as a guarantee of economic stability, with long experience in managing public expenditure; in short, a party-state built over thirty years and capable of reconciling different interests in society. It was therefore divided into a number of organized currents, each organically linked to certain social layers, regions, public corporations or branches of the state apparatus, but strongly united in believing that the party had to maintain its supremacy. The trump card of Christian Democracy

1. With a background in the left opposition within Christian Democracy, Giuseppe Chiarante moved towards the PCI in the late 1950s and served variously as a Communist parliamentarian and senator. He was closely identified with the Berlinguer leadership, and later opposed the 'Bolognina turn'.

2. Aris Accornero: industrial sociologist, especially noted for his analyses of Fordism and post-Fordism.

was that it could point to the expansion of the economy under its rule, and to the wise way in which it had distributed the benefits.

This did not mean that the DC was an impregnable fortress, since the decline in economic growth had reduced its scope for mediation among its constituencies. The cycle of workers' struggles had had a clear impact on the thinking and behaviour of labour organizations traditionally associated with it, such as the CISL and ACLI; even the farmers, under pressure from agribusiness and deals imposed by larger European countries, were beginning to escape the total control of Coldiretti and the Federconsorzi.[3] The parliamentary alliance of the Centre had broken down, and repeated underhand attempts to reach ad hoc agreements with the far Right created tensions with the DC more than they provided a solution. Above all, the Catholic turn at the Vatican Council, though superficially reversed, still had an effect at the grass roots and had even led to some new thinking among intellectuals close to the hierarchy. At a little-known but important conference (Lucca, 1967), Ardigò and Del Noce[4] had asked: 'After decades of government by a Catholic party, ordinary people are wondering how it is that the Christian imprint on society is on the decline.' Yet, although the Communists, for all their greater strength, were now considered less of a danger, the Christian Democrats remained intransigent in refusing to consider any real agreement with the PCI – precisely because its strength could throw the party-state into question, threatening the grip on power that was what bound the DC together. No deal ever materialized – and none could have, without provoking a crisis and break-up of Christian Democracy and releasing the forces bottled up inside it.

But Berlinguer and the PCI leadership refused to draw the conclusions from these obvious facts. On the contrary, they were becoming convinced that only a gradual shift in the DC as a whole, through an experience of shared government with the PCI, could bring about an alliance of the Communist, Socialist and Catholic masses. At the end of his essay, Berlinguer therefore got around the problem with a sophism:

3. See Chapter Six, notes 7 and 8.

4. Augusto Del Noce: Catholic philosopher and political theorist, elected Christian Democrat senator in 1984.

> The DC is not a metaphysical reality but a changing historical subject: it was born in opposition to the old liberal and conservative state and crushed by fascism, then it took part in the war of liberation, contributed to the drafting of the Constitution, and took part in the Cold War on the opposite side to our own, and in worse forms. Today it may change again, and it is up to us to help and force it to do so.

Thus Berlinguer ended by committing himself to a proposal for the government of Italy: a 'new great historic compromise', led by the two major parties. What the compromise would involve, and how it might become 'historic', remained something of a mystery. It is still not clear to me why such a risk was taken. Perhaps he really thought he had found a way out, in a complex situation that urgently required answers. Perhaps overconfidence in the impetus and solidity of the PCI's principles made him believe that it would be immune from the risks. More likely – although the one does not exclude the other – he did not think he would be forced to make the choice so soon, before the situation was ripe, or that the Christian Democrats would make such paltry offers; he probably overestimated Moro's extraordinary ability to say yes and no at the same time, to promise and to procrastinate. In reality, instead of finding a way out, Berlinguer had put his hand in a trap, and by the time he pulled it back, it was too late.

15

From Apogee to Defeat

In my background reading for this book, I came across a sentence that caustically sums up what happened to the PCI in the 1970s. It comes from Ramsay MacDonald, towards the end of his not exactly brilliant experience of National Government, answering an American journalist's question about the lessons he would draw from it: 'I'd already learned how frustrating it is to be excluded from government for a long time, but then I understood that there's something worse: to go into government and realize that almost nothing can be done.' This pithy conclusion, if not its wit, might have come from the mouths of those involved in similar experiments in other countries, including Italy, from the Centre Left of the 1960s to the present day. But it is most pertinent to the fate of the PCI's endeavours in the mid 1970s.

The story began with a surprising victory in the regional and local elections of June 1975, which radically changed the relationship of political forces and seemed to open the door to government for the PCI after decades of exclusion. The Communists suddenly jumped to 33.5 per cent of the vote, taking first place in nearly all the large cities (except Palermo and Bari): three million more votes than in 1972, mainly from young people, not always cast for reasons consonant with the Party's objectives, but expressing a common resolve to change the state of things. The Socialist Party won 12 per cent and seemed prepared, though not yet decided, to end its subaltern participation in DC-led governments. The PdUP took 2 per cent, having stood in ten regions out of fifteen. The DC dropped to 35 per cent, losing two million votes not to the Right and the Liberals but to the Left and secular parties of the Centre Left. With general elections due soon, it was clear to everyone that it would not be able to govern the country without the participation, or at least the support, of the Communists. Yet this very success lit up problems that had until then been hidden or deliberately evaded. First, paradoxically, it had come too soon. The PCI had intentionally remained ambiguous about the time frame of the historic compromise. Was it a long-term, or least a medium-term, strategy (Berlinguer fulminated against anyone who denied this), or was it an immediate proposal for government, necessary to confront an urgent crisis (as quite a few other leaders, including Amendola, believed)? Now the knot would have to be disentangled in a few months, or at most a year.

This gave rise to another problem. While the Left as a whole now stood at 47 per cent, the Socialist Party was refusing to join another DC government and was toying with the idea of an agreement with the PCI. How was this to be interpreted: as a shaky or even mischievous position that required caution, or as a lever to push the DC onto the ropes and force it into a clear turn, or into opposition?

In an editorial in the recently founded, but already authoritative, daily *La Repubblica*, Eugenio Scalfari did not mince his words. It is worth quoting him, because he expressed a view common in intellectual and social circles not traditionally on the Left:

> The last Christian Democrat conference showed that the DC is now a debased expression of a broad alliance of parasitic clienteles. Until it changes its nature – that is, until it becomes the party of democratic Catholics, instead of the representative of arch-fraternities of power – any idea of a 'historic compromise' is untimely. It will therefore be necessary to present an alignment of the Left and a programme for a Left government at the next general elections.

Shortly afterwards Francesco De Martino, then secretary of the PSI, is said to have put forward the same proposal, making it rather more digestible to the PCI: the door should be kept open for dialogue with the DC, but starting from the strength and ideas of a united Left. In this version, the proposal did not require anyone to make a turn or to give anything up. Even those like Berlinguer, who were convinced that the strategic aim had to be to find common ground with the Catholics, and who thought there might be a shift in the DC to make this possible, seemed to have no reason to refrain from using the strength of a united Left to impel the first steps. But, to be serious, there were reasons for him to tread warily. Two major obstacles loomed, and his mistake was not to have recognized and dealt with them while there was perhaps still time.

First of all, to rebuild a solid and durable political unity between Communists and Socialists that could sustain even a temporary rapprochement with the DC, it would not be enough simply to turn the clock back. Too much water had flowed under the bridge, both ideologically and at the level of each party's social implantation. Both sides would have to make a partial correction – one in its judgement of the nature and evolution of the Soviet Union, the other in relation to the discipline of Atlanticism. One would have to moderate its passion for having 'some button to press' in a government office, and the other to contain its impatience to acquire visible legitimacy as part of government. On both these points, there was space for innovation but also problem areas. The two international blocs were in crisis, with weakened leaderships, but for this very reason the policy of coexistence was in difficulty and each bloc was preoccupied with issues of control in its own ranks.

At the same time, the election results of 1975 offered scope for successful initiatives in many cities where the Left already had the resources and capacity, but in other regions, and in many peripheral parts of the country, the tempting new opportunities were more ambiguous: that is to say, they pushed in the direction of any old broad alliance, with a lot of booty-sharing among the parties and not too close an eye on items of expenditure. This explains why the PCI was quick to suspect a trap in the proposal to prioritize a relationship among the Left; and why the Socialist advocates of a Left alternative later helped to replace De Martino with Craxi, who did not disguise the fact that he had quite different ambitions.

The key problem that came to light in 1975, however, was the lack of a programme. The question of a new government and new alliances was appearing on the agenda at the very moment when it was most difficult to tackle it, since 1975 was also the year in which the structural crisis shaking the world economy came to a head in Italy. There is nothing to say that crisis situations rule out a bold programme of reforms – sometimes the opposite has been the case. But that required the development of new policy ideas, a capacity for running the country and forming stable coalitions, and the understanding and support of the public, especially among those who had voted for you and were counting on the fruits of reform. However, not even a start was made on the work necessary to achieve this. Paradoxically, the programmatic baggage the Socialists had taken to the Centre Left in the 1960s had been bolder and clearer than that which the Left carried with it in 1975. The number one priority was to fill the gap with a new programme, and to mobilize a social bloc around it.

I would like to quote from the courageous and far-sighted verdict that Luigi Longo, by now in failing health, expressed at the leadership discussion of the 1975 election results: 'Our proposal for a "historic compromise" is enigmatic and ambiguous, and this ambiguity probably contributed to our electoral success, but the proposal remains impracticable and will lead us into passivity.'

THE DILEMMA OF 1976

The chickens came home to roost in 1976, when De Martino's demand for 'greater balance' in government policy was followed by the PSI's exit and the calling of early elections. Berlinguer spotted a trap. His judgement was ungenerous, but his predictions proved accurate. In fact, the election results were doubly surprising: the PCI continued its forward march (from 33.5 to 34.4 per cent), a gain which, though modest, this time embraced regions that had long been DC preserves; but, contrary to forecasts, the Christian Democrats jumped back up to 38.8 per cent, at the expense of their smaller allies.

At this point, the mathematics seemed to require some involvement of the PCI. A straightforward coalition of the two main parties (DC and PCI) was out of the question in the immediate future, especially as the DC campaign had sought and obtained support from moderates with the explicit aim of shutting the Communists out of government. (The prominent journalist Indiro Montanelli had written that 'we should hold our noses and vote Christian Democrat again'.) Could the DC go back on its own positions? Besides, a meeting of Atlantic governments had recently fired a shot over the bows by excluding Moro, the representative of the Italian government, on the grounds that he was considered unreliable. On the other hand, the Left lacked both the figures (48 per cent) and the political will to form a government, since the PSI, which had floated the idea, was now weaker than ever, the far Left was marginal, divided and mostly reluctant, and the Social Democrats did not agree to lend their support. It was therefore a tough dilemma. One possibility was to hold fresh elections, with different line-ups and programmes, and to repeat this until a new balance emerged; the other was to form a broadly based emergency government, excluding the extremes, which would address the most urgent problems facing the country and continue acting on them until they were resolved, or until there was a change in the balance among the parties.

The first option – which quite a few, including myself, favoured – was probably the correct one, but also implausible and risky. Implausible because it implied a sudden, radical change in the strategy of the PCI, at a time when it considered itself victorious. Risky because, as we have seen, Left unity had not been built beforehand among parties or in the country, and because there was no convincing common programme for the future. The outcome might therefore be a long period of instability, with no clear solution in sight.

The second option – a broadly based coalition – might have been tried, as the first stage in a more developed turn; explicit participation of the major parties of the Left, with powers in proportion to their weight, would have been the logical corollary. But that solution too was problematic, and of uncertain outcome. Problematic because the DC was a long way from openly accepting it, since it would put an end to its supremacy and disrupt its unity; a bitter tug-of-war would therefore have been likely. Of uncertain outcome because a provisional coalition government would, by its nature, have been inadequate to tackle the real problems, whose origins went back a long way, and a solution to which would necessarily require a long time and affect substantial interests.

Amid the uncertainty, a formula nevertheless emerged that was accepted with no visible sign of resistance. In a way it was a bizarre idea: a monochrome Christian Democrat government, with no binding agreement on programme and no recognized parliamentary majority, supported simply by the fact that the PCI and the PSI would refrain from declaring 'no confidence' in it.

It was a bizarre idea in principle. Minority governments had existed before (though rarely) in other parliamentary democracies, but in such cases a dominant party close to holding a majority had relied on open support from a minority not dissimilar to it. A single-party government with 38 per cent support in the country, facing a line-up of 48 per cent and resting on 'no no-confidence', was unprecedented. So, the government whose first novelty was to have been a legitimation of the PCI ended up legitimating the quasi-monarchical right of the DC to govern the country, and to govern it alone, without a majority. The second bizarre aspect was that the 'emergency government' had no 'emergency programme', was not limited to a precise period of time, and consisted entirely of people who had long been in power with the most diverse allies. The third bizarre aspect, no less important, was that any programme the government might be kind enough to present to parliament would not correspond to a shift in the centres of real extra-institutional power, or in the state bureaucracy that was supposed to implement it. For its part, the Left was offered a symbolic role in chairing a few parliamentary commissions, which, as everyone knows, have had a say only in marginal amendments or occasional trifling pieces of legislation (real direct power: zero). I have never been able to ascertain who came up with this solution. Both PCI and DC leaders from the time have sincerely assured me that the idea originated in their own ranks. Anyhow, the fact is that it was widely accepted – and that, for the Left, it was a 'losing proposition' to assume responsibility for a government in a spurious role. Not a marriage of convenience, nor even an alliance, only a casual adulterous liaison.

Beyond this division of powers – which had frequent disagreement and shaky compromises built into it – we should examine the actual people who played their role in government. The premiership, especially crucial in such a murky situation, fell to Moro's candidate, Giulio Andreotti – on grounds that he offered guarantees to quarrelsome elements on the right of the DC, who, with considerable strength in society, might at any moment have demanded greater consistency with the policies outlined in the election campaign and sanctioned by the extra millions of votes. This argument had some weight, but it was not very convincing. Andreotti was not a straw figure, nor a *trasformista*. Behind an appearance of flexibility and extreme realism, his career displayed a constant identity and a consistently tough approach to politics, so that, though nearly always a member of government, he had nearly always chosen to organize a dissenting minority in the party. He was a right-wing De Gasperian, who not by chance had built his following in Sicily and Lazio. He had always been trusted by the most traditional section of the Church hierarchy, and had, within the limits of possibility, repeatedly sought the support of parties of the Right and Centre Right. He was on good terms with all the big industrial and agricultural employers, and with some pretty shady characters in the world of finance. But above all, thanks to his long service at the heart of government, he enjoyed the confidence of Washington and had an excellent knowledge of the civil service, with many friends in high places. In the 'no no-confidence government', he was flanked where necessary by men from other currents in the DC (mostly 'Doroteans'[1]) not unlike himself. The DC that now took the reins of the state was undoubtedly a changed party, therefore – but it had not changed for the better.

It is true that, in parallel, a political leadership with a different orientation advanced a few steps: Moro and Berlinguer. Nor was it just for show, since they shared a wish to look further ahead and to convert a provisional agreement born of need into a lasting, more substantial convergence. But, aside from the banal yet important fact that neither man had the skill or interest to make a real impact on government action, the dialogue between them generated mutual liking and trust but ended only in postponements or half-agreements. There were two reasons for this. The first had to do with their asymmetrical functions in their respective parties. Berlinguer enjoyed unlimited trust in the PCI, which allowed him to make decisions when he liked, even when mistaken. Moro, on the other hand, had authority in the DC, but as a source of inspiration or a mediator. Two episodes clearly showed this asymmetry: Berlinguer's statement that he felt more secure in the Atlantic alliance, which was accepted without rebuke, even though it was a dubious and gratuitous remark; and Moro's speech in parliament arrogantly defending those implicated in the Lockheed scandal.[2] The second and more important reason for the stop-go dialogue was that both men looked far ahead, but in different directions. For

1. See note 1 on p.157.

2. A scandal involving kickbacks, which engulfed, among others, the president of the Republic, Giovanni Leone, and forced his resignation in June 1978.

Moro, a period of cooperation with the PCI might lead to a new political order, in which the two main parties would democratically represent two alternative projects; whereas for Berlinguer it might pave the way for a compromise and a new social order, in which both the Communists and the Catholics would make a dynamic contribution. They were two different perspectives. One was meant gradually to bring about what the Centre Left had failed to achieve, implicitly accepting that the PCI, by far the largest force in the Left, had gone further than declaring autonomy from Moscow and respect for the Constitution to change its Communist identity, and adhere to the Western camp. The other emphasized an 'Italian road to socialism', however gradual, and the overcoming of the blocs. Both, however, were a question not just of words but of deep convictions, rooted in a history and shared by those whom the respective parties represented. A hasty political operation born of necessity was certainly not going to resolve the difference between the two conceptions; Moro's sincere but generic statement about the need for a 'third stage' or Berlinguer's more committed moves (his talk of 'austerity' or his letters to Monsignor Bettazzi[3]) fell on stony ground or, worse, gave rise to distortions and protests.

So, what forces did the Left really have at its disposal to shape the action of such a skewed government? It did have two cards: a parliamentary presence reflecting its 47 per cent share of the vote, and the pressure in society of a trade union that had grown considerably in size and was united by agreement with other unions. But these two strengths showed cracks even before the Andreotti government took office, or immediately afterwards, and the new government later weakened them still more.

The new political unity between Socialists and Communists, which had seemed to appear from nowhere and led to dissolution of the previous parliament, just as suddenly began to look precarious. The replacement of De Martino as leader with Bettino Craxi was conceived and presented as a necessary renewal after the PSI's defeat at the polls, and a sign of political autonomy to curb the excessive power of the two main parties – not as a change of line away from Left unity. A large part of the Lombardy Socialists and even of De Martino's supporters therefore went along with it. But

3. Between 1976 and 1978 Berlinguer had a public exchange of letters with Monsignor Bettazzi, the bishop of Ivrea, about the relationship between Catholicism and Marxism.

Craxi, like Andreotti, was not a man of straw: he was a capable politician, with well-defined ideas of his own. Always a follower of Nenni, and of the kind of politics that Nenni had conducted during the Centre Left period, he thought of autonomy mainly in relation to the PCI rather than the DC. He was profoundly convinced that, in order to challenge the supremacy of the DC, it was first necessary to change the relationship of forces in the Left – and to this end the PSI had to edge away from the 'grand coalition'. He gradually carried this plan through as he consolidated his power in the party, cautiously, but without wavering or concealment.

The situation was changing in the union movement too: its organizational strength had grown and held up in every sector, but the same could not be said of its determination and fighting capacity. The economic crisis made it more difficult for the rank and file to take the initiative in disputes, and when this happened the results were more meagre. To go beyond mere resistance, and to gain wider support among the workers as a whole, the union movement had to find a way of influencing economic policy, while the employers, for their part, needed the unions for a return to normal relations in the factory, as well as public funding for restructuring projects. The employers, though divided among themselves, had an effective resource for this kind of three-way bargaining: that is, their tried-and-tested affinity with the political layer already installed in government and the civil service, and the blackmail exercised by powerful international groups. The union movement, on the other hand, faced a particular difficulty. Objectively, it was no longer 'factory councils' and industry-wide structures but branch organizations that played the leading role. This changed things considerably. For, unlike in nearly every other country, these structures had deep roots in their respective areas and constituted a precious resource against craft or trade corporatism, fostering unity among workers for common objectives. But their alignment with one or other of the rival national parties had long been a factor of division. The great wave of struggles in the 1960s had led to the conclusion of pacts, which in theory were soon meant to result in organizational fusion, as in the case of the engineering workers. But in reality this process had become stuck, since the national federations were not involved in the dialectic between union apparatuses and autonomous rank-and-file movements that had transformed the thinking and action of the main groups of industrial workers. They tried to replicate it by setting up area councils and launching campaigns on housing and healthcare issues, but this was not successful, either because of internal resistance or because of nervousness in the major political parties. They therefore built a top-down leadership that was vitiated by parity principles and distorted the balance of representativity in the real world. It also incorporated moderate social strata and, in some cases, clientelist relations, while bearing residual traces of past ideological conflicts. All this acted as a brake on the build-up of pressure when it was a question of coming into conflict with a 'friendly' government. On the other hand, even the most combative and radical sections, which had established their autonomy especially from the parties, distrusted any kind of dealings with political institutions (*pansindacalismo*).

All these problems might have been overcome if there had been a reform-minded government in office, but the 'no no-confidence government', divided in its intentions, vague or evasive in its programme and policies, could only make them worse. In the name of trade union unity, any mediocre compromise could pass muster – and the most varied forms of dissatisfaction could appear among the workers.

In conclusion, it seems clear to me that the political expedient devised as a first step to push the DC to the left, by handing it nearly all the levers of power, was doomed from the beginning, not only to fail but to facilitate a restoration of the old order.

Buscar el Levante por el Poniente: seek the East by way of the West. Columbus's gamble succeeded in defiance of all logic, because he discovered not just a new wheel but a whole unknown continent, with only small numbers of hospitable inhabitants. It was altogether unlikely that the miracle would repeat itself here and now, when all the continents were known and presided over by people who would not be fobbed off with coloured beads.

THE FAILURE OF THE GRAND COALITION

The 'grand coalition' did not last long – less than three years. Almost every day a new bone of contention would arise, only to be settled by a shaky or murky compromise. Signs of discontent, sometimes of protest or revolt, also emerged in the country. Having committed themselves, the main forces of the Left were obviously reluctant to see them, or to accept their own responsibility, but little by little they became convinced that 'things can't go on like this'.

It is surprising that neither at the time nor later, neither internally nor with one another, did the Left parties open a debate or engage in public reflection on the experience. Each went its merry way, preferring to gloss over what had happened. But gaps do not remain empty for long in the historical memory, especially when they relate to such stormy periods full of drama for all concerned.

For a long time the gap was filled with a stream of personal testimony, partisan revelations, and special pleading that was unreliable as to the facts and their temporal sequence. Later, as always, the victors' memory took a more coherent shape, becoming the commonly accepted version and gaining credence among intellectuals – easy to summarize in a few lines, which are now trotted out at every commemorative event or other opportunity. The 'grand coalition' of the 1970s is here touched up, domesticated and revalued. The whole brief experiment, it is said, was born of necessity, and if it was not handled well this is because the time was not yet ripe; there were therefore many misunderstandings and over-generous concessions to the DC, but also some positive results, because the arrangement gave support to democratic institutions at a time of danger and achieved some important reforms. It was interrupted by terrorism and the calamity of Moro's murder, which could perhaps have been avoided if more flexibility had been shown in the negotiations. The experiment might then have lasted longer and borne greater fruit, since the thinking behind it was good and reflected a historic process then under way – if only Berlinguer had revived it along the lines suggested by Craxi, instead of breaking it off prematurely, reasserting a specific Communist identity and stiffening in his personal moralism. We would then have arrived earlier and in better conditions at a democratic system in which Left and Right alternate in government, with the shared framework of a capitalist society and the Atlantic alliance. So, we should not talk of a defeat, but rather of a first step forward, still insufficient, but positive for the Left and for everyone else.

Such an argument hangs together, and of course it has had increasing success, because it offers a historical background suitable for present political purposes. Its weak point, especially in relation to what happened thirty years ago, is that 'any resemblance to real events or to persons living or dead is purely coincidental'. To convince ourselves of this, we need only recall the salient moments of these past decades, put them in a logical and temporal sequence, and add a few things that were not known at the time but have since come out (or which I have been able to gather from the archives or the disclosures of key players). The main requirement is to have a nose for the truth, to be able to pick out the little grain of wheat from all the chaff. I admit that, both then and later, I too failed to take some accurate analyses into account. Having said straightaway that the strategy of the historic compromise was fundamentally mistaken, and having predicted its collapse all the more after 1976, I took its eventual demise for granted – and therefore I failed to give sufficient thought to the particular form it took at government level.

OMISSIONS, SILENCES AND LIES

Our first modest step should be to clear the collective memory of gross errors of fact. Here are a few.

1) It is evidently untrue that millions of people who, through their struggles and votes, made the PCI necessary for the government of the country were motivated simply by a desire to create the conditions for future 'alternation'. Even those convinced of the rightness of Berlinguer's project not only hoped for but willed a profound change in economic and social policy, and in Italy's international position, mode of governance and distribution of power. A compromise maybe – but not subaltern cohabitation. If anything, younger and more combative sections of the population, less accustomed to discipline and delegation, wanted to participate in decision-making and to see the results sooner rather than later. The mere sight of a monochrome DC government was therefore bound to turn enthusiasm and hopes into suspicion or watchful waiting. A moderate minority had chosen to vote left for the first time, with the idea that the PCI might help to bring back order and honesty, but in their way they too wanted a new government capable of taking decisions, not the subtleties of 'say one thing and then the opposite'. Disappointment began to spread at once, as early as the festival of *L'Unità* in September, when Berlinguer met a frosty reception trying to sell the government to the crowd in the square.

2) It is not completely false, but marred by omissions, to argue that objective factors made the 'no no-confidence government' inescapable. What this leaves out is that the objective necessities constrained the DC as well as the Left, since the conservative Right had already contributed to its tally at the polls, and the reactionary Right was no longer willing to offer its support without getting something in return. So what prevented the Left, united for once, from saying that if the emergency required a temporary grand coalition it would have to be a case of 'everyone in or everyone out'? I agree that the DC would have found that hard to accept, and even that things would not have gone very far if it had, but its refusal would then have led to fresh elections and saddled it with the blame for the obstruction. It might be objected – and such arguments were heard in the PCI – that the Socialists would soon have wriggled out of their commitments. But that is not true, because De Martino, then still secretary of the PSI, had proposed such an approach immediately after the elections of 20 June: Lombardi had supported him, and Nenni had had nothing else to offer except a humiliating return to the failed Centre-Left experience. The turn in the PSI and Craxi's election took place afterwards, corresponding to the formation of the monochrome DC government and Socialist fears of a stifling duopoly.

3) The real 'necessity' lay elsewhere, in the American veto. This is a serious matter, because at other points in time, both before and after, it constituted a looming threat. But that was not the case in 1976. The Americans had their own economic and political troubles: defeat in Vietnam, Nixon's impeachment, instability in Latin America and the Middle East, oil-price rises and the dollar crisis. In Europe there were the Portuguese revolution, the collapse of the colonels in Greece, the acute competition with newly emerging economies, Mitterrand's surprising re-launch of social democracy and the Programme Commun with the PCF in France. This did not mean that the top people in Washington had lost interest in Italy, still less that they had dropped their opposition to the PCI's entry into government; they continued to exert official pressure, and encouraged one or two plots. But it was scarcely credible that they were planning a more radical intervention, and the 'strategy of tension' had proved counterproductive in the end.

4) It is thoroughly questionable to suggest that the incoming government gave any encouraging signals to its generous allies, in

the period prior to its formation and take-off. In fact, the opposite is the case. In terms of method, the proposal of Andreotti as prime minister and the allocation of the key ministries pointed to an Andreotti-Dorotea coalition, rather than something more uniform. Moreover, since the choices could not be based on an explicitly agreed programme, nor on an explicit alliance with the PCI, they were thrashed out hour by hour around various tables, or more often around none, in confidential private meetings with go-betweens (Chiaromonte, Barca, Di Giulio, Evangelisti[4] and Galloni[5]) whose mandate was unclear. It was, and would remain, a common method: secret diplomacy instead of open dealings in front of the public. As to content, the immediate decision was to go for a major devaluation of the lira, perhaps inevitable by then, with its concomitant of steep price rises. And Andreotti added another item, not agreed upon with anyone: a decree-law suspending labour disputes at company level, partly eliminating wage indexation, and increasing certain charges that affected workers in particular. The Left parties and the unions opposed these measures. The government then backtracked, but not completely, and the message got through to the factories; there were some spontaneous strikes in the next few months, and a number of regional warning strikes.

5) Soon afterwards, in February 1977, a youth revolt flared up briefly. Opinion is still divided today about this movement, but in my view both sides are wrong. It is not true that it had the character of a new '68, nor that it represented a phenomenon that we have seen more recently in the peace and ecological movements and the movement against free-trade globalization. The differences are clear from a number of facts. It was mainly a student protest movement in a period of general downturn, mostly driven by anger and disappointment, and kindling huge hopes for a new world. It was a mass movement, yet concentrated in a few areas of the country (big cities, but not all of them: Rome, Bologna, Florence and Turin), and although it lasted only a few months it left deep marks on society. Its habitat was the university or the piazza, but its social base was new and heterogeneous: various marginal

4. Franco Evangelisti: prominent journalist and DC politician, close to Andreotti.

5. Giovanni Galloni: founder of the Left current within the DC, vice-secretary of the party in 1965 and again in 1977.

groups (unemployed youth, rank-and-file union activists in the railway and health sectors, jobless graduates) clustered together, or tried to cluster, around the students, whereas industrial workers were neither much in evidence nor the social subject centrally at issue in the protests; a major player that outlived them was the new radical feminism, although it was quite distinct, often contrary, in its aims, culture and political practices. As to the forms of struggle, total spontaneism alternated with a quasi-military organizational thrust. The movement was not only diverse but wide open, and therefore destined to fall apart – but also to shape lasting convictions in thousands of young people. I shall return to many of the issues and new social subjects that blossomed for the first time in the movement and largely outlived it (radical feminism, environmentalism, crisis of politics, critique of dogmatic ideologies and bureaucratic apparatuses), but at this point I wish to clarify its origins, the main dynamic in its evolution, and its impact on the overall political situation. Again a simple chronology of events will suffice, so long as we look beyond the media reports (all centred on spectacle) and filter the passionate memories of those directly involved. A genuine mass revolt suddenly exploded, seemingly by chance, on a precise day and at a precise place: the furious attack on the stand where Lama was trying to speak, without prior notice, at the occupied University of Rome.[6] In order to understand this, we need to bear two key points in mind. The first is the formation of the Andreotti government and the subaltern role that the PCI had agreed to play in relation to it. A generation formed in the 'long '68', which, despite the downturn, had prolonged it in other struggles (over housing, unemployment, the secret webs of the 'second state', recurrent scandals left unpunished), experienced this political solution not as a compromise but as a provocative piece of horse-trading. Such feelings were neither a product of 'armed-struggle extremism' nor an indication of its strength, but were shared by the great majority of those who participated, in various ways and for various ends, in the Italian '77. The second point, whose importance is often overlooked, is the crisis of the 'New Left'. It is not true that the extra-parliamentary political formations of the early 1970s were hot-headed *groupuscules*,

6. Luciano Lama, secretary of the CGIL from 1970 to 1986, was driven from Rome university by rebellious students, when he tried to make an impromptu speech in the grounds on 17 February 1977.

destined to disappear and productive only of a diffuse irrationalism. Between 1969 and 1972 they had played an important role among students and intellectuals and in a number of major factories. They were real organizations, with a trained cadre, several daily papers, and influence in the intellectual debate. They ran into difficulties in the downturn, because it dented the basic hope on which they had thrived: the hope that a revolution was imminent. This led to the disappearance of the smallest or most dogmatic groups, while the larger ones not only survived but tried to come seriously to grips with politics. They did not refuse to present a joint list for the elections (which even the extra-parliamentary Lotta Continua insisted on joining): it was a shaky coalition, but united around the call for a 'government of the Left'; in clear disagreement with the 'historic compromise', but not hostile to all institutions as such.

The poor results of this initiative led Lotta Continua to divide irretrievably between feminists and proponents of armed struggle, and its leadership decided to dissolve the organization. Others remained in the field (Il Manifesto-PdUP, Avanguardia Operaia, MLS), trying to save the '77 revolt from a sterile counterposition between an alternative political course (now refuted by events) and an extremist will o' the wisp more and more tempted by violence. That this was not purely fanciful is shown by the often sharp clash between the two lines in much of the country; the extremist lurch was not at all a foregone conclusion and in many cases remained under control, partly because the Communist Youth agreed to enter into dialogue. But it was too little, too late. The PCI leadership was not exempt from blame: it again showed no preparedness to differentiate between the real risks of the youth revolt and the justified criticisms it had raised, and certainly not to correct anything in its own policy; it tarred everything to its left with the same brush, accusing the young rebels of being no more than 'hooligans, dyed-in-the-wool fascists, collaborators with reaction'. The attack on Lama's stand was therefore followed by a large demonstration in Rome, at which the extremist wing – now referred to generally as Autonomia – not only preached armed struggle but took command and attacked two gunsmith's shops. The police, or rogue services within it, tried to use the opportunity for a head-on confrontation.

In Bologna, in September, the revolt thought it was celebrating its new self-assertiveness when it developed the thesis that Italy was an authoritarian state ruled by the PCI-DC duo, and that this justified action by proletarian youth against a regime already veering towards fascism. Some intellectuals in Italy and France were seduced by the argument. But in Bologna the movement had really been celebrating a rite of impotence, precisely on the question of forms of struggle and violence, and it was not long before it fell apart. The consequences were momentous: an unbridgeable gulf between the PCI plus unions, and the section of young people who had opposed them; a crack in the forces that had tried to escape the polarization (crisis in Avanguardia Operaia; a 'left' breakaway of PdUP from the group led by Vittorio Foa, and then a growing distance between PdUP and the journal out of which it had been born, *Il Manifesto*); and a permanent milieu of comrades and sympathizers who, unsure of what to do next, were tempted by armed struggle or a withdrawal from political activity – a potential recruiting ground for terrorism.

6) It is not true that the working class remained solidly behind the Party, the union and the government supported by them. In fact, what should have been worrying was that the opposite was the case. I am not speaking of a revolt, but certainly of unease and growing discontent. On 24 January 1978, in a long interview in *La Repubblica*, Lama offered the government a three-year truce on union wage demands, partial de-indexation, and a right to lay off 'the several tens of thousands of workers who are actually surplus to factory requirements'. Berlinguer (let alone the workers) had not been consulted, and he made a non-public protest. Lama then sent a note of disavowal to the paper, but it did not change the substance. Moro himself let it be known that he was surprised by Lama's offer, and he thought it would be an obstacle to PCI support for a political turn. Nevertheless, a General Meeting of the trade unions took place at the EUR centre in Rome on 14 February. The word 'general' here is rather a euphemism, since in reality it was a joint meeting of the leadership councils of the union federations, expanded to include a number of specially invited workers. The offers made to the government were the same as Lama's, with a little verbal softening (labour flexibility instead of lay-offs). The union Left (Trentin, Carniti) reluctantly went along with it, in return for a commitment by the parties and parliament to draw up sectoral restructuring plans that guaranteed employment in general and support for the South in particular; the certain was traded for

the uncertain, as we can see from what became of the sectoral plans. In any event, the workers made a last offering of trust: they gave up sectoral struggle in support of an industrial restructuring that would provide jobs and investment not funded mainly through their own sacrifices. They did get something: irrigation aqueducts in a few regions of the South. All the rest remained on paper. So, on 2 December 1978, when the national engineering negotiations provided an opportunity, a large demonstration of workers marched past PCI headquarters on Botteghe Oscure – this time not only to give greetings but to protest.

7) Berlinguer was aware of all this: he could not have been otherwise. He wrote to Moro (and hence to Andreotti) with a clear and unequivocal message: 'Things cannot go on like this. We have to go beyond the no non-confidence government. There must be a real coalition of which the PCI is an explicit part – a coalition with a well-defined programme. A clarification and a choice are necessary.' As usual, only part of the message got through; everyone agreed that there should be a discussion of programme, and that this should be publicly announced. The discussion dragged on for weeks and ended in a vague formula that satisfied no one. Yet, like it or not, everyone signed up. The real stumbling block was whether everyone who was supposed to implement the common programme should also have a place in the government. Was this a sine qua non or was it not? It is not easy to give a simple answer, because there was real uncertainty on either side. Many in the PCI leadership were opposed to an ultimatum, and Berlinguer accepted a provisional compromise: for now we'll step up our criticism of the government. He went to parliament in person to step it up, so sharply that Andreotti felt compelled to resign, without knowing what other government might be formed. In private and confidential talks (but this time also in a public speech at Mantua), Moro said that he now personally considered the PCI to be a democratic force worthy of a direct place in government, but that he was not yet in a position to gain DC approval for it. The talks therefore ended by postponing a final decision until Andreotti appeared again in parliament with his proposed ministers. This leaves a grey area on which I, at least, am unable to shed further light. Many reports insist that Moro spent three days trying to convince the DC National Council to accept the existence of a formal parliamentary majority and a common programme; yet Chiaromonte,

who was present at the meeting, claims in his memoirs to know for sure that Moro privately told Andreotti to do the opposite (that is, to form a government not to the PCI's liking), since, with the Lockheed scandal still raging, the main danger was of a revolt within the DC. The fact remains that the new government was, if possible, worse than the previous one, and that when the PCI leadership saw the list of ministers it moved towards withdrawing its support. I have gone into these details to make it clear that, on that fateful morning of 16 March 1978 (the morning when Moro was kidnapped), the 'grand coalition' was already in an irreversible crisis.

8) It is therefore a deliberate falsehood to claim that a difficult but fruitful experiment was stopped in its tracks by the kidnapping and murder of Aldo Moro. The opposite is the truth. That iniquitous act helped to prolong for more than a year a 'grand coalition' government that was by then on its last legs. During that time the political conditions were assembled for a rerun of the Centre Left.

These facts are so obvious that it would seem pointless to enter into the tangle of confessions, memoirs, court proceedings and parliamentary enquiries that have multiplied in connection with that dramatic event. Out of scruple I did read much of this material, and came away with certain convictions. First of all, some overlooked but important questions emerge from the verified facts – important both for an assessment of what happened and for clarification of its darker side. Why did the kidnapping and especially the killing happen, when it was perfectly clear to everyone that the 'grand coalition' was done for? What interest might 'dark forces' opposed to Communist participation in government have had in encouraging or provoking the crime? Why did the Red Brigades, whose aim it was to destabilize the system and to increase their own base of support, kill Moro after a long and risky period of confinement during which they had wrung from him various incriminating statements and credible revelations? Why did they conceal and destroy the most shocking parts of the material from their interrogations of Moro? How are we to explain the careless and inefficient manner in which the state apparatuses had been combating terrorism and now confronted its most dangerous operation so far? Why did the 'toughness' displayed by all the pro-government parties sow division and suspicion among them, instead of producing greater unity? I would not presume to provide exhaustive answers to these questions, and I do not think that anyone else will be able to, until many skeletons have come out of the cupboard. But a few things can be said and proven. As far as the Red Brigades are concerned, it is absurd to suggest that they had long been the expression or instrument of a grand plot by other reactionary forces. Tens or hundreds of individuals – if we include those arrested plus new recruits – do not kill hundreds of (often blameless) individuals, or prepare to die or spend their life in prison, unless they have a strong ideological identity to sustain them; nor can they live alongside one another for years in a closely knit, commune-type organization without realizing that they are being used for other ends. Equally groundless and misleading, however, is the idea that the Red Brigades were born and degenerated as part of a PCI 'family album' – that is, that we already know everything there is to know about them. The PCI can be reproached with many things, including its former integration of armed insurrection into revolutionary strategy; but never in the long history of Communism, anywhere in the world, can it be said that it was soft on terrorism – that is, on violent action outside the context of a people's war and broad mass support. The group behind the Red Brigades, throughout its existence, never had any leaders or activists who had come out of that historical experience: most lacked a political background, either personally or through their family, and very many had roots in the Catholic movement. So, how did the group originate? What was and remained its founding element? This is well known. The organization appeared late in the day, in comparison with the real social conflicts of the 1960s, to which it paid limited attention and from which it soon separated itself. Its ideology was that of the Latin American guerrilla *foco* (when Castro had already dropped it, and Guevara had died an isolated death trying to revive it); and its decision to opt for an underground mode of organization in 1970 froze that ideology in ever more delirious form. It is not true that organization is always the product of ideology; it can and does happen the other way around. To grasp the mechanism, one has only to read the autobiographies of Franceschini, Curcio and Moretti.[7] A

7. Alberto Franceschini and Renato Curcio: the founders of the Red Brigades. Mario Moretti was head of the operational group responsible for Moro's kidnapping and confinement.

clandestine existence, especially in a small isolated group, shapes the ideas in people's heads. A life apart, the imperative of secrecy, the constant danger, the use of weapons and exemplary gestures to communicate a message to the people; the need to select targets commensurate with one's strength more than with their guilt, to keep raising one's sights to increase the impact, and to recruit new members to make up for losses: all this produces an extreme variant of the guerrilla *foco* and makes the organization itself increasingly self-referential, so that its analysis of reality becomes distorted and instrumental. This explains much about the Moro case. For the Red Brigades, it was not mostly about destabilization of the state and the political establishment (this was, in their view, anyway inevitable); their main aim was to give a display of strength that would win over a good number of the militants who had been wavering since '77, and eventually persuade the masses of the utility of armed struggle. Something like that did happen after the Moro kidnapping: an impromptu formation of new armed groups, one-off assassinations. Any real accommodation, not recognizing them but ratifying their organizational credibility, could easily have triggered a barbarous escalation.

These points by no means exclude the possibility that the Red Brigades were infiltrated and corrupted, but they do reduce its significance and provide the key for a partial but convincing reading. No underground group is impervious to penetration: that was shown clearly enough in the PCI and the anti-fascist movement, as well as among anarchists and the Carbonari secret societies of the early nineteenth century. In the case of the Red Brigades, we may mention some of the clearest evidence. A first clue was the arrest of their two leaders, Curcio and Franceschini, at Pinerolo in 1974: an anonymous telephone call warned of a trap twenty-four hours before, but the information was not passed on to them. This showed a number of things: obviously that the organization could be penetrated, not even by some James Bond but by a shady, squalid character like Frate Mitra;[8] obviously too that it did not have channels of protection and internal communication for emergency situations; probably that there were and remained police collaborators in its ranks; and probably that the aim of the state

8. Frate Mitra: pseudonym of Silvano Girotto, directly responsible for the police entrapment of Curcio and Franceschini.

apparatuses was not to nip the terrorist phenomenon in the bud, but to freeze it and operate selective arrests, in order to deprive it of an accomplished leadership and encourage its further descent into militarization. That is what happened until the killing of Moro.

A second indication, much more important but difficult to decipher, concerns the Moro case itself. Let us pass over the form of the kidnapping: that is, the fact that, at the height of the terrorist wave, the protection given to the country's top leader was so ineffectual that he followed the same schedule every morning, travelling the same route without any surveillance of the surrounding area. The crux of the matter lies elsewhere. In relation to the Red Brigades: the location of their operational base within easy reach of the SISMI;[9] the 'lucky' and needless discovery of their hideout at via Gradoli; the final harrowing decision to execute Moro, when he had already 'talked' and an attempt to negotiate was dividing the government; and, above all else, the non-publication of the disclosures that had already been torn from him. In relation to the Italian state: infiltrators who suddenly disappeared or went silent; the farce of the Lago della Duchessa;[10] the stenographic records of interrogations that remained for years in via Montenevoso,[11] before being seized and censored by the Carabinieri, then hidden away instead of released to the courts. Although some suspicions remain unproven, one conclusion seems clear. There was a more or less conscious convergence of two tendencies in the Moro case: the Red Brigades – which not by chance divided from that point on, and dissolved after a desperate flurry of senseless, random executions – placed the search for a spectacular outcome above any political rationality; while the state needed, not, of course, to have Moro kidnapped, but to avoid the consequences of what he had already said or what he might say or do if he were freed (Andreotti later frankly admitted that Moro at large could have caused a lot of trouble). Craxi, on the margins, without ever taking responsibility for a practical suggestion, adopted a 'humanitarian' discourse to

9. SISMI: Servizio per le Informazioni e la Sicurezza Militare, Italy's reorganized military intelligence agency, active from 1977 to 2007.

10. An initial communiqué, purportedly from the Red Brigades, stated that Moro's body lay in the Lago della Duchessa on the border of Lazio and Abruzzo; soon afterward it was found in a parked car in central Rome.

11. Via Montenevoso: location of one of the main secret bases of the Red Brigades, in Milan, discovered in 1978.

attack the PCI's 'toughness' and to stress the freedom-loving character of the new PSI. We can now understand better why the Moro case not only sealed the end of an alliance, but worked against the PCI and contributed to the development of a new political order. It also underlined the gravity of the Party's failure to have ever adequately tackled the 'dual state', before it went on to play a role in supporting the government.

It is therefore not false but completely inaccurate to say that the formal break-up of the 'grand coalition' was decided by the PCI in an overhasty and dramatic manner. In fact, if we consider the dates and the archive material, the opposite seems to be the case – and I must say this even if I do not like it. On 7 January 1979 Berlinguer drew his conclusions and proposed to the Party leadership that the experience of the grand coalition should be called off. Pertini[12] tried to patch things up by giving a post to La Malfa, but the attempt failed because no one believed in such things any more. When a proposal for a DC-PSI-PSDI government then failed to gain acceptance in parliament, it was agreed to call new general elections. On 30 March, at the Fifteenth Congress of the PCI, Berlinguer finally said straight out that 'the PCI will remain in opposition to any government that excludes it', but he also confirmed that a 'broad agreement' was the objective for which the Party should fight. With this line the PCI went to the polls on 20 June, and it alone paid the price for the common failure. It lost 4 per cent of its vote, most notably in working-class areas and among young people. But the election result as such did not signify a general shift to the right: the DC, PSI and the far Right gained virtually nothing, while the PCI's losses benefited the various other lists on the Left, particularly favouring the Radicals and the PdUP (left alone and bereft of a paper, and generally given up for dead). The real defeat of the PCI was political, and it fully came to light in the subsequent months. Craxi's Socialist Party did not merely accentuate its distance from the PCI, but made its ideological turn explicit (a more pronounced break with Marxism than in other social-democratic parties, in the implausible name of Proudhon, to put the whole past history of Italian Socialism behind it) and performed a radical shift in political strategy (a competitive but

12. Alessandro ('Sandro') Pertini: Socialist leader and president of the Republic from 1978 to 1985.

permanent coalition with Christian Democracy in government). The DC congress, for its part, toppled Zaccagnini[13] and entrusted the party to Flaminio Piccoli and Arnaldo Forlani;[14] it also approved a binding document whose preamble ruled out any agreement to govern with the PCI. One of those involved in the turn – indeed, its *metteur en scène* – was Donat-Cattin: I mention this because he had kept a special relationship with the CISL and ACLI, and paved the way for a growing rift among the union federations. Only in 1980 did Berlinguer decide on a truly radical turn, receiving wide support among the Party rank and file but also encountering strong resistance at the top, which Amendola, as usual, was the first to express clearly in an article in *Rinascita* that caused quite a stir. It took particular issue with 'all the concessions made to extremism since 1968'.

13. Benigno Zaccagnini: one of the founders of Christian Democracy and national secretary from 1975 to 1980.

14. Flaminio Piccoli: national secretary of the DC from 1980 to 1982. Arnaldo Forlani: briefly DC prime minister in 1980–1, then vice-premier in the two Craxi governments of the 1980s.

16

What Was Brewing in Italy

In my long discussion of the 1970s, I have concentrated on events that dominated the political scene and paid little or no attention to latent, irregular tendencies that were just starting up and would only later acquire decisive importance.

THE DOWNWARD MIRACLE

The first such tendency concerns the form of the economic crisis in Italy and the role played by capitalist power. Here we must first clear up some misunderstandings about the course of events and their actual conclusion and long-term consequences.

To speak of economic crisis in Italy is not to speak of permanent recession or structural immobility, devoid of alternatives. The statistics bear this out. National income continued to grow in the 1970s, with various ups and downs but at an annual average of 3.7 per cent: nearly half the rate of the 1960s, and still higher than in other large European countries (France 2.8 per cent, Britain 1.8 per cent). On the other hand, it should not be overlooked that, although Italy was generally less advanced and internally much more uneven, it had considerable unexploited resources, and even its backward regions might become a resource if properly used.

Let us take a few examples. The tax burden was still below 30 per cent of GDP (10 to 15 per cent less than in other advanced countries), and therefore offered considerable scope for revenue increases. Moreover, although Italy was on average a poor country, net savings stood at 20 per cent of family income (less than in Japan, but more than in other advanced countries). The question was how these reserves should be tapped and how they could be most usefully invested. Large-scale industry, both private and public, had the capacity, knowledge and potential to keep pace with the new technological leap visible on the global horizon. This was true of many sectors: electronics and home computing (Olivetti); chemicals, both basic and refined, and pharmaceuticals (ENI, Montedison); fossil and alternative energy (ENEA); perhaps high-grade steel and new shipbuilding methods. Even agriculture, more mechanized and less fragmented than in the past, might underpin a modern quality-food industry; the artistic and natural heritage, if properly managed, could sustain an orderly tourist influx; the construction industry had scope for new housing and urban redevelopment on land cleared by public intervention; and the rail system was suitable both for workers and for companies in general.

None of this was 'beyond reach', but it required courageous structural reforms, coherent planning, efficient public administration and far-sighted entrepreneurs. The road taken was quite different, however, owing both to policy defects and to the obtuseness of the employers.

The first clear sign that the employers were not up to the tasks came in 1970, even before the international crisis began. In their response to the struggles of '69, the main idea was that the block on development that needed to be removed post-haste was the wage rises being won by the workers. I was not among those on the far Left who thought the incipient crisis was purely an invention of the employers, still less among those in the PCI who fretted that the middle layers were being squeezed out of the spoils. The rises in wage costs for large firms had been consistently above 19 per cent, and disputes then under way were spreading this level to other firms and depleting the reserves for self-financing. But the importance given to these figures, and the typical responses to them, were false, one-sided and fanciful: false because the unusually high increases were due to compression over a period of decades and, even now, wage costs remained below those in Italy's competitors; one-sided because the legacy of '69 was not so much high wage demands as a challenge to working conditions and factory despotism, and because the workers needed to pay for essential new needs (housing, transport, health care) not covered by public expenditure; and fanciful because the accumulated strength of the unions and factory councils, now backed up by the Labour Statute, would not permit wage cuts or a drastically higher intensity of work. Between 1970 and 1973 the number of hours lost in strikes was close to the level of previous years, and a rise in absenteeism occurred if a strike failed or was repressed. Unlike in 1964–5, then, head-on confrontation was even more damaging to the employers than it was to the workers.

Spurred on by the election advance of the Right, the government tried to give a helping hand to extremist tendencies among the bosses – the 'Decretone' raising public charges was beginning to have an inflationary effect – but, despite everything, industrial output continued to grow in 1970 because of earlier investment. In 1971, however, the wind began to change a little as the utilization level of industrial capacity declined.

It should be said that the union movement – or, rather, its most advanced sections – showed greater far-sightedness than the government, parties or bosses in the new conditions. Without bowing to diktat or simply going onto the defensive, they put forward a new kind of struggle and new priorities for action. Inside the factory, they concentrated on quality demands (a single pay scale, job designation, 150 hours a year for further education) rather than the wage chase; outside it, they developed new organizational forms (neighbourhood committees) to fight for social needs across the board, uniting different occupational groups, North and South, employed and unemployed, and appealing to non-parasitic middle layers. The union federations accepted this line, but showed little conviction or readiness to support it, while the political parties, including the PCI, saw it as poaching on their territory and remained indifferent. Everyone spoke of 'a producers' pact', but the unions did not have the strength to impose it, while the employers were not willing to concede anything that affected their interests, their political allegiances (the DC) or their social claim on revenue.

Now began a second phase, whose importance has escaped everyone. After the end of the gold-dollar standard and the ensuing currency fluctuations, and especially after the oil price hikes, the government in Rome – that is, the DC – understood that policy rigidity plus a head-on confrontation with labour were not enough to address the complexities of a much wider crisis. A new season therefore opened with the Colombo government,[1] supported by the PSI; it too ended in failure, but not without leaving traces of a 'mongrel reformism', as its opponents called it. This would characterize the running of the economy throughout the decade: no 'historic compromise', but an assortment of compromises, often with a sting in their tail. A section of the employers went along with it, setting clearly defined limits, while another tried sabotage by means of capital flight and an investment strike ('the horse won't drink', it was said at the time).

What were the reforms, then? It would be a mistake to underestimate them. Some were substantial, especially those which directly affected the economic system but offered the opposition something at institutional level in return for greater moderation: the creation of regional authorities all over the country; the law on referendums; uniform and compulsory education for all up to the age of fourteen; the establishment of a Constitutional Court; a requirement for all local authorities to draw up regulatory plans; a reform of the tax system. All these provisions were stipulated under the Constitution, but had always been left in suspense. It was no small matter to achieve their introduction: they were stepping stones towards a wide-ranging participatory democracy in which a new economic policy might also come into play. But here too all was not clear, as we may see from the fate of two important reforms. 1) The establishment of regional authorities was not accompanied with a decentralization of ministerial powers, a precise definition of what was actually delegated to them, or even direct responsibility for their budget. So, whereas some regions tried to emulate the German *Länder*, a larger number were dragged down the 'Sicilian road' (that is, major central funding for aid programmes plus rampant political favouritism). 2) The reliance on indirect taxation was replaced with a system centred on decidedly progressive personal taxation. However, the assessment and deduction of income tax at source mainly affected dependent labour, while all other types of income had many ways of escaping the net; the fixed rate for all income from financial assets meant that many were able to avoid the progressive scale to which they would otherwise have been subject. The total yield therefore remained limited, and the

1. The government headed by Emilio Colombo, in office from August 1970 to February 1972.

redistributive effect turned into its opposite (workers paid a higher share of their income than their bosses).

The worst aspect of 'mongrel reformism' was most apparent in other areas of social and economic policy. New institutions (GEPI, EFIM, EGAM[2]) were created to channel massive grants to state industries or loans to private ones, with no aim or constraint other than to rescue ailing firms (the socialization of losses) or temporarily to boost employment in depressed regions by means of giant factories that lacked markets and had no lasting effect on the surrounding economy. The government, or the parties supporting it, then chose directors to head all the firms or consortia – men who often migrated to and fro between the public and private sector (Cefis being a typical example[3]). This was the triumph of what a brilliant little book dubbed the 'employer breed',[4] referring to the pernicious interlocking of public and private in key positions in the economy.

In the short term, this economic policy served to stimulate demand and output and partly to protect employment and wages. In the medium term, however, it produced not only a rising public debt but a further degeneration of the public sector, which in the past had played a role in promoting growth. In short, it was a mutilated and perverse Keynesianism: Keynes's paradox (public deficit spending to kick-start growth, digging holes and filling them in) was applied literally, with no guarantee that it would result in growth capable of absorbing the deficit and creating stable employment. The employers not only tolerated this policy but actively exploited it to their advantage, as a well to draw from and an instrument for binding the public and private sectors together. Even the wider negative consequences of this policy – inflation and currency devaluation – suited the most powerful party to it (large-scale industry), by promoting exports, cutting real wages, facilitating layoffs, and even reducing their past debt in real terms.

2. GEPI: Società per le Gestioni e Partecipazioni Industriali; EFIM: Ente Partecipazioni e Finanziamento Industrie Manifatturiere; EGAM: Ente Gestione Attività Minerarie.

3. Eugenio Cefis: adviser to AGIP, chairman of ENI and Montedison, involved with the Propaganda Due secret masonic lodge, who suddenly left the public scene in 1977 and went to live in Switzerland.

4. *Razza padrona - Storia della borghesia di stato* (Milan: Feltrinelli, 1974): title of a topical exposé by the two senior figures in the weekly *L'Espresso*, Eugenio Scalfari and Giuseppe Turani.

But it could not last. In 1974–5 inflation rose above 20 per cent, and the devaluation of the lira jumped to 16 per cent. Wage indexation was by now greatly reduced for workers, but the middle layers (especially the increased numbers in public employment) also suffered; internal demand shrank, and companies felt the effects; the crisis was turning into a recession. All this was reflected in the political balance of forces, as the election results of 1975 showed.

In the brief interlude between the Centre Left government and the 'no no-confidence government', two serious attempts were made to reach a direct compromise between capital and labour: the Lama-Agnelli agreement on full wage indexation and flat-rate adjustments for all workers, and the government-backed agreement on more extensive temporary redundancy payments. The core of both these agreements was well-intentioned, and in fact Agnelli, the chairman of Confindustria, was sharply criticized then and later by other employers. But on closer inspection things are not so clear. The indexation agreement did seriously protect wage-earners, especially the weaker categories, but – and this was a grave omission – it ignored the immediate effects of taxation on cost-of-living rises. At the same time, the principle of flat-rate adjustments, in a future context of galloping inflation, threatened an excessive levelling of wages and offered the employers scope for making bonuses dependent on the behaviour of individual workers, thereby opening cracks in the workforce and facilitating an eventual attack on wage indexation in general. As for the wider use of temporary redundancy payments, this too was originally a good idea. It protected surplus workers during changeovers to new technologies and products, on the assumption that they would return to the workforce at a later date. This presupposed that the redundancies in question really would be linked to a restructuring that did not permanently cut the workforce, and that they would therefore affect all workers in turn – but the problem was that the source of funding, the central state, did not insist on either of these conditions. On the contrary, lay-off periods became longer and longer, there was no talk of job rotation, and the redundancy fund effectively became a form of unemployment benefit, while the recipients prepared to take work elsewhere at lower rates or off the books. The two specific compromises could therefore function either as a way for capital to continue with its previous policies, reaping the full benefit of restructuring and offloading the costs onto the state, or as the starting point for a genuine turn in economic policy.

So, the crunch came after many resources had been used up and no counter-cyclical measures would have been sufficient. It was necessary to look further ahead, to develop a new power structure and a new growth model. The major capitalist countries (USA, Japan, Germany, France, Sweden and, more slowly, Britain) became aware of the problem and took steps to solve it, on different roads, at different paces and in line with different class orientations. But all imposed or promoted an element of 'virtuous' synergy between public intervention and strong powers in the economy. The idea that 'neoliberal globalization' arose spontaneously out of market laws is a fable spun in the capitalist heartlands.

In Italy, more than anywhere else, the economic crisis called for structural reforms, a new institutional structure and a new plan to ensure that it did not end in decline. Yet no one tried to do what was necessary to achieve these. I have already referred to the programmatic deficiencies involved in the 'historic compromise', and to the wall the DC placed in the way of genuine reforms. But, as often happens in history, there was also a strong dose of misfortune: chance had it that the election victory which made it impossible to govern without the Communists, and the short-lived unity of the Left, coincided with the height of the economic crisis, making the choices more urgent and difficult. The employers also bore a heavy responsibility, both because of their long tradition of obtuseness and because of the new corporate interests they were defending. In fact, there was a glimmer of insight on their part that it was necessary to choose between continuity and risky innovations. This makes me think of a curious episode, which has remained secret until recently and is absent from all the records. On the initiative of the National Unity governments, Guido Carli, the new head of Confindustria, asked for a face-to-face meeting with Luigi Longo, whose authority and independent judgement he knew from experience. Surprisingly, however, Carli was not asking the PCI to swallow new workers' sacrifices or a general cut in social spending. 'Short-term measures or special assistance are no longer enough,' he said. 'Either you Communists manage to bring some morality into social spending and public administration, push through a strict but efficient economic policy, and get rid of political kickbacks, or there's no reason why a certain part of the country should accept your participation in government.' Of course, what he meant by 'bringing in morality and efficiency' was different from what the Left understood by such words, but he recognized that the problem was to get out of the swamp by making a break with the past. If, as Barca writes, Longo listened with 'irony in his eyes', it was for a different reason. For what Carli said was completely contradicted by what the employers had been saying and doing every day. The signals were crystal-clear. The Agnelli family itself had become involved in politics for the first time (Umberto standing for the DC in an election campaign mainly designed to keep the Communists out of power; Susanna for the Republicans, at a time when La Malfa was undertaking to legalize the secret financial backing by oil men). The main dailies, like Montanelli, urged readers 'to hold their nose and vote DC'. The employers spoke perfectly calmly about the Sindona case,[5] the Banco Ambrosiano[6] and later P-2, in which many of them were implicated. The parliamentary term witnessed resistance to a real reform of town planning; full-scale polemics against public industry deficits, but not against the stream of credit facilities and the building of 'desert skyscrapers'; a failure to campaign for a higher scientific research budget in the face of a brain drain and reliance on the purchase of foreign patents; a reorganization of big private finance in line with the elite 'Chinese box' model, to which top members of the 'employer breed' also had access. Scalfari's preaching was good (see p. 268), but the Italian big bourgeoisie as a whole did not practise it. In fact, in the National Unity period, economic policy continued in much the same way as before: generous public deficit spending, to prop up ailing companies and to reduce the social impact on those able to press ahead with restructuring.

Let us look at some aspects of this, so that we do not tar everyone with the same brush. To be socially equitable and economically plausible, a new project had to pass muster on three questions. First,

5. Michele Sindona: corrupt banker and the Vatican's *homme de confiance*, criminally linked to the Mafia, found guilty of murdering a Milan lawyer in 1979 and eventually poisoned in prison in 1986.

6. In 1978 the Banco d'Italia had already produced a report on Banco Ambrosiano that led to criminal investigations and finally, in 1982, to public revelations about a huge hole in the bank's finances and links with the P-2 secret masonic lodge.

the short-term distribution of income: where could those saddled with past debt find the resources for a new and dynamic type of growth? Berlinguer made an important and courageous speech on this, in which he said that 'austerity' was generating distrust or cynicism on both the Left and the Right. I was not among those who denied that austerity had any value; I had used the word myself in my own way, as an indication of a real problem and as part of a forward-looking critique of consumerism and status symbols. To shift income towards collective consumption, basic needs and an enlargement of the productive system, without squeezing overall demand, was at that time a necessary condition for future prosperity and a higher level of civilization. But Berlinguer's speech actually avoided spelling out who should bear the main burden of austerity. The whole country (as Amendola argued), to show a sense of responsibility to the national interest? Or more selectively and rigorously, protecting real wages and employment, allowing more generous benefits in money and services to the poorest layers of the population, and taxing high incomes and luxury consumption more intensely? An incomes policy? Yes, an incomes policy – not with restrictions on collective bargaining, however, but with an effective taxation system and freedom for the unions to act independently. On these questions, the DC and the employers stonewalled, but the PCI too, apart from Trentin and the FIM, hesitated to give answers – either to avoid breaking the recently concluded political agreement, or because it was dangerous, amid a vast archipelago of benefits and entitlements, to separate off the sacrosanct rights of the poorest layers, large or small unearned incomes, tax evasion in small businesses and all the way up to giant bequests and footloose capital. Whether inefficient or complicit, the civil service was not equipped to combat tax evasion or close loopholes. Essentially, then, nothing was done.

The second knot to be untied was more important and more difficult. What use should be made of the resources that a coherent project might identify and make available? What credible perspective could be offered in exchange for possible sacrifices? The most obvious and serious problem related to planning, in a country where the state had a huge presence in large-scale industry and banking. In the past it had been capable of stimulating and steering growth in the difficult environment of the postwar years. In the abstract, it should have been possible to give it the key role in major investments with a delayed return, but also in the provision of research and grants for private enterprise, channelling skills and experience into the industries of the future. But in reality a lot of murky water had passed under the bridge. Public industry was overloaded with debt (11,000 lire per 1000 lire of turnover) as a result of various rescue operations and white elephants, and because it was being run by a new generation of managers accustomed to silent obedience. The banks often handed out state-backed loans that had riddled their balance-sheets with debt and threatened them with insolvency. It was therefore not credible to speak of planning unless you had the will and the power to revolutionize the whole structure. The DC's fine talk of putting its own house in order sounded far from convincing; the employers had every interest in continuing to milk it for maintenance. The unions were compelled to be flexible in order to save jobs.

At that time, planning was also running up against other obstacles, not only in Italy. The international market still did not allow reliable forecasts to be made that might guide investment decisions. What is more, once the basic needs threshold had been crossed and production had acquired the capacity to steer consumption, the drawing up of a scale of priorities became a free and complicated choice, in which different conceptions of culture or civilization were expressed. The material conditions and values of people around the world still showed huge differences, and new issues such as environmental protection had to be either tackled or left unresolved. Yet it cannot be honestly said that these questions of planning featured in the policy debates of the 1970s, except in so far as the PCI, in a limited way that was extremely short on ideas, tried to put them at the centre of a new economic policy. The leaders often had different positions concerning instruments or objectives: some (the strictest Amendolans) still pinned their faith on improved public intervention; others (who took their lead from Franco Rodano[7] and had an influence on Berlinguer) thought it necessary to set stricter limits, and to act on the quality of growth indirectly through the creation of social demand. Such discussions, which only took place at the top and remained quite generic, did not lead to any organic plan and added little that was

7. Franco Rodano: radical left-wing Catholic philosopher and politician of the postwar years.

constructive to the argument with Christian Democracy and the government. One commitment, wrested from them in 1977, led to the statutory earmarking of funds for sectoral restructuring – although the ministerial committee in charge failed in its task of precisely defining and coordinating the plans. The unions took the legislation at its word and began a number of disputes, with strikes and mass mobilizations, but the result was extremely disappointing: an executive plan for building nuclear power stations (which got under way but was then cancelled because of local opposition). The rest of the earmarked funds went unused or were dished out at random; planning remained little more than a fantasy.

Our judgement on the third aspect of the supposed reform – the construction of a modern 'social state' – needs to be more nuanced. This was a burning issue, both because it would offer a tangible quid pro quo for wage moderation, and because it would generate new, non-parasitic employment and general support for production. Only one initiative in this direction actually came off, however, when an innovative law towards the end of the parliamentary term established one of the most advanced public health services in Europe, intended to provide free treatment as well as preventive medicine for all. But it was not easy to get it going, not only because of the high expenditure involved but also because of the realities it had to face on the ground. The previous health systems had reflected the two Italies: the North had long had a partially public service that functioned reasonably well, with a generation of doctors who believed in it and were not chasing after riches; but the Centre and South had remained with a private system, often ruled by a speculative logic, which left the state to handle the most difficult and costly cases while picking up the most profitable for itself. If we add to the picture a fragmented regional administration, excessive use of hospitals, the lack of a national health plan, the over-prescription of ineffectual medicines and the exorbitant bills of private practitioners, it is easy to see the roots of later inefficiencies. Nevertheless, a general principle had been established and would remain in force.

Other welfare initiatives – above all, in housing – could have played a more important role in relation to the economic crisis, but it was no accident that they failed. Housing was superabundant in some areas, but scarce in others where internal migration had pushed up demand. Rent was the largest item in most family budgets. The private sector, weighed down by ground rents, charged unaffordable prices when it built any housing at all, while the public sector – which despite everything had put up an average of 361,000 units a year between 1962 and 1967 – was down to 198,000 in 1972–4, and 140,000 in 1977. Its recovery was an acute social problem but also a production problem, with multiple ramifications.

The government appeared to be taking important decisions in this regard. Sizeable resources were allocated for public housing, and an incentive was offered in the form of the right to buy suitable land at the price of agricultural land, thereby covering the costs of urban development and the provision of services. But regulations full of traps and obstacles, combined with passive resistance from businesses and stubborn hostility on the part of central and local administrative bodies, were enough to sabotage the project. Out of a thousand billion lire earmarked for popular housing, only 24 billion reached their target; the rest went on the purchase of private housing or to phoney cooperatives, as it had done before and would do in the future, causing various social and economic distortions. For it meant that the place of residence was often a long way from the place of work, alongside an increase in home ownership for the sake of future children or inheritance breaks, and a growing tendency to resort to petty abuses. In short, the whole thing was a failure. Another unsuccessful reform imposed a system of 'fair rents', which were supposed to open up the market by removing the postwar rent freeze that had blocked new entrants and made housing repairs unprofitable. But, since the law did not define any grounds for eviction at the end of a lease, and since public housing was in ever shorter supply, the 'fair rents' proved to have the opposite effect to the one intended: landlords left properties empty in hopes of selling at a higher price when the opportunity arose, and a large number of unregistered leases completely escaped the fiscal net.

I will not speak of education and scientific research, which should have played a key role in growth perspectives, because there is nothing to say. Let us simply note that, with little funding and no reform in teaching methods or syllabuses, mass education led to an 'easy time' and a decline in cultural and professional training, to a new kind of class differentiation, and to disaffection among poorly paid staff who often lacked job security. Meanwhile the paucity of public investment in scientific and technological research was offset, not by a growth of private facilities, but by the purchase of foreign patents, a brain drain, and the takeover of the most promising firms by large multinationals.

In this absence of new policies and reform initiatives – a void it had itself contributed to and exploited – Italian capitalism eventually found its way to defining and imposing a solution of its own. It was certainly not a lucid project: the aim was not to produce another economic miracle and to join the front ranks of a future world order, but rather to adapt pragmatically, so as not to be left entirely out in the cold. But for that there existed a real basis, which Italian capitalism itself had built over the previous decade by seeking and finding the necessary supports. Within limits, I therefore reject the term restoration or ultra-conservatism (*immobilismo*) and have instead used the paradoxical expression 'downward miracle'. Restructuring took place, Italian-style, and as the National Unity governments failed to produce results the employers cautiously but clear-headedly took over the leading role.

This economic restructuring advanced on two fronts, with two parallel initiatives. Large and medium-sized modern industry, already feeling its age, found the means to hold up and even to update itself, by cutting the workforce (by an average of a third) but not overall production. It did this not with the classical instruments of sackings and speed-up, nor only with low-interest credits, but essentially with the help of the temporary redundancy fund and by farming out parts of the productive process to a network of formally autonomous, but actually dependent, small or medium-sized firms, where wages were lower, rights less secure and production more flexible. At the same time new forms of work organization, tried and tested in Japan or Sweden, were introduced to raise productivity, shorten the command chain and make shopfloor workers more directly responsible for the quality of the final product; sales and marketing were also made more autonomous. Finally, there was an early but major relocation to countries such as Poland and Brazil, where labour costs were very low and new markets could be tapped. Fiat is the clearest case in point. Since then, employment in large-scale industry has steadily fallen in Italy, whatever the economic situation. Balance-sheet surpluses have been restored mainly through cost-cutting, and part of these surpluses has then been transferred into investments outside the core business, particularly in attractive sectors of finance. The other, negative, aspect of this restructuring was not only higher unemployment and lower-paid, less secure employment, but also the sacrificing of ever more firms and sectors that might have been at the forefront of technological progress, had they not required major investments with no prospect of short-term returns. Typical examples are computers and chemicals (Olivetti, Montedison), the big pharmaceutical corporations and the food industry.

The second front in the industrial restructuring witnessed the exponential growth of small and very small firms, which had already played an important role in the take-off period in Italy, and were associated with the stable migration over short distances of sharecroppers with latent entrepreneurial skills. In the growth years, firms of this kind had become more common and more diverse. At least some of them, with the help of a favourable social environment and the support of local authorities, had discovered for themselves, as it were, the advantages of territorial specialization theorized by Alfred Marshall, a great economist of the early twentieth century. In some cases these firms had even taken on advanced technologies and established direct links with the international market. Their common foundation was low wages and tax evasion, but very often also a high degree of professionalism and entrepreneurial imagination. In the 1970s the economic crisis, the new international division of labour and new individual patterns of consumption enabled this model to spread to many more regions, and as time went by they became more differentiated in terms of firm size and type of specialization. They also found major opportunities in the market interstices that industry had abandoned in the most advanced countries, and which newly developing countries were not yet in a position to occupy. Such 'industrial districts' were viewed everywhere in the world with great interest, but the life pulsating in them, or in other zones, came from small businesses on the fringes of legality. It was the 'secret weapon' of Italian capitalism.

Nevertheless, the restructuring of the late 1970s brought political and social costs and economic weaknesses from which Italy has not since recovered. It is easy to enumerate them, because the evidence is still plain to see: growing splits in the sphere of wage labour and hence an objective shift in the relations of class forces (wage differentials, insecure or unregistered labour, co-opting of the most active and intelligent employees into the entrepreneurial middle layer and the fragmented world of services); decline of the newest and most advanced sections of industry, which might have shaped and controlled the future; new regional imbalances that underpin other, more degenerate, trends, such as the interpenetration of organized crime and economics, and the collusion between organized crime and politicians; an almost structural preponderance of tax evasion and widespread trade-offs between money, fiscal tolerance and electoral support. And, summing everything up, a bottomless pit of public debt: 20 to 25 per cent of GDP in the 1960s, 41 per cent in 1972, 60 per cent in 1975, 80 per cent in 1979; over 100 per cent in 1988 ...

Am I not right to speak of a 'downward miracle'?

17

What Was Brewing in the World

THE LAST COLD WAR

The analytical blank that most strikes one in relation to those years concerns the evolution of the international situation. As in 1946 the PCI, but also its Left critics, did not realize that a new phase of the cold war was already beginning, and that it was necessary to get to grips with it while it was still in its early stages. We all rightly went into the streets to support the Vietnamese struggle and rejoice at its success, or to denounce the overthrow of the legitimate government in Chile. But we saw both as evidence of revolutionary stirrings amid the crisis of imperialism, which had no way of fighting back other than brute force. We divided between those who concluded that we should be prudent and seek to build broader alliances, and those who proposed quickening our pace in support of the global ferment and making an active contribution to it in the West. But the real canvas as a whole, the new train in motion throughout the world, escaped us. So, when a change of government in Italy came onto the agenda, the issue of an active new policy towards the East dropped to bottom place.

The last phase of the cold war initially manifested itself as a rivalry between two crisis-ridden superpowers, both in their heartland and in their respective alliances; the crisis affecting them was economic, geopolitical and hegemonial (though still under the shelter of the nuclear balance of terror). I should immediately add two points here on the theme of economic crisis.

The first is that the ruling classes of the largest Western countries were quick to grasp the scale of the crisis. To be sure, their governments were not at all solid. Nixon won the presidential elections, but in his early weeks already declared: 'We live in an age of anarchy, both abroad and at home.' He was partly right, because the United States was then mired in a costly war that it was losing, while the youth revolt and the anti-racist movement had eroded popular trust, and in Europe social-democratic governments that had come to power on a wave of economic growth and welfarism ran into difficulties as soon as the expansion lost steam. But in 1973, and above all in 1975, they found an informal meeting place – Kissinger's 'Trilateral Commission' – where political rulers, big business and authoritative academics could thrash out an analysis and agree on a line to keep chaos at bay. Its name was a little imprecise, because the United States and Japan participated in the Commission as real powers, whereas Europe was still only a common market and not an independent political subject. Nevertheless, the Trilateral produced some important results.

First of all, it dismissed the facile idea that the crisis was mainly due to the oil price rises, and refused to tackle it by resorting to protectionism and the defence of individual currencies (the disastrous policies of the 1930s). Second, it committed everyone to pursue two initial objectives straight away: real wage cuts, with an end to disorder in the factories, and cuts in social spending to bring it back below danger level. These two objectives were taken up in different ways and to different degrees, and were partly achieved through an alternation of inflation and deflation and the wearing down of trade union resistance. The Trilateral urged two further steps: free but ongoing harmonization of economic policy among the various states, and a gradual building of supranational, rather than international, bodies to regulate the world economy. These recommendations were not immediately acted upon – indeed, the various countries often resorted to devaluation to cope with emergencies and give a temporary boost to their exports. But, in the longer term, powerful organizations were created or strengthened under American tutelage – the International Monetary Fund, the World Bank – which took their place alongside the burgeoning multinationals and stimulated and protected the development of global private finance. Finally, an undeclared but well-funded theoretical counteroffensive was launched against the hegemony of Keynesian economics. This was somewhat chaotic at first: a number of different schools blossomed (the Chicago school being one) but then mostly sank into confusion and disappeared (Paul Krugman's perceptive writings offer an ironical survey of the muddle and how it was cultivated). But the supremacy of a generic neoliberalism remained behind as a sediment, in governments, universities and the media.

A second point, banal though often overlooked, underlines how precarious the real process in the economy was for a long time. In nearly all the large Western countries, on both sides of the Atlantic, stagnation dragged on without precipitating a recession (the average GDP growth-rate in Europe was lower in the 1980s, and for some time after, than it had been in the 1970s). Even when the maximum neoliberal programme could be applied (in Britain and the United States), the results were disappointing and in the early years alarming (the crisis of 1983). In the same period, inflation first peaked and was then merely contained, not overcome. It created major social inequalities, while unemployment reached levels reminiscent of the 1930s, sometimes offset by low-paid and precarious forms of work. Thus, it soon became clear that capitalism would exit from such a crisis only by further squeezing the workers, for the sake of profits; it needed a more profound restructuring so that it could regain a higher rate of productivity increase and larger markets. These were not easy problems to solve.

In the years after the war, it had been relatively simple to deal with such problems. There had already been an engine in the shape of Fordist industrialization and the production of mass consumer goods, including exports to defeated or semi-ruined countries that were nonetheless capable of participation, politically integrated and economically open to a common market (Western Europe, Japan). Now, however, things were much more complicated. The power of the trade unions, though somewhat reduced, meant that unemployment was less effective in lowering wage costs – but even where this happened, it was only the beginning of an answer. It was not as if the problem of a new technological leap had already been solved and only required everyone else to imitate the solution, for now the dominant economy itself was in trouble, closely followed by countries to whose modernization it had contributed. The US did have reserves with which to meet the challenge: the role of the dollar as a world currency, and the store of knowledge and capital accumulated over decades by the military-industrial complex. But to draw on this, as it had already begun to do in the production and use of computers, it needed time and the capacity to extend its advantages to the whole of the productive apparatus (even if at first the costs were higher than the returns). Most important of all, the weight of industry – where it would be easiest to increase productivity – had been declining, and the service sector, where productivity gains were slower and less profitable, had been expanding. Finance and relocation partly made up for this, but it was still necessary to find a new international division of labour, and to integrate a large new zone of the world into growth. Such a zone existed, but it was economically backward and politically unreliable.

This is why, in my view, the main problem in the early 1970s, even at the limits of the capitalist economy, was already geopolitical. Who could organize a new world order and impress its own stamp on it, and by what means? Two camps continued to be organized around rival superpowers, but a large part of the world remained outside them, freed from colonial domination, subjectively unsure of itself and objectively lacking the power to determine its own future. This was the 'ball game' in those days, a reality to which the European Left was blind and toward which it was devoid of initiative. The outcome would depend less on the strength of capitalism than on the dissolution of those who had hitherto sought, with some degree of success, to challenge it.

CRISIS IN THE EAST

The main factor in this dissolution was the crisis of the Soviet Union, whose leading group was completely incapable of – indeed, intransigently averse to – any innovation in the country's economy, political institutions, ideology, party organization and international alliances. This was rather more than an economic crisis, which took some time to emerge: it was a crisis of the entire system. Yet no one in Italy or elsewhere seemed to know – or at any rate, seriously discussed – its nature, scale and implications.

The PCI leadership, and a good part of the membership, was already convinced that the USSR had little to do with socialism, yet continued to trust in its capacities as a great power. Openly critical of that kind of society, but wary of making any contribution to its evolution, the PCI maintained a kind of diplomatic truce with Moscow. European Social Democracy, for its part, saw no reason to revise its long-standing views about the authoritarian character of the regime, but good reasons to live with it. Those like myself and the whole *Manifesto* group, who since the Prague Spring had openly argued that the Soviet Union was no longer socialist in its class structure and political institutions, and who did not believe it had the capacity to reform itself consistently, failed to predict its imminent collapse and spent little time thinking about the likely consequences. We contented ourselves with the evocative formula 'A left exit from Stalinism', without really asking ourselves how, when, with which forces and in how many stages that might be achieved.

Today we all know that the crisis led in twenty years to the collapse of the Soviet state and society, without a war but also without a legacy. How and why it all happened, and what consequences it had, is a highly complicated question (even more than in the case of the Second International in the First World War). But it will be useful to mention some of the events in the 1970s that already pointed in that direction.

The long 'Brezhnevite ice age', whose noxious role has received too little attention, was not a form of *immobilismo*, or only in appearance. If you stand still while reality is moving, unable to find the energy to keep pace with it, first you fall behind, then you make a belated effort, and finally you grow demoralized and bow out of the scene. That is precisely what happened. At a strictly economic level, the USSR in the 1970s looked reasonably healthy in comparison with the crisis-ridden West. For a number of years, political stability and a return to central planning (after Khrushchev's improvised and half-hearted attempts at reform had mostly ended in failure) ensured a respectable growth-rate, higher than that of the Western countries. But it was a sick model, still centred on heavy industry and the military sector, and largely unconcerned about productivity; new sectors such as chemicals, petrochemicals and electronics (for which there were abundant raw materials and developed scientific-technological skills) were being neglected; the structure of prices remained arbitrary; light industry was still the Cinderella and turned out poor-quality consumer goods. Agriculture was improving after a long period of stagnation, thanks to the enlargement of arable land and the greater autonomy given to farmers under the Khrushchev reforms. But when the stagnating chemicals industry failed to produce the necessary fertilizers, a new decline set in. The slow and patchy transport system made the delivery of orders, and therefore economic coordination, generally unreliable – especially in the case of food supplies to the cities.

I could continue, but this is enough to demonstrate the structural impasse. Central planning had achieved extraordinary results in creating and extending the country's industrial base, but it no longer worked in a more complex economy where individual and collective needs could only be guided, not imposed. Still less would it serve for the establishment of advantageous trade relations with friendly countries, where labour productivity and product quality were essential to success. In the absence of an effective tax system, the statization of all productive activity had made some sense as a way of avoiding the rapid formation of social classes, at a time when the high degree of political and ideological mobilization could replace the use of material incentives. But statization no longer functioned in the growing area of service activity, especially as the revolution became a distant memory, the danger of war receded, and even the regime worked to depoliticize the masses in order to stabilize itself through a perverse trade-off between political discipline and social apathy.

This impasse of the economic system made itself felt directly at a geopolitical level. The cycle of liberation struggles was ending. The new states resulting from it needed not only military support or weapons, but also technical, organizational and even ideological assistance to resist the lure of neocolonialism, which tended to foster antagonistic interests in the form of a 'comprador' bourgeoisie – either inherited from the past, or recruited within the liberation movement itself. Brezhnev proved to be the true gravedigger of the Russian Revolution, precisely at the moment when other possible paths were opening for it.

KISSINGER, AN EVIL GENIUS

The game of a new world order, with the Communists the main losers, was already shaping up in the 1970s. For, although it is true that the economic crisis and restructuring processes made it necessary for capitalism to expand into a large new space, the point is that this space was offered in advance by a crisis in the opposite camp, and that capitalism seized the opportunity with an intelligence and political acuity that have not often been recognized.

For the United States, the geopolitical situation at the beginning of the 1970s was as difficult as the economic situation. I know that nowadays to speak ill of Kennedy is like speaking ill of Garibaldi. But Garibaldi, though ultimately defeated, left a united Italy behind him; Kennedy presented himself as a new Roosevelt, but was far from being one. The social reforms of the Great Society were a genuine compromise – in the face of the civil rights movement, a youth revolt and growing casualties in Vietnam – conceived and implemented by the essentially conservative president who replaced him: Lyndon B. Johnson. In foreign policy, however, Kennedy was a shiftless and in some respects execrable president. The construction of the Berlin Wall in 1961 – appalling in itself, but ultimately meant to prevent the collapse of the GDR – did not lead him to consider negotiating a reasonable treaty on the reunification of Germany as a neutral, non-nuclear state (in line with the Rapacki Plan[1]). Instead, he retaliated by cranking up the cold war. And to the Cuban revolution, which was not at first Communist or an appendage of Moscow, he responded with a foolish landing at the Bay of Pigs. When Khrushchev, with matching adventurism, then sent Soviet missiles to Cuba, in America's backyard – US missiles had, it is true, been deployed for some time on the borders of the USSR – Kennedy threatened to launch a hot war; against Castro's wishes, Khrushchev made a rational decision to withdraw the missiles, receiving a guarantee from Washington in return that it would refrain from another invasion in the future. Above all, it was Kennedy who gave the go-ahead for the Vietnam war, breaking the Geneva accords on the reunification of the country, and sending the 'Green Berets' to support a government that refused to negotiate. Soon after his assassination Johnson continued on the same road, first encouraging and funding the military overthrow of the legal government of João Goulart in a major Latin American country (Brazil), then ordering the escalation in Vietnam (even though he was convinced, like his defence secretary Robert McNamara, that it was a senseless tragedy). Meanwhile, in 1965, a military coup in Indonesia led to the massacre of 800,000 Communists.

1. Named after the Polish foreign minister, Adam Rapacki, who in 1957 submitted a plan to the United Nations for a nuclear-free zone in Central Europe comprising the two Germanies, Poland and Czechoslovakia.

By 1970, however, this had still not been enough to ensure US domination – indeed, American prestige was beginning to wear decidedly thin. The war was going badly in Vietnam, Allende was winning the presidential race in Chile, guerrilla campaigns were becoming endemic, and Cuba had established closer ties with the Soviet Union. Much as I dislike saying it, the real mix of repression and political intelligence was only then taking shape, in the person of Richard Nixon and the brains behind him, Henry Kissinger.

Kissinger was no more fastidious than his predecessors in the use of force and arbitrary powers – quite the contrary. But he knew how to make an analysis and to use a range of instruments. In Latin America, where the balance of powers imposed no clear constraints, the first stage in the *reconquista* proceeded to restore order by every method in the book. Hence the swift and impressive series of coups d'état, replete with torture and murder, carried out by loyal military allies of Washington in Chile, Uruguay, Peru and Argentina. The reaction of European governments? None. Nor were many people protesting in the streets. Only later were there ritual expressions of solidarity with the Mothers of the Plaza de Mayo,[2] excitement over the songs of the Inti-Illimani ensemble from Chile, or demands that the guilty should be punished – the wretched local culprits, that is, not the respectable ones in the State Department.

Familiar scenarios? Not entirely. There was one novel aspect that we did not appreciate at the time. The military coups of the 1970s had new protagonists and were less blinkered in their objectives. The officers who led them were no longer a well-paid, ideologically para-fascist force intervening to prop up an oligarchy of absentee landowners. Still less were they unreliable populists à la Perón. They had been taught modern repressive techniques in military academies of the United States, and their economic advisers had graduated from North American universities. They seized power with unprecedented violence and went on exercising it directly – not to restore the old order, but to lead a managerial elite into a new kind of dependent industrialization, replacing import substitution with a strategy geared to exports. This was not so easy to achieve: it required raising finance from world markets and

2. The association of Argentine mothers which mounted an ongoing presence in the Plaza de Mayo in Buenos Aires, demanding to know what had happened to the sons and daughters who had 'disappeared' under the military dictatorship.

gaining the support of the multinationals, and it needed members of the ruling class to reinvest their money in the country, instead of frittering it away or stashing it in American banks. In the early 1980s, then, development gave way to a debt crisis, but the IMF and the US Treasury mounted a costly rescue operation in return for a decisive say in economic policies.

A second, more subtle, kind of *reconquista* took place in the Middle East. The stakes were high: nothing less than oil. But it was more difficult to establish political control. Despite the military defeat by Israel in 1967, the failure of the federation of Egypt and Syria, the ambiguities of the Iraqi Baath Party, leadership changes and splits in the Algerian FLN and civil war in Lebanon, the tide of Arab nationalism, secular and progressive, was still going strong. Nasser had a firm hold on power, in alliance with the Soviet Union, which had accepted his dissolution of the Egyptian Communist Party, a small force with a highly skilled cadre. Saudi Arabia was the only solid American ally in the Arab world, thanks to the web of financial interests that linked the two countries. As for Israel, although Washington assured it of military support, it still hesitated to treat it as a direct representative of its interests, for fear of losing even more popularity in the Arab world. At the end of the decade, America's main military partner in the region, the Shah of Iran, was overthrown by a non-violent Islamic fundamentalist insurgency fiercely hostile to the West.

The opportunity for the Americans had come with the death of Nasser in 1970. He had not named a successor, and Sadat, though vice-president, was tenth in the real hierarchy of power. But he was smart enough to use his caretaker position to launch a semi-coup and jail his rivals. With a shaky base in the Nasserite party, and limited support among the masses as a result of persecuting the Muslim Brotherhood, Sadat sent all the Soviet advisers back home (seeing them more as a liability than a useful presence) and turned to the West for political and financial backing. Kissinger offered him more and more, and after a little skirmishing over Sinai he ended up recognizing Israel and signing a substantive agreement between the two countries. The process influenced the Jordanians and the Iraqis, who were later pushed by the Americans into a decade of war with Iran. At this point the US relationship with Israel could become more open and full-bodied, a kind of proxy arrangement. Another part of the Third World was thus brought under control. Pakistan, always on the brink of war with India, left SEATO in 1973 and came under a variety of influences, but it remained essentially under American control. Indonesia, for its part, had a military regime and was a secure ally.

But the Far East remained decisive. The regimes in Taiwan and Korea were pushed into a land reform to gain some mass support – another sign that this imperialism was not stupid – and then used the economic aid they received, as bases for the Vietnam war, to become small capitalist 'high-flyers'. Japan was a very loyal ally, but also an economic rival that exported much and imported little – certainly not a space into which the US could expand.

The big outstanding problem for a new world order was therefore the People's Republic of China: a gigantic market for the future, a formidable opponent due to its size, its Communist revolution and its glimmerings of autonomous economic development. In the past the Americans had refused to recognize this country with a population of one billion, and repeatedly blocked its admission to the United Nations. For their part, the Chinese had considered the US their principal enemy, and criticized the Soviets for accepting peaceful coexistence with it.

As we knew, relations between the Chinese and the Soviets had never been easy. The main source of intermittent tensions was that, although the Chinese had recognized the Russian revolution as an ideological reference point and a pillar of support for common action in the world, their own revolution, like the Yugoslav, had been not only Communist but nationalist, achieved with their own forces and therefore entitled to its own autonomous space. Even in the years when they had been closest (the war in Korea, the first steps in industrialization), the Chinese had regarded cooperation between the two countries not as a duty but as a matter of choice and convergence. The first sign of discord came in 1956, in relation to the judgement of Stalin, but this was set aside during the Hungarian crisis and indeed for a brief period the Sino-Soviet relationship took on the character of a partnership. New and graver differences emerged in the early 1960s, when Chinese criticisms of Moscow effectively rejected the principle of a 'leading state' and attacked its over-conciliatory relationship with Washington. At this point Khrushchev made the worst mistake of his life: he suspended all economic and military aid to China and withdrew the technicians it needed for its economic development. It was a disastrous decision, not only because it created difficulties that Beijing would never forget, but because it converted a sharp ideological and political debate into a break between states. It was what Togliatti had feared so acutely, even before the Cultural Revolution.

As for the Cultural Revolution, its most damaging aspect was not the radical critique of the social and political model emerging in the USSR, but the identification of the Soviet Union as the main enemy in the global contest. Whereas Zhou Enlai and Tito had responded to Zhdanovism with Bandung – that is, with a defensive and autonomous but effective foreign policy – the China of the Cultural Revolution was unable to develop anything similar in answer to the Sino-Soviet split (which instantly wiped out the greatest change in the geopolitical balance since the second half of the nineteenth century). The 'three worlds' strategy, elaborated by Lin Biao, had no basis in reality and was not put into practice even at the stormiest moments of the Cultural Revolution. The Chinese had no resources to offer the Third World, and no message except the maxims in Mao's Little Red Book. In reality, however, Beijing's foreign policy – at both the inter-party and inter-state level – was extremely cautious. It mistrusted or condemned the various guerrilla movements around the world, and distrusted Cuba even when it was still completely independent of Moscow; it was prepared to negotiate advantageous economic agreements with right-wing regimes, and viewed the building of alternative Communist parties with scepticism (because it rightly feared they would cause trouble rather than provide support). The only effective contribution it could make to the anti-imperialist struggle was to give real aid to the Vietnamese. And this it did – paradoxically side by side with the Soviet Union, though without looking it in the face.

I remember one little incident in 1970, soon after I and other *Manifesto* comrades were expelled from the PCI. We asked for a meeting with the Chinese CP, so that we could better understand its position and make ours known to it. Not only was our request accepted, but we were asked to go to Paris, where a senior Chinese leader was present at the time. This seemed a good sign, because we thought a discussion would be interesting and we were certainly not orthodox towards anyone. We were given a very courteous and friendly reception, but when we moved on to the discussion the Chinese became very formal and reluctant to speak of their own experience, their current situation or their plans for the future. Instead they asked us many well-informed questions: mostly about Fanfani, the Italian Centre Left and its likely foreign policy; less about the PCI and the reasons for our expulsion; even less about our intentions and capacities; and nothing at all about mass movements in Italy and the West, or the little Marxist-Leninist groups in Italy that claimed to speak in the name of the Chinese. We therefore returned from Paris more than a little disappointed – leaving aside the exquisite dinner. There were only two possibilities: either the situation in China was now so unclear and complex that it was impossible to speak candidly about it; or else the Chinese were convinced that a 'cultural revolution', a call to revolt, could not happen without a charismatic leader to launch and steer it and an established power to be put on trial but not swept away – convinced, in short, that in the end it was necessary 'to rely on your own forces'. In fact, both sides of the alternative were true. For my own part, I came back with the idea that we would have to revise some of our thinking – not so much about them as about the world situation.

But a burden of proof still existed concerning the Sino-Soviet relationship. After Khrushchev, the main wrongdoer on the Soviet side, was deposed, the new leadership in Moscow had considerable material resources that it could have offered to the Chinese, as well as an interest in drawing on the huge pool of eager, skilled manpower. China had a large market and a still fledgling industry; it was potentially an important ally, still threatened by the United States and shut out of the United Nations; and it had a great need of natural resources and basic skills. As for the Cultural Revolution, Mao reined in the radicalism in 1968, without by any means disowning or liquidating the movement. The opportunities I am speaking of were not momentary. The Soviet economy was still enjoying a degree of development. In China, for some ten years, both Mao and Zhou Enlai tried to guarantee and bequeath a balance between radical principles and realistic policies. The Vietnamese struggle was nearing a climax, though with the possibility that it might be defeated.

Many Communist parties, not only the PCI, were becoming averse to the discipline of the camp, sharing Togliatti's idea that international solidarity should exist without overriding difference or autonomy. The PCI could not impose anything, of course, but, as a major party in the West, with influence in many other countries, it could have taken an initiative to revive a much-needed degree of convergence between China and the USSR. As things were, the relationship was heading in the opposite direction: on the Soviet side, the occupation of Czechoslovakia in the name of a theory of 'limited sovereignty'; on the Chinese side, the liquidation of Lin Biao, with accusations that he of all people had been in league with Moscow.

Here we can appreciate the skill and speed with which Kissinger moved, not crudely seeking to exploit the divisions in the opposite camp, but making them the lever for a new strategy. In 1972, at the height of the Vietnam war, without ceasing to blow hot and cold towards Moscow, an American president sought and obtained direct contact with the staunchest of enemies, Mao Zedong and Zhou Enlai. It was a historic turn, not simply an offer of détente. In little more than a fortnight, the changes came thick and fast: Washington would recognize the People's Republic for the first time and sanction its admission into the United Nations and the Security Council (causing uproar in Taiwan and South Korea); Beijing would create a number of special zones from 1978, where joint ventures could be formed and trade freely on the world market (mainly exporting their goods to the United States); these would set the pace for the rest of the Chinese economy, the only condition being that the currency would remain non-convertible. There was an element of caution, because state ownership of industry would remain intact in other regions, as would collective ownership of the land, with farmers authorized to sell their produce individually or collectively. The final stages in the process only occurred later, but it is an indisputable, though little-known fact, that it involved changing the entire system, and that the groundwork for the new economy was laid in the geopolitical turn of the early 1970s.

Deng Xiaoping, who gradually took charge of the policy, did not hesitate to proclaim: 'No matter if the cat is white or black, so long as it can catch mice.' But the change of direction was made when Mao was still alive. An account of his talks with Nixon has recently been published in the United States, and though the text is of doubtful authenticity it contains a statement by Mao that Nixon later reported and which has never been repudiated. 'If I'd had to vote in America I'd have voted for you – because in the West people on the Right do what they say, whereas those on the Left say one thing and do another.' In a jokey, provocative way, this showed that Mao was not engaged in skilful diplomacy but was making a firm decision that carried risks for everyone. Resistance in the Chinese leadership, and the confidence that Mao ultimately expressed in the results of the Cultural Revolution, suggest that he thought China could block the kind of capitalist restoration he considered to be under way in the USSR; for him the game was still wide open, and could not be won by digging into a posture of immobility. The short period left to him, as well as his tendency to see history in the *longue durée* of the class struggle, prevented him from setting limits in advance, defining the mechanisms to 'turn an evil into a good' (or, as we would say, 'to make a virtue of necessity') and predicting the shape of things to come. But he was fully aware that his China was making a historic gamble. Paradoxically, the real pillar that remained after his death – and has still not collapsed, however debatable the effects – was the solid pyramid of power in the hands of a single party.

Anyway, what is sure is that today's neoliberal globalization was already brewing in the 1970s. Perhaps it could have been better contained and shaped in its early stages. But the European Left was ignorant of the whole question. If, in this context, I use the expression 'dissolution of the socialist camp', it is precisely because the final split between China and the USSR, and the path that each country then took, had a political and ideological impact on other countries and regions: witness the difficulties that Vietnam faced after victory, the economic problems of Cuba, or the isolation of the Palestinians.

THE NEW WIND FROM THE WEST

In 1980, when a long period of conflict was coming to an end without a new world order, a new political leadership suddenly emerged in parts of the West, not at all by chance, and gradually prevailed over a quite different alternative.

1) The key event was the almost simultaneous accession to power of a new Right in Britain and the United States. For decades we had been used to thinking that the alternation of conservative and social-democratic governments in the West did not lead to major or permanent turns. Economic and foreign policy might change, but not essentially because one or another party was in power. The gap was small between moderate conservatives and

liberal socialists, and on critical issues (Atlantic loyalism, peaceful coexistence, a welfare state within the limits of the possible) no one wished to deviate from a bipartisan approach. Conflict shifted to peripheral areas of the world, where it took a different form or became more circumscribed. This was the fruit of a hegemonic culture and a certain relationship of forces. Ronald Reagan's new Right stepped outside of this framework, however, and proposed a clean break with the past compromise. In respect of political objectives, this meant freeing the market from the fetters and costs that had been increasingly hindering its expansion and efficiency. The goal was to move beyond the postwar social compromise and the labour-market rigidities that had underpinned it; to redefine fiscal policy and shift budgetary resources away from remuneration to accumulation; and to sweep away firms that were unprofitable or on the verge of becoming so. Reagan quickly achieved this first, destructive, part of the programme by methods that would have a permanent effect: tax cuts for the well-off, but real wage cuts for the workers; mass unemployment or reallocation of labour to inferior, non-unionized jobs, a longer working week, the hiring of more women and immigrants without employment rights, a reduction in welfare spending and services, and measures to curtail strikes and to break the power of the trade unions. But none of this was enough to guarantee a revival of the economy or a reassertion of American supremacy; it even threatened to trigger a recession.

What was required was to expand the market within and outside its existing areas of application; to achieve significant productivity increases (hence a technological leap) that would confound international competitors, and to nurture businessmen with a higher degree of market-focused entrepreneurial competence. It was also necessary to find ways of obtaining consent among the majority of the population whose security was being eroded. The first steps in this direction involved supporting new sectors of production (information technology, biotechnology), large multinational corporations, trends associated with financialization, a monopoly of the culture industry to shape the new common sense of the age, and the export of patents and import of brains. But these steps did not work fast enough, and needed an engine to drive them. It was therefore a second objective that became the driving force of 'Reaganism': a high-profile ratcheting-up of the cold war, already begun under Carter, especially through a newfangled arms race centred on such dangerous projects as the neutron bomb, a missile shield and 'Star Wars'. This turn was of fundamental importance on two fronts. The military-industrial complex, based on public funding but run by private firms, had the twin tasks of accelerating the technological leap at a time when it could not guarantee short-term profits, and of forcing the Soviet Union into ruinous military expenditure of its own if it was not to fall behind. Domestically, this orientation rebuilt the myth of an 'American mission' to unify the world, while externally it revived the idea of American supremacy and control over key policy decisions. It gave the United States the economic role of a safe haven for overseas capital, which it needed to overcome its growing international disadvantages. The ideology of the new Right underlined the necessity, and possibility, of rolling back the major turn produced by the Second World War and Roosevelt's New Deal. But it remains to be explained how such an explicit ambition went unchallenged, even though it offered American citizens more headaches than hopes, and flew in the face of the model that had been built up in Western Europe. The answer is obvious. Europe – which alone had the resources to oppose or correct this strategy – was not a united political subject; and the European Left lacked the ideas, the strength and the will to propose an alternative.

2) Events in France were proof of this strong wind blowing from the West. At that time France was the only country which, by virtue of its size and political orientation, could promote resistance in Europe to the new Anglo-American Right. It had twenty years of Gaullist rule behind it – not left-wing, to be sure, but more autonomous than any other from Atlantic discipline – and a centralized but efficient state apparatus ready and able to intervene in the economy. In previous decades the Left had been bitterly divided between a strong Communist Party (around 25 per cent of the vote), which was nevertheless isolated by its ideological dogmatism and subordination to Soviet policy, and a Socialist Party that participation in postwar governments and the colonial war in Algeria had reduced to a shadow of its former self. A skewed election law meant that the Left could not aspire to govern until this internecine conflict was healed. In 1971, however, a new course seemed to begin, in France of all countries. The initiative came from François Mitterrand, a prestigious but capable leader, though short on organized forces and haunted by a less than spotless past.

Without changing its name, he pulled the Socialist Party from the verge of collapse and set out to rebuild it around groups of intellectuals and politically unaffiliated trade unionists. The venture was not without success, and its sponsor had the intelligence to propose a lasting entente with the PCF to aim at the presidency of the Republic. The Communists, for their part, had the intelligence not only to accept the proposal but to suggest an even more ambitious agreement around a 'Common Programme'. To this end they greatly toned down their dogmatism and their links with Moscow, and agreed that Mitterrand should run as the Left's joint candidate for the presidency. The Common Programme was a little antiquated, but dense and binding. The core of it was a 'Left Keynesianism': pay rises and higher social spending, public intervention to promote the growth that would cover budgetary deficits, and limited nationalizations – the exact opposite of the Reagan programme. The Socialists added to this a rather general discourse of self-management. Within a few years the Union de la Gauche, unique in Europe, succeeded in capturing large numbers of votes. The outlook was promising, until some cracks began to show. The voters who were now turning left – often the very same who had defected to Gaullism in the 1950s and '60s – naturally inclined more towards the Socialist Party, which regained its traditional strength in the middle layers and even won over some Communist 'fellow-travellers' (opinion polls showed the PCF vote down from 25 to 20 per cent). At this point the PCF made a serious mistake. It could not tolerate the idea of losing its primacy on the Left, and thought it could avoid this by partly reviving its traditional image; Mitterrand profited from this to downplay the Common Programme. Meanwhile neither the Communists nor the Socialists applied themselves to filling the gaps in the Programme, such as its scant reference to trade union struggle, its paucity of ideas about how to make the project more in tune with the times, its failure to involve new social subjects, and above all its indifference to international issues and the 'European question'. Nevertheless, Mitterrand won the presidential elections in 1981. The PCF vote dropped to 15 per cent, but the agreement was loyally applied and Communists joined the government. It took only a few months for all to appreciate the difficulties involved in a reform project, particularly at a time of economic crisis. Power is not made up only of votes, but also of unity among those who exercise it, the mass mobilizations that it generates or nurtures, and the international relationship of forces in which it is inserted. The bosses responded to wage rises (and similar measures) with massive redundancies and a flight of capital; the franc became a target for profit-hungry speculators and had to be devalued on two occasions; the trade unions were divided or uncertain; and the leaders of '68 had turned into *nouveaux philosophes*, cheerleaders for the West and a new anti-Communism. In this context, the Socialists soon turned their economic policy round in an ultra-liberal direction. Mitterrand built an 'iron axis' between France and Germany (where Kohl's Christian Democrats had returned to power); his policy towards the Third World degenerated into an often unsavoury collaboration with the corrupt governments of France's former African colonies. A few years later Chirac's Gaullists won the general elections, and the long-suffering Communists finally quit the stage. Nor was France an isolated case: Craxi in Italy and Felipe González in Spain were headed in the same direction as Mitterrand. The British labour movement, after fighting and losing a hard battle against Thatcher, underwent a split, and it would be another twelve years before the next Labour government. The European alternative to Reaganism failed even before it started.

Reality, then, was demonstrating two things. On the one hand, Keynesianism in a single country (but existing in an unregulated international market) produced inflation, unemployment and deficits in greater measure than it generated new investments or new jobs. Perhaps, intelligently applied, it could have worked if the whole of Europe had adopted it, and if in the medium term there had been popular support for a programme of essential but costly reforms. But neither of those conditions was present, and no one had tried to create them. On the other hand, although circumstances eventually forced the Union de la Gauche to abandon its original project, the parties that made it up had not started out from the halfway house of traditional social democracy. As time went by, the European Left came to a crossroads: either it could isolate itself in resistance, accepting the prospect of a long decline ahead, or it could move much further to the right, towards liberal democracy, effectively endorsing the American model and trying to contain its excesses – or to derive some advantage for itself. The world was still in turmoil, but the prospects for the Left were by no means rosy.

18

The Fateful Eighties

I confess that at this point, a profound doubt paralysed my work on the book for weeks and months.

In 1980, after all that had been happening in Italy and the world, politically, economically, socially and culturally, was there still any real possibility for the PCI to influence the course of events, or at least to preserve the greater part of its forces and identity for the future? It was a legitimate doubt, but much depended on it: if I answered yes, it would mean judging Berlinguer's turn in 1980 to have been fanciful and irrelevant, and Occhetto's endorsement of the PCI's dissolution in 1989 to have been correct. I therefore combed through my memories of that decade and the historical accounts of it that have since become the accepted version. And I came to the conclusion that the history of the 1980s was less linear and straightforward than is generally believed. Two 'surprises', as it were, convinced me of this.

First, not only was the decade chock-full of important events; virtually no one had predicted most of them, and few attempts were made to analyse their dynamic or their likely consequences. The fact that such a radical and extensive turnaround took place in such a short space of time, without a war or an economic catastrophe, implies that it was the result of tendencies that had been at work for some time – which makes it all the more interesting to consider how they eventually emerged and developed in the light of day. On the other hand, if all these new events were unexpected yet took a long time to arouse discussion, then they were the fruit of complicated endeavours, successful or unsuccessful, later compounded by right or wrong political choices or suicide on the part of the various protagonists still in the field.

This brings us to the second 'surprise'. To what extent were all aspects of the final outcome determined in advance, and to what extent could they have turned out differently in the specific historical conditions of each country, given its material and human resources and its political strategies for tackling the crisis? Simply to file everything away under the heading 'Death of Communism' is not consistent with the facts.

Let us be clear. It is undeniable that in the 1980s the history of Communism as a world movement, inspired by the Russian Revolution, came to an end. It is also undeniable that this weighed heavily on all the forces that had participated in that history, even those that had gradually gone their independent ways and developed autonomous cultural traditions. No surprises there: the 1980s led where they had to lead, to a general crisis of twentieth-century Communism. But is also true that, when a crisis affects large forces with deep roots in society, it can be addressed in more ways than one; it can produce various outcomes, either completely writing off the past or salvaging part of it as a resource for the future. The long-term fate of the French Revolution is enough to convince us of this evident truth. And, within these limits, the events of the 1980s have given me much unexpected food for thought.

Let me mention a few examples. It was not inevitable or foreseeable that Gorbachev would suddenly appear at the head of the Soviet Union, nor that he would make such a radical attempt to reform the system, nor that this would end so quickly in failure, nor that the failure would open the way to dissolution of the state and society in the turbid years of the Yeltsin regime. Likewise, it was not inevitable or foreseeable that in China – after the Maoist revolution was put on ice though not disowned, and in a context of cautious political continuity – a state would consolidate itself across the huge land mass and promote explosive development that would make it a pillar of the new world economy. It was not a foregone conclusion that the extraordinary Yugoslav experience would transmute, with some goading from Europe, into a ferocious ethnic conflict, or that the situation in the Middle East, with the active intervention of Israel and the United States, would take a tragic turn with the rise of religious fundamentalism. Nor was it a foregone conclusion that the European Union, instead of taking the economic road suggested by Jacques Delors and the political road proposed by Willy Brandt, would supinely accept the logic of Reaganism and resign itself to political impotence by putting its institutions out of reach of popular sovereignty.

In this set of circumstances – in which the 'crisis of Communism' dominated the scene, but possible variants were not yet ruled out – the originality of Italian Communism reasserted itself for good or ill, in new forms, with many challenges, and in a series of distinct stages.

THE SECOND BERLINGUER

On the eve of the 1980s, Italian Communism was out on a limb. The PCI found itself in serious difficulties. The result of the 1979 general elections had not been as dramatic as the press claimed: the Party kept 30 per cent of its electorate, two points more than in 1972 – which meant that, in comparison with its peak, it had lost less than the major European social-democratic parties; and a good part of the lost votes had gone to the far Left, not to the Right. More worrying was that the defections had mainly occurred in the big cities and among workers and young people – the sections of the population that had enabled its previous successes. But the greatest problem was the political shift in the two main forces on which the PCI had built its project – the DC and the PSI – which were now governing in coalition, competing with each other, but united in their resolve to keep the Communists out. So, the PCI was not just missing a few parliamentary deputies; it no longer had a credible political perspective.

At first the leadership refused to face facts, reluctant to make an explicit self-criticism of the recent past, and convinced that the new Centre Left was too divided to govern a country in crisis and would not hold out for long. The plan, then, was to keep up the pressure on the government until the hour struck again for a 'grand coalition' to be proposed, with fewer limitations this time.

Inside the Party, however, heated arguments frequently broke out in closed meetings, more over tactics than strategy. The main issue was how the PSI's evolution should be judged. Authoritative leaders thought that Craxi's 'new course' could be reversed by playing on extensive alliances in the union movement, the cooperatives and local authorities (while turning a blind eye to questions of morality), and that the PSI's presence in government might eventually help to undermine the supremacy of the Christian Democrats, to win the more modern, middling layers away from them, to build a new unity on the Left, and to open channels of communication with the European Left. Other leaders, close to Berlinguer, took a much harsher view of Craxism, seeing it almost as the greatest danger, the laboratory for a new kind of anti-Communism and the symptom of a voracious redistribution of power. On the other hand, they pinned some hopes on the social and political contradictions of the Catholic world that were still coursing through Christian Democracy.

Both these positions lacked foundation. The turn in both the PSI and the DC had not only been dictated by necessity, or by the lure of power, but expressed deeper tendencies in society and more firmly rooted convictions. To have brought the still powerful PCI back into the government game would have revived the idea of major reforms and involved concessions that even the most modern sections of the ruling class now opposed; it would also have aroused the hostility of rightward-moving Atlantic governments and of a Vatican now ruled with a firm hand by the Polish Pope. In any event, for all of them it was a pointless risk to give the PCI succour at a time when it finally seemed to be floundering. Dialogue could resume only when its strength had been reduced and its identity modified.

In 1980 Berlinguer proposed a turn that he hoped would take account of the real situation, and give the Party some breathing space. Neither then nor since has there ever been any real discussion about the content of that turn, the way in which it was to be applied, its value and shortcomings, its initial successes and its eventual failure. In fact, one misunderstanding after another has arisen to obscure the facts and to distort judgements. Worse: a curious mechanism has been more or less consciously used to erase it from historical memory.

The moving circumstances of Berlinguer's sudden death in June 1984 rapidly turned him into a myth: a positive, well-deserved myth of an honest, modest and tenacious man, loyal to the democratic Constitution that Italy needed then and would need in future. For this reason his political work was endorsed en bloc. His supporters considered it an insult to highlight what separated his original idea of a 'historic compromise' from the drastic reformulation he attempted in the final years of his life; his critics, though also paying homage to his personal virtues, claimed that these in the end had led him into an ideological rigidity and moralistic enthusiasm which prevented him from playing a truly forceful political role. In both these views, there was no real change in or of the PCI: a second Berlinguer never existed. Hence the history books have little to say about it, and only in the language of edification.

My own view is certainly different, and more problematic. What I believe, and hope to show, is as follows:

1) In the early 1980s Berlinguer attempted to make a turn that was not only tactical but strategic, not only political but cultural.

2) The idea behind the turn was not only, or not mainly, to recover a past identity, but also to renew that identity in a profound way that took account of a rapidly (and dangerously) changing reality.

3) It was not restricted to denunciation or good intentions, but became a definite, political line of action that obtained important results for a number of years.

4) It was hindered, and eventually thwarted, not only by the overarching objective factors of which I have spoken, nor only by the action of its opponents, but also by resistance and dissent within the Party that Berlinguer had helped to shape.

5) The turn never took a complete or finished form, but it was no less radical for that; it emerged mainly through a series of eloquent choices.

6) Berlinguer encouraged and often called for the turn on the basis of changes in his own thinking, using particular situations as a peg to hang them on, and drawing on a charismatic power that chimed with popular sentiments.

7) I therefore think it is correct to speak of 'a second Berlinguer' – without upholding him as an icon, but also without reducing him to a dreamer of 'imaginary realms'.

THE REVIVAL OF CLASS CONFLICT

What were the first signs of a turn?

The journalistic vulgate, as well as later histories, have seen them in one of two events: either the Fourteenth Congress of 1979, which approved the PCI's decision not to support future governments that excluded it; or the special meeting of the leadership after the earthquake at Irpinia in 1980, which called for a 'government of honest people' resting on the PCI. Public opinion interpreted these two decisions as marking the end of a political cycle. However, this dating of the turn seems to me inexact and misleading. For the congress decision by no means ruled out another set of 'broad agreements' in the near future, subject to certain conditions. And the proposed 'government of honest people' had no chance of becoming a reality: who were these 'honest people', and how many would have been prepared to take part in a PCI-led government? In short, there was no new policy, only an attempt to keep some doors open.

The real turn began to manifest itself in some specific actions. First of all, the PCI successfully opposed the decision of the new government to dock a small amount from pay packets to fund new investments – a measure the unions had accepted, but not the workers. Shortly afterwards, Berlinguer personally intervened in what was perhaps the most important company dispute anyone could remember.

In the summer of 1980, Fiat sent out 15,000 redundancy notices. The workers rebelled en masse, bringing production to a standstill and blocking the factory gates for thirty-five days. Other workers in similar jobs across the sector staged a protest strike in solidarity. Everyone knew that the sackings were part of a general counteroffensive by the bosses, intended to claw back some of what they had been forced to concede or tolerate in 1969. On the trade union side, it was clear from the start that the confrontation would end badly, for a number of reasons. Fiat really was in trouble: not because of a market downturn or productivity problems, but because it had itself created a labour surplus by building a network of subcontractors based on precarious or underpaid labour. The 15,000 redundancies were directed not only at 'hotheads' but also at workers who no longer had a function on the shopfloor; they registered a fait accompli and heralded a reorganization that would blackmail thousands of other workers, before they too were put on the scrap heap. The unions, especially the national federations, were partly unwilling and partly unable to spread the conflict, although, given the high level of unemployment, this would have been the only way of imposing a different kind of restructuring. Moreover, the workforce included a layer of white-collar workers and technicians who in '69 had sided with the shopfloor, despite its demands for equal pay rises for all. These were now wavering in the face of a threat that had not yet struck at them directly, though they had already lost out heavily as a result of flat-rate cost-of-living increases in a period of high inflation. Elsewhere in Turin, the mere possibility of disruption at Fiat – always the apple of the city's eye – reduced public opinion to silence, if not indifference.

Eventually a con trick was tried, with government backing. The sackings would be withdrawn, but a temporary redundancy fund would be set up for 20,000 workers. Why 'con trick'? I use the word advisedly, because the huge state-financed lay-off fund did not involve any commitment on the employer's part to take back the laid-off workers at a later date. This was not 'job rotation' but a 'zero hours' prelude to redundancy, on an income partly guaranteed by the state while the affected workers hunted for a job elsewhere on worse terms. Such was the background to the spontaneous but organized 'March of the Forty Thousand'[1] in central Turin, to demand that the strikes be called off. In the end, even the FLM signed – one might say, imposed – an agreement, despite workers' protests, and though it knew it spelled defeat.

Why then did Berlinguer go to the factory gates to offer his unreserved support, in a dispute that was always on shaky ground? Why, having kept his distance from a series of victorious struggles, did he now commit himself to a seemingly lost cause, gaining enthusiastic and moving acclaim from the workers but opening a gulf (as Romiti immediately put it[2]) between the Party and the most modern and powerful employers? We need only read what he said there – not the false version reported in the press – to understand his motives. It is not true that he called for the occupation of Fiat. 'It's up to you to decide on the forms of your struggle, up to you and your unions to say what agreements are acceptable. But you should know that the Communist Party will be there beside you, in good times and bad.' It was a language that had not been heard for years, a reaffirmation of the PCI as a national party of the working class. Nor was it just tailored to the situation:

1. The name commonly used to refer to the demonstration by Fiat white-collar workers and managerial staff on 14 October 1980, following a meeting at Turin's Teatro Nuovo. The figure of 40,000, an evocative allusion to Garibaldi's army of 40,000 volunteers, was disputed by the unions and the Left.

2. Cesare Romiti: chief executive of Fiat from 1976.

Berlinguer's words expressed a much meditated choice, with a degree of self-criticism on his part. In any case, the political situation had changed, and a new path had opened up for the PCI. What it needed to do now was restore mutual trust with the workers and rely on their combativity, without undermining the autonomy of the unions, but also without renouncing the presence of the Party as such in mass struggles.

This choice was followed up even more clearly, and with greater success, in the next few years. The key focus for everyone in the early 1980s was the battle over wage indexation.

For a while lower oil prices seemed to reinvigorate the economy, but this soon proved to be an illusion. Double-digit inflation continued, and a credit squeeze in the United States plus the debt crisis in developing countries made competition even fiercer in international markets. That is why all Italian employers saw the Fiat agreement as the way forward, and why the workers experienced it as a defeat that exposed them to blackmail. The scope for bargaining at company level was reduced, especially where productivity remained flat and price competition was fierce, but even where productivity rises cut employment. Tax evasion among the now sizeable contingent of the self-employed, together with the spiralling pressure of public debt, pushed tax rates upward – especially for workers in full-time employment. The wages question was back at centre stage, while unemployment, concentrated among young people and in the informal economy, not only weakened union bargaining power but impacted on family incomes. The only real cushion was the wage-indexation agreement that Lama had signed with Agnelli a few years earlier. In 1981, therefore, a press campaign got under way to 'persuade' trade unionists and intellectuals that it was necessary to correct some of the perverse effects of indexation, especially the narrowing of wage differentials and the fact that it only protected a certain section of workers. Calls for an 'incomes policy' were again in the air.

Although these arguments related to real problems, they did not hold water and pointed to much more ambitious purposes behind them. It was not true that wage-indexation was the privilege of a minority; it also protected the growing numbers of workers in small firms who had little or no bargaining power. Nor was it true that its flattening effect hit skilled workers especially hard, since the widespread system of 'perks' mainly rewarded loyalty to the company, and strike-breaking. What was true was that wage-indexation did not exist in other European countries, although there were other protections such as minimum wage legislation, decent unemployment benefits even for young people, study grants, and so on. Finally, it was not true that real wages were growing in Italy; the weight of indirect fiscal burdens meant that they were actually falling.

But the greatest myth in that campaign against wage-indexation had to do with so-called 'incomes policy', which journalists waved like a red rag at a bull. In a context of persistent stagflation, an 'incomes policy' was a necessity and already did exist, partly dictated by the new labour market, partly imposed by the public authorities. Ideological and material support for relatively superfluous consumption, generous aid, with no strings attached, to rescue insolvent companies, subsidies to large exporters, tolerance of massive tax evasion, cash handovers to clientelist networks, protection and privileges for sundry unearned income: all this went on outside the framework of any development plan, largely resting on public debt, at the price of high interest rates that pushed inflation skyward. The dismantling of indexation, and with it a weakening of union bargaining power, was thus a price that the workers were called upon to pay to keep the economy afloat, so that other interests could continue to be protected.

The campaign of 'persuasion' made headway in some sections of the union movement (the CISL and the pro-Socialist current in the CGIL), as well as in part of the middle layers, but it did not win over the working classes, or the democratic intellectuals who realized what was going on. In 1982 Confindustria therefore stepped up the pressure by threatening to pull out of the 1975 agreement. The response from the Palazzo Chigi[3] was a devastating blow. In 1983, soon after his appointment as prime minister, Bettino Craxi arrogated the right to settle the issue on behalf of the government, thereby asserting himself as a decisive leader and giving the Socialist Party a role far greater than its paltry 11 per cent of the vote would have implied. When he then issued a decree lopping a few percentage points off the indexed wage scale, the workers realized that this was not just tinkering around but amounted to direct government control over the wage dynamic: it was the end

3. Palazzo Chigi: official residence of the Italian prime minister.

of wage-indexation as a right freely agreed between both sides of industry. A wave of spontaneous strikes spread throughout Italy, and the factory councils called a national demonstration in Rome. Berlinguer not only helped to spur the protests, but also denounced Craxi's decree as unconstitutional. Risking a split in its ranks, the CGIL decided to take the helm of the demonstration, which turned out to be a major event also involving local branches of the CISL. The PCI raised the matter in parliament, using the instrument of obstructionism (which it had employed only twice before, against the *legge truffa* in 1953[4] and against the NATO pact) and announcing that it might have recourse to a referendum.

It cannot honestly be denied that this intransigent struggle marked a turn in both method and substance. Nor can it be honestly claimed that it led to isolation from the broad masses, or that it narrowed rather than widened the base of opposition in the country. If there was a weakness, and there was, it consisted in the lack of a solid attempt to accompany the struggle with a convincing alternative economic policy.

THE MORAL QUESTION

A second element soon came to characterize Berlinguer's turn. This was the so-called moral question, which addressed a larger part of the country, though also in a radical and deliberately 'scandalous' manner. I add the epithet 'so-called' for two reasons, one polemical, the other self-critical. Polemically it targets the legend of 'Berlinguer the moralist', incapable of formulating a real policy and given only to denunciation and preaching. Self-critically, it indicates that I did not grasp the full value of his orientation at the time, nor the impetus it offered for a new development of Communist thinking on the question of democracy – focused more on Marx and Gramsci than Togliatti. I considered it too close to the invective of Salvemini,[5] Dorso[6] or even Spaventa[7] against

4. See note on p.92.

5. Gaetano Salvemini: noted anti-fascist thinker of the interwar period, who went into exile in the United States.

6. Guido Dorso: early opponent of Mussolini and polemical anti-fascist writer, who later became a leading figure in the Partito d'Azione.

7. Silvio Spaventa: political theorist and major bourgeois-liberal figure in the second half of the ninteteenth century.

Depretis[8] and Giolitti;[9] and I feared it might take the Party too far from the central question of the class struggle. But that is not how things were.

One has only to reread the long interview Berlinguer gave to Scalfari in 1981:

> The parties have degenerated, and that's at the root of the mess in Italy. The parties today are mainly power and clientelism machines: poor or mystifying knowledge of people's real lives and problems; scant or hazy ideals and programmes; zero feelings or civic passion. They manage various interests, often contradictory, sometimes shady, but anyway unrelated to emerging human needs. Unless that political machine is broken up, you can rule out any economic recovery, any social reform, any moral or cultural advance.

Moralism? It was a radical critique of the whole political system. On a key point, it overturned the analysis underlying the proposed 'historic compromise' and a fortiori the national unity governments, but it also corrected Togliatti's judgement (plausible at the time) of the main parties which, because of their mass character and the ideas then inspiring them, had taken part in the anti-fascist struggle and cooperated in writing the postwar Constitution. Berlinguer's new verdict was thoroughly grounded in reality, and therefore easily intelligible to the majority of public opinion, at that moment more than any other.

One incontrovertible fact after another had been and still was coming to light: the secret funding of government parties by big corporations or financial interests in return for favours; the murky channelling of relief funds for the earthquake victims at Belice and later Irpinia; illegal construction and breaches of planning regulations; widespread vote-selling in return for personal recommendations or subsidies; rampant cronyism governing access to academic, health service and public television jobs; cases of embezzlement in local and regional councils (e.g., Turin and Genoa). And these were just the minor misdeeds that everyone was used to. Mega-scandals at the top included the Lockheed affair, which, in Italy alone, engulfed members of government and even brushed

---

8. Agostino Depretis: early disciple of Mazzini, leader of the nineteenth-century parliamentary Left, and intermittently prime minister between 1876 and his death in 1887.

9. Giovanni Giolitti: variously interior minister and prime minister of Italy between 1892 and 1921.

the Quirinale;[10] huge kickbacks on oil imports, involving the state-run ENI and mostly ending up in Socialist hands; the Sindona and Banco Ambrosiano scandals, which revealed collusion among the Mafia, financiers and politicians, and ended in two murders. (An eyewitness told me of a meeting in prison between Sindona and the parliamentary enquiry charged with the investigation, at which the financier icily replied to a Christian Democrat's question: 'I have nothing to say to you, because you know how generous I was with you people.')

Finally – and most explosive of all – there was the uncovering of P-2. Two young magistrates stumbled almost by accident on the secret masonic lodge, which was not only involved in business but planned to bring about a revision of the Constitutional Charter. And they found a partial list of the members. It still makes one gasp as one reads it: forty-five parliamentary deputies, from every party (except the PCI, of course, which was its main target), two ministers, the leadership of the three secret services, 195 senior officers in the armed forces, including twelve Carabinieri generals and five Guardia di Finanza generals, owners and directors of newspapers and television channels, and top judges in a position to shelve investigations and halt trials.

To reproach Berlinguer for raising the moral question, or for giving it too much weight, is therefore quite unreasonable. If anything, one could make the opposite criticism: that he did not do so earlier, before too many people became inured to the degeneration or found a way of profiting from it, and before the system had set up such dense protective networks; that he did not fully grasp that the tendency to corruption was not an anomaly, nor peculiar to Italy. Past history, and trials all around the world, have shown that corruption grew deeper for structural reasons in the evolution of the capitalist system, much as bureaucracy and political authoritarianism recurred in a socialist system as a result of prolonged curbs on political pluralism and individual liberties.

In any event, Berlinguer's battle bore fruit, both in electoral terms and in the evidence it gave that the PCI was 'different'. The results could have been greater if it had lasted longer and had probed more deeply at every level.

10. Palazzo del Quirinale: official residence of the president of the Republic.

THE BREAK

A third distinctive element of Berlinguer's turn concerned the PCI's international position and its relationship with the Soviet Union.

The opportunity was offered – or, to be more precise, imposed – by two decisions that Brezhnev took in the vain hope of competing with Reagan on his own terrain. In 1979 the Red Army entered Afghanistan in support of a 'friendly government' that had not been able to quell a revolt against it; and in 1981 the threat of a similar intervention in Poland compelled General Jaruzelski to declare martial law to end an impulsive workers' protest.

In itself, neither of these operations forced the PCI into a break. The 'friendly' government in Afghanistan was of doubtful legitimacy, but it had extended women's rights and secularized the state and the educational system, in the teeth of a fundamentalist guerrilla force, the Mujahideen, organized in Pakistan and funded by the United States. Amendola, for one, actually opposed condemnation of the Soviet action. But Berlinguer, seeing that the real issue at stake was strategic control of Central Asia, persuaded the leadership not only to condemn the intervention but to add a general rejection of power politics. The repression in Poland was a graver matter, because it was directed against a workers' protest supported by the Church in the name of religious freedom. But, in declaring martial law, Jaruzelski had avoided the threat of Soviet intervention and struck a compromise. The occupation of Dubček's Czechoslovakia had been much more serious.

What now led Berlinguer to go beyond simple condemnation was the repetitive character of Brezhnev's two choices: the fact that together they expressed the incapacity of the Soviet system to acknowledge its own crisis and to tackle it in any way other than with force. The PCI leadership agreed on a severe criticism, but Berlinguer then went on television to make a much more explosive statement, off his own bat, without consulting anyone. I do not mean, of course, his judgement on the Polish events, which he repeated more clearly and put in the context of more general problems in Eastern Europe. I am referring to remarks of far greater import, delivered to an audience of millions: 'The impetus that showed itself over long periods, going back to the greatest revolutionary event of our epoch, the October Revolution, is now exhausted. We have reached the point at which that phase is ending.' The substance and manner of this declaration created unease and resistance among Party activists and even in the leadership, but Berlinguer did not correct it and subsequently gained the support of the leadership with a single vote against, that of Armando Cossutta.[11] And Cossutta made his disagreement public in the most dramatic way, declaring that Berlinguer's statement constituted a real break in the history of the PCI. That seemed undeniable, even to those like myself who considered the break urgent and fruitful.

A major break is never pleasant, but it can be handled in several different ways. Take a jacket to which you have become attached – one with a fine cut, made of quality material and generally in good condition, but which has worn away at the elbows and has seemed for some time in danger of coming apart. You can leave the hole for the time being, if it does not show too much, because you know the jacket will not last much longer and is anyway going out of fashion. Or you can send it for invisible mending until you make up your mind to buy another, perhaps one you have already seen in a shop window, although it is not of such good quality and not entirely to your taste. Or you can have some pieces of leather sewn onto the elbows, making the jacket more resistant to wear and perhaps even nicer to look at. Such was the PCI's situation, more or less, after the 'break' of 1981. Berlinguer chose the third option: the hole could not be hidden, but it could be the occasion for a major repair.

This was an arduous undertaking nonetheless. First of all it meant answering two sets of historical and theoretical questions.

1) Recognition of the past. Had there really been an impetus from October? Did it achieve important results that could be taken up and used, or was it a brief and high-minded illusion, vitiated by its Leninist matrix and then scuppered by Stalinism? When and how did the revolution become exhausted, and attempts to reform it break down? Should the PCI's links with that experience (not with a model to be imitated) be set aside as a regrettable error, or should they be critically reviewed in their various phases, in the belief that they were kept up for too long?

11. Armando Cossutta: leader of the wing of the PCI most favourable to the link with Moscow; future founder of Rifondazione Comunista.

2) Present situation and future prospects. What did the exhaustion of that impetus leave behind? A victorious capitalism that could not and should not be opposed with a systemic alternative, or new contradictions and newly emerging forces, needs and purposes for the construction of a different society? Could a critique of the Soviet Union focus only on its lack of pluralism and total statization of the economy, or should it include the progressive abandonment of its original aim of moving towards a new civilization – one that deserved (or at least gave meaning to) the name Communist?

It is evident from this simple list of questions that, for the PCI, the 'break' was only the starting point for a new labour of cultural elaboration, without which the 'difference' of Communism was bound to fade away.

The PCI had a number of resources for this task: Marx's thoughts on the ultimate goal of Communism, which he refused to visualize in greater depth because he did not want to 'cook up the future', and which the revolutions of the nineteenth century were not capable of setting themselves; Gramsci's thoughts on revolution in the West (which Togliatti admitted had not yet been used), an anti-dogmatic Marxism that re-emerged in the 1960s within and outside the Party; the best stimuli to come out of Italy's long '68, before it finally ebbed; an original tradition of Italian socialism; and the real anguish that neocapitalism had aroused in a Catholic world shaken by secularization. It was a labour against the current, however, which required time, brains, great and single-minded determination and much honesty, if it was to enter the common sense of the age.

Berlinguer did not possess the genius of Gramsci, nor the stature of Togliatti. But he was aware of the problems, and he showed this in a couple of pieces he wrote. On the one hand, he tried to erect a barrier to liquidationism in the name of 'the new': 'There can be no invention, imagination or creation of the new if it begins by burying itself, its own history and reality.' On the other, he clarified the innovative nature of the research task ahead: 'We need a Copernican revolution; the entry of new social subjects (women, young people, peace activists) should change the terms and style of our politics, from which they have been excluded until now.' *Vaste programme!* as de Gaulle might have commented, with his customary sarcasm.

But the break posed another problem, which required an answer and an initiative in the short term. If the impetus of the Soviet Union was spent, it was logical to expect that its role as a great power would decline. The bipolarism that had ruled the world was on the wane, but no other balance was replacing it, and no steps were being taken towards disarmament and an increased authority for the UN. Indeed, Reagan was counting on a new arms race to force his opponent into unsustainable military expenditure: that is, to use it as a way of converting Soviet decline into collapse. The problem of war and peace was more urgent than ever. Everyone knows that in history the hegemony of one power or civilization over others is not asserted always and only through war, even if it usually arises and concludes in war, and that US supremacy had many other means of asserting itself. But everyone also knows, or should know, that the two unequal powers then in conflict with each other had a button with which they could drag the world into a common conflagration.

I consider it Berlinguer's greatest political and intellectual merit that, in the final years of his life, he was alert to this danger and genuinely tried to defuse it. The clout of an opposition party in a second-rank country was perhaps slight, but the attempt was neither fanciful nor pointless. What it achieved was due to its character as a policy turn – from mere preaching of peaceful coexistence (or even tepid 1975-style Atlanticism) to active promotion of peace and a proposal for bilateral disarmament. The first definite step in this direction – apart from repeated interventions in support of the Palestinians massacred in Lebanon – was a 'touring visit' to the main centres of the Left in the Third World: to China, where (after all the polemics of the past) he was greeted as a head of state; to Cuba, for a long discussion with Fidel; and to a Nicaragua already under attack from the Contras. These contacts served not only to mend the cracks in some amical relations, but also to measure the influence and prestige that the PCI still had for a range of different parties and states, united by a wish to revive the spirit of Bandung. The tour was an unexpected success, owing precisely to the political way forward that it offered.

A similar attempt to reach agreement in the European Left on peace and disarmament met a very different reception. It struck a chord with some leaders – all in a relatively weak position (Olof Palme, Willy Brandt, Tony Benn, Bruno Kreisky) – but not with major party leaders. The differences soon became clear, centring on the burning issue of 'theatre' missiles that was successively manipulated, truncated and erased in the historical memory.

In December 1979 the Atlantic Council decided to instal medium-range missiles in Europe that would be capable of striking the Soviet Union in a matter of minutes, before it could easily respond. Brezhnev, in his unsubtle way, responded by immediately deploying equivalent nuclear missiles. NATO then went ahead with deployment in West Germany and Italy (France and Britain had already had missiles of similar power for some time). The situation was growing steadily worse, since the whole issue of a 'first strike' capacity lay behind these moves. Fortunately, two new developments applied a brake. Brezhnev died and his replacement at the head of the Soviet Union – Yuri Andropov – had a different outlook and a finer intelligence. He broke new ground by proposing a verifiable bilateral reduction in theatre-level nuclear weapons, prior to their total elimination; in response, the broadest and most forceful mass movement since '68 sprang up almost throughout Europe. In Italy too a grass-roots movement began to develop; PdUP and various Catholic groups were especially active in a varied and visible membership that expressed itself in a demonstration in Rome, and in a blockade of the US base at Comiso that was brutally repressed by baton-wielding police. Berlinguer sent a message of solidarity, and from that moment the PCI mobilized all its forces (in Sicily with the support of Pio La Torre,[12] who was assassinated by the Mafia). Another demonstration was held in Rome, this time with a truly impressive display of unity. Andropov's proposal came to nothing when Britain and France refused to include their nuclear weapons in any disarmament pact, but the movement did slow the build-up of tensions for a few years and stimulated the agreement between Reagan and Gorbachev at Reykjavík in 1986 (which the US Congress refused to ratify).

Can it honestly be denied, then, that Berlinguer's PCI took on a new international role during those years, that it achieved results, and that it actively helped to lay the basis for a new kind of peace movement? Or that many others sabotaged it?

12. Pio La Torre: leader of the PCI in Sicily, member of the parliamentary anti-Mafia Commission, assassinated in April 1982.

A PROVISIONAL BALANCE SHEET

Our review of speeches, stated intentions and policy decisions shows that the PCI did attempt a major cultural and political turn between 1980 and 1985, which went beyond words to express itself in a definite political initiative: that is, to generate mass struggles and keen opposition to the government in both parliament and the country. Its dominant feature was not a return to the past, nor denunciation of the present, but a search for new directions.

Some legitimate doubts arise, however, as to the effectiveness of this turn. To assess a new policy on the basis of its intentions, projects and public reception, or even of its early successes, is always risky. And it was especially so in the case of Berlinguer.

Many of the strategic innovations took the form of guidelines or principles, rather than a precise programme based on searching analysis and explicit self-criticism. Some of the hard struggles that were begun in this period had a solid foundation and therefore achieved undeniable results, but their final outcome was still uncertain. The political line certainly had a coherent thread, but it left open a number of questions that would be decisive for the future: for example, the educational system, commercial television and the culture industry, and the growing damage to the environment; that is, the diffuse area of culture that the new Right would use as its launching pad. The driving force of the turn was Enrico Berlinguer, in command of wide support and authority in his party and beyond; but the degree of conviction in the PCI leadership, and the Party's capacity to translate the turn into definite initiatives, remained uncertain. With a will, all these knots might have been disentangled over time. Instead, Berlinguer died in 1984.

This raises a difficult question. How much of the proposed new policy was achieved, or achievable? It would not be serious to answer this on the basis of the facts and experiences available in 1985, still less of a forecast for the years ahead made on that basis. All we can do is update the situation in which the PCI found itself five years after the turn of 1980, trying to identify its existing and possible future strengths and the difficulties that had emerged in the meantime: in other words, to define the legacy that Berlinguer left to his successors. In my few brief reflections on this, I will concentrate on points that can be reasonably demonstrated.

To identify the positions of strength, it will be useful to start by assessing some banal election results. The idea was born then, and later widely accepted, that in 1979 the PCI entered a period of steep electoral decline, as did all other Communist parties. But that is a false idea, especially if it is applied to the years of the 'second Berlinguer' in order to downplay the effectiveness of his turn. In the general elections of 1983 the PCI won 30 per cent of the vote (still up on 1972), whereas the PCF dropped from 25 per cent to 15 per cent, the main European Social Democratic parties lost much of their support, Italian Christian Democracy fell to 32 per cent, and the PSI, despite its new government levers, remained stuck at 11 per cent. The most surprising result came in 1984, when the PCI vote shot up to 33.5 per cent, the highest of any Italian party.

It has been repeatedly said that this was only an apparent success, prompted by the outpouring of emotion and respect after Berlinguer's sudden breakdown on live TV and subsequent death. There is certainly some truth in this, but it is an explanation that itself needs explaining. Feelings can carry activists away, and respect can express itself in many forms, but there is nothing to say that it should spread to a wider electorate and express itself in support for a party's policies, especially at a time when they were taking clearer shape and being challenged on all sides. That happens only if emotion links up with currents of support which, though unevenly distributed, exist on a huge scale.

Moreover, intensity is a better measure than figures. Footage of Berlinguer's funeral presents us not only with vast numbers of mourners, so varied and so deeply affected, but with a people on its feet. It graphically shows a renewed relationship of trust between the Party and the working class, a denunciation of political corruption, a readiness to dialogue with the new feminism, an unmistakeable autonomy from the discipline of international blocs, and a revival of the peace movement – all united with a resolve not to abandon the goal of transforming the social system. Each of these elements still had many open questions and major obstacles, which I have not hidden and shall not hide. But it seems to me wrong to present the PCI in 1984 as a weakened, rapidly declining force, politically isolated and cut off from the country, immobile in its thinking and devoid of initiative. Swimming against the current, it had managed to increase, or at least consolidate, its strength and to create some new openings. In short, the 'turn' had some results to show for itself, even if it still remained a gamble.

What were the weaknesses that continued to weigh on the Party during these years? First and foremost, of course, the overall relationship of forces on the economic, social and cultural levels – not only in Italy but in the world. I might add that Berlinguer's policy turn would have had greater resources, and greater results, if it had happened ten years earlier, when the situation was more fluid and the forces it could influence were broader and more assertive. But here I will simply consider the greatest difficulty, which Berlinguer hesitated to recognize or perhaps did not have the strength to face: the question of the Party.

Again it will be useful to start with some figures. Logically, a new policy – one involving clearer opposition, more geared to social and cultural mobilization, and more innovative with regard to ongoing social change, without giving way on ideals – should have won proportionally more activists than occasional voters, more young people than old, and more participation than diffuse sympathy. One would also have expected it to have made most headway in geographical areas where the social and cultural conflict had been sharpest (even if it was now declining), and to have been met with greater doubts in areas of long-standing attachment to the Soviet Union. However, the organizational statistics did not respect that logic. The PCI's electoral support held up, even slightly increased, but its membership figures continued to show a gradual decline; the Party's social composition, level and quality of involvement, age structure and geographical implantation did not correspond to the character of the political turn, and did not provide it with sufficient means to overcome the monopolistic media wall and the clientelist network at the disposal of its opponents.

It was therefore clear to many, including Berlinguer himself, that pockets of resistance, misunderstanding or passivity were limiting the effectiveness of policy innovation. But he was rightly convinced that he could build on his rapport with the Party rank and file to press ahead with clearer policy decisions, in a clearer, more forthright language, even if it meant that he risked paying a price or being pushed aside. He also felt sure that, as it accumulated new experiences, the Party would be able to change without tearing itself apart. *L'intendance suivra*, Napoleon would have said. The basic idea of 'lead and others will follow' is frequently at work, for good or ill, in the practice of Communist parties.

But this time there was another aspect that escaped him. The peculiarity of the PCI, as Togliatti already saw, was that it was a 'mass party' that 'conducted politics' and acted in the country, but also positioned itself in institutions and used them to achieve results and to build alliances. This was part and parcel of the democratic road. The other side of the coin, however, was not only a parliamentarist temptation (and a nagging urge to get into government) but something that asserted itself more gradually. Over the decades, and most especially in a period of great social and cultural change, a mass party becomes more necessary than ever, as does a capacity to pose problems of government. Little by little, however, processes of change alter the material composition of the party itself. In this case, new generations, among subaltern classes too, were now mainly educated in the state system and by the culture industry; new lifestyles and consumption habits overtook all of society, including groups who could still only aspire to them; the 'fortifications' of political power became increasingly important but spread out to many decentralized positions, favouring those who came to occupy them; politicians, even if in opposition and uncorrupted, mingled daily with members of the ruling class, sharing mores and language, if not ties of friendship, with them. All these phenomena had a positive side, since a democratic road benefits from higher levels of general education, personalities no longer in thrall to poverty or superstition, and a larger, more diverse, number of public institutions. Also larger and more diverse, however, were the mechanisms of integration and standardization.

Nineteen sixty-eight injected a number of anti-systemic elements, but it also sowed the notion that a social system can change without a project, organization or alternative power, simply through spontaneous, intermittent revolts. For symmetrical reasons, the experience of the Historic Compromise speeded up the process whereby the material composition of the Party became more uniform. So, what really was the PCI on which Berlinguer tried to base a new politics? The bulk of activists concurred in the new direction he wanted to give it, but had difficulty understanding and practising it. Party branches had ceased for some time to do regular work among the masses, or to engage in the day-to-day education of cadres; their only real bursts of activity took place around *L'Unità* festivals or national and local election campaigns; workplace cells were thin on the ground, and left almost everything up to the union. The distribution of roles in the leadership had changed: the greatest importance, and the best cadres, had been switched from political functions to positions in local and regional government, or in parallel organizations such as the cooperatives. This meant greater competence, but also less political passion; feet closer to the ground, but narrower political horizons. Intellectuals were stimulated by the discussion and debate, but tended to involve themselves less in political organization – and even the discussion among themselves was often eclectic. One exception was the women's section of the Party, where a direct link between leaders and ordinary members kept things productively on the boil.

Of course, the waning of the ideologically defined mass party, linked to and nurtured by a clear-cut social base, did not affect the PCI alone. Other real parties, such as the DC, had long since shed those characteristics and undergone a kind of voluntary degeneration – in order to keep its sights on power, come what may. The PCI too was threatened with a discrepancy between what it thought and what it was.

In any event, Berlinguer's attempt in the early 1980s to reassert the PCI's distinct identity won widespread, though not always total or active, support in the middle echelons of the Party. A different discourse, lacking schematic formulas, was in order at leadership level, and for better or worse that was what it got. The real leadership group, whose importance did not stem only from the offices it held, was not made up of newcomers. It still had some valuable cadres from the period of illegality, and in its great majority it represented the generation that took part in the partisan struggle and organized the fight-back in the harshest years of the cold war. These leaders had mostly been selected at the Seventh Congress, then. The Ninth Congress had marginalized a minority, but the appointment of Longo and then Berlinguer as national secretary had been intended to ensure a certain balance among various orientations, without allowing the now dispersed Left through border control. It cannot honestly be said that the new secretary faced internal opposition (except, paradoxically, for Longo) during the long and losing phase of the Historic Compromise. Occasional criticisms came from Giorgio Amendola, but they would subside without causing a rift, partly because they were well taken. Berlinguer avoided a change in the composition of the leadership, except in dribs and drabs that had no special political significance.

The picture changed profoundly with the 1980 turn, however: the unity of the leadership broke down. Both the policy decisions – which Berlinguer often made alone – and the general line of which they afforded a glimpse met with explicit, sometimes fierce, dissent at the top. He did not give way, and challenged his critics to oppose him publicly; they did not think they had the strength to do this. But, since the disagreements linked up with doubts and hesitancy in the middle cadre (still hopeful that it might be possible to return to broad political understandings and even effect a reconciliation with Craxi), they prevented the kind of general shake-up and clarification without which it would be rather difficult to recruit new forces. The PCI's mode of thinking and working did not make its proposals secure, nor did they invite participation. Thus a vicious circle began to operate. I have reason to believe – a turn of phrase I use because it is wrong to attribute definite intentions to someone who cannot reply – that in the final months of his life Berlinguer determined to break this vicious circle: that is, he became convinced of the need to open a real political battle within the Party and about the party form as such. He did not have the time to do it.

There remains one delicate matter to clear up. Could Berlinguer have fully counted on the support of a sizeable majority of the leadership to thwart the so-called Right in the PCI? Among his supporters some were still nostalgic for the Historic Compromise, and quite a few thought that, in difficult times, the Party should present the image of a complete unity that was no longer there. His opponents included not only the long-time Amendolans, who now called themselves *miglioristi*, but also some of those who had always thought of themselves as belonging to the pro-Longo Centre: prominent figures such as Bufalini, Lama, Pajetta, Di Giulio, Perna and, in some respects, even Cossutta. The old New Left too (Ingrao and Trentin, for instance), who supported the turn, still bore some understandable grudges towards its sponsor.

After this provisional balance sheet of the PCI in 1985, including both the successes and the obstacles of the previous five years, I cannot honestly identify a consistent, settled framework or main trend that would allow a safe judgement to be made. But I do find the elements for a non-fanciful hypothesis to measure and explain the events of the subsequent years. It goes as follows.

Berlinguer's turn was driven by the ambitious medium-term objective of actually taking a step along the democratic road to socialism in Italy and Europe. For objective reasons, but also because of subjective immaturity, this ambition did not stand up to the test of the facts; the goal was out of reach, but the strength it had preserved and the new choices and ideas that had entered into it did make it possible for the PCI to escape being engulfed by the crisis of the Soviet Union, to avoid dissolution and abjuration, and to refound a Communist-inspired Left that was vibrant and meaningful. Such an objective was challenging, but not impossible. If such a Left had still been standing in 1992, when the First Republic unravelled, the story not only of the PCI but of Italian democracy would have been very different.

19

Natta, the Conciliator

It is indisputable that the last few years of the 1980s marked a watershed between two epochs.

The decades during which world history had unfolded within a basically bipolar order could be considered at an end. The competition between two economic systems and ideologies, each involving hundreds of millions of people, had assumed the character of a contest between two blocs of states that also served as a reference for other existing or newly emerging states; the competition had centred on various goals, in various forms and regions, but it had been stimulated, contained and underwritten by the equilibrium between two superpowers. Now, however, a new and more unified, though also uneven, world order was emerging, in which spontaneous market forces supposedly ruled supreme, but which in reality was governed by the military might, financial supremacy, technological advantage and media monopoly of one power: the American. It is also indisputable that, in the absence of another great war, such a major change could not have happened at a stroke or as the result of a political decision at the top; it must have come about in stages, based on multiple tendencies and processes with deep roots in society. But the real qualitative leap occurred at the end of the decade, with a suddenness that no one had predicted; it was not due to a stunning success of capitalist restructuring – which, in fact, had run into difficulties and could anyway promise little – but rather to the collapse of its long-standing adversary and the passive acquiescence of the European Left. The PCI could not remain immune from such a dramatic upheaval, and still less did it have the strength to prevent it. But what of the second half of the 1980s, when the general crisis of Communism was gathering momentum and the power of a new hegemon was becoming more and more apparent? Could the PCI not have taken a different road then, to keep a strong, Communist-inspired movement alive on a new basis, and at the same time to have a positive influence on the international situation?

Berlinguer's death weighed heavily on the Party: it was not easy to find a successor. The 'Right' had enough ideas and cohesion to aspire to form a new leadership, and in fact it did talk, behind closed doors, of making Napolitano or Lama secretary – even though both men had expressed a line different from the Right's on more than one occasion. But this choice did not command a majority. The waverers too considered it risky, and so the meeting did not even decide to put the idea to the test.

On the other hand, although Berlinguer's supporters had the numbers to prevail, they were not homogeneous and did not have a properly heavyweight candidate. It was therefore decided to opt for a wider process of consultation, organized by Pecchioli[1] and Tortorella.[2] The method already entailed the selection: a large majority favoured a man of great virtues (culture, decency, experience, independence of judgement) but also of great caution, who hesitated before expressing or provoking disagreement, not out of conformism, but because his main concern was party unity and the likely effects of discord on public opinion. That man was Alessandro Natta. He had been standing aloof for some time, with no ambition to become secretary, but he enjoyed great respect and some popularity in the Party. As his right-hand man he chose Aldo Tortorella, who certainly had fervent ideas but was equally inclined to prudence.

One might, in slightly jocular vein, sum up the brief period of Natta's secretaryship as an attempt to continue Berlinguer's policy without its rough edges and, as far as possible, with the support of Giorgio Napolitano. In normal years, against a background of unity, such conciliatoriness – which did not rule out tactical differences – might have succeeded. But those were not normal years.

---

1. Ugo Pecchioli: a well-known figure in the partisan war, later leader of the PCI in Turin and Piedmont, and a member of the national leadership since 1983.

2. Aldo Tortorella: editor of *L'Unità* in the early 1970s, close to Berlinguer in his final years and responsible for the PCI's cultural policy.

The first sign of trouble soon appeared in relation to the referendum on wage-indexation and the assessment of its outcome, in 1985. The decision to call a referendum had been taken by Berlinguer, against the opposition of the right of the Party. And, in truth, it was a risky undertaking – though one I supported at the time.

A referendum to abrogate a law involves the whole of the electorate, and in this case the law did not strike directly at most people's interests; some voters indeed benefited from it; and all the other parties and newspapers presented it as a necessity, due to the economic crisis. Hence, despite the large-scale mobilization of workers, and despite the democratic importance of the issue, it was always going to be very difficult to win the referendum. The man who had proposed it was no longer with us, and mistrust was spreading in the ranks of those who were meant to support it. Natta accepted the challenge, mainly to honour the commitment made by Berlinguer, but he was not able to mobilize the Party on a large scale and he did not want to force a campaign on the unwilling (part of the trade union movement, the retailers' associations and the regions with a Communist government). The negative result therefore came as no surprise, nor was the Party completely blameless. But it was a surprise that the PCI – though out on a limb and not solidly united – managed to obtain 46 per cent of the vote: this demonstrated great strength and did not call for recrimination. However, those who were only waiting for an opportunity read it as proof that Berlinguer's turn had gone a little too far and needed to be corrected. This was how the right of the Party argued, and it met no opposition. Take, for example, one whole boring issue of *Critica Marxista* published in 1985, which contained a collection of essays on Berlinguer by nearly all the top leaders. It is easy to see that, with the exception of Garavini's article, and laying stress on different points, the common aim was to establish an essential continuity between the Historic Compromise and the turn of the 1980s. This idyllic construction, justified by the commemorative occasion, did not cause much of a stir – indeed, it passed unnoticed. But the same cannot be said of a (still moderate) proposal to the Central Committee for a correction of the recent political line, which was backed by part of the secretariat. This formed the main theme of a special Party congress held in Florence in 1986. Rather than a compromise, it involved a reconciliation that for the present simply glossed over recent disagreements and, as for the future, corrected the turn without explicitly saying so.

I do not think I am being overcritical, nor would I have any right to be. For I too was a silent participant: partly because I had only just rejoined the Party and did not want to appear a busybody, partly because I did not understand the mechanism that was being set in motion. But, when I reread today the bulky Proceedings of that congress, I feel sure that criticism is in order.

The first point that strikes me is the inadequacy, not to say deliberate lack, of analysis of what was going on in the real world (which Togliatti considered the essential prerequisite for a correct policy). Just a few important cases in point: the nature and duration of Reaganism, the rightward shift in Europe and its major social-democratic parties, the crisis of the Communist camp and, at least initially, the reform initiatives of Gorbachev in the USSR and Deng in China. As to society and economics, the key developments were not only new technologies (post-Fordism in industry) and a redistribution of income to the detriment of much more than 'a third of society', but also the 'financialization' of capital and a global unification of markets in line with the interests of the multinationals.

At the cultural level, the same years had seen a general widening and deepening of individualism and consumerism, a growth in the power of commercial television and an erosion of educational standards, with the aim of forcing the much-heralded freedom into a standard mould. Many of these issues had featured in Berlinguer's rethinking, while others fell outside it. All in all, they added up to a picture less favourable than the one presented in the congress proceedings, but they also offered a number of possibilities. There was little discussion of these in Florence or subsequently, and in some cases no discussion at all.

The 'parsimony' of analysis was not due to ignorance or to a wish to downplay what was new; indeed, in the PCI and elsewhere, overblown rhetoric about new directions was beginning to obscure what was really essential in the situation. More or less consciously, however, the analytic deficit served to make a correction in the political line, and in the Party's political practice, both more plausible and more acceptable.

From the Florence congress on, the PCI again saw its main role as being to hasten the formation of a new government majority, a 'democratic alternative' government to confront the crisis in the country; restored unity with the PSI would help to bring this about, but that did not exclude a broader coalition. There appeared to be nothing very new in this vision: it essentially resumed the discourse of a decade earlier, shorn of errors of subalternity and minimalism, and set within the framework of an emergency government or a 'government with a programme'. Had not Berlinguer himself been the first to speak of a 'democratic alternative'? The problem was, though, that the objective no longer had any basis in the real situation and therefore should have been scrapped. It is easy to demonstrate this, just with reference to Italy.

As far as the PSI, DC and the secular parties were concerned, although they remained in competition with one another, they had all shifted to the right under the political and ideological pressure of the neoliberal wave washing over much of Europe. Their shared resolve to exclude the PCI from government had therefore actually hardened, even though it seemed ever less justified. With the situation in the economy and society still critical (14 per cent unemployment, a public debt higher than annual GDP), electoral support for the government coalition was flat, sometimes falling, and so the parties in it were forced to close ranks around an even greater recourse to clientelism, new public spending sprees, indulgence towards tax evasion, and a false image painted over all. Craxi was a master of such operations ('the ship sails on', 'the leader's personality is winning political support', 'how well he handles the media!'), surrounded by people whom even Formica described as 'dwarfs and ballerinas'.[3] In this situation, how could the PCI have thought that an 'alternative government' based on a new agreement among the parties was credible? Which parties? And what would be the programme of the 'government with a programme'?

Nor is this all. For four years Berlinguer had often sprung surprises in his attempt to advance the turn: the 'moral question', the wage-indexation battle, the critique of consumerism, the dialogue with young people over the experience of the peace movement, and the new feminism that assailed conceptions of the family and ways of conducting politics. The break with the Soviet Union and the opening to social democracy went together with a foreign

3. Salvatore ('Rino') Formica: PSI apparatus man during the Craxi years. He was referring in 1991 to the large numbers of people from the theatrical world who took part in its decision-making National Assembly.

policy geared to bilateral disarmament and independence from both blocs.

Berlinguer's underlying conviction was that Italy needed a profoundly new politics, focused on gradual but structural change, and that the conditions for this had to be built in society and the national culture, over and above any political manoeuvring. He rejected extremist approaches and saw the need for alliances, but he also believed that the way forward required clear opposition and real mass movements. This was what gave meaning to the idea of a 'democratic alternative' government, associated with the term 'hinging on the Communist Party' or 'a new stage in the Italian road to socialism'.

I repeat that, given all the events of the 1980s after his death, this vision erred on the side of optimism and displayed a number of weak points and areas of abstraction. It needed to be rounded out and deepened. But the Party that could have been the basis for this no longer existed, while the PCI neither recognized the real situation nor did anything to try to change it.

In fact, its immediate emphasis on an inter-party agreement for government, which pushed new areas of social and political conflict to the sidelines, was not only more abstract but also more costly. It involved relinquishing various pillars of support: the 46 per cent vote in the referendum on wage-indexation; potential leadership of the still active peace movement; links with the women's movement, which had lost its mass character (at a time when the crisis was especially affecting the material conditions of women); and any ambition to head the new ecological movement (an issue on which it had numerous doubts that left the way open for a Green party to emerge). Above all, it involved giving up on a wide debate in and about the Party, which remained stifled by the spirit of conciliation at the top.

In this detailed, perhaps overcritical, analysis of the Natta leadership, which I can permit myself to make because I too was to blame for not criticizing it, I have intentionally refrained from dealing with one novelty over which there was unanimity at the Florence congress. I am referring to the sentence: 'The PCI is an integral part of the European Left.' It was important because it sought to define the Party's international location at a time when the global balance was rapidly changing. But it was also so general as to be ambiguous. Did it indicate an urgent need to overcome the barriers to dialogue in the Left, so that Europe could play the role of a third force beyond the bipolar world order – a dialogue to which the PCI could contribute by virtue both of its tradition and its renewal, as well as its influence in the newly emerging countries? Or did it indicate a readiness to join the Socialist International, whatever the outcome of the heated debate that was then taking place inside the PCI? If the former, it pointed to a development of Berlinguer's recent initiatives on disarmament, multipolarism and the critique of any great power hegemony. If the latter, it meant a new choice of camp and the gradual liquidation of a distinctive Communist identity (at least as much as would be necessary to obtain Craxi's consent to its joining the Socialist International).

The choice had not yet been made. But the general direction of the Florence congress was clear enough: a partial, non-explicit correction of the Berlinguer turn, toning it down and making it strategically less ambitious. Nor did it take long for the results to become apparent: in the elections of 1987 the PCI won 27 per cent of the vote, down from 30 per cent in 1983 and the exceptional 33.5 per cent of 1984. It was a sharp and unexpected defeat, but not yet a rout. The lost votes had not gone to strengthen the government parties, but had spread around a galaxy of small unstable forces to its left.

But there were other worrying signs. In a number of local contests the setback was more severe, as authorities led by the united Left showed symptoms of exhaustion or decline. Internal divisions as well as labour market difficulties were exacerbating the crisis of the union movement, and neo-integralist tendencies and organizations were gaining a firmer hold in the Catholic world. The uncontrolled public debt limited the scope for further spending, and was being used as a pretext to block any progressive economic policy. As both cause and effect of all this, the Centre-Left coalition government was shaping up as a power-sharing deal among the most conservative elements in its constituent parties (the so-called CAF: Craxi-Andreotti-Forlani[4]). So the prospect of a 'democratic alternative', already inconsistent in its origins, receded more and more each day, while the size and especially the structure of the Party membership steadily deteriorated. As we can see, there was

4. Arnaldo Forlani: briefly DC prime minister in 1980–1, then vice-premier in the two Craxi governments of the 1980s.

no shortage of issues for a bold political and strategic discussion, yet the PCI avoided having one, for a combination of reasons. The change that the state of things required therefore simply took the form of a generational change. The occasion for it was a (fairly minor) heart disorder that afflicted Natta. He was politely requested to resign, and, gentleman that he was, he acceded to the request without expressing the bitterness to which he would later give vent. Achille Occhetto became secretary, and a leadership coalesced around him that lacked homogeneity in all respects except one: its rhetoric of 'newness'. I do not use this expression ironically or scornfully: it really did herald an ideology, political line, method and organizational form that would carry the day and lead to the dissolution of the PCI.

Before we come to that, however, we should look at the most important event in world history during those years, which had even greater influence than the other factors on the evolution of Italian Communism. I am referring to what happened in the Soviet Union between 1985 and 1990.

20

Andropov, Gorbachev, Yeltsin

On 11 March 1985, Mikhail Gorbachev was elected general secretary of the Communist Party of the Soviet Union. It was a great surprise all round, and a great hope for the Left. The surprise was understandable but exaggerated; the hope had real but weak foundations.

The turn, made necessary by a looming economic crisis and widespread discontent, had begun soon after Brezhnev's death in November 1982 and his replacement by Yuri Andropov. But it had not been evident at first. The economic crisis was still obscured, not only by official statistics but by the fact that the real rate of growth, in quantitative terms, continued to be no lower than in the West. (The social discontent was due not to wage levels or the performance of the social state, but to the poor quality of goods, the privileges of the *nomenklatura*, rising crime rates and the growth of a shadow economy.) As for Andropov, what struck everyone first of all and made it difficult to form a judgement was that he had been head of the KGB; perhaps this indicated that an authoritarian tightening was on the cards. His advanced age and poor state of health also made it unlikely that he would toy with renewal.

Yet the opposite turned out to be the case. It would be interesting – but for me impossible – to reconstruct the story of his life as a way of explaining this. What is sure is that his long experience in the security services allowed him to have an accurate grasp of the real state of the country, and to foresee the mortal dangers that threatened it if there was not a profound structural transformation.

And he was the one who began it, as a number of immediate decisions testify. His foreign policy proposals included the bilateral scrapping of theatre missiles in Europe, and a national unity government plus the withdrawal of all foreign troops in Afghanistan; while inside the Soviet Union he chose the young Gorbachev, an intelligent but low-ranking leader with limited experience, as his right-hand man and prospective successor.

To gauge how radical and focused were Andropov's intentions, it will be useful to look at a lengthy piece he wrote on the hundredth anniversary of Marx's death. It was the first time any top leader had offered the public a truthful analysis of the situation in the Soviet Union, together with a balance sheet of the past and a commitment for the future. He was certainly blunt, admitting that socialism had by no means been achieved. 'Despite the socialization of the means of production, the workers are not the real bosses of state property. They did obtain that, but they never actually became its bosses. So who are the bosses in the USSR? All those who, with a camouflaged privatism, refuse to convert mine into ours and want to live on the backs of others, on the backs of society.' It is hard to imagine a sharper criticism of the parasitic bureaucratic layer, of corporatist greed, and of the underground economy that took advantage of public inefficiency to acquire undeserved profits. The conclusion, addressed to the mass of the population, was not demagogic:

> To overcome the stagnation of the economy, growth must be not only quantitative but qualitative; it must improve the quality of work and offer consumers what they really need. What must be called into question is not planning as such but planning based on administrative fiat, which is indifferent to technological development or product quality and incapable of gauging the results of investment. Let us put an end to the system of 'Communist decrees' that has allowed managers to build their careers and share part of the proceeds with their dependants.

These were only thoughts on his part, but they showed a will to reaffirm the ideals of socialism at a time when their application was being criticized, and a determination to restore a central role to class struggle. Illness and death stopped him from doing more. The subsequent election of Viktor Chernenko as his successor showed how strong was the resistance of those who defended the status quo. But the economy continued to stagnate, the gerontocracy became intolerable to everyone, and finally Gorbachev emerged as the leading candidate to take over as secretary. Though originally in a minority in the Politburo, he was backed by Andrei Gromyko, the best-known and most authoritative figure from the old guard, who knew enough about the world to understand that the USSR might soon go under if it did not 'get a move on'. In addition to running a country in crisis, the new secretary was therefore subject to many influences. But he took the plunge and boldly launched the process of perestroika.

PERESTROIKA

The Russian word is quite generic: it can denote anything from a moderate adjustment to a semi-revolution. That is why nearly everyone accepted and used it, but not always with the same meaning.

Gorbachev (as Eduard Shevardnadze later revealed) had been convinced since 1978 that the whole system was 'rotten'. And he stuck to the slogan of *perestroika* through years of hard political battles, to indicate the need for a 'great reform' that would transform the system without giving up the foundations on which it rested. Western capitalism had tried something similar at mid-century, to face up to a major economic crisis and the spread of fascism in Europe, and to arrive at a new global order. But that, of course, had lasted a couple of decades and involved a world war, and the West had used the emergence of new antagonists to gear itself up for the attempt. Could it succeed in the Soviet Union, which was now in much worse straits both internally and internationally? Could it at least ensure its survival as a state?

Potentially, the USSR still had considerable resources to navigate its way in the modern world without being overwhelmed by it. It had huge reserves of raw materials (oil, gas, rare metals) that it could use and export without much difficulty, and plenty of land in relation to population density, which, if well cultivated and distributed, could ensure complete food independence. Its heavy industrial apparatus was by now technologically backward, heedless of productivity and unsuited to new consumption needs, but the country had the know-how and scientific capacity to catch up, as well as a level of education that could provide the cadres for new cutting-edge sectors. Its planning system was increasingly ossified, but it had shown in the past that, when necessary, it could suddenly concentrate its energy on long-range priorities. The people were frustrated and demotivated, because their needs were not being met and they had been pushed into political passivity. But it cannot be said that they were yearning for the veneer of affluence.

All these opportunities had been available at the time of the Twentieth Congress, and they were still present in the 1980s – plus one more. Throughout its history the Soviet Union had had to bear the economic burden (and the resulting ideological rigidity) of an arms race, first to counter external threats, and then to guarantee a bipolar balance; its military expenditure was completely disproportionate to its national income. The pressure lifted a little in the period of 'peaceful coexistence', but then Brezhnev's senseless policy of 'limited sovereignty' and the costly adventures in Afghanistan and the Horn of Africa offered Reagan the chance he was looking for. A pharaonic project to achieve definitive US military supremacy with the help of new technology (neutron bomb, missile shield, Star Wars) would force the USSR into responses that brought it to the verge of economic ruin. This time, however, the military threat was partly bluff. Vietnam and Afghanistan had shown that state-of-the-art weaponry was not enough to swing a large-scale guerrilla war, and it was all the more absurd to dream of a pre-emptive nuclear attack on a country the size of the USSR, which already had a developed military capacity of its own. The Soviet Union could therefore have remained secure from threat for a long time, without pointless imperial adventures, and reallocated much of its military expenditure and scarce human and material resources to other sectors.

On closer consideration, however, it becomes clear that structural reforms were necessary to take advantage of the opportunities mentioned, and that success in one area would require advances in others. If the system in crisis was already rotten, it needed a complete overhaul to pull through. All this helps to explain why Gorbachev came to power, why his efforts obtained impressive results and widespread support at first, and why growing obstacles finally inflicted a defeat that contributed to the collapse of the Soviet Union.

As many historical examples teach us, a 'great reform' is no easier than a revolution; it calls for audacity and strength to sweep away what is already 'rotten' and decayed. But a realistic assessment of the situation is also required, as are clear ideas about what should replace the old and how it should function: a grasp of the feasible objectives, the timescale necessary to achieve them, and the forces that might continue to give support for the long haul.

Gorbachev was not lacking in audacity. His first aim was to release society and the Party from their cage of prohibitions, conformism and silent conspiracies, which had developed during the twenty years of Brezhnevism and sunk roots in a vast bureaucratic apparatus numbering sixteen million. This objective was achieved by the simple means of conceding, and stimulating, free speech and press freedom. In the space of a few months the Soviet Union saw an explosion of debate among intellectuals of every stripe, the headlong growth of a critical and widely read press, and new scope for television to tell the truth and sometimes broadcast lively debates at the top of the Party. It was a real structural reform, the sine qua non for anything else. It gained widespread support. Sceptics had neither the courage nor the arguments to oppose it, and whenever they tried, they simply added more fuel to the flames of argument. Nevertheless, problems started to show amid the innovation. The discussion mostly involved intellectuals, who expressed the most diverse and irreconcilable opinions, but were very far from constituting a new ruling class. The masses were intrigued but remained on their guard. A scathing quip began to do the rounds in Moscow: 'I read lots of papers, but the shops are still empty.'

The dismantling of a petrified system could no longer be halted. But the problem of creating a new vision came hot on its heels – one that could mobilize tens of millions, offering some immediate improvement in living conditions and beginning a clear-out of the institutions.

It cannot be said that Gorbachev did not try. At the Twenty-Seventh Congress, late in 1986, he proposed an ambitious and structured programme of reforms, mainly centring on the economy, which addressed real problems but, in almost every case, pointed to a radical choice that had yet to be completed. Above all it failed to say which subjects and which instruments would implement it, within what timescale. The difference with Deng Xiaoping is immediately apparent. I will give just a couple of examples.

1) Was greater enterprise autonomy enough to raise labour productivity, to upgrade the technological base, to shift investment towards light industry and to improve the quality of consumer goods, if there was no fiscal system to reward or redistribute results, and no directive plan to steer decisions? In the absence of these, would greater autonomy not give a further advantage to large monopolistic enterprises, inducing them to produce the same things as before in the same old way, only with pointless new plant and for higher prices? 2) Was it enough to tolerate the growth of a hazy private or cooperative initiative, without entrepreneurs or a market, and without controls, transparent accounting or contractual guarantees to ensure that the result was not a speculative underground economy?

The obvious shortcomings in this economic programme certainly did not make it easier to implement, nor did they promise swift or imposing results. Yet the programme was encouraging and open to correction. The better company managers, of whom there were not a few, were initially in favour of taking on greater responsibilities, and at the same time were aware that an overhasty elimination of planning would threaten to sow disorganization. At the other extreme, the majority of workers demanded an immediate improvement in the supply and quality of basic consumer goods, a reduction in the privileges of the *nomenklatura* and a war on crime and speculation. All these goals were achievable; the regime only had to achieve them before moving on to other things. At the Twenty-Seventh Congress of the CPSU Gorbachev scored a great success, even if many had been expecting a balance sheet of what had been done.

When it was realized, less than two years later, that results were slow in coming and popular support was on the wane, almost everyone, Gorbachev included, did not dwell on the real reasons but blamed everything on the failings of the existing personnel and political institutions. Hence the idea of giving priority to political reform. In my view this was a correct decision, though also unwise. Correct, because a major political reform was impossible without a change in the ideas of the ruling class and the active involvement of broad masses, without new institutions and new ways of thinking and acting at both top and bottom. Unwise, for equally obvious reasons that were undervalued and negated.

For seventy years, political power had been in the hands of a single party; the state was only one of its instruments, its secular arm. But it was a peculiar kind of party, which ensured unity by suppressing dissent, yet organized and activated many millions within its limits and beyond, disseminated or imposed a world view, and secured the virtually constant mobilization of an entire people to face great emergencies (patriotic defence) or to attain great objectives (rapid industrialization, mass literacy, universal social protection, great-power status, the struggle against colonialism). Towards the end of that period, however, the Party had gradually changed its role and nature, while still ruling alone and remaining authoritarian. Its re-definition of itself as a 'party of the whole people' seemed to recognize a plurality of ideas and interests, but behind this a dominant stratum had welded political *nomenklatura* and technocracy into a bloc, reduced ideology to a catechism in which few believed, and encouraged the passivity of the masses by offering in return a tolerance of absenteeism (and hence of moonlighting and the black market). To clip the wings of this party and to separate it from the state would therefore be of little avail unless it recovered an identity at the level of ideas, and unless it rebuilt a relationship with the underprivileged masses. Nor would it help much to allow partial scope for contested elections, for micro-parties with a local base, or for individual demagogues who might later join forces in coalitions to weaken the CPSU. The most that would achieve would be political segmentation and a power vacuum, whereas a major reform, at least for a transitional period, would require a united and determined political force to lead it. The refoundation of politics, more than of any other domain, would take a long time and demand much hard work. And yet it was precisely a reform of politics, greater than at first envisaged, which was now happening piecemeal, without a cohesive project, as a set of fait accomplis, expressing local initiatives and interests and contradictory, sometimes fortuitous, positions. This move from an ultra-centralized authoritarian system to a scattered diaspora set up effects in all the problematic areas of Soviet life: the economy, national unity, international politics.

FROM GORBACHEV TO YELTSIN

Is it right to speak of a shipwreck of perestroika, and if so, when and how did it occur? The judgement at the time, as well as the memory still dominant today, has presented a rough-and-ready version for the purposes of edification.

Gorbachev himself is seen solely, or mainly, as the man who extended democracy to a sizeable area of the world (the fall of the Berlin wall being its symbol) and promoted a reshaping of the world market. The breakdown of the Soviet Union as a state; the rise of a corrupt oligarchy in what remained of it, resulting not from energetic enterprise but from the greatest pillage in history; the collapse of production, the scandalous inequalities, the prolonged tragedy for tens of millions left unprotected and forced back into poverty, the sharp fall in life expectancy, the explosion of violent and still unresolved ethnic conflicts: all this is regarded as the transitory 'collateral damage' of a great civilizing enterprise, the last bitter fruits that the distant year of 1917 rendered inevitable.

In my view, this is false both as judgement and as factual analysis. The happy period of perestroika lasted only three years, after which it broke down more and more visibly and rapidly. The process would not have begun at all had Gorbachev not become general secretary of the CPSU; only that gave him the strength to 'demolish the cage', to introduce free speech and press freedom, to promote the idea of a 'great reform'. Behind him stood a party which organized nearly twenty million people, from every social layer and every region, exercising power in all the nerve centres of society and of a state accustomed to discipline and unity. Like it or not, that party was the force that drove the extraordinary, triumphant mobilization of an entire people. But, from the very first experiences, it was agreed that the reforms had to have a precise content if they were to succeed, and that the party of which Gorbachev was secretary was at the same time both necessary and inadequate. This is why a special congress was convened, early on, to transform it – to limit its tasks in running the country, while imparting new life and vigour to its culture and placing its ideals on a new foundation.

Between 1988 and 1989 things went very differently. Even before 1988 they had begun to deteriorate. The first shock of

Gorbachev had aroused hopes of renewal, especially among young people, who, lacking experience or a clear line of sight, bounced off in every direction, forming endless microparties (below 5000 members) and thousands of political associations on disparate issues. The Party felt mistrustful and closed itself off defensively, with the result that it suffered many little splits and a growing number of individual defections. But the worst damage came during the congress: not through the re-emergence of a nostalgic opposition (that had always been there, and only now came into the open), but on two much more important levels.

First, cracks appeared among those who had supported perestroika and Gorbachev, not merely on topical or organizational issues, but on questions of strategy. A party cannot be founded or refounded without a relatively cohesive leadership, without a vision of the past and the present, without goals shared by a majority of its members. Indeed, the more one wants to permit and encourage free debate within a party, the more necessary it is to have a common perception of things.

Gorbachev's people, or at least many of them, discovered that they were divided into two camps. One side – not out of principle but to prevent the economic and political break-up of the country – argued that even deep reforms should not erase the socialist character of the system: there was no need to write off the whole past, or to capitulate wholesale to the market and private property. The other side was equally convinced that it was necessary to go *jusqu'au bout*, as quickly as possible: to close the parenthesis of the October Revolution and to build a coherent new system modelled on Western democracies (wide scope for the market, multiparty parliamentarism, economic and cultural openness to the world), which was now finally accessible to the Soviet Union. Otherwise the reforms would remain on paper, unable to produce results because of sabotage by powerful conservative forces. This second position was held by a minority within both the Party and the country. Gorbachev helped to criticize it and, for the moment, avoided a showdown. But the first position too had little to be complacent about, since it was an arduous task to proceed with comprehensive reform while keeping the socialist system intact. Culturally, it was necessary to invent a completely new socialist system, which relied on not only the support but the active involvement of millions of individuals, especially among the popular classes, and neutralized those who had always sworn by socialism but actually feathered their own nest and avoided taking personal responsibility. In short, a battle was joined.

Many delegates to the congress remained above the fray, however, passive and suspicious, partly for fear of losing their established role, partly for the deeper reason that they did not know what to say. With regard to the past, for example, it had been easy to encourage debate, or a real fight, so long as the choice had been between Stalinist nostalgia and liquidation of Lenin and his revolution. But now that greater discrimination was required to separate good from bad in a long and complex history, debate was not possible for the simple reason that the Party cadre did not know the history. For years it had studied Stalin's official version, then Khrushchev's secret report, and that was the sum of its knowledge. Nor did Gorbachev try to fill the gap: he spoke of a return to Lenin, but as if all Lenin had done was invent the New Economic Policy in 1921.

The consequences were onerous indeed: failed revitalization of the Party, plus cracks in its leadership. But that is not why the Party split apart. The truth is that it had simply been vanishing from the centre of the stage, as it grew ever weaker and tried to perpetuate itself at the edges in the form of pressure groups. Although its members did not realize it at the time, this was the starting point for the future waves of secession.

Gorbachev tried to react by changing the agenda of perestroika, refocusing the political reform on democratization of the state (greater powers for the soviets of the constituent republics, elected by popular suffrage with a real choice of candidates). Here too the intentions were excellent, the results terrible. The elections were a stunning defeat for the CPSU, especially in the big cities, where small parties and individual demagogues banded together to marginalize it.

Of even greater import was the concentration of the whole of Russia into a single union, which, by virtue of its size, became a counter-attraction to the central government of the USSR. Political power was now thoroughly fragmented, not only horizontally (among regional fiefdoms) but also vertically: soviets had legislative powers in their respective territories, permanently vying with one another over the division of central resources; the Soviet of the Russian Federation carried much greater weight than any other, undermining the authority of the central government, whose thirty-seven ministers did not know where to turn for their orders and anyway often made light of them. Each of these centres and levels claimed that its laws prevailed above all others in its territory. Headlong democratization turned into utter confusion. It also boosted the ethnic and religious conflicts that led to the break-up of the Soviet Union two years later and, in what remained of it, the rise to power of Boris Yeltsin, director and inventor of a new populism, who, in the name of liberty, ended up bombarding the parliament building, and in the name of the people divided up the public patrimony among corrupt oligarchs and mafiosi. The point I want to make is that the collapse was already under way in 1990: the economy was lurching into recession; it was difficult to distribute what was being produced; crime and speculation were booming; a real state no longer existed. Gorbachev was losing his authority, his only real power now over foreign policy. In fact, this was the realm that most clearly showed the best aspects of perestroika, and illustrated the heavy responsibility of the European Union (especially the European Left) in not only failing to seize the opportunity in its own interests but actually sabotaging it. Moreover, Gorbachev himself had certain illusions that made him unsure of how to handle foreign policy.

Already in 1985 the Soviet Union took up the idea of a completely new order in international relations, which would involve gradual and mutually verifiable nuclear disarmament; self-determination for every country in the world; the referral of disputes to the United Nations; democratization of the UN and other major institutions, and progressive dissolution of the blocs. To make this more credible, Moscow proposed a number of immediate agreements and concessions that often caught the Americans by surprise. Moreover, after some hesitation, Gorbachev withdrew the Red Army from Afghanistan, unilaterally reduced military expenditure and showed himself more open to trade. The other side seemed gratified but was only half listening: the American weapons modernization programme proceeded apace; the Mujahideen kept up their offensive in Afghanistan; and the terrible war between Iraq and Iran remained as bloody as ever, with US political and financial support for Baghdad. The Palestinian question smouldered on, while no one – even after the massacres in Lebanon and Jordan – tried to make the Israelis respect the resolutions passed at the

UN. Gorbachev's peace proposals thus began to turn into a creeping capitulation, with nothing in return from the other side.

That is precisely what happened between 1989 and 1990. Gorbachev made minimal efforts to influence how the East European countries – whose full independence was absolutely just – passed from one bloc to the other, or to shape their future economic relations with the USSR. One cannot fail to value the freedom of passage that came with the demolition of the Berlin wall – an event that soon acquired mythical status – but it is perfectly reasonable to discuss whether reunification of the two Germanies should have taken place immediately, in the form of an annexation of the one by the other (which even the SPD did not call for).

The lack of a Soviet initiative on the war over Kuwait was equally resounding. There was nothing to object to in the UN-backed decision to re-establish the frontiers of an independent country, but it is more doubtful whether this should have been achieved by a massive armed force rather than through political means. And there was every objection to the fact that a war, and then an inhuman blockade, were unleashed in support of Kuwait's international sovereignty, when no measures were taken concerning the fate of the Palestinians and the Golan Heights. Saddam was accused of possessing fabulous, non-existent weapons, while Israel was allowed to keep its nuclear arms. On these issues, a tough and clear position from the Soviet Union would have carried weight in the United Nations and on the ground. But none was forthcoming.

What amazes me most is that Europe did not realize how much it would gain from having an economic and political partner in the East, which could have allowed it to escape a subaltern role in the new American empire; and that Gorbachev imagined he could convert Reagan to the Roosevelt line by sheer force of example. It was too late in the day when he realized that democracy by itself was no Aladdin's lamp.

21

The End of the PCI

This brings me to the last part of my work: the end of the PCI.

I come to it after a brief interlude, in the worst of conditions, above all because of a deep personal loss. The death of my beloved companion, Mara, is not only a source of pain but feels like an amputation that will never heal, making my mind opaque and my will sluggish. On her deathbed, though, she made me promise to struggle on without her, at least until I finish the work I began during the years of her suffering. And I know that if I break it off now, I will not be able to keep that promise.

As it happens, I now find myself facing the complex, and in its way also painful, theme of the end of the PCI at a moment when not just the PCI but the whole Left seems to have vanished, or to be in total disarray, while the adversary that defeated it is in the throes of a serious crisis that makes the Left more necessary than ever. Furthermore, Italy in general – which for decades was a laboratory of political-cultural debate and social struggles of interest to the whole world – has been demoted to the rank of a minor, sometimes rather indecent, country, so that a new historical cycle appears unlikely to begin here amid the global turmoil; indeed, for the moment, it seems more likely that the worst consequences will play out here. If the systemic crisis proves to be long-lasting, new opportunities might present themselves, but in the short term it is difficult to see where to start: the reconstruction of a genuine Left will be a problem for future generations.

But perhaps this very observation should prompt us to ask

whether the PCI's legacy of ideas and forces should not have enabled its demise to be less abrupt and barren.

I should like to hazard an answer – sounding two notes of caution. I shall be delving into my own memories to fill the gaps in the archives and recent historical studies, with all the risks that this involves. And I shall also be inserting occasional autobiographical material, given that I had a not insignificant role and responsibilities in the events.

THE OCCHETTO OPERATION

I know for sure that if I were to ask competent figures when the end of the PCI began, I would receive many different answers: in 1979, after the collapse of the Historic Compromise to which it had been so committed for so long; in 1984, when the death of Enrico Berlinguer, the only high-quality leader of his time, drew a line under the Party's attempts to tack against the prevailing wind; in 1989, when the 'Bolognina turn' that was supposed to lead to the Party's revival rapidly ended in disaster; or in 1991, when a larger than predicted breakaway led many waverers to end their membership.

I see some truth in each of these answers, because each moment contributed in turn to the advance of a poorly diagnosed and poorly treated disorder. But if one wishes, as I do, to identify what triggered the really terminal stage, then one would have to choose Occhetto's performance at Bolognina – relating it both to what went immediately before and made it possible, and to what followed in the next two years. The 'Occhetto operation' was launched at the Eighteenth Congress, with much audacity but muddled ideas, rather in the manner of Gorbachev's perestroika. And it followed the same trajectory: a rapid ascent, with broad support, then difficulties and bitter disputes, and finally, three years later, the collapse.

Unlike in the time of Togliatti or Berlinguer, the turn did not gradually develop from a particular set of risky choices into a new strategy; it began with an ideological revision.

The revision was not closely argued, but it was radical. Indeed, it concerned how the Party saw its own past. In an interview Occhetto said: 'The PCI feels itself to be the child of the French Revolution (the revolution of '89, that is, but without the unfortunate Jacobins) and not, as is always said, the heir of the October Revolution.' In a speech shortly afterwards, he accused Togliatti of having been 'Stalin's unwitting accomplice'. And, finally, he hit out at Berlinguer as well: 'A third way does not exist; we don't think we can invent another world. This is the society we live in, and we want to work in this society to change it.' The class struggle no longer had a primary role, 'since the main contradictions of our age concern the whole of humanity'. In short, it was necessary to 'move beyond' the democratic road to socialism, conceived as a distinct society, antagonistic to capitalism.

Such iconoclastic fury dismayed even an authoritative old-timer such as Norberto Bobbio, who wrote in *La Stampa*:

> I ask myself whether what is happening in the PCI is not a real about-turn. One has a sense that there is a lot of confusion there. The haste with which they have been throwing their old cargo overboard seems suspect to me. They are still afloat, but the hold is empty. It would be an illusion to think that new merchandise can be easily found in any port. Be careful: there are a lot of damaged goods around, a lot of stuff that does not work and is passed off as new.

It could not have been better said, but one important point escaped Bobbio. Behind the ideological iconoclasm lay an all too elementary political project. By eliminating the 'difference' of Communism, Occhetto – and not only he – thought it would be possible to break the exclusion and to form a government with the PCI inside, a better one than anything previously seen. But here precisely was the strategy's weak point.

For, to fuel such hopes and to make them seem credible, it had not only to obscure reality but to construct a fantasy world. It had to ignore the fact that, although the bipolar world order was going up in smoke, it was being replaced not with a multipolar system but with a world dominated by one superpower; that, where that power could not peacefully impose its neoliberal policy and a reassertion of class domination, it would do so by force of arms; that the new financialized global capitalism did not protect the majority of nations and individuals, but excluded them from prosperity; that Italy, in particular, was heading for bankruptcy and social conflict, with a divided and weakened union movement; and that the government parties resisted the inclusion of the Communists not for ideological reasons, but in order to defend the interests and forms of rule on which they had always based themselves. Et cetera.

Thus when platforms, alliances and the real international situation were discussed at the Eighteenth Congress, there proved to a vacuum at the heart of the 'Occhetto project'.

A SURPRISING UNANIMITY

Despite all this – liquidation of an often revised but deeply rooted theoretical tradition, analytical void on newly emerging realities, 'newness' as the only criterion for a political proposal – Occhetto's 'new course' won almost unanimous support at the Eighteenth Congress.

Before we go any further, we should consider the reasons for this surprising unanimity, which explains much of what happened immediately afterwards. It would be ungenerous and misleading to claim that Occhetto won it mainly because he was secretary of a party in which, for the sake of unity, the secretary could not be overruled on crucial questions at a congress. The fact is that he also displayed political intelligence, and his lucid reading of the party allowed him to gauge what he could promise each section to gain its approval, and what he should refuse so as not to be its prisoner.

The *miglioristi* did not care for Occhetto's movementist rhetoric or his impromptu solo acts; indeed, they had once voted against him when he was made vice-secretary. But he now offered them an end to Berlinguer's talk of 'Communist difference' and planned to apply to join the social-democratic International, without calling a ceasefire with Craxi over policies (which would have caused a strong adverse reaction in large sections of the PCI).

Occhetto knew he could count on the goodwill of Natta and Tortorella, because it was they who had made him secretary of the Party. Knowing their affective ties to Togliatti and Berlinguer, he moderated his direct criticisms of them and even threw in a generic appreciation of what they had done to distance themselves from the Soviet camp (the affirmation of democracy as a universal value). These were knife-edge compromises, but they worked.

Much more difficult to explain is the support, or at least the lack of hostility, of the Left within the Party to Occhetto's 'new course'. *Ingraismo* had 'dissolved' after the Eleventh Congress, remained silent throughout the period of the Historic Compromise, and failed to take full advantage of the opportunity offered by Berlinguer in his final years. It had received a modest shot in the arm from the convergence with PdUP in 1985, but in normal conditions it would have been wrong to think of it as an active and recognized force within the PCI. Occhetto's turn, however, sanctioned by the Eighteenth Congress, was not within the bounds of normality. It already signalled a break – one which, if challenged, would have had immediate repercussions and cracked the unanimity.

This was not an abstract possibility but something already under way, unbeknown to anyone, and which I now feel that I ought, at last, to reveal.

The shape of the 'new course' was already clear before the congress, and a group of comrades with a certain profile and authority decided rightly or wrongly to oppose it from the left – in the name not of conservation but of a different kind of renewal. They therefore drafted a resolution to put to congress, together with a longer supporting document. They were Ingrao, Garavini, Bassolino[1] (a little less resolutely) and myself, who for this purpose was assigned to the small committee in charge of preparing the congress theses. At that point Occhetto, wary of appealing to democratic centralism, moved with undeniable skill. He invited Ingrao to meet him and generously asked: 'What would you like to put in my speech in return for giving up an alternative motion?' Ingrao replied, more or less: 'A strong emphasis on the environmental question and, to be consistent, a strong denunciation of the multinationals that now make all the main decisions for the economy.' Occhetto promised to do this, and kept his word after a fashion: he inserted a few high-flown general phrases, including one on Amazonia that caused a bit of a stir. Ingrao too felt bound by the agreement, so that within a few hours the alternative document was filed away in a drawer. I should add that those attending the congress were very satisfied, because they came away with the impression that the new course had united the Party and would pave the way for a dynamic and fruitful initiative. I, and perhaps not only I, was convinced of the opposite, but I resigned myself to acquiescent silence. When I look back on my life in politics, I think this was

1. Antonio Bassolino: Communist deputy with roots in Campania; he eventually joined the PDS after the dissolution of the PCI, and served as mayor of Naples in the 1990s and president of Campania from 2000 to 2010.

the only error which had some cowardice mixed in with it. For on one point Occhetto was right: the PCI could not survive on a line of continuity. An opposition needed a completely different analysis and political line, organic and innovative in equal measure; it therefore needed to run the risk of confrontation.

But reality is much less malleable than words. In the months after the congress, two disturbing developments occurred. Economic crisis, institutional disarray and breakaway tendencies heralded the end of perestroika and the collapse of the Soviet Union (and its zone of influence), not only as a regime but even as a state. And Occhetto's 'new course' in Italy elicited sympathy and encouragement, but completely failed to modify the alliances or the policy of the forces in government. Occhetto, like Gorbachev, therefore found himself at a crossroads: he could modify his chosen course, or he could speed it up by means of risky political actions intended to raise its profile in society at large. The latter was the rational basis of the so-called Bolognina turn; it provides us with the key to understand the timing, form and content of a decision that would otherwise appear as the work of a would-be demiurge.

THE BOLOGNINA TURN: THE AYES AND THE NOES

The timing. Occhetto sprang his proposal immediately after the fall of the Berlin wall, because he intuited that, symbolically at least, the event offered the PCI one last opportunity to present its dissolution not as a surrender to the inevitable but as part of a great democratic advance, which legitimated its history and its function in society.

The form. If his proposal had followed the normal rules (discussion in the leadership, then in the Central Committee, then in the local branches), not only would the process have taken longer, but the motion would have risked being defeated. The Party therefore had to be presented with an irreversible fait accompli, even if it meant that the man who carried it out would be brought down.

The content. Its two bombshells were: the opening of a constitutive phase for a new party of the Left, into which the PCI was willing to merge; and a change in the name of the PCI as a stimulus to, and logical consequence of, this phase. Someone had already floated the idea of a name change, but the leadership had explicitly ruled it out on the grounds that it might look like an acceptance of defeat, such as other Communist parties had suffered – not a recognition of the specificity of Italian Communism and the beginning of a well-deserved re-launch. But, according to Occhetto, now that such a misunderstanding had been cleared up, a new name might benefit the construction of a great new force of reform, bringing together various social and cultural components and finally unblocking the Italian political system.

So, on the morning of 12 November 1989, Occhetto unexpectedly showed up at a small gathering of Resistance veterans in the Bolognina district, on the outskirts of Bologna. He made a speech that said nothing of names, but emphasized that the fall of the Wall showed how much the world was changing and how much the PCI had to change if it were not to lag behind. Then, as the meeting was coming to an end, a young editor from *L'Unità* – a welcome guest who looked implausibly innocent – finally asked whether we would also drop the name 'Communist'. And 'the wretch responded':[2] 'Everything is possible.' In a few hours the rest of the press heard of this and had no difficulty decoding the phrase: the next day's headlines read 'The PCI Changes Its Name' – without a question mark. I was dumbfounded and, coming upon Natta at Montecitorio, I asked him: 'Did you know about this?' To which he replied, sadly raising his arms: 'Absolutely nothing.'

Twenty years later, although I have often repeated the question to others, I have still not managed to discover exactly who knew what. My hunch is that the secretary's most trusted friends (Petruccioli,[3] Mussi,[4] the Rodano family[5]) were fully in the picture, and the idea had been run past a number of others, but that the majority of the top leadership knew as much as I did: nothing.

2. The allusion is to Canto XXII of Dante's *Inferno*.

3. Claudio Petruccioli: Communist Youth secretary in 1966, parliamentary deputy in 1983, PCI national secretary in 1987. One of Occhetto's main associates in the camapaign to wind up the PCI. Appointed head of RAI television in 2005.

4. Fabio Mussi: joined the PCI at an early age in the 1960s and was in the Direzione by 1984. Although he supported the dissolution of the PCI, he joined the left 'Correntone' in the PDS which later converged with much of Rifondazione Comunista in the new Sinistra Ecologia e Libertà party headed by Niki Vendola.

5. Franco Rodano: originating in the Catholic Left of the wartime period, he became an infuential figure in the PCI, though without ever holding any position. Co-founder of *Rivista trimestriale* (1962–70), which expressed a critical position toward 'official Marxism' and attracted a significant group of intellectuals and economists (including Napoleoni, Chiarante and Magri).

That same day, the secretary called a meeting of the secretariat and, after a brief report, asked for its collective endorsement. Noticing a certain unease, and a few teary eyes, he pointed to an empty page intended for resignations if he was denied its support. But he received it, even though the statutes specified that the secretariat was only an executive body, with no power to make important policy decisions. Apparently everything was up for renewal, except the time-honoured tricks of the Via delle Botteghe Oscure. The next morning, when the matter was discussed in the Direzione, the secretary put forward a more detailed argument, without varying the content. I was the first to jump up and utter a flat 'No': both to abandonment of the name 'Communist' (which remained justified in the case of Italy, and might yet be enriched by events taking place elsewhere in the world); and to the formation of a new party, which seemed premature and therefore threatened to wreck what already existed, instead of creating something larger. On the first day my 'No' stood alone, and *L'Unità* carried a headline: 'Only Magri Against'. But two days later Castellina and Cazzaniga[6] added their 'noes' and two others abstained (Chiarante and Santostasi[7]), while some further speakers (Natta, Tortorella) raised doubts but stopped short of a vote against. Ingrao was in Spain at the time, but he would soon return to express his total disagreement, lending greater solidity and visibility to the scant forces of the opposition. Meanwhile, however, the ground floor of the building was full of journalists and TV cameras, and the news rapidly spread to the whole country. This prompted the first active and public intervention from the grass roots: lively federal committee sessions, packed branch meetings (some convened on the initiative of the members), noisy protest marches in front of PCI headquarters, dissenting statements from intellectuals. Everyone wanted to have a say, with no beating about the bush.

On 20 November the Central Committee met for a three-day session. The atmosphere was tense, and hundreds had put their

---

6. Gian Mario Cazzaniga: originating in the extraparliamentary Left, he joined the PCI in the late 1970s and gravitated towards the 'orthodox' Cossutta current. As such he entered the Direzione in 1989 and opposed the dissolution of the PCI, later turning to academic life in Pisa.

7. Mario Santostasi: Puglian labour leader, who joined the PCI Direzione in 1986. A supporter of Motion 2, which opposed the dissolution of the PCI, and later head of *Il Manifesto* (2000–5).

name down to speak. The secretariat wanted clear statements from everyone, and put forward the briefest of agendas: a yes or no vote on the proposal as a whole. This was followed by the calling of a special Party congress. Someone tried to head this off by expressing a commendable fear that it would harden the various positions – but to no avail. It was later said that Pietro Ingrao was the one who insisted on a congress. But that is not true. There would have had to be one, for reasons of legitimacy. The Central Committee had been elected by a party that actually existed; it did not have the right to create another party. Besides, you can't quieten people in ferment by making them discuss but not decide.

Of course, both the Central Committee session and the hastily convened Nineteenth Congress were well attended, and sparked lively debate. But, to tell the truth, the discussions were neither very interesting nor creative – mostly a rehash of old positions, with a little added varnish but no real substance. I shall therefore not go into the details. Two novelties that emerged did have considerable importance, however, both immediately and in the long run.

First, the dissent was far greater and more tenacious than expected. This is clear from the figures. At the meeting of the Direzione there had been three clear 'noes' (four after Ingrao arrived), plus two abstentions and one no-vote. At the Central Committee, out of the 326 people present, 219 voted 'yes' and 73 'no', while 34 abstained. At the Bologna Congress the 'no' delegates represented 33 per cent, a third of the registered membership. Nor do the figures tell the whole story. Many other elements allow me to affirm that the scale of dissent was even larger. There was an exceptional, and sometimes rule-bending, mobilization behind the secretariat, regional apparatuses and local administrations; wide regional disparities, with an overwhelming 'yes' in the 'Red areas' (containing more than a third of the Party) but widespread or even majority opposition in a number of large cities; and a campaign in the Party press and independent papers that left dissenters without an organization or a means of conveying their arguments. Two opinion surveys of the Communist electorate (whatever their value in such a situation) recorded 73 per cent against. And, last but not least, considerable numbers just walked quietly away: the Party membership fell by nearly 400,000 between 1989 and 1990.

But a second new feature worked against the oppositionists, contributing to the general unease. The 'No Front', though unexpectedly large, was politically and culturally heterogeneous. It was united in opposition to Occhetto's proposal, but it had not formulated, nor did it wish to formulate, a common and convincing alternative. It lacked reflection on the past (critical, not liquidationist) and it lacked analysis of the present (not complacent, but conscious of new developments in society and the world). So, in the end it appeared as a source of resistance rather than a more serious, more ambitious project to build on the best of the PCI's legacy.

This posed a delicate and complex problem. The congress finally backed Occhetto's proposal, and so he had every right to call upon the whole Party to implement it, without further consultation, dissociation or verification. But it was very risky to begin building a new party by losing a third of the existing one, amid constant uproar. On the other hand, the opposition also needed time – to define its purpose more clearly, to develop its own central and regional leadership, and above all to decide what to do in the future. A compromise was therefore reached whereby preparations would get under way for the new party, but would be subject to checks at another congress in a year's time, when only those still registered as members would have a right to vote. This semi-postponement certainly kept a lively contest going, but it also provided for more serious discussion, in the most interesting and least predictable phase of the process that had begun at Bolognina. It is worth reconstructing this period, since it was badly reported at the time and later forgotten.

The majority around Occhetto was determined not to change its course, and in fact a member of the secretariat was given the task of approaching forces outside the Party to gain their support; this was meant to show that the work of preparing the new party was bearing fruit, and to reduce the space for a future split. But the hunt did not live up to expectations. The small parties showed interest, but no positive intent. Prestigious left-wing intellectuals were divided, but generally non-committal with regard to themselves. The 'scattered and submerged Left', already sceptical of the party form as such, refused to have anything to do with the unresolved conflict. But what was decisive was the effect of the turn on those at whom it was mainly pitched. The DC and especially Craxi (the man who held the balance) were not spurred by the prospective dissolution of the PCI to involve themselves in discussion about the reshaping of politics, but rather saw it as the expression of a crisis that would cut Italian Communism down to size; only afterwards might it be possible to engage in advantageous parley. The new integralist organizations were making the running in the Catholic world, while the Polish Pope had been playing a lead role himself in the evolution of Solidarność and the collapse of the East European regimes. Dissident Catholics close to the PCI had made their choice years ago: they felt they could be more useful as independents active in new social movements than as members of the new party. So, poor old Petruccioli returned from his trips with a game bag half-empty at best, causing rifts in the majority that never seemed to heal. One section, the *miglioristi*, thought they would get nowhere without revising their judgement of the PSI and their attitude towards it. But Occhetto demurred, because he knew this touched a raw nerve in the PCI membership and might increase unruliness in the ranks – precisely what Craxi was waiting for before he committed himself.

The 'No Front' was not in good shape either, or at least it had to clarify many things before it could pull itself together and decide what to do next. A general meeting was held in June, but it was here that the first cracks began to show. Ingrao and Bertinotti[8] suddenly proposed shelving the question of the name until the next congress and concentrating instead on programme and political line. Santostasi, who was the coordinator and reporter at the meeting, did not share this view of how to proceed – neither did I. This was not only, or not chiefly, because of the symbolic importance of the name, nor only because the proposal to change it was an integral part of a political and cultural turn begun a year earlier; the point was that, in facing the problem of whether to retire or reaffirm the word 'Communist', we too would have to make an effort to enrich its meaning and to think more critically about the past. It should not be shelved but become central to our discussion. Santostasi put a rather bald motion along these lines to the vote, and it was rejected by a large majority. But behind this lay a more burning question, about which nearly everyone was undecided. What would we do after the congress, and what could we threaten to influence its outcome?

8. With a background in the CGIL, Fausto Bertinotti joined the PCI in 1972 and became one of the union leaders most opposed to consensus politics. He went on to play a leading role in Rifondazione Communista.

All this favoured some timid attempts to reach a compromise between the majority and the opposition. One glimmer of hope, proposed in an article by Michelangelo Notarianni,[9] was a federal solution that would allow a Communist minority to be recognized, on condition that there was a basis for agreement on short-term policies. But the majority showed no openness to the idea and nothing ever came of it. Part of the reason for this was the onset of the Kuwait crisis in August, and the later Italian involvement in the war against Iraq (which the majority supported); for the first time ever, a sizeable number of PCI deputies broke discipline in parliament. This made it all the more necessary for the 'No Front' to develop a more advanced platform, before it launched into organizational initiatives. A long and wide-ranging seminar was convened for this purpose in the autumn; I was commissioned to write a text for it, and this kept me busy all summer. After consultations with many other comrades, a finished document was produced in time.

The seminar took place at Arco di Trento, in late September, with a large attendance and an unusual and interesting agenda. Since the document was very ambitious and consisted of many parts, it was decided not to have a personal introduction setting out its main points. Participants were given a copy on the first evening and asked to spend the whole of the next morning reading and reflecting on it. The result seemed encouraging: people were generally appreciative, there were no disagreements in the discussion, and since the text was neither trivial nor repetitive the support did not mean that it represented a lowest common denominator. At one point, though, a sudden clap of thunder made everyone jump. In fact, the storm had been building up for some time; we might call it 'Hurricane However'.

Armando Cossutta took the floor and said some nice things about my proposed platform, but then came the first 'however'. If the Party changed its name, he and others would create another, Communist, party. Soon afterwards Ingrao, who until the previous evening had approved of the text, added a 'however' of his own: he would take part in the preparations for a new party proposed by Occhetto. With these two 'howevers', any power to reach a

9. Michelangelo Notarianni: editor of the peace movement weekly *Guerra e Pace*.

deal – assuming that one was possible – was greatly diminished. The outcome of the Twentieth Congress, to be held in Rimini, was a foregone conclusion: there would be a sung mass, followed by a split unworthy of a news item.

THREE SPLITS

Separations and splits have punctuated the whole history of the workers' movement, in nearly every country and in many eras: between Socialists and Communists, but also within the ranks of both. In every case a heavy price was paid. Gramsci, who played a leading role in the split of 1921, said that it had been a necessity but also a misfortune. This is not to say that all have been equally disastrous, or have proved with time to be equally sterile or irreversible. Nor have all been the straightforward reflection of a great ideological and political divide. Their gravity and finality have depended in large part on their historical context, on who executed them and why, and on the nature of the project behind them.

The split of 1991 was one of the worst. Much later Bertinotti painted a seductive but misleading picture of it, when he simply said: 'Sparrows went with sparrows, blackbirds with blackbirds.' If the split had led to a strong reformist party on one side, linked to the best in the social-democratic tradition, and to a genuinely refounded Communist party on the other side, then Bertinotti's summary would have been appropriate. But that did not describe what was happening in 1991, still less what would happen subsequently.

In reality, there were two or even three splits. The first – the most important and conspicuous – saw the birth of two new parties that fought over the inheritance: one devised by Occhetto, the Partito Democratico della Sinistra (PDS), with the oak as its symbol; and one launched by Garavini, Cossutta, Libertini, Serri and Salvato, which, after much discussion, took the name Rifondazione Comunista (PRC). A second cleavage, less important and visible, but with important indirect effects, opened up between nearly all the national and local leaders who had waged the 'No' battle before joining the PDS (and remaining there for many years, generally dissatisfied and reduced to silence) and their base, which mostly moved towards Rifondazione. In this case too, Occhetto and others persuaded themselves that the split would fail or that it would soon be possible to mend it.

But new members did not flock to the PDS, even when the wind of Tangentopoli[10] began to break the PSI and DC apart, whereas Rifondazione recruited 119,000 in just a few months. The 'grand new party' therefore celebrated its debut with a membership 50 per cent down on that of the PCI, and a score of 16 per cent at the general elections of 1992.

This second cleavage also weighed on the political project of Rifondazione. For its recruits were predominantly working-class activists, trained in operational tasks or trade union disputes, full of enthusiasm and a sense of belonging, but unaccustomed to political reflection and rightly enraged by any 'newness' that produced no results. To build, or rebuild, a party out of them – as Togliatti knew – calls for organization, clear thinking and sharp struggles, and minimum demagogy; it requires, above all, a cohesive leadership, rich in ideas and prestige, capable of pedagogy, and united by common experience. Without that, a popular breakaway from a mass party, burning with a sense of betrayal, could easily fall into maximalism or harden into uncritical worship of the past.

A third split was even less visible but in my view perhaps the gravest of all, because it struck not only at the PCI but at Italian democracy.

Italian democracy was already a weakling at birth, because of its late delivery and the elitism of the Risorgimento. Held back by illiteracy and the Vatican's *non expedit*,[11] it was later regimented and undermined by fascism, which – let us not forget – was in its way a reactionary regime with a mass character.

The PCI made an essential contribution to the renewal and completion of democracy, not least through its role as a mass party that educated millions of people, involved them in politics and infused them with confidence that their collective action could change the world. Most of these men and women belonged to the subaltern classes, which, as everywhere, are the most distrustful of institutions, and especially distant from international politics. A party of this size and character, supported by a range of flanking

10. Tangentopoli, from *tangenti* (bribes or kickbacks) and *polis*, is the term commonly used for the whole edifice of political corruption uncovered by the Mani Puliti investigation team between 1992 and 1996.

11. See note 9 on p.58.

organizations, was unique in Europe. Over the decades, however, these features became much less pronounced. There were advantages in this (for example, a move away from ideological dogmatism and hierarchical structures), but the downside outweighed them (separation between leaders and workers, political careerism, a paucity of young people, assimilation of mainstream culture). By the late 1980s, the mass party was quite different from what it had been. Yet the fact remains that the PCI still had 28 per cent of the vote, and of its 1,400,000 members, many active and politically aware, with roots in the world of the proletariat, 40 per cent had been in the Party for more than twenty years.

This was what even Occhetto called the 'bedrock' – a resource and a bond. The need for renewal above all else was evident, but so too was the fact that any sudden break in identity and symbols, while perhaps not provoking a rebellion (because of habits of discipline), would produce an exodus. And an exodus there was, on a colossal scale: careful research, going beyond official statements, shows that roughly 800,000 people moved away from active politics. And since it is not true that the subaltern classes are by nature of the Left – and since television will take over if there is not an organization to persuade and orient them – an exodus on this scale and of these classes is worse than a political split: it creates an opening for populist demagogy.

At this point I can say that my work is done, as I have fulfilled my principal objective. I can also say that it has been worthwhile. I have restored the memory of twentieth-century Communism, especially the PCI, filling in some of the gaps and refuting some of the manipulation. Perhaps I have even provided serious evidence that twentieth-century Communism was not a calamity and did not leave only a heap of ashes behind. I have not concealed, or hidden from myself, anything of what I knew and thought. I did fail in one objective, though – or, better said, one hope.

I had hoped that my probing of a distant past would give me a better purchase on the word 'communism' and reveal a wider range of meanings. But I did not find enough, either at the level of thought or at the level of experience. Marx was very cautious in this regard. Asked what a Communist society would look like, he gave no more than a few hints. Gramsci added to this the whole theme of a 'new human type', and Togliatti said that Gramsci's thought made it possible to 'go beyond' progressive democracy. The movement of 1968 expressed the same demand, but often contradicted it in practice, while the main workers' parties (Communist and social-democratic) basically set it aside. The words 'communist' and 'socialist' were used as equivalents, each indicating a long transition, in a different way, but without much concern for the final destination. This was understandable, because the times were not yet ripe: economic development, class struggles and mass education would automatically define the goal and enable it to be reached.

By the late 1980s, however, more than a century had passed. Economic prosperity, mass education and the running of the state had not produced a new civilization, still less a 'historic turnaround' or a 'new and higher type of human being'. The time had therefore come to explain what Communism meant, in contrast to actually existing capitalism, and to specify both its goals and the forces capable of upholding it; or else to adapt to the present state of things. Here lay the almost incurable weakness of the Left, in every country and every school. Only the developed West could try to remedy it, over a long period of time. Other countries still had other questions to address, and either they did this well (China) or they collapsed (USSR). But once again the European Left shirked the test, either by dissolving or by throwing in the towel. The PCI too, which had persisted for so long in its distinctiveness, shrank from the challenge and paid the price, suddenly finding itself face to face with the Berlusconi phenomenon (much as Italy's relative backwardness had once led to the first fascist regime).

I cannot exorcise this disappointment, since historical reality has to be recognized for what it is. But, in this case, it allows for an attempt at a 'counterfactual' conclusion.

Counterfactual history is not a retrospective flight of fancy built upon experiences that came later. It must apply to the situation that it is meant to cover, on the basis of ideas present at the time; it is a hypothesis that did not, but could have, become reality.

So, it is legitimate to ask whether there was still a possibility in the 1980s that the PCI would not crumble as it did. Did it still have an untapped cultural legacy on which it could draw (the 'Gramsci genome')? And were there any contradictions and forces in the real world it could have used as a lever to begin a Communist refoundation, instead of melting into the neoliberal globalization already under way? I think there were. And, to avoid sounding like a crazy visionary, I will resort to a little expedient: I will append a large part of a text I wrote in 1987, without corrections of any kind. It is not a personal text: it was intended as the basis for a collective resolution to be presented to the Eighteenth Congress of the PCI, as an alternative to Occhetto's resolution. Two years later it was taken up and inserted into the agreed platform of the 'No Front', which represented a third of the PCI. Then it was again put away in a drawer. It must have been a good drawer, because twenty years later, to my eyes at least, it does not seem to have aged so much.

Envoi

A New Communist Identity

The crisis and restructuring that we have been living through is certainly not the first in the history of modern capitalism; others no less innovative and even more dramatic have marked its development. Capitalism emerged from each of these moments profoundly transformed, often gaining the impetus for further expansion and new forms of domination. And in each of them, the workers' movement and progressive forces suffered huge blows in various countries and were everywhere forced to revise their previous theories, programmes and organizational forms.

In the past, however, albeit unevenly and over a period of time, the crisis and systemic changes always spurred a general development of the workers' movement and the Left, in terms of organizational strength, spaces of power and cultural hegemony. This happened at the end of the nineteenth century, after the First World War and in the 1930s. For example, the darkest period of the 1930s also saw the great mobilization inside the USSR, the mass struggles of the Popular Front, and even the rise of a new progressive bourgeois thought (Roosevelt, Keynes), not to speak of the tide that followed it.

Today this is not the case, or does not seem to be. Years of economic crisis and political instability have been accompanied with a decline of the political and cultural forces that have in various ways opposed the trend and should have profited from it. To say that this is because they were unprepared for that trend, and were therefore unable to understand its significance or formulate a response, is true but not enough; the lack of preparedness must itself be explained, and so too must the fact that the initial bewilderment has not yet given way to fresh initiative and reflection.

A plausible and widely recognized explanation is the following. The greatest novelty of the massive changes under way – and certainly the most important for our discussion – lies in something over and above the crisis and the capitalist restructuring: that is, in what is commonly called the 'epochal shift from industrial to post-industrial society'. Of course, this statement should be treated with considerable caution and many qualifications: we should not think that what matures over a period of time is totally new, nor confuse what is still only a tendency with something universal and complete.

It is evident that many of the phenomena we define as 'post-industrial' gradually developed within the previous historical phase of Fordist mass industrialization; this may be useful to recall, because they could then have had a 'left' expression if the cultural, social and political referents for it had been present. Even more evident is the fact that industrialization is only now taking off in many parts of the world, or attempts are being made to clear the obstacles in its path; while in the advanced countries of the West itself, not only do traditional forms of industry continue to occupy a large part of the labour in society, but industry has been most successful in applying innovations, raising productivity and organizing concentrations of power, so that it remains the core that carries along and orients the whole. This reminder may help us not to lose sight of an important part of reality and its contradictions. Indeed, as we shall argue, the decisive element that allows us to understand and intervene in the world is perhaps, once again, this structured coexistence of different levels and forms of production, this dialectic of 'uneven development'.

Three facts are nevertheless true. 1) Industrial production, at least in the West, is tending to decline in terms of value and employment levels, relative to the production of services or immaterial goods. 2) In industrial production, productivity depends less and less on the direct input of general labour or the quantity of investment capital, and more and more on skill levels and the organization of consumption: in short, on what happens outside industry. 3) These phenomena impact on backward societies less explicitly and directly than in the past, but even more coercively, proposing or imposing technologies and a consumption model that are hard for them to adopt, and an international division of labour in which they cannot usefully participate, or which actually has a disruptive effect on them.

The capitalist restructuring of recent years has enormously accelerated these long-term processes. It has speeded up the introduction of new labour-saving technology (much of it available for some time), which narrows the industrial foundations; it has boosted the expansion of services and the production of immaterial goods; and it has shaped the industrialization of emerging economies through the replacement of natural raw materials, the intensive transformation or revival of mature industrial sectors, or the permutation of capital resources within the circuit of core countries to enable them to live 'beyond their means'.

In this sense, and for this reason, we may say that the 'post-industrial transition' is the horizon within which we must operate. What dominates the scene is a capitalism that strives to outlive the historical factors that produced its birth – to guide the next epoch too with its values and rules.

This presents all variants of Marxist theory and all components of the workers' movement with radically new and disturbing problems of perspective and purpose. On the one hand, it seems to offer new and unexpected historical justifications for the capitalist system: the market provides for the flexible, swift and decentralized decision-making required by ceaseless changes in technology, organization and consumption demand; the entrepreneurial function may once more extend to large numbers of people, either directly integrated into the economic trusts or guided by their decisions; and intense competition at an individual level stimulates the development of necessary skills and the deployment of labour in areas that the Taylorist organization of work cannot reach.

On the other hand, class polarization in terms of ownership of the means of production and struggles over the division of surplus value seems to have become increasingly obsolete, now that new trends shape and fragment different figures within wage labour, enlarge the realm of autonomous, semi-autonomous or precarious labour, and bring into the open social subjects and contradictions external to production.

This has fortified the cultural offensive of which neoliberalism is only the most visible component, precipitating what is presented as, and partly is, a crisis of Marxism.

The very idea of the socialist revolution and communist society, in all its possible forms, is now said to be baseless, since capitalism seems better able to ensure its development by means of, not in spite of, its fundamental elements (market, profit, individualism) – those 'animal spirits' which are more than ever the engine of progress and its necessary 'material basis'. Should this no longer hold true in the future – it is said – a system transformation would anyway have no affinity with the conceptual apparatus of Marxism, which operated entirely within the horizon of industrial society.

These views are now widespread in the major parties of the Left, which think that, in the present historical period and perhaps for ever, it will be necessary to manage – and impossible to change – the capitalist social-economic formation.

But they are also widespread in the new (anti-war, ecological, feminist) movements, which challenge existing society yet often think it marginal or distracting to define and change it as capitalist; they situate themselves either this side or the other side of the problem of capitalism.

It may be objected – indeed, it is crucial to object, so as not to throw away a precious historical and theoretical legacy – that the hypothesis of a 'post-industrial transition' was not only present in Marx but underpinned his idea of communist society. Perhaps he was the only thinker who, seeing the nexus of capitalism and industrialism so far in advance, linked the overcoming of the one to the overcoming of the other. 'The exploitation of living labour will become a paltry basis for the general development of wealth'; 'production for the sake of production' will lose all meaning when the primary measure of progress is 'the enrichment of distinctively human needs, and in particular the general need for non-alienated activity'.

This and only this prediction, contrasting with any 'primitive' theory, allowed him to see capitalism as the necessary premise for socialism, and to conceive of communism as a reversal, not a development, of previous history: the realm of freedom opposed to the realm of necessity, the 'critique of political economy'. It was this prediction which gave to his radical conception of communism – the overcoming of commodity relations, alienated labour, the social division of labour and delegated democracy – the character of a rational project rather than an empty utopia. The fact that human history is moving beyond the threshold of basic needs, that new technologies permit a reduction in necessary labour, that educational levels and the speed of information allow a great diffusion of power and decentralization of decision-making, that quantity is no longer the only or main criterion of progress, should mean that the discourse of communism, in its original, emancipatory meaning, has come of age for the first time in history.

All this is true: we were arguing it in 1968 and we are still convinced that it is the key to a communist identity that involves both recovery and profound innovation.

But the ebbing of '68, at the levels of both theory and practice, has taught us that things are less evident and much more complex. First of all, the reference to Marx is too simplistic, and like every return to the sources, to 'something that used to exist but was later misunderstood and betrayed', it is arbitrary. It is neither irrelevant nor fortuitous that Marx himself felt neither able nor willing to formulate a theory of revolution that integrated the radical emancipatory aspects which seem most topical to us today. His theory of revolution never departed from the sketch presented in the *Manifesto* of 1848: neither the themes of his Paris manuscripts nor the more solidly grounded reflections in the *Grundrisse* and the *Critique of the Gotha Programme* ever served as the basis for a real theory of the transition to socialism. The revolutionary break would pave the way for a radically changed horizon of history, but it would occur before that horizon took shape, owing to the strength of the contradictions and social subjects within the phase of industrialization; the incapacity of the system to guarantee development of the productive forces would lead to the conquest of power by a proletariat that industry had made ever larger and more united. The rest would follow by itself, or at least could not be theorized without 'cooking up the future'.

This schema was never criticized or revised in the theory and practical history of the workers' movement. Even those, like Lenin, who concentrated all their theoretical work on the intertwining of modernity and backwardness, the need for social alliances or the limitations of workers' spontaneous consciousness, and who occasionally tried their hand at some of Marx's more radical themes (*State and Revolution*), never departed from that approach. Spontaneous consciousness would be overcome with a purely subjective external instrument (the party), while alliances would be built essentially around 'completion of the bourgeois revolution'; the 'withering away of the state' was left to salvation through technological development. Most important of all, however, actual history yoked the workers' movement and industrialism ever closer together. Twentieth-century revolutions happened in parts of the world still on the threshold of industrial development, whereas the Western labour movement willy-nilly stimulated capitalist growth while distributing its product by means of trade union struggle and political democracy. All this accentuated an economistic vision of progress in 'actually existing Marxism', and an emphasis on the state as the only possible alternative to the domination of the market.

A post-industrial society, with its new contradictions, therefore introduces a disturbing novelty with regard to a tradition built up over many decades. What can be the point of insisting on a communist identity, if we are talking about two such different things?

Nor is this all. The founding element of Marxism is not only its critique of capitalist society and its affirmation that a different society is abstractly conceivable, but also that communism is a 'real movement that abolishes the present state of things'. Its theoretical coherence and practical efficacy depended, and still depends, on the possibility of demonstrating three things: a) that the real dialectic of capitalist society generates material contradictions that lead towards its dissolution; b) that these contradictions are expressed in the struggle of social classes, which to liberate themselves have to subvert the existing order, but which have in themselves a real capacity to build a new order; and c) that, at varying speeds and with varying degrees of violence, all this requires breaking the mechanisms of the system and establishing new mechanisms, a different kind of transitional class power, without which another system will never be 'mature'.

If none of this was true, or was true no longer, it would make no sense to speak of Marxism or communism. The central role that Marxism gave to the contradictions within industrial development were therefore the result not only of historical contingency but also of its own theoretical statement: the industrial development of capitalism produced a social subject, the proletariat, which in its contradictory position – maximum dispossession, maximum links with modern production – had both a radical need and a real capacity to emancipate itself, and with it the rest of humanity. To be sure, it remained unclear how this dialectical leap might take place. On which material forces could the proletariat base itself to escape its inherent dichotomy between the pure negativity of total alienation and the 'bad positivity' of heteronomous technological progress? Perhaps Gramsci was the only one who took this theme seriously, by focusing on the relationship between the proletariat and 'preceding forms', between productive base and superstructure, between political and cultural reform.

In retrospect, one might doubt whether Soviet society and the Soviet regime were really socialist, or whether the social-democratic experiences really were an alternative. But on the whole it was evident to everyone that a historical process was under way in that the working class not only grew in size but gradually asserted a political and cultural role as a ruling class, as the driving force behind major processes of economic and democratic development.

So, what remains of this strong identity of Marxism and the Left in general, at a time when industrialism is on the decline but a revolutionary break is not emerging in the most developed countries, and when revolutions in backward regions have not produced a solid point of reference or a credible alternative model, but have themselves fallen into difficulties as a result of the competitive pressure of modern capitalism?

Is the crisis of society continuing to express itself in devastating material contradictions, or producing no more than disappointment, an atomized unhappiness? Do these material contradictions ultimately derive from the production relation, and condense in oppressed social forces capable of assuming a directive role in society? Or do the various prospects for the future depend on a non-hierarchical plurality of contradictions and once more compete within the circuit of elites as their 'unhappy consciousness' and possible options? Can the oppressed social forces unite in a common project, and does or does not the system create its gravedigger in the shape of class antagonism? Finally, and perhaps most important of all, is a systemic break (that is, a different economic and political system) still necessary, or is it possible for a new social order gradually to assert itself in the interstices of the old, using and steering its propulsive force without overturning its constituted power?

On these matters there is a new, more problematic, divergence between communist identity and both radical utopianism and liberal democracy. Neither of the latter is capable of responding to all these questions today in a theoretically rigorous and empirically grounded manner, or of giving an equally convincing answer to each. But it is possible to glimpse some of the answers.

Let us try to give a few examples, without making any claim to exhaustiveness. We shall refer to the 'great issues of our age', especially the new ones that are seemingly most remote from the traditional class conflict, but we shall consider them in their most prosaic, empirically verifiable forms, as they present themselves and operate today.

DEVELOPMENT AND NATURE

No one now denies that the threat of environmental disaster is an explosive problem of our age, a contradiction that people already experience today as an element in the collective imagination. It is a new and far from trivial issue, which not only agitates the vanguards but is forcing broad masses to reconsider the meaning and criteria of development.

Human production and demographic growth have always been based on the assumption that nature is a virtually inexhaustible resource, immune to the consequences of the productive process deployed to utilize it. This belief did not flag, indeed it became all the more unqualified, when science and technology stamped an exponential rate of growth on production, consumption and population in the last few centuries. The myth of science and technology fuelled confidence in their unlimited capacity to absorb the disasters they produced. Nor was it entirely a myth, because even in environmental terms the trade-off between what economic and demographic growth underpinned (hygiene, health, protection against catastrophes) and the costs they involved was indisputably positive.

We now know that this was ceasing to be true. For many natural resources were running short before they could be done without; production had increasingly destructive effects on the environment; this was already worsening the situation with regard to new qualitative needs as well as basic needs of health and survival; and, if this kind of feverish quantitative growth continued, it would lead to real catastrophe in a relatively brief time.

Less clear perhaps is our awareness of two equally evident facts. First, environmental disaster does not only affect the more developed parts of the world but is also reflected, indeed compounded, in backward regions as a result of demographic pressure and breakdown of the old economic fabric based on self-sufficiency. In short, it is the product of development and underdevelopment alike. Second, what is at stake is no longer only the natural external environment but also the social environment (lifestyles, not just the speed of production growth) and even the biological human species (both through effects on physical and mental health, and because of new possibilities opened up by genetic engineering).

These two facts mean that any fundamentalist position, any romantic critique of development, is contradictory and fundamentally unstable; rather, they compel us to establish a link between ecological and social critique, to raise the question of a different kind of development. For the mere slowing of quantitative growth would not be enough to cushion the environmental disaster in Third World countries without resorting to ferocious Malthusianism, and it would be quite illusory to force them into conservation policies while denying them the option of a more expensive road to modernity. Nor can the threat of repressive anti-human uses of genetic engineering be combated simply in the name of preserving human nature, since the attenuation of natural selection by the increased capacity of the weakest to survive compels us to find new ways of averting biological decay.

Nevertheless, it is significant that a high awareness of the scale of these problems finds very little expression in individual and collective behaviour, featuring only sporadically as a criterion for decisions and planning.

But this is precisely where the 'question of capitalism' comes into play, both as an economic system and as a political form.

By its nature, capitalism is based on certain mechanisms that have constituted its historical legitimacy and underpinned its extraordinary dynamism: the market as a guiding standard, the firm as a subject of decision-making, and profit as a motive and as proof of results. The capitalist – or 'entrepreneur', as he is called nowadays – is not only an organizer of production; he takes over various innovations, respecting those mechanisms, stimuli and rules.

But, apart from other implications to which we shall return, all this is closely bound up with the environmental question. For it is this fundamental logic – not a degenerate 'pillage capitalism', however important that has been at certain times and places – which makes it necessary to think of production as the production of commodities, and to calculate productivity mainly, if not only, in a narrow time frame and within the limits of the productive process *sensu stricto*. Indirect or long-term costs cannot enter into the economic calculus of the great majority of decision-makers, just as a development process not involving the expansion of commodities for sale and consumption is systemically incidental or marginal.

It might be objected that new frontiers opened up by modern technology and increased knowledge seem to allow for less resource-hungry development, or that the spread of immaterial goods and services may make the environmental fall-out from development less burdensome. Perhaps, in other words, the contradiction between development and environment applies with somewhat lesser force in post-industrial society.

This is absolutely true, and it offers the material basis for a different logic of development. But reality shows that the investment and location choices characteristic of the system are not taking us in that direction, nor are the prevailing consumption model, the addition of new subjects to the market crush, or the extreme concentration of powers to plan research, technology and growth strategy in the hands of decision-making centres remote from the regions and populations affected by them. Instead, what we sometimes see is the replacement of scarce, and therefore costly, raw materials with artificial products whose impact on the environment or human health is no less uncertain and dangerous; or the dismantling of noxious industrial plants in the capitalist heartlands, to be relocated in other regions where they are even harder to manage, or replaced with totally decentralized but even more polluting forms of production; or the combined consumption of material goods and immaterial goods and services, in forms no less damaging to the urban and natural environment (fast food, city traffic, mass tourism); or minor limitation and regulation of the use of chemical fertilizers, together with export monoculture, intensive farming techniques and shrinking biodiversity; or the ever greater domination of pharmaceutical and biological research by interests and agendas that make its results unreliable and disturbing; or the spread of suburbs and the ghettoization of city centres, leading to a chaotic degradation of life seen at its monstrous worst in the mega-cities of the Third World.

A new spurt in consumerism, for those who can indulge it on an individual basis, is taking place around the need for protection and withdrawal from the consequences of this spiralling collective impoverishment.

This economic mechanism is compounded by political and cultural trends. However grave the environmental question may be, and however much the awareness of it is growing, it still essentially appears as a long-term issue concerning numerous scattered populations; those who will suffer the consequences are often a long way from those who produce them. Or, in particular regions, the problem presents itself as a set of contradictory needs. The political authorities, on the other hand, are intrinsically unfit for planning, tied to short-term consumption, more sensitive to pressure from small but determined social groups than to broad but fluctuating public opinion, organically impotent and, of course, subordinate to big private interests. They therefore produce regulations that remain a dead letter, and, even when their declared intentions are acted upon, these are undermined by far more weighty factors.

Under these conditions, the ecological movements themselves keep oscillating between radicalism on single objectives and chameleon-like *trasformismo*, between an effective and sometimes positive apocalyptic culture and an underlying reticence when they have to take political sides.

As always, of course, we are not speaking of absolute contradictions. Just as it was partly possible at times to modify the spontaneous thrust of the system by steering income distribution or constructing a social state, it may be possible, even in the existing system, to implement 'environmental policies' as the need arises and as awareness develops. But it is much more difficult. For an environmental policy cannot operate only, or mainly, 'downstream' from the productive process, redistributing for various uses the resources that it makes available; such forms of restrictive or reparative intervention would make it not only ineffectual but hugely expensive. Besides, the fate of the environment depends precisely upon long-term choices, whose comparative fruitfulness can be measured only on a global scale.

Powers are needed to intervene prior to the production process, in the setting of research agendas, the making of strategic investment and location decisions, even the organization of the international division of labour; and it is necessary to foster a new public awareness, so that people are capable of conceiving a different hierarchy of needs and experiencing it as their own within a long-term global perspective.

Thus the environmental question not only offers new ground on which a communist project could base its critique of the system, but also provides a momentum to transform and qualitatively enrich that critique, taking it beyond economistic ways of thinking. At the same time, the environmental question needs a communist project and organizational form to unite different social subjects and interests, to identify the real roots of the problems, to assert a power capable of addressing them as a whole, and finally to change people's very minds.

ABUNDANCE AND POVERTY, NEEDS AND CONSUMPTION

The history of society until now has been dominated by the problem of scarcity. Not only have the great majority of men and women been forced to live at the limits of survival, but the appropriation of the surplus product by ruling elites formed the material basis for civilization.

The great historical merit of capitalism is precisely its capacity to channel much of the surplus product into accumulation. This made it possible to accelerate the development of the productive forces to an extraordinary degree, thereby laying the material basis for the broader satisfaction of basic needs, and to involve a growing part of society in the circuit of civilization (education, mobility, socialized labour).

But the history of capitalism has not been one of ever widening prosperity. Indeed, in certain phases ('primitive accumulation', colonialism, the early industrial revolution), the priority given to accumulation and the creation of generic wage-labour produced forms of inequality and exploitation that were even more brutal and widespread than before. In the last hundred years, however, the convergence of two major impulses – the need to develop markets for capitalist production itself, and the rise of mass struggles that modern production made more conscious and organized and the modern state made more capable of political action – eventually created the conditions for growing prosperity and, in many cases, for greater equality. At the peak of this correlation of development, welfare and equality, represented by Fordism, the welfare state and the anti-colonial revolution, the workers' movement found favourable terrain for its struggles, even though at some points the necessity of systemic change seemed to diminish. On this view of things, what is now happening to prosperity in the period of emergent 'post-industrial society'?

The first thing that strikes one is a new tendency to inequality and poverty at the simple level of basic needs.

Not only does the gap in living conditions seem to be widening again between North and South, but a considerable part of the South, trapped between population pressure and the break-up of traditional forms of self-sufficiency, is spiralling downward below subsistence level. Meanwhile, in the most developed parts of the world, income differentials are increasing again after a period of relatively narrowing, and a substantial fringe of society is falling beneath the historical threshold for a minimum existence.

It seems to be the most traditional of all possible contradictions, but in fact it is not traditional at all. The main reason why it is not is that the injustice and poverty appear not as 'residual' or transient phenomena, but as the direct result (or the other side of the coin) of modernity and its governing mechanisms. The other reason is that the new injustice and the new poverty express themselves in cumulative processes of marginalization, creating a large social stratum bereft of hope and pushing it towards degenerate cultural forms (fundamentalist fanaticism or barbarism among new marginal layers in the Third World; racial conflict, widespread violence, rejection of politics in the capitalist heartlands) which may open the way to a spiral of repression of revolt.

To dismiss all this as a secondary issue, manageable with the instruments of aid or welfare with no need to question our lifestyles or modes of production and consumption, seems not only deluded but foolish. Here, after all, is 'ultramodern' terrain for the revival of communist thinking and struggle; this large mass of the marginalized and impoverished is the organic link between the workers' movement and the new social subjects emerging from the qualitative contradictions of post-industrialism.

But our reflections on 'prosperity' cannot end there. If they did, that link would be very difficult to make.

Other aspects concerning the quantity and quality of consumption, and the mechanisms by which consumption needs are actually formed, have been no less important in challenging confidence in a linear relationship between development and growing prosperity. Such confidence has therefore also become problematic in countries or social sectors that participate in the process of enrichment, or hope one day to do so.

The theoretical presupposition underlying the rationality of the capitalist mode of production was the existence of an autonomous system of needs, which formed the basis for demand and hence for the market. This autonomy was always partial and problematic, if only because the order of priority for the satisfaction of needs depended on the distribution of income: that is, on which needs could be translated into effective demand.

And yet, so long as the majority of basic needs remained to be satisfied, the development of production had a secure reference measure, and policies for growth and income distribution converted into rising individual and collective prosperity.

Today this presupposition is beginning to fade. For, now that productive capacity, in some parts of the world, has gone well beyond the basic needs threshold, and now that the productive apparatus and the organization of society are increasingly capable of steering consumption and forming new needs, real prosperity depends on the fact that individuals and society have sufficient income to convert their needs into actual consumption, plus the capacity to enrich the quality of their needs.

This very fact ought to permit an extraordinary leap in civilization: the enrichment of distinctively human needs associated with personal growth and relationships – and previously connotative of upper-class privilege – could for the first time in history become the goal of an entire society. The spread of information, rising levels of culture and emancipation from age-old static systems of relations could open the way to the revaluation of individual freedom, including in the realm of consumption; they could strip away from consumption its repetitive, predetermined, passive character; above all, they could remove its logic of individual appropriation (that which is taken from others) and make it a mediating force in the relationship with others.

Although the new technologies still bear the mark of past history and the present system, they appear to offer important instruments for such an advance, since they permit a gradual reduction in necessary labour time and create the scope for hugely differentiated products. 'Quality' is within the realm of possibility, both in the case of the subject who consumes and in that of the things to be consumed.

But this is not the direction in which 'post-industrial capitalism' seems to be heading. On the contrary, the tendency is to make differentiation the vehicle of the illusory, the serial and the ephemeral, to subordinate consumption even more to changing external imperatives, and to perpetuate elite consumption models in a squalid, second-hand repetition.

The first aspect to consider is the 'inducement of consumption' in accordance with the easiest and most convenient priorities. This is not a new phenomenon: it was present in the classics of economics and has been widely discussed in the past thirty years. What is new is the leap in the manipulative power of the mass media and in their inter-relationship with the major centres of economic power, which makes it more and more possible to transform consumption into a function of production, and to impose world-wide consumption models with an impressive capacity for standardization and deep roots in the consciousness of the masses. New is the fact that, beyond a certain threshold, expanded individual consumption in relation to basic needs (especially mobility and food) generally produces a qualitative decline in the satisfaction of those same needs. New is the fact that other areas of consumption uncoupled from basic needs are much more liable to manipulation. New is the fact that some growing needs of unquestionable importance (health care, education, urban planning) are restricted and marginalized by the mechanisms of inducement, precisely because they can be satisfied only in the form of collective production and consumption. And new too is the fact that the intertwining of individualism and mass culture impels people to look for 'positional' forms of consumption, the ever more vacuous symbols of an immediately self-defeating differentiation.

No less important, though less discussed, is what is happening in the underlying process of needs formation. The idea of human nature or human needs outside history, requiring only the necessary means to express their richness, has no basis in reality. Human needs, beyond the threshold of necessity, are both the product and mirror of social relations. The privilege of upper-class consumption consisted not only in the ability to satisfy one's needs, but often also in the capacity to shape them in a relatively more creative and meaningful way, precisely in relation to the individual's function in society and to the social system of values.

Well, we are dealing with a society where wage labour, though less wearying, remains largely fragmented and operative, while directive or creative labour has income and profit as its overwhelming reference; where education is more and more blatantly subordinate to occupational training, and its wider function supplanted by fast-moving mass media and their message of passivity; where intellectuals have been losing their autonomy and becoming absorbed into the circuit of production; where old schemas of interpersonal relations are giving way to individual atomization, and the logic of the market is invading the most private spheres of life. By its very nature, this society produces subjects who are incapable of expressing qualitatively rich needs, over and above the simple expansion of material consumption. And, instead of generalizing the positive side of upper-class consumption, freeing it from parasitism and privilege, it generalizes the essential poverty of mass consumption and strips from privilege even its quality.

If all this is true, then three things follow from it. 1) New and richer reasons exist for a critique of the society in which we live, as well as more solid ground on which to build a different society by appealing to the needs that affluent consumption deadens, to the diffuse unhappiness fuelled by the blockage and impoverishment of needs, and to real possibilities that the present historical level affords. 2) This critique attacks more directly and radically than ever before the foundations of a certain mode of production and a certain structure of power. The 'alienated character of consumption' does not derive solely from cultural mechanisms or the dominance of technology; in fact, both are bound up with a class contradiction, even if they do not exhaust themselves in it. 3) What is happening in the realm of consumption hinders the formation and unification of an alternative social subject, and so today, more than ever, there is no exit from the vicious circle of integration and revolt without a powerful political intervention; without a subject capable of influencing the major apparatuses that shape individual and collective consciousness, and of promoting a moral and cultural reform, a critique of everyday life and a 'new human type'.

Is this not a strong basis for a communist project and a communist identity, one that is radically new but no less antagonistic to existing society?

THE QUESTION OF WORK

The greatest novelty that capitalism introduced into the history of society related to work. It brought, on the one hand, the progressive transformation of all living labour into wage labour (commodity-producing labour, itself a commodity); and on the other hand, the ceaseless incorporation of living labour into capital, into a system of machines.

Industry was the most effective terrain and vehicle for this process. Here the separation between labour and ownership of the means of production, between managerial-organizational functions and general operative labour, between labour and its product, between 'dead' and 'living' labour (with the former supreme), permitted the most extraordinary increases in productivity. The fragmentation of tasks, and the resulting impoverishment of job content, produced a huge rise in the social capacity of labour; and, by virtue of its homogeneity and cohesion, wage labour acquired a collective bargaining power that offset the decline in individual power associated with job specialization.

All this permitted not only real wage rises but also improvements in conditions (continuous across-the-board reductions in the working day, lower levels of physical exhaustion, bargaining over line speed and the factory environment, and a degree of control over recruitment and work assignment).

Taylorism and collective agreements represented the high point of this process, both in the extreme fragmentation and alienation of labour (the mass worker) and in the control that workers had over the workplace, the growth of collective identity and the political weight of organized labour.

Although the transformation of autonomous or self-sufficient labour into market-oriented wage labour sometimes involved extreme displacement and pauperization, it generally offered a quid pro quo in terms of higher incomes, greater mobility and freedom from suffocating social relations. What does the gradual decline of industry and the factory system imply for the future of labour and its forms?

A totally new opportunity for human emancipation has arisen: both emancipation *from* work and emancipation *of* work. The further reductions in the working day that are now possible, indeed necessary in order to provide work for everyone, offer space not only for relaxation and entertainment but also for a widening of interests and social activity beyond the horizon of 'paid work', without which free time becomes a hollow and frustrating state of restless agitation.

At the same time, productive activity has become increasingly necessary and possible in sectors where wage labour cannot ensure either control over employment or a sufficient degree and quality of involvement. This applies to major collective services such as health care and education, to cultural activity and the distribution of information, and to the organization of leisure time.

In industry itself, complex new technologies, a more flexible and differentiated product range, and expanded functions of organization, planning and quality control, point beyond the great concentrations of production to a decentralization of operational decisions, requiring greater skills and a higher level of active participation and cooperation.

Finally, the increase in average cultural levels, or at least in the amount of time spent in education, together with the general availability of high-speed information circuits, helps to make roles more mobile and to socialize management and productive strategies (the main entrepreneurial functions being connected more to overall organization than to individual capacities for risk-taking and command).

Now, some of these labour reorganization processes have gone ahead through simple force of circumstance, as they should, even in the context of the existing social system: for example, the growth of diffuse entrepreneurial activity in services and industry, as decentralized points in a productive cycle governed by large-scale concentration, or market interstices unsuited to large-scale enterprise; the growth of a stratum of workers involved, however peripherally, in the management of large businesses; and the spread of jobs and roles with a high professional content in all sectors of the economy. The surprising productivity successes of the 'Italian model' in certain sectors, and of the (quite different) Japanese model in others, are widely recognized to stem in large part from the social capacity to promote and mobilize these new and diverse job-creating energies.

This is not the main tendency, however.

What we face are two disturbing, and closely interconnected, macroscopic phenomena. The first is the new mass unemployment and the growth of precarious forms of employment. Despite a stable population level, the labour supply has been rising throughout the West as a result of profound and irreversible social trends such as the declining productive and reproductive role of the family, increased life expectancy, and the irrepressible need of everyone – particularly women – to have their own independent livelihood and mode of insertion into society. Job opportunities are generally declining, however, or do not offer an income level or quality of work that everyone finds acceptable. A sizeable and increasing section of the population therefore does not find steady employment, while some of the demand for labour can only be met by immigrants.

The fact that unemployment or underemployment does not appear suddenly, as part of the business cycle, but represents a chronic and gradually rising tendency, particularly affecting groups (young people, women, senior citizens) who survive on benefits or family support, means that the problem is less immediately explosive. But it also means that the phenomenon is more serious in the long term, since it results in systematic and permanent marginalization from the mainstream labour market, and expresses itself in forms of dislocation that damage the whole society (drugs, violence, gang culture and organized crime).

No doubt much of this is linked to a particular phase in the economic crisis and the restructuring of production: that is, to the decades-long fall in growth rates, new labour-saving technologies, the irreversible decline of certain traditional sectors, and the elimination of old occupations or roles at an initially faster pace than new ones are created. It is therefore possible that unemployment will decline as a result of renewed growth, the take-off of new sectors of production and effective retraining schemes.

We simply need to ask ourselves – as we shall do in a moment – how things stand today from this point of view; whether a new period of extensive growth is in sight, and, if so, when it will come and at what price.

But it seems to us that, in the new unemployment and job insecurity, we can and should see something deeper and permanent, which touches precisely on the overall question of work in a post-industrial society.

It is now generally recognized that, at least in the industrial sector and the production of material goods for sale, the developed countries are unlikely to return to stable growth, whatever their economic circumstances, and that for them stagnation, if not rapid decline, in employment levels is an irreversible tendency. It may be possible to recover from degenerative processes of advanced deindustrialization (as the United States is trying to do, and regions such as southern Italy should be doing), and certain industries or products (such as steel or basic petrochemicals) may be replaceable with others. But the fact is that by its very nature – not only because of various temporary objectives – the present technological revolution does better at producing the same goods more efficiently than at creating new ones; that the demand for the new goods it produces is rather less elastic, and that their unit cost and labour content soon start to fall; and that, in their case, productivity rises much faster than production, so that more labour is shaken out than is taken on. In short, not only will industry lose relative weight in the total labour of society – as it has been doing for some time – but the developed countries will not experience another phase of sharply rising employment.

Furthermore, it is doubtful that this tendency can be reversed through the extension of modern development to new areas of the world. For, not only does the present shape of the world set major limits to this, but, in comparison with forty years ago, the application speed of new technology is so great, and technological supremacy so hard to convert into steady commodity flows, that new processes of industrialization rapidly threaten competition in the consumer goods sector that more than offsets the absorption of investment goods from the dominant power. In any event, a new international division of labour would not result in major all-round expansion of the industrial base in the capitalist heartlands. It would probably take the form of either a trade-off between material goods and know-how, or a surge of financial speculation.

The basic issue for developed societies is therefore whether a new type of production and consumption – not material goods and industry, but immaterial goods and services – can offer adequate long-term outlets for the labour supply, comparable to those that emerged with the historical passage from an agrarian to an industrial economy.

The analogy certainly raises some doubts. For, in the advanced societies, what we call the service sector has for some time been undergoing constant – and, in some respects, hypertrophied – expansion. In a number of traditional services, developed under official auspices and funded by continual industrial growth, the costs have proved unsustainable, and new technologies themselves have permitted a rationalization of work and the elimination of overmanning. Since the sectors in question often fail to cover real needs, and since their institutional structure is more likely to guarantee job security, it is possible this tendency will be curbed. But it remains difficult to see how greater efficiency in those services will consistently create new jobs.

Our hopes should rather focus on new types of services, which replace residues of self-sufficiency, provide support to industrial forms (applied research, insurance and finance, consultancy, marketing and legal assistance) or produce new immaterial goods (training, information, health care, cultural activities, regional administration).

This brings us to the fundamental point. As Alfred Sauvy and Giorgio Ruffolo have noted, two conditions are necessary for a new sector to create employment more quickly than the old sector sheds it: 1) productivity in the new sector must on average be higher, so that it can offer better wages while leaving a margin for growth; and 2) production in the new sector must grow faster than productivity. Industry did indeed achieve this in its time. But it is not so easy in the case of the 'new services', some of which replace non-market labour with wage labour (fast food, personal services) or answer new social and individual demands (from security guards to services connected with traffic congestion), which, useful and necessary as they may be, have considerably lower levels of productivity than any industrial activity. Others, such as finance and distribution services to firms, do not produce new goods, are part of the costs of production, and, however profitable, result at least partly in parasitism and checks on growth. Still others – the newest and most promising – involve the production of immaterial goods. Here the form of stable waged employment is rather less suitable than in industry, not all end products actually sell, and both production and consumption have a social character, involving deferred profitability and a less direct, more diffuse utility. On the whole, then, productivity in capitalist terms is relatively low in these new services. And, precisely because the labour market functions as a market, job opportunities either come with inferior wages and conditions (and are therefore aimed at layers without social protection) or expand too slowly to satisfy the growth in demand.

So, there is good reason to believe that steady employment at a decent wage is tending to stagnate, if not decline, in the advanced societies.

This being so, the redistribution of work becomes a structurally important and strategically central issue. The idea of such a social operation is not something that a capitalist system is capable of conceiving. Yet the general rise in labour productivity, partly expressed in reduced work time, means that it has kept recurring for the best part of a century. In periods when aggregate productivity is flat, however, the system's invariable tendency has been to reduce total work time by means of endemic unemployment, underemployment, part-time work, and lack of security for general unskilled labour, while lengthening the working day for stable, highly skilled employees. Nor is naked capitalist interest the only obstacle to a redistribution of work, since employed workers cannot reduce their hours if it means losing part of their income. A cut in working hours is therefore impossible unless a way is found to increase individual productivity in sectors where waged employment does not function well, and to ensure greater prosperity by other means than the pay cheque – through modern forms of non-market work and a revaluation of socially useful activities outside the form of sellable commodities.

Similar points apply to the second major phenomenon we face, which concerns not the quantity but the quality of work. A new polarization is taking place in the most advanced societies today. On the one hand there is an enhancement of skills and professionalism, itself highly differentiated and hierarchical, among a minority in society, at the price of atomized specialization and subordination to production goals (the 'mass intellectual' working for capital), so that personal enrichment through work proves more apparent than real, measured more in terms of income or power than freedom or meaning. Here the Japanese model is paradigmatic for the future. On the other hand a process of further fragmentation, de-skilling and subordination of labour takes extreme forms among the insecure, downtrodden service proletariat, but also affects stable jobs in large corporations, reaching far beyond directly productive manual labour into the sphere of white-collar work, commerce, health care and public employment; the image of an information society based on high skills, creative labour and workforce involvement is sheer mystification. Here American society is a good illustration: the much-vaunted creation of millions of new jobs is a function of the new de-skilling, sometimes beyond the limits of social maladjustment and neo-illiteracy.

We would not argue that these phenomena exhaust the horizon of work, nor that it is impossible to envisage or impose employment policies and revaluations of work that might have some effect even within the present system. We only want to stress four points. a) In the post-industrial future, there will be new and different, though no less abundant, material to fuel the class conflict between capital and labour. b) The major issue of employment and the quality of work will appear more, not less, bound up with the essential logic of capitalism. c) Even more than yesterday or today, tomorrow will pose the question of gradually overcoming (not only protecting) wage labour, and perhaps the more radical one of freedom from work. d) Structural changes in the labour market are weakening the homogeneity and direct power of labour; its unity and destiny will depend less than in the past on trade unions and more on a political project, and on instruments that directly impact on the structure of the state, the economy, technological strategies and educational apparatuses.

Is this radical yet underdeveloped part of the Marxist critique of capitalism – the emancipation of human labour from its commodity character – not a sufficiently solid base on which to rebuild a communist identity?

THE IMPOTENCE OF THE SOVEREIGN

The infatuation with neoliberalism that has marked the whole of the past decade is beginning to fade – not because of changing fashions, but because of hard facts. The major social contradictions of which we have just been speaking now stare everyone in the face, making it harder to trust that the market and the 'animal spirits' of individualism, released from the chains of politics and public intervention, can provide a brighter future for the community and the individual. Even those who think it unnecessary, or indeed dangerously mistaken, to question the capitalist basis of the economy are again forced to recognize the wisdom of regulating and balancing it with an efficient and independent public power.

The waning of neoliberalism is matched by the recent fortunes of its friend-enemy: movementism. For hard facts also eat away at the notion that diffuse struggles and the molecular growth of alternative cultures and movements expressing social solidarity will suffice to correct the ferocity of the market and individual competition. Each day brings crushing evidence of the logic that, despite appearances, really governs the system, and of its capacity to fragment, integrate or redirect whatever opposes or challenges it.

The question of democracy in the strong sense is therefore coming back onto the agenda: that is, democracy not only as a system of guarantees for the autonomy and freedom of action of individuals and groups, but also as a political and institutional form capable of condensing a general will and interest, equipped with effective instruments to ensure that they prevail.

This, however, is precisely the terrain on which the situation of the Left is so paradoxical. At the moment when it might have been celebrating complete success and regained unity, it displays a new and disturbing impotence. Let us explain.

Modern democracy came into being in a direct relationship with the capitalist system, and the mark of this origin was present within it as an underlying contradiction: political equality among individuals who are *un*equal in their real power and effective rights. The 'abstractly equal' right of citizens covered over the reality of class domination and guaranteed its objective character, but at the same time offered a principle and a powerful instrument to those wishing to change things. The history of Western political thought and institutions in the past two centuries is entirely dominated by this tension. On the one hand, the liberal state guarantees that subjects who are unequal in their fortune, talents and power are formally able to compete with one another; on the other, universal suffrage provides an instrument to correct that inequality and allows everyone to exercise their essential rights. It was not only a tension between the logic of political liberty and the logic of social justice. For political liberty itself was only meaningful in so far as citizens had the minimum education, income and security to enjoy it; while the ruling class was prepared to revoke the political institutions it had created as soon as the substance of its social domination was threatened.

We might say that, for more than a century in the West, the workers' movement that had grown up outside and against the political system became its champion and guarantor – the whole workers' movement. Even those like Lenin, who dwelled on the limitations of bourgeois democracy, the illusory character of parliamentarism and the need for a 'proletarian dictatorship', not only recognized the representative state as an 'enormously favourable terrain for the class struggle' but insisted obsessively that socialism called for even broader and more radical forms of political democracy. So, the true paradox of this century is that movements that criticized liberal constitutions often defended their formal elements more effectively, and with greater sacrifices, than did the most convinced apologists for those constitutions.

Yet what divided the workers' movement for a whole epoch was precisely the question of political democracy. For the Leninists held that the historical period in which democracy could coexist with a capitalist order had come to an end, and that socialist democracy could blossom even while denying – or only by denying – the exercise of universal political rights. It might be argued that these convictions were justifiable in their time, and that they were in the end part of a real movement that contributed much to a general process of liberation and emancipation, including politically. But there can be no doubt that they were formulated, and practised, as a general theory of a new and higher form of political power. And at that level Leninism suffered a harsh defeat, whose full scale is only today becoming apparent.

As far as the Soviet Union is concerned, Lenin's hopes of a higher democracy (workers' councils, recallable mandates, elimination of the state apparatus as a separate force) not only clashed with the problems of building socialism in an isolated and backward country; it gradually proved incompatible with a political system (single party, centralized power, equation of dissent with the class enemy) that hardened into bureaucratic privilege, inculcated political passivity in the masses, petrified critical thought into dogmatism, and finally paralysed the country's social and productive dynamism. History thus demonstrates that the full exercise of political democracy is not less, but more, important for socialism than it has been for capitalism.

Meanwhile in the West, first the struggle against fascism, then the experience of the welfare state showed that political democracy – even in a bourgeois society and in the form of a representative state – offers huge scope for specific changes in social relations. It may result in real and substantial gains (mass education, trade union bargaining, social security systems), and permits continual growth in the organization and consciousness of the exploited mass of the population.

Everything now suggests that the long and troubled historical controversy is at an end. All the countries of mature capitalism (including Spain, Greece and Portugal, and tomorrow perhaps Korea, Taiwan and Brazil) are now governed by representative democratic institutions that no significant political force or cultural component seeks to subvert. The state decides on the destination, and organizes the spending, of more than half the national income, intervening directly in a number of sectors of production. Education, health care and pensions are largely organized as universal public services. The level of education and information ensures that public opinion has a certain sway. There are powerful trade unions and professional associations, and social conflicts are a permanent fact of life. At the same time, a truly revolutionary process of self-critical reflection has begun in the Soviet Union around the question of political democracy.

In this situation, we used to say that the Western Left could celebrate a historic victory and rebuild a new unity. A political form for which it long fought, and which is largely its own historical achievement, has asserted itself as a universal model and the most realistic instrument for the progressive transformation of society.

It would therefore appear that, at least on the level of political institutions, a critique of the system no longer serves any purpose. That the question of a 'third way' does not exist, and that a communist identity and tradition have rightly disappeared, without regrets, into the mainstream of democratic thought *tout court*.

But, as often happens, the hour of success threatens to be also the hour of a rude awakening. Just when the representative democratic state has achieved mature expression, with the power to intervene in the whole of society and to make popular sovereignty and equal civil rights a reality, it seems to be regressing in a new form to its origins: that is, to an appearance behind which a quite different de facto power grows and operates unchallenged.

What we have in mind is not only the ideological and practical attack on public intervention in the economy, on employment protection policies, universal welfare benefits, labour market regulation and formalized trade union bargaining – an attack that has done grave and lasting damage, but that might be part of a particular economic phase and a transitory relationship of political forces. Nor do we have in mind only the fact that, in most parts of the world – economically underdeveloped as they are – political history has recently been going into reverse, as the states that emerged from great liberation movements degenerate into oligarchies riddled with privilege and arbitrary power, or into fanatical theocracies: all of which might be the reflection of an economic impasse and a cultural dependence that political democracy in the leading countries could, and should, seek to modify.

We are mainly referring to something more profound and general, intrinsic to the political institutions of a capitalism turning post-industrial: the growing structural irrelevance of politics. What used to be, for good or ill, the nerve centre of decision-making, the instrument of an armour-plated hegemony, the principal arena of the most heated conflicts, is tending to become an empty ritual for rubber-stamping what has already happened, a mediation and administrative support for power that exists elsewhere.

The empirical evidence of the last few decades is enough to raise the alarm. Is it not true that, during those decades, various coalitions and political forces in Europe have taken turns to form governments, pursuing the same set of policies in certain periods and another set in other periods, following ties of obligation and impulse whose strength overrules theirs? Is it by chance that the advanced capitalist country where the state has most effectively operated a plan for economic growth is Japan, the one without a system of political alternation, the one resting on a committee of all the major economic powers, a consensus of organized clans and clienteles and a high degree of conformism among the masses?

In short, if people are losing their esteem or passion for politics, it is because they think it not only alien and corrupt but, above all, pointless.

What lies behind all this? Is it, as many believe, mainly the bloated inefficiency of a state machine which, apart from being extremely costly, has yielded too much to the purposive logic of welfarism and the functional logic of bureaucracy? Is there a congestion and paralysis of political decision-making, an organic incapacity to draw up and impose priorities, precisely because democratic powers are too diffuse and a thousand rights of veto are present in society?

That is certainly a factor. And it tells us that the existing political-institutional system has reached crisis point, entailing a need for innovation and non-neutral choices.

But there are also deeper phenomena, linked precisely to the epochal shift of which we have been speaking.

The first set of phenomena stem from the economic globalization process and the force dominating it: finance and the multinational corporations. It is strange that something of such obvious and overwhelming significance for the real shape of power remains so marginal in political reflection, and that the whole Left accepts it uncritically, or anyway as a neutral fact, about which very little can be done.

The progressive unification of markets and technologies is not in itself a novelty. What is new are the enormous acceleration of this tendency, and the power mechanisms that govern and sustain it. I am thinking, above all, of the headlong growth of international centres of political and economic management, endowed with normative as well as market powers: the European Economic Community, the International Monetary Fund, the league of central banks, the effectively unified international system of scientific research. These structures, which are taking over the most strategic areas of political power, elude any form of democratic control or influence: not only because they reject it in principle (IMF) and the institutions that should guarantee it have no real power (the European Parliament), but because it would anyway be a formal control or power, one that lacked a political subject minimally capable of self-organization, understanding and involvement. What is developing is a kind of federal state 'by conquest', where the king, a narrow economic and technocratic oligarchy, faces a 'people' divided by national histories and local corporate interests and capable of mounting only sectoral resistance (one thinks of European agricultural policy, or the Babel of trade union organizations and the social state). Universal suffrage, the much-vaunted lynchpin of modern democracy, plays little or no role in the decisive choices.

Next, we need to consider the new reality of finance and the multinationals. Not only has their weight grown enormously in individual countries and sectors, but their base and role have changed. Compared with the still recent past, the great economic concentrations give less and less priority to a national base and industrial activity. First and foremost, they are a financial force stretching across sectors, with a global, or at least continent-wide, theatre of operations and the function of producing organizational capacities, research programmes and market organization, integrating apparatuses of training and information, organizing myriad dependent firms, and guiding the choices made by governments and major institutions.

These are private power centres that play a full role in the social planning of development, with their own mass base (shareholders) and their own system of forming a consensus.

Here an even larger part of political power eludes universal suffrage. It is not only that big capital has the means to stifle or distort the exercise of democracy, but simply that it can commandeer state power and empty democracy of any real meaning. It is rather pathetic to imagine that this power could be 'governed' with the traditional instruments of the national state, or that it could be regulated by anti-trust legislation or the like.

Finally, globalization also means a uniform consumption model, integrated information systems and unrestricted circulation of people's savings: in other words, a mass of micro-decisions standardized in accordance with objective mechanisms and interests that the power system determines, and which radically limit, from below as well as from the top, the real scope for intervention on the part of what is still constitutionally defined as the democratic national state.

To counter this transfer of real power, the democratic state should field a strong resolve and capacity to pursue forceful long-term projects. But here we come up against a second, no less grave, set of phenomena that threaten a crisis of democracy. Let us mention a few in no particular order, without drawing out the deeper links that unite them.

The decline of the large factory, the segmentation of occupational profiles, the varied and often random or arbitrary distribution of income, the concentration of social injustice in marginalized or subaltern sectors and zones: all this makes social conflict less unified and transparent, and removes the cohesive, organized subject that for decades breathed life into political democracy. The pervasive drumbeat of the mass media not only makes it possible to manipulate consensus – which is obvious – but shapes an inherently atomized public opinion and clouds political awareness with a uniform and jumbled surfeit of ephemeral stimuli and data. These objective elements, together with an ideological crisis linked to general social attitudes, produce the decline of mass parties as activist organizations capable of unifying interests and behaviour in a common culture and project. Massively expanded public intervention in a thousand areas of life, and in the management of national income, involves a specific trade-off between a corporatized society, which offers consent in return for protection and favours, and a layer of political professionals who are also tending to become a corporation. Politics in the strong sense, in so far as it can survive at all, cuts itself off from this consensus machine and moves into a parallel realm of power, where the real ruling class, very small in size, unifies governmental, technocratic and economic elites, but by its nature interprets market impulses and acts forcefully only in response to them.

Democracy without hegemony transmutes into a ritual, a reign of the ephemeral, degenerating in the corporate market and, in the best of cases, merely dealing effectively with tasks and objectives that are decided elsewhere. Meanwhile, a parallel oligarchic power grows not only as a fact but as a necessity.

The tasks and objectives of the state do not diminish, therefore. But the state no longer plays a propulsive, synthetic role, and the people that legitimates it is less and less sovereign, at most its opposite party. The Leviathan is no less invasive, but it has now been tamed.

Some would say that none of this is so serious: that, if a way is found to correct the symptoms of degeneration, this kind of 'light politics' – in which the state is no more than guarantor and administrator in the hands of those with the necessary know-how – will leave society free to come alive, and finally banish the political and ideological spectre of totalitarianism. We do not think this likely, since the resulting universe is no less totalitarian in its apparent complexity. In any event, if these are the only political institutions we have, the idea of 'governing' development, of changing the sign of modernity in accordance with a collective project, has no credible foundation.

Some classical, and radical, themes of the Marxist critique of the bourgeois state are thus re-emerging in the most modern reality.

The first such theme is the mystified, illusory, ultimately unsustainable character of a democracy that is neither able nor willing to attack the sanctuaries of an ever more centralized and determinant economic power, or to take public control of areas that the socialization of the productive forces already makes intrinsically public, well beyond functions of income redistribution and including the very mechanism of accumulation and the fundamental choices of resource allocation. Not everything can be planned, to be sure. But it is absurd that, on the pretext of the market, such planning as is possible is becoming a function of the private economy.

A second theme is the need for an internationalism that matches the process of global unification, offering a real force with the capacity to manage and control it democratically – and, in the process, valuing the distinctive richness of national identities against a pure standardization that feeds the resurgence of particularism.

We should not delude ourselves that it is possible to influence the process of supranational unification if the ruling classes are the only forces that unite culturally and organizationally; political institutions must not only sanction certain rights, but be occupied by real forces capable of upholding them.

The final theme is the need for a collective political subject: one capable of imposing a complex long-range design on immediate impulses and particularist interests, and capable of promoting cultural and moral reform among those who wish to change society, but are constantly conditioned by its values and mechanisms. Democracy is not alive without a collective sovereign, and that collective sovereign cannot exist in the form of an atomized multitude, a jumbled mix of impulses and cultures: fragmentation is not pluralism but disguised uniformity.

These classical themes, however, now appear in a thoroughly new form, or one so ancient that the memory of it has been lost. For the statist solution dominant until now in the workers' movement has not only proved inadequate and costly, but seems more than ever powerless to solve the problem of democracy. Public power run as bureaucratic power is caught in a spiral of inefficiency and arbitrariness, which causes the masses to reject the public sphere as such. If popular sovereignty is confined to the selection of a representative at the polling booth, it not only marginalizes the section of the population who exercise no other powers, but produces in them a regression to cultures of subalternity and demands for protection rather than participation in government, transforming sovereignty into consent, and consent into the market. To govern society from the centre, or simply with laws, is a sheer illusion. In today's world, the development of democracy goes together with daily, structured appropriation of the various functions of government, with a socialization of power, with a gradual withering of the separateness of the state. And none of that is possible without questioning the statism reflected in the organizational forms of the workers' movement: that is, a conception of the party as the exclusive locus and instrument of politics (distinct from a mass movement as locus and instrument of social-economic conflict), not as the stimulus and synthesis of a whole system of autonomous political movements, through which a multiplicity of social subjects together weld a new historical bloc. The very richness of a long-cultivated democratic field, the cultural diversity of the political subjects confusedly yet actively present in society, the thousand articulations of state power resulting from a succession of experiences and struggles, the irrepressible though subaltern multiplicity of national subjects: all this offers extraordinary material for a similar but very difficult attempt to reconstruct democracy on new foundations.

In short, and perhaps a little crudely: to recognize democracy as a universal value does not at all mean abandoning the old Leninist, and especially Togliattian, assertion of a link between democracy and socialism. In fact, we may today speak rather of a two-way link, whereby each element is not only essential to the other but confers a different form and content upon it.

Does not all this have something to do with the search for a 'third way'? Is there not a strong basis for a refounding of communist identity around the more complex and controversial question of the institutions and forms of politics?

The various points as well as the general argument we have summarily presented concerning the 'major contradictions' of our time would appear sufficient to define a fairly solid, non-subjectivist, field of possibility, but not to provide any reasonable certainty. As a first step, these contradictions allow us to affirm the following.

1) Capitalist society, as it emerges from its new transformations, does not appear either to be unified or to be governed by a stable hegemony. On the contrary, it is already today – and will be more tomorrow – shot through with material and ideological conflicts that do not concern only peripheral or marginal areas, nor express only needs for liberation that are still historically unripe and limited to a minority in society. These conflicts and needs also assert themselves at the heights of modernity and involve the great bulk of society. If their depth is not duly appreciated, and a rational way forward is not offered, they may generate a slide towards barbarism.

2) The contradictions besetting society are and will be less and less straightforwardly attributable to the conflict between capital and labour. In fact, the conflict between capital and labour can itself find full expression only if its contents and goals are enriched to include a critique of the quality of development, and not only of its quantity and the distribution of its product. The autonomy of new social subjects and new needs must be recognized (ecology, women's liberation, species diversity, meaningful work and consumption), as these are essential to lend hegemonic capacity to the struggle of the working masses, and full scope to its emancipatory project. Yet all these various contradictions are linked more profoundly than ever to the structures and values of the capitalist mode of production: that is, they pose in even more radical terms the problem of overcoming it, while offering the bases on which this might be done. If this link is not grasped, and if unity is not achieved around it, it seems inevitable not only that the new movements and subjects will be defeated, but that they will come into conflict with one another and take part in a passive revolution. In this light, the class struggle continues to be the engine or nodal point of an alternative.

3) A different society cannot come about through a sudden break, a revolution from above; it must advance as a long transformation of the mode of production and consumption, of technologies and ideas and lifestyles, both individual and collective. But this new society does not grow in tiny increments within the interstices of existing society (as was the case with the bourgeois revolution): it

needs power, a project, an organization; it is a social transformation that must not only conclude but originate in an antagonism, a hegemony, a political rupture. All this definitely offers a solid basis and possible mass audience for the full recovery, or the refoundation, of a communist identity. Above all, it shows up as quite abstract and unrealistic any idea that the Left today can present itself as a credible alternative by conforming still further to the system. For that would mean no longer speaking (except rhetorically) about the most acute problems in society; it would mean cutting oneself off from the needs of the most oppressed, and losing a strong motivation for one's own political commitment.

But the above considerations also point to another side of reality that it would be impossible, or dishonest, to censor. They realistically force us to recognize the following.

1) The social forces antagonistic to the system today appear largely divided, or boxed in, between subalternity and revolt, integration and utopianism; a unifying perspective still lies far beyond their practice and culture. In addition to what we have already stressed in relation to the advanced societies, the Third World has been undergoing the regression of national bourgeoisies, new agrarian contradictions, and the emergence of a huge, marginal proletariat eking a precarious existence in the cities. Meanwhile, in the countries of 'actually existing socialism', passivity and contradictory impulses make it difficult for the working class and the broad masses to play a role on the social stage.

2) The main political forces that might possibly counter this fragmentation are still sunk in a deep crisis of culture and identity. Apart from the trends we have already noted in the Western Left, the Soviet Union is witnessing an extraordinary and unexpected reform process, but its historic turn is based on a theoretical model and will take quite a while to settle down, recover and take effect. Gorbachev speaks sincerely, and correctly, of 'more socialism and more democracy', but it is difficult for this to become immediately evident or successful, and produce reforms instead of crisis.

3) The redefinition of a communist identity appears to be a long haul theoretically and culturally, which involves switching away from a decades-long mode of thinking. It has to pass through a period of trial and error, with all the risks of eclecticism and false trails, within a horizon dominated by new bourgeois ideas and old

working-class ideas; it will require a long educational effort before it acquires the strength of a diffuse culture, a new world view and a common store of deeply rooted ideas.

In conclusion, it seems that we can give the following answer to our initial question: for the PCI and the whole European Left, the refoundation of an anti-systemic identity is a necessary and possible condition for a political revival. But it is not an easy condition to fulfil, nor is it sufficient by itself.

On the contrary, it can happen only in so far as a crisis of the system persists and grows more acute in economic and political terms, creating scope for intervention to force through partial yet trenchant structural changes around which a longer-term perspective can take shape. If, instead, the capitalist system attains economic growth and relative political stability in the near future, it is hard to see how the main forces of the Left will again manage to express a strong anti-systemic identity in respect of long-term perspectives. In that case, the 'main contradictions of our epoch' would probably manifest themselves in the form of a diffuse malaise, scattered experiences of struggle and eccentric cultural statements, threatening over time to regress rather than move beyond the present state of society. And a force such as the Italian Communist Party would find it very difficult to avoid decline and growing conformism. That is why any serious reflection on the PCI, and more generally on the European Left, must mainly be tested on the terrain of analysis, prediction and 'phased' proposals.

THE PARTY FORM

The matter of the party is the one on which we must honestly recognize that Occhetto's turn has greater justification, but also the one on which his proposed solution is most debatable and dangerous.

The justification is that collective theoretical reflection has been especially impoverished with regard to this problem, and practical innovation timid and inconclusive. There has been some renewal, but by force of circumstance; the new has been superimposed on the old, in the absence of a project or real decisions. Without the injection of new energies, experiences and cultures, and without a change in organizational forms, the 'instrument' therefore now seems to everyone incapable of putting even the best policies to good use.

But then it must be asked what kind of break in continuity is required, tilted in which direction. What are the real 'evils' that need to be corrected or excised? What kind of party can be useful in the transformed society – and for the process of transforming it?

What is developing is the idea of a modern 'light party' – not light in the sense of low membership (that would, if anything, be an unintended consequence), but in the sense that its members and activists have less weight in relation to the electorate and regional associations. It means a party that uses the skills offered in the intellectual marketplace; that marshals its forces around specific issues and programmes; that aims to listen and to interpret (a part of) society more than to transform it – an instrument more than a subject, and above all a form of institutional representation and electoral aggregation.

Now, there can be no doubt that this marks a profound break, not only with certain traditional forms of Communist organization – those at which criticism has been easily and rightly levelled (centralism, discipline, political activism as an all-absorbing practice, and so on) – but also with their theoretical foundation. A break, in other words, with the idea that the party should be not only 'for the workers' but 'of the workers' – the instrument through which a class that by its nature occupies subaltern roles, within a subaltern culture, gradually but directly turns itself into a ruling class, and without which the proletariat (different in this respect from the bourgeoisie) cannot become a class 'for itself'. In fact, we might add that such a break is even more radical with regard to Gramsci's conception of the party than to Lenin's. In the Leninist model (at least until the advent of socialism), there was always a real dichotomy between, on the one hand, a proletarian mass confined in an economic-corporatist logic and politically mobilized only at certain moments for general objectives, and, on the other hand, the cadre party bearing a 'science of revolution', basically identified with the science of seizing power. Gramsci, by contrast, posited an intellectual and moral revolution – the collective self-education of an entire class – as the central premise of hegemony, and sought a material basis for it in the dialectic between proletariat and intelligentsia, or between working-class practice and pre-modern values present in the society and culture. The party was the locus and instrument of this not only because it was an activist mass party, but because it was a 'collective intellectual'. To tell the truth, this conception never materialized in an actual party (not even Togliatti's new party, at its best moments), but nor was it simply confined to books. Before, and especially after, Gramsci, one of the original features of the Italian workers' movement (even of the old Prampolinian socialism[1]) was precisely its function as a civilizing force, provider of a collective ethical and cultural foundation that Italy's bourgeois revolution had never had. In short, a break of no little import.

The first point to make, however, is that the break now being proposed is not at all with the type of party that dominates politics in the West – the type that the PCI has often become in practice, and towards which it spontaneously tends.

What is being proposed as an 'innovation' tends to equate with the 'party form' as it presents itself in today's Western democracies. This helps us to understand it better. For when we look at the facts, it is easy to see that a so-called 'light party' of this kind – even if it is on the Left – is not light at all, and that it has a rather peculiar way of 'listening to society'. It is a 'light party' that compensates for its tenuous links with the masses and its poor connective tissue by strongly emphasizing the personal role of the 'leader'; that is run by power apparatuses no less complacent and aloof than the old ones, by an establishment of almost irremovable parliamentarians, information and administration technicians, managers of cooperatives and trade union bureaucrats; that it has to build a consensus mainly by using the mass media (or, rather, seeking its not disinterested support) and by mediating between various corporate interests, good and bad. The direct consequence is a political passivity of the subaltern classes, both outside its ranks (voter absenteeism) and within them ('how can you become a leader if you don't have the know-how or the power?'). The direct consequence is a kind of electoral consensus that does not hold together and cannot withstand harsh tests of government – hence a watering down of programme, and a 'listening to society' that selects and respects the essence of the existing balance of forces.

1. Camillo Prampolini (1859–1930): a founder of the Italian Socialist Party in 1895, and a leading figure in its gradualist–reformist wing.

'Low-profile reformism' becomes less a choice than a necessity. We are not only describing conservative and centrist parties (which in Italy take on the character of a party-state), but also trends within the 'progressive' parties: the US Democratic Party, the French or Spanish Socialist parties. To some extent the same is already happening in the PCI.

Everyone in the West knows, and some say, that this is the greatest weakness of the Left: a democratic deficit that exposes it to electoral abstention by the poor, media blackmail, and the cultural hegemony of its opponents.

None of this is fortuitous or due simply to political errors; it is directly attributable to the new features in society that the Left would like to address, and has to address, by renewing the party form.

Let us schematically mention a few points already touched on.

a) Segmentation of society. The working class itself is becoming much more differentiated, by physical location and function or level within the production process; and greater social mobility (spontaneous or forced) is continually subtracting from its vanguards. The importance of intellectual workers is growing, but they are heavily conditioned by their formative culture and the role they take on. Intellectuals in the narrow sense are an organic part of powerful, structured apparatuses. A large part of 'the poor' consists of marginal layers (the unemployed, pensioners, precarious workers). The 'new subjects' associated with horizontal contradictions in society are by their nature physically dispersed and often at odds with one another.

b) The role of the mass media enables them not only to manipulate political decisions, but also to mould cultures, lifestyles and values, especially among subaltern classes, and to keep shaping and reshaping the common sense of the times; this gives public opinion a confused and indecisive character. This is the typical constituency of the 'primaries', the lynchpin of the electoral machines in the United States.

c) The real power behind (and indeed thanks to) the apparent plurality is highly concentrated, and claims to act objectively on the grounds that its decisions are the only rational ones possible.

d) Last but not least, although the choice of 'democracy' and its associated rules is correct and obligatory, it comes at the price of establishing for decades a large stratum of political professionals, whose everyday existence integrates them into the modes of thinking and acting (and often also the privileges) of the dominant layers in society. The parties of the Left, then, not only occupy the state and society, but are in turn occupied by them.

As a result of the changes under way, if there are to be real reforms (I do not speak of a revolution), it is more necessary than ever that the protagonists of change should have an organized, autonomous subjectivity that makes them capable of self-transformation. In this sense, the question of an activist party that not only has a 'mass' character but operates as a collective intellectual should absolutely not be consigned to the archives; and to do no more than update it, rather than treat it as a problem to be discussed, would be to surrender to an absolute *continuismo*. On the other hand, it seems absurd to throw away an experience that has been of such vital significance.

What would real innovation mean, theoretically and practically?

The PCI was only ever partly an 'activist party with a mass character that operated as a collective intellectual'. For some time it has no longer been that at all; but it could not and should not have remained the way in which it used to be conceived. As regards its mass character, let us start with some factual observations, rather than with how the Party thinks of itself. There is a need for in-depth research and analysis, but some points stand out at once.

a) Age composition. The membership of 1,400,000 now has an average age above fifty. The under-twenty-fives (1.9 per cent) are outnumbered by the over-eighties. The percentage of members under thirty (the truly dynamic force in society) is smaller than the percentage of those over seventy. The Youth Federation has begun to decline again, after its moderately successful re-launch.

b) Class composition. Apparently the PCI still has a very largely working-class and popular base; its composition seems to have been stable for decades. I say apparently because the percentage of pensioners has greatly increased, and new occupational categories of dependent labour do not have a significant presence. Moreover, it has become incredibly difficult to ensure that the social composition is reflected in leadership positions. When one thinks of the extraordinary blossoming of working-class elites in the 1970s, one is struck by how little of that has remained in the PCI's leadership groups. All the more reason to fear that the trend will worsen in a period when those elites are no longer forming spontaneously.

c) The Party's grass-roots structures have become extremely narrow in their political activity, mainly focused on self-reproduction (recruitment) or propaganda (election campaigns, *L'Unità* festivals), or in the most energetic cases on local administration in small and medium-sized towns. Their links with real struggles, on the other hand, appear tenuous, or operate via the trade unions or social movements (peace, ecology) from whose everyday activity they stand relatively apart. The only positive exception, not by chance, is the Communist women's organization.

d) The Party's local leaderships experience mounting difficulties: their selection base has become narrower, drawing less on real experiences of social and cultural struggle, and they lead a tough life materially, with little compensation in terms of role and ideals. Their real power is spread among a number of apparatuses, of which the Party's is neither the most important nor the most valued. The central leadership lost its undisputed authority long before the recent crises, yet it acts more through impulses and instructions than through a mechanism for discussion and decision-making that might provide a check on the implementation and results of decisions.

e) Educational activity is much slighter than in the past, in terms both of cadre training and of the development and transformation of the intellectual sector. The typical relationship between the Party and intellectuals now recognizes the latter as 'independent' – or anyway as 'experts' separate from active political life. The Party press is clearly in crisis, and even political information is disseminated independently of it.

The list could go on. But these remarks are enough to show that a break is necessary in relation to the Party and its organizational forms.

This obviously cannot be achieved by reverting to a classical model. For not only experience but changes in society have called into question Gramsci's conception of the Party as a 'totalizing' subject and his emphasis on its educational role. Today, the Party is only one component, though an essential one, in an anti-systemic subjectivity. What are its functions in this respect, and which organizational forms are appropriate to them?

The problem is among the most complex and difficult that the Party faces; it cannot be solved in an armchair without the benefit of ongoing experience, without a clear idea of the potential forces to be fielded that will require adequate organizational forms. The main thing that can and must be achieved is some clarity about the direction in which we wish to find an answer.

But let us just raise a few problem areas and risk a few emphases.

a) If a new party form with the features we have mentioned is to exist, it needs something to grow outside it, if not before then at least together with it, so that the 'boundaries' of the party – a correct but also ambiguous concept – are not simply represented by an amorphous society or atomized individuality. The party needs an organized democracy and autonomous mass movements, which, though starting from particular issues and conflicts, have the strength and durability to become political subjects and to be recognized as such. Hence the relationship between party and masses – the so-called mass character of the party – can no longer be conceived as the superimposition of 'general consciousness' on economic-corporate spontaneity, still less as the superimposition of a political-institutional apparatus on an atomized public opinion from which no more than consent is required. The last two decades have witnessed some extraordinarily rich, if embryonic, experiences in Italy: first in the working class (the factory councils of the 1970s), then the peace and ecological movements and, above all, the women's movement. Today only the latter has really retained the tension of which we have been speaking. Environmentalism has been too quickly sucked into corner-cutting electoralism, the peace movement has gone into a period of decline, and the factory council structures are going through a grave crisis. Yet a capacity for self-organization still exists in all these areas, and in some cases has been growing for the first time (the anti-Mafia struggle, voluntary work on health or drugs, the immigrant question). Because of its culture and its mode of operation, the PCI has not really recognized the necessity of this dialectic: sometimes it has been suspicious, sometimes it has tried to absorb the movement, and sometimes it has established a relationship only with its institutional expression. But the goal of unifying the various movements inside a party, or in American-style electoral alliances, is a false solution. It is necessary for Communists to work 'inside' the movements, each recognizing the other's autonomy; the party must engage with them, not simply 'represent' them. Without such a dialectic, there is no 'material' on which to build a new hegemony.

b) For this reason, however, it is also necessary to create the minimum structural and institutional conditions for the growth of an organized democracy, a collective subjectivity. Here I am referring, above all, to the two major structures that shape subjectivity in modern society. First, the bureaucratic-centralist character of the educational system makes it incapable of creating a critical spirit or a sense of personal identity, while at the same time widening the rift between elites and subaltern classes. Unless a break is made with this system – without falling into a conception of education as a conduit for the requirements of capital and the market – it will be impossible for any mass experience to overcome the limits of particularism and pressure groups. Second, unless the mass media are liberated both from the oppressive powers that stand over them and from the market logic that has them in its grip, the problem of constituting an autonomous subjectivity will be impossible to solve.

c) This premise leads to radically new features in the conception of Togliatti's 'new party', and even more in our present organizational forms. First there is the very meaning of the term 'mass party', characterized by the joint presence of two fairly separate realities: the cadre party, whose members, though highly active and enthusiastic, take little part in policy formulation; and the 'Communist people' to which it is linked by broad ideological orientations (anti-fascism, 'actually existing socialism') and immediate struggles (trade unions, cooperatives, occupational associations). Today this separation – between a political layer and public opinion – has become deeper.

Today, then, it is necessary to distinguish between party and institutions; to emphasize the party as an agent and organizer of society, whose role is to promote struggle and stimulate intellectual and moral reform. It is what Gramsci called the 'splitting mentality' – I hope I am not stupidly mistaken here – when he regretted the absence of a Reformation or Enlightenment in Italy as the basis for a new collective identity. He meant by this more than mere cultural autonomy, and much more than a general choice of values: he meant the fusion of values, analysis and transformative project that bestows on politics its profound significance, and which, day in, day out, serves as an instrument for the criticism and transformation of personal life. An ethical, not only intellectual, foundation. Is this not the radical meaning of women's critique of male politics? Does it not lie at the root of the unexpected and often fundamentalist revival of religion, and of the new and greater 'wretchedness' of modern left parties and of all who proclaim ourselves communists? Now that the perilous drift towards populism and the equally false conception of a 'party-church' have exhausted themselves, the reality left behind is that of the party as a public apparatus. In a society as fragmented and secularized as ours, is there a real basis – excluding the short-cut of fundamentalism – for a revival of that tension of ideas which, in Marx's view, constitutes a material social force? The answer will probably lie in whether qualitative social contradictions allow the party of the subaltern classes to break out from the confines of integration or revolt, and to express a radically anti-systemic but also 'positive' point of view. Decisive importance – which we have no wish to deny – therefore attaches to the relationship with other cultures and subjectivities, some of which conflict with our own tradition. The only provisos are that this not be degraded into the banality of 'contagion' or eclecticism; that a provisional synthesis be sought at every moment, and that each element in the relationship value its own richness and identity.

Index